Moral Visions

Moral Visions

Ethics and the Book of Mormon

Edited by
COURTNEY S. CAMPBELL
AND KELLY SORENSEN

UNIVERSITY OF
ILLINOIS PRESS
Urbana, Chicago, and Springfield

Cataloging data available from the Library of Congress.
LCCN 2025001976
ISBN 978-0-252-04671-1 (cloth : alk.)
ISBN 978-0-252-08881-0 (paper : alk.)
ISBN 978-0-252-04811-1 (ebook)

Contents

Introduction

COURTNEY S. CAMPBELL
AND KELLY SORENSEN

That most fundamental ethical question—How should one live?—often sends its askers searching through religious and philosophical texts. The Book of Mormon is centrally concerned with the question of how one should live. But for its wide circulation and central role in the lives of millions who take it as a sacred text, and its status as a curiosity for those who do not, it is remarkable that the present text is the first collection that takes as its shared focus the moral and ethical visions of the Book of Mormon. The Book of Mormon is consulted regularly by adherents for guidance about specific choices and, more broadly, about how to live a life. The book has had significant practical ethical influence, and scholars have sought to interpret the various kinds of guidance it offers. But a certain kind of study of the book's ethics has been underrepresented. It is that kind of study this volume aims to represent, spotlight, and encourage.

Of course, much has been written about what we might call the book's *doctrinal vision*, which includes substantial moral and ethical content. The Book of Mormon offers a God who acts and interacts with humans in history, who guides them to distant places and away from social decay to an opportunity to start anew. It offers a God who establishes structures of revelational exchange with persons. It offers warnings about the choices and conditions that lead to civilizational corruption, and it reports the emergence of a peaceful, egalitarian society under the influence of the teachings of Jesus Christ. It offers a world where God will help bring about wonderful things, and might not always prevent terrible things, but also a world where a particular kind of goodness can come into existence only under conditions of choice among opposites. And it offers a variety of more specific doctrinal teachings about, for instance, faith, covenants, repentance, and religious discipleship.

In a second zone of inquiry, some have looked to the Book of Mormon for its treatment of various issues in *applied ethics*. Scholars have analyzed the way that normative questions about war and violence, distributive justice, law, indigeneity, and the normative significance of meaning in life are embedded in its narratives and the implications of its teachings on moral life in families, religious communities, and political associations. Still others have seen in the book a meta-critique of less obvious ethical issues, such as racism or sexism and misogyny.[1]

This book takes a third approach, putting the Book of Mormon in conversation with contemporary ethics and asking what the book has to contribute to broader academic conversations about personal, religious, and social morality in the twenty-first century, and what claims about human nature, moral knowledge, and moral psychology are necessary to provide both clarity and coherence. This third approach overlaps in part with the doctrinal and applied ethics approaches. But academic work specifically on ethics and the Book of Mormon is still largely at an early stage, and much in this collection charts new ground. Until recent developments in literary and theological interpretation, interpretive energy in the last several decades has focused on questions about the book's historicity and its reception history. The authors in this volume hope to spark more interpretive energy on the book's moral and ethical content.

Daniel Becerra, a leading scholar in examining the ethical aspects of the Book of Mormon, has recently written, "One simple way to further develop scholarship on Book of Mormon ethics in the coming years would be to expand the range of topics examined in it, thus bringing this subfield of Book of Mormon studies into closer alignment with its sister field, biblical studies."[2] As Becerra points out, there is an extensive field of study in biblical ethics. Theologians and philosophers of religion alike turn to the Bible as a resource for exploring ethical issues, for the development of normative theory in contemporary philosophical work, and for interpreting the worldviews within which the ethical norms and practical teachings are situated. In the burgeoning field of Mormon studies, work parallel to that in the field of biblical ethics might productively inform ongoing reflection on the Latter-day Saint and other restorationist traditions.

The chapters in this collection illustrate that morality and ethics are not simply about decisions we make, actions we engage in, or even about our ideals and aspirations as persons but, more fundamentally, about how we see the world, our relationships with others, and our connections with a divine or sacred presence—that is, our *moral vision*. Moral vision highlights the importance of context, narrative, worldview, and the capacity for perception within which moral questions are situated and moral problems resolved. It invites the exercise of imagination and empathetic engagement to see a moral world through the experience of other persons. Moral vision is central to ethical readings of a sacred religious text and provides a focus and clarity of perspective on ways that moral values are embedded within a reality of religious beliefs.

We have titled the book *Moral Visions* not only to highlight a view of morality and moral life that is more expansive than assessments of actions but also to underscore the pluralism about ethical approaches that suffuses the book. The chapters that follow present different forms of ethical interpretation and method, including virtue ethics, narrative ethics, casuistical ethics, indigenous ethics, prophetic ethics, and an ethics of memory. The Book of Mormon is represented as an important text for a religious community, certainly, but also as a resource for moral formation, a source for normative ethical teaching, and as a moral critic against authoritarianism and paternalism. The authors highlight and investigate meaningful differences and pluralism among the Book of Mormon writers themselves on matters like moral epistemology; moral authority; moral assessments of agency; cultural moral integrity; and responsibilities to past, present, and future communities. The chapters likewise offer different moral visions of what it means to read the text ethically, including as a community formed by the text, as a historical artifact, and as a form of resistance to assimilation.

Moral visions and pluralism are no less displayed in the shared aim of the collection's authors to model a variety of ways in which the Book of Mormon's ethical themes can sustain academic attention. The collection brings together the voices of an interdisciplinary group of scholars from fields including ethics, literature, philosophy, political science, religious studies, and theology, and policy practitioners with an interest in the relationship between religious texts and ethical conduct and character. The hope is to show the potential for productive dialogue among scholars with diverse practical, religious, and theoretical interests—and in conversation with a text that is normative for millions of twenty-first-century human beings.

The diverse moral visions and methodological approaches discovered in these chapters intimate a background of textual and scholarly conversations from which conceptual and substantive connections have been forged, interpretations deepened, differences candidly investigated, and questions opened and examined in a community of inquiry. Our project includes certain chapters on how the Book of Mormon could shape the ethical practice of the community of believers in the book's religious value, offering a resource to make that faith community a place of greater understanding and empathy. This aim focuses on the practical potential of the text within a specific religious community. Other contributors have begun the work of descriptively understanding ethical teachings of the Book of Mormon, a second aim that seeks to account for its complexity before prematurely harmonizing its themes. Still other contributors use the text in thinking about issues in moral philosophy and moral theology writ large. This third objective underscores the potential of the text as a resource in religious ethics and even social ethics.

All the contributions to this volume share the idea that the Book of Mormon repays sustained attention. By bringing together readers from different fields but uniting them in thinking about one aspect of the Book of Mormon, we hope to deepen the shared understanding of the Book of Mormon's ethical messages as well as to enlarge the range of ethical issues that might be brought into conversation with the text.

The chapters in this volume are organized around two primary considerations, those of "ethical foundations" and those of "practical applications." The chapters organized through the concept of theoretical foundations examine ethics in the Book of Mormon as informed by broader philosophical, theological, psychological, and literary questions and methods. These chapters explore issues in moral psychology, moral conflict, moral epistemology, the meaning and value of life, moral pedagogy and motivation, and moral agency.

Daniel Becerra's chapter, "Moral Psychology and the Book of Mormon," provides a comprehensive overview of the claims of the text regarding what comprises good moral character and conduct. Becerra maintains that the religious and moral teachings of the Book of Mormon portray the human psyche as the locus for moral formation. In a textually rich exposition, Becerra finds that the text consistently understands the human person to be comprised of five constituent features—heart, mind, soul, spirit, and body/flesh—that are interrelated with the psychological faculties of cognition, emotion, and volition. While the Book of Mormon situates human persons within the narrative of fallen human nature, it also affirms the possibility of a transformation in moral character that Becerra refers to as the "saintly ideal." This ideal is illustrated through different forms of moral discourse, including moral exemplars, figurative analogies, psychological descriptions of virtuous persons, and instruction on virtues (and vices). Becerra constructs a comprehensive portrait of the moral person from these psychological and moral resources of the text. In this account, moral character formation and being good are necessary to fully realize humanity's psychological potential.

In his chapter "The Moral Reality of the Book of Mormon," Courtney S. Campbell contends that the Book of Mormon is not only a witness of religious truths but is also revelatory of a profound moral reality in human experience. Campbell uses the methods of moral philosophy and moral theology to explore the relationship between religious belief and moral practice, the prospect of general moral knowledge, normative moral content, and the kinds of moral situations presented in the text. This analysis leads Campbell to discern and distinguish between two types of morality in the text, a common minimalist morality of prohibitions necessary for moral agency and communal cohesion and a gift-based morality of covenantal responsibilities that promote personal well-being and communal flourishing, including care for the vulnerable. In this regard, the Book of Mormon offers moral meaning and accountability for all communities.

The moral perspectives and narratives of the Book of Mormon can speak to profound philosophical perplexities, as illustrated in the chapters by Joseph M. Spencer and Ryan Davis. Spencer's chapter, "What Is the Good and How Does One Know It? Ethics and the Book of Mormon," addresses the foundational questions of the nature of the good and knowledge of the good. The sermons of two prominent religious teachers—Alma$_2$ and Mormon$_2$—"go right to the heart of the ethical," Spencer contends, but his close-to-the text analysis strikingly discloses tension and diversity: the text "sets forth two different ethical ontologies and two different ethical epistemologies." Alma$_2$'s sermon, directed to a community lacking belief but seeking truth, offers a kind of ethical naturalism through an analogy between the word about Christ and a "seed," while Mormon$_2$'s sermon invites a believing community, the peaceable followers of Christ, to rely on the "Spirit of Christ" to acquire a "perfect knowledge" of good and evil. Spencer's comparison suggests these approaches to knowing the good are "diametrically opposed" and reflect philosophical and theological contrasts between a natural and a Christological epistemology.

Ryan Davis's chapter, "Do Values Depend on Other Persons? The Book of Mormon's Apocalyptic Solitude," brings the vision or experience of apocalypse of the Nephite community to bear on a philosophical thought experiment posed by Samuel Scheffler. Scheffler's "communal value thesis" affirms an integral relationship between personal values and community such that the collective afterlife of one's community following personal death is of greater significance for one's valuing and meaning than a personal afterlife, and, correlatively, loss of community undermines personal values and life meaning. By contrast, Davis contends that the stories of Nephi$_1$ and Moroni$_2$ the first and the last Book of Mormon authors, who anticipate or experience the end of their social communities but affirm their personal convictions, challenge Scheffler's position. As with Spencer's analysis of Alma$_2$ and Mormon$_2$, Davis likewise observes divergence between Nephi$_1$'s and Moroni$_2$'s values and purpose. While Nephi$_1$ finds the meaning of his writing to consist in a witness to future generations and a reconstituted social world, Moroni$_2$ learns that his salvation requires his self-perfection through divine grace and is not intertwined with a community. This leads Davis to a provocative interpretation of the theological virtues of faith, hope, and love in the Book of Mormon: faith and hope may fail as appropriate responses to the prospect of the end of one's social world, but love must remain and endures even in the absence of faith or hope in personal or communal change.

Kimberly Matheson highlights the ethical claims of the text on its imagined audience and readers in her chapter, "Epic History, Ethical Pedagogy: The Book of Mormon's Scene of Instruction." This means the Book of Mormon's moral power lies less in application to contemporary sociopolitical conversations and more in the persuasive forms it exerted on its earliest readers and continues to exert in the twenty-first century. Matheson portrays the Book of Mormon as a "powerful piece of moral instruction," and she draws on the concept of a "scene of instruction" to explore the "how" of moral formation in a text that "moves bodies" to action, whether as critics or as communities of believers. These scenes of ethical pedagogy include the act of reading a printed book and its resonant biblicism and the discourse of a sacred, and heretofore unknown, historical narrative: The narration of the history of a lost civilization is a form of moral instruction as readers are inscribed into the text and learn they are the culmination of this history. This rhetorical device invites a moral vision of the present as laden with regenerative possibilities, particularly as the covenant relationship embedded in the text extends to contemporary peoples. Moreover, the text's self-acknowledgment of its fragmentary incompleteness is itself a stage of moral instruction as it extends promises of more records, more history, and more knowledge contingent on moral reform. This promissory persuasion offers what Matheson considers a "road map of moral progress" that generates an intensified dramatic tension when juxtaposed with the anxiety expressed by the book's authors that the persuasive project may fail.

Kelly Sorensen likewise explores the moral claims of the Book of Mormon on readers. In "The Moral Visions of the Book of Mormon: Ethics and the Gospel of Agency," Sorensen maintains that the Book of Mormon presents an "agentic and participatory ethics" or "gospel of agency." This gospel displays a pattern of divine engagement with and extension of human moral agency, as reflected in a question from God to a prophet: "What will ye that I should do?" Sorensen illustrates his thesis through a method that highlights different choices made by persons or communities in three comparable moral narratives—communities who escape oppression, community choices regarding the defensive use of violence, and prophetic confrontations with nonbelievers or anti-Christs. These narratives disclose both morally adequate and morally superior ways of exercising agency; moral agents and communities who participate with God in their agency experience more desirable life conditions, including peace and covenantal relationships. This pluralistic moral vision of the Book of Mormon, Sorensen contends, invites readers to exercise their own moral agency in interpretation and action.

The chapters organized through the concept of practical applications examine ethical choices in communal practices embedded in the text, such as integrity and resilience, dress and nakedness, sources of moral authority, and covenantal witness. This section concludes with a chapter outlining and extending practical ethical engagement with the Book of Mormon.

Rachel Esplin Odell's chapter, "Moral Agency, Resistance, and Resilience in the Story of the People of Anti-Nephi-Lehi," presents an indigenous and decolonizing interpretive method to convey that readers have a "moral obligation to grapple with how the Book of Mormon has been and is still used as an assimilation tool." In developing her argument, Esplin Odell offers a provocative exposition of the moral agency and resilience of a community of converts known as the Anti-Nephi-Lehies, whose story "subverts" assimilation and erasure from history from within the text. Esplin Odell identifies how the moral reasoning of this community, especially regarding its decisions about the use of violence for self-defense, is characteristically misunderstood or neglected by the text's primary narrators. Yet, this moral reasoning, inculcated within families—particularly by mothers to children, both sons and daughters—persists through generations and becomes a source of community resilience, integrity, and resistance. The story of the people of Anti-Nephi-Lehi discloses how indigenous and antiracist interpretations of the Book of Mormon display different "ethical alternatives in the text" and serve as "the prophetic voice of warning to the dominant group."

Ariel Bybee Laughton likewise explores how the Book of Mormon's moral teachings can be a form of moral criticism for contemporary communities. In her chapter, "The Perils of Apparel: Clothing and Dress Ethics in the Book of Mormon," Bybee Laughton contends that textual teachings and practices regarding clothing and nakedness are imbued with communal meaning and values, particularly regarding social and economic justice, relationship with God, and humility. Bybee Laughton's comprehensive overview of dress ethics in the text discloses that "fine dress" and "costly apparel" are markers of communal moral decay; social stratification; oppression of the poor; and of the vices of pride, vanity, and self-promotion. Similarly, textual proscriptions against nakedness are situated within broader prophetic critiques of societal corruption and neglect of the poor, needy, and naked. Such critiques presume normative precepts of communal solidarity and an ethic of work: Producing clothing should be a community project on behalf of the community. Bybee Laughton concludes by invoking these ethical guidelines in a moral critique: Ecclesiastical teachings on "modest" dress in the contemporary Church of Jesus Christ of Latter-day Saints (LDS) are deeply gendered, focused on sexual morality, and hence are "deeply at odds" with the egalitarian and solidarity principles for dress embedded in the church's formative text.

Michael D. K. Ing likewise invokes the Book of Mormon as a moral critic in his chapter, "An Ethics of Authority and the Authority of Ethics: The Book of Mormon Talks Back." Ing addresses the relationship between moral authority and ecclesiastical authority in the context of deference within LDS church culture to the teachings of ecclesiastical leaders on moral issues. Ing contends that the LDS faith tradition lacks a robust discourse of moral deliberation, which has been supplanted by a conflation of ecclesiastical with moral authority, or a tradition of "priesthood might makes right." Ing argues against this moral deference of loyalty by relying on Book of Mormon narratives that highlight moral vulnerability and fallibility, the usurpation of moral authority by ecclesiastical authority, and illustrations of extra-ecclesiastical religious teachers. These narratives inform Ing's contention that moral authority is based on virtues that emulate Christ and his articulation of moral limitations on ecclesiastical authority. Ing concludes with a "serenity prayer" that reflects commitments to open space for legitimately disagreeing with LDS ecclesiastical teachings as a matter of conscience, for church leaders to acknowledge wrongdoing, and for developing a robust mode of ethical reflection in church culture.

In "The Ethics of Memory in the Book of Mormon," Courtney S. Campbell provides an exposition of the textual and communal imperative of "remembering" narratives, norms, and moral legacy to shape moral cultures of the present and the future. He explores the moral memory of the Book of Mormon through an interpretation of the moral voice of prophetic criticism, a construction of the moral logic of covenantal relationships and responsibilities, and an application of the concept of a moral witness. The ethics of memory fuses together responsibilities of remembrance of preceding generations and commitments of care to future generations, articulating moral visions that offer constructive alternatives for creating moral communities out of strangers. Campbell contends that the moral trajectory of the ethics of memory and responsibility to future moral communities confers upon the entire text the character of a moral witness.

The possibility for the narratives and teachings of the Book of Mormon to inform and engage with an array of practical ethics issues are explored in the concluding chapter by Kelly Sorensen, "Further Visions: Practical Ethics and the Book of Mormon." Inviting further scholarship, Sorensen briefly situates these practical applications within an array of expanding communities, including responsibilities to self, to family, to community, to particularly vulnerable others, to those perceived as having other identities, to the political state, and to nature. Ultimately, questions of practical ethics invite more substantive reflection on the question of what makes a life go well.

We are aware that the Book of Mormon narratives, communities, and characters may be unfamiliar to many readers who we see as the audience for the book. We have positioned two resources following this introduction and preceding the thematic chapters to provide background. Joseph M. Spencer, a pioneering scholar in philosophical and ethical studies of the Book of Mormon, has composed "A Brief Reader's Guide to the Book of Mormon" to assist readers in situating the concepts, communities, and characters within the broader narrative arc of the text. There is also a resource titled "Names in the Book of Mormon," which provides short descriptions of the figures in the Book of Mormon who are referenced or discussed in the volume's chapters, and a section titled "Abbreviations of Books in the Book of Mormon."

We wish to express our appreciation to the Neal A. Maxwell Institute for Religious Scholarship at Brigham Young University for hosting a series of seminars between 2019 and 2023 on "Ethics and the Book of Mormon" that provided the basis for scholarly conversations between the authors and other scholars and from which many of the chapters received their initial inspirations. We also express appreciation to Alison Syring Bassford, her editing team at the University of Illinois Press, and peer reviewers of earlier versions of this book.

Notes

1. The chapters by Joseph M. Spencer, "A Brief Reader's Guide to the Book of Mormon," and Kelly Sorensen, "Further Visions: Practical Ethics and the Book of Mormon," discuss important literature in the field of Book of Mormon studies as well as in the doctrinal and practical approaches to the Book of Mormon.

2. Daniel Becerra, "Ethical Approaches to the Book of Mormon," *Journal of Book of Mormon Studies* 32 (2023): 100.

Names in the Book of Mormon

The following is a list of names of persons from the Book of Mormon who are discussed in the subsequent chapters. There are several Book of Mormon characters who bear the same name in the text, some of whom were named after an exemplary predecessor. The field of Mormon studies has adopted a convention of differentiating persons with the same name in the Book of Mormon by a subscript notation.[1] The subscript sequence used within a particular name follows the chronological introduction of a particular person in the biblical text and the Book of Mormon narrative; for example, the Book of Mormon prophet Jacob$_2$ is preceded historically by the biblical patriarch Jacob$_1$; the father and religious leader Alma$_1$ precedes his son and prophet, Alma$_2$.

Aaron$_2$ (c. 100 BCE)	Son of King Mosiah$_2$; following conversion, he refuses the kingdom and participates in a missionary effort to the Lamanites
Abinadi (c. 150 BCE)	A prophet to King Noah$_3$ and his people; the first martyr in the text; his teachings convert Alma$_1$
Abish (c. 90 BCE)	A servant of a Lamanite queen, she invites Lamanites to witness the conversion of the queen and her husband, King Lamoni
Alma$_1$ (c. 130 BCE)	A priest of Noah$_3$ converted by Abinadi's message; he establishes the church of God and leads his people to the Nephite society ruled by Mosiah$_2$
Alma$_2$ (c. 100 BCE)	Son of Alma$_1$; he rebels against the church of God and experiences a miraculous conversion; the first chief judge and the high priest leading the church during the rule of the judges

Amaleki$_1$ (c. 130 BCE)	Last Nephite record keeper of small plates, in the book of Omni.
Ammon$_2$ (c. 100 BCE)	Son of King Mosiah$_2$; following conversion, he coordinates a missionary effort to the Lamanites and leads converted Anti-Nephi-Lehies to a refuge in Jershon
Amulek (c. 80 BCE)	Missionary companion of Alma$_2$
Anti-Nephi-Lehies (c. 90 BCE)	Lamanites converted through the preaching of Ammon$_2$; following a speech by King Anti-Nephi-Lehi, they assume a covenant of nonviolence
Benjamin (c. 150 BCE)	Righteous king and Nephite record keeper at the beginning of the book of Mosiah; his sermon on Christ and moral teachings invites his people to accept a covenant relationship with God
Enos (c. 420 BCE)	Son of Jacob$_2$; Nephite record keeper; and author of the book of Enos
Gideon (c. 100 BCE)	Nephite leader who opposed Noah$_3$ and provided counsel to Limhi; killed by Nehor
Helaman$_2$ (c. 70 BCE)	Son of Alma$_2$; a Nephite religious and military leader and record keeper
Helaman$_3$ (c. 50 BCE)	Son of Helaman$_2$; Nephite record keeper, religious leader, and chief judge
Jacob$_2$ (c. 570 BCE)	Fifth son of Lehi$_1$ and brother of Nephi$_1$, whom he succeeds as leader of the Nephites; author of the book of Jacob
Jared, brother of	A prophet at the time of the Tower of Babel narrative; he receives revelations and visions from God that lead the Jaredites to a land of promise
Jesus Christ	Prophecies of his appearance are fulfilled following his resurrection; he reorganizes the church, blesses the people, and provides religious ministry and moral instruction (3 Nephi 11–28)
Korihor (c. 70 BCE)	A skeptic or "anti-Christ" who challenges the teachings of the church and the authority of Alma$_2$
Laban (c. 600 BCE)	A record keeper in Jerusalem who is killed by Nephi$_1$ to procure records of Lehi$_1$'s genealogy and biblical prophecies
Laman$_1$ (c. 600 BCE)	Eldest son of Lehi$_1$; he contests the leadership of Nephi$_1$ and is the progenitor of the Lamanite communities

Lamoni (c. 100 BCE)	Lamanite king who is presented the gospel by the Nephite missionary Ammon$_2$; his conversion experience leads to the formation of the Anti-Nephi-Lehi community
Lamoni, father of (c. 100 BCE)	A king over all the Lamanite lands, he is converted by an ecstatic experience following the teaching of the Nephite missionary Aaron$_2$; he appoints his son, Anti-Nephi-Lehi, as his successor
Lehi$_1$ (c. 600 BCE)	A prophet in Jerusalem at the time of Jeremiah; commanded by God to leave Jerusalem with his family for a land of promise
Lehi$_3$ (c. 70 BCE)	Nephite military leader with Moroni$_1$
Lehi$_4$ (c. 40 BCE)	Son of Helaman$_3$, missionary to Nephites and Lamanites with Nephi$_2$
Lemuel (c. 600 BCE)	Second son of Lehi$_1$; joins his brother Laman$_1$ in rejecting the leadership of Nephi$_1$
Limhi (c. 120 BCE)	Son of Noah$_3$ and king of the Nephite colony subject to Lamanite tribute; he leads his people to unite with the general body of Nephites under the rule of Mosiah$_2$
Mormon$_2$ (c. 350 CE)	Primary anthologizer of the text, a religious and military leader at the end of the Nephite civilization; author of the short book of Mormon
Moroni$_1$ (c. 100 BCE)	Nephite military leader, extolled by Mormon$_2$ as an exemplar of faith and commitment to Nephite liberty
Moroni$_2$ (c. 400 CE)	Son of Mormon$_2$; concluding author following the destruction of the Nephite civilization; completes the Book of Mormon, anthologizes the book of Ether, authors the book of Moroni
Mosiah$_2$ (c. 130 BCE)	Nephite king and record keeper succeeding Benjamin; he reconstructs political governance by a system of judges and ends monarchy
Nehor (c. 90 BCE)	Introduces priestcraft and presents teachings contrary to the church; slays Gideon and is sentenced to death by Alma$_2$
Nephi$_1$ (c. 600 BCE)	Son of Lehi$_1$; author of first two books, 1 and 2 Nephi; first leader of Nephite community
Nephi$_2$ (c. 40 BCE)	Son of Helaman$_3$; gives up the judgment seat to preach to both Nephites and Lamanites with Lehi$_4$
Nephi$_3$ (c. 40 CE)	Son of Nephi$_2$; a disciple of the resurrected Christ

Noah$_3$ (c. 160 BCE)	An unrighteous Nephite king who rejects Abinadi's message and orders his death by fire
Omni (c. 360 BCE)	Nephite record keeper; initial author in the book of Omni
Samuel$_2$ (c. 5 BCE)	Also known as Samuel the Lamanite; a Lamanite prophet to the Nephites who testifies of Christ and the evils of the Nephite community
Shiblon$_2$ (c. 70 BCE)	Son of Alma$_2$; Nephite record keeper and missionary
Sherem (c. 540 BCE)	A learned man who denies Christ and confronts Jacob$_2$
Zeniff (c. 200 BCE)	Founder of Nephite colony in the land of Lehi-Nephi; father of Noah$_3$

Note

1. See Grant Hardy, ed., *The Book of Mormon: Another Testament of Jesus Christ* (Provo, UT: Neal A. Maxwell Institute for Religious Scholarship, Brigham Young University, 2018), 634–43.

Abbreviations

1 Ne.	1 Nephi
2 Ne.	2 Nephi
W of M	Words of Mormon
Hel.	Helaman
3 Ne.	3 Nephi
4 Ne.	4 Nephi
Morm.	Mormon
Moro.	Moroni

A Brief Reader's Guide
to the Book of Mormon

JOSEPH M. SPENCER

The Book of Mormon presents itself as a modern translation of an otherwise unknown ancient record. A young American farmhand named Joseph Smith (1805–1844) claimed that an angel directed him to the hiding place of the gold plates on which the record was anciently inscribed. After a period of preparation for the task, Smith said, he unearthed the plates and translated them into modern English over the spring and early summer of 1829. The resulting text, nearly six hundred pages in length, appeared in print for the first time in 1830. Just weeks after the book went on sale at the Grandin Book Shop in Palmyra, New York, the earliest believers in the book's inspiration organized themselves into the Church of Christ—the ecclesiastical nucleus of what later became a larger religious movement distributed among a variety of formal churches. The largest of these churches today is the Church of Jesus Christ of Latter-day Saints, popularly known by a nickname (Mormons) drawn from the title of its sacred book.

During the nearly two hundred years since the tradition's founding events, the Book of Mormon's spread throughout the world has been dramatic. Due to vigorous missionizing, in fact, the Book of Mormon is among the world's most-printed books. Its contents nonetheless remain unfamiliar to most. The book is long and complex, setting the entry fee for developing serious familiarity with it at a high price. In addition, many of the volume's adherents have historically prioritized acquiring a divine witness of its truth over reading the book for deep comprehension. It is only in the last forty years that the Book of Mormon has become the primary guide for the devotional life of lay Latter-day Saints and only in the last twenty years that the book has become a serious and sustained object of scholarly inquiry. Recent work, both pastorally inclined (and therefore facing inward) and academically oriented (and therefore facing outward), has helped to clarify greatly the content of the Book of Mormon.

A Sketch of the Book of Mormon

The Book of Mormon presents itself as the literary work, predominantly, of three figures.

Nephi₁

The first major contributor is Nephi₁, a young man who is described as leaving Jerusalem with his parents and his siblings just years before the Neo-Babylonian empire (in 586 BCE) conquered the small nation of Judah. The decision to leave is precipitated by the prophetic activity of Nephi₁'s father, Lehi₁, but the decision divides the family in two. Despite hard feelings and recriminations, the family travels across desert and ocean to arrive eventually in "the promised land," the ancient Americas. As time goes on, the fracture in the family creates two parties, headed respectively by Nephi₁ and his oldest brother, Laman₁. As the division deepens, especially after Lehi's death, the factions grow into two rival nations, the Nephites and the Lamanites. The Nephites are portrayed throughout the Book of Mormon as the carriers of the Christian gospel, while the Lamanites are initially characterized by their alienation from God.

Nephi₁'s record (kept on what are usually called "the small plates" and divided into the first and second books of Nephi) recounts the above history: the family's removal to the promised land, the conflicts within the family, and the eventual division of the family into two warring nations. In addition, Nephi₁'s record interlaces this history with a series of revelations and prophecies about the distant future for both his own and his oldest brother's peoples. From the very beginning, Nephi₁ learns in a vision that the Nephites (because of their waywardness) will ultimately be destroyed by the Lamanites. The latter will then be preserved until the New World is discovered by "Gentiles" centuries later, when a series of divinely orchestrated events will trigger a promised "redemption" of the Lamanites: their restoration to a knowledge of Jesus Christ and of their own status as part of Israel, God's covenant people. Nephi₁ frequently draws on the language and ideas of the biblical prophet Isaiah to give form to all these predictions.

At first glance, Nephi₁ consistently presents himself not only as a prophet and a gatherer of prophecies but also as a stalwart hero and a key example of faith. A closer reading of Nephi₁'s narratives, however, shows him to be a nuanced storyteller. In both subtle and not-so-subtle ways, he raises questions about how his own anger and impatience toward his brothers' doubts and questions may have contributed to the family's division. And his narratives—and occasionally his prophecies as well—are punctuated by events that raise serious ethical questions for readers. In one early and often-discussed story, Nephi$_1$ claims to have been divinely "constrained" to kill a helpless man named Laban in a dark Jerusalem street. In various passages, Nephi$_1$ presents himself as potentially overzealous or impatient with his brothers. Throughout his record, women are underrepresented and sometimes indelicately spoken of, something Nephi$_1$ may subtly signal awareness of. And in a key vision, and later in part of his larger storyline, he uses apparently racializing language that sounds problematic for twenty-first-century readers, despite his clear affirmation that God "denieth none that come unto him, black and white." Nephi$_1$'s stories thus cry out for moral and ethical analysis.

Toward the end of his life, Nephi$_1$ passes the small plates on to his brother Jacob$_2$, who adds a much shorter record of his own: the book of Jacob. Jacob$_2$'s few chapters follow Nephi$_1$'s prophetic program, adding further visionary and scriptural resources for understanding the much later redemption of the Lamanites. Jacob$_2$ also, however, includes in his brief record a sermon of key importance for readers hoping to make sense of the ethical bearings of the Book of Mormon. Jacob$_2$ claims to discern after Nephi$_1$'s death an emerging Nephite culture of abuse toward women, racism toward Lamanites, and classist elitism among Nephites. The sermon consequently contains some of the Book of Mormon's strongest words against marginalized and vulnerable populations.

The remainder of the small plates consists of three particularly short records written by Jacob$_2$'s descendants—the books of Enos, Jarom, and Omni—that sketch several centuries of Nephite history that are otherwise unrecounted in the Book of Mormon.

Mormon$_2$

The second major contributor to the Book of Mormon is the titular figure of Mormon$_2$. In a brief transitional document called "The Words of Mormon," which appears at the end of the small plates, he introduces himself. He describes himself as living "many hundred years after the coming of Christ" (it is later revealed that he lives and dies in the fourth century CE), hence as living long after Nephi$_1$ and even long after the distant descendants of Jacob$_2$, who conclude the small plates. Mormon$_2$ explains right away that his own historical context is that of the Nephites' predicted destruction. He has "witnessed almost all the destruction," and he anticipates that his son (Moroni$_2$) "will witness the entire destruction." He interrupts at this point in the Book of Mormon, though, not to recount that later history but, rather, to explain the circumstances under which he has discovered the existence of the small plates and to explain the effect they have had on his own literary project.

Mormon$_2$, it turns out, has written a summary account of more than four centuries of Nephite history, from the time of Nephi down to the reign of a Nephite king named Benjamin. He draws his knowledge of the history from a library of records the Book of Mormon often calls "the plates of Nephi" (and what students of the Book of Mormon call "the large plates" to distinguish them from the small plates). But, Mormon$_2$ explains, once he had finished the first part of his own telling of early Nephite history, he "searched among the records which had been delivered into my hands" and found the small plates. The contents of the small plates "pleasing" him, he says, he "chose these things, to finish [his] record upon them." Readers, it seems, are meant to understand that Mormon$_2$'s encounter with the small plates redirected his literary efforts substantially. For "the remainder" of what he now intends to write, he will take the themes and "prophecies" of the small plates as guidance and orientation.

There follows a series of historical books—the books of Mosiah, Alma, and Helaman, and two books of Nephi (usually called the third and fourth books of Nephi)—all inscribed by Mormon$_2$. Collectively, they tell the story of the Nephites and the Lamanites from the time of King Benjamin, in the mid-second century BCE, until the beginning of Mormon$_2$'s own lifetime, early in the fourth century CE. Each of Mormon$_2$'s several books covers a unique period of Nephite political history.

The book of Mosiah recounts a period when the Nephites are settled in the land of Zarahemla (rather than in their original land of settlement, the land of Nephi) and are governed by monarchies. The book closes with the reorganization of the Nephites' governmental structure, replacing the monarchy with a system of judges oriented by a strong sense of the rule of law. The book of Alma then recounts the first four (rather rocky) decades of the judges' reign. It details a series of conflicts internal to the Nephite state, conflicts that repeatedly lead to larger conflicts—and even protracted wars—between the Nephites and the Lamanites. The book of Helaman opens with the rise of a different problem for the reign of the judges: the formation of covert organizations that work from within the Nephite government to seize power over the state. Early in the third book of Nephi, these "robbers" actually trigger the total collapse of the Nephite state, provoking the people's reorganization into a loose collection of clans or tribes—this shortly before a series of massive climatic disasters occur and a substantial portion of the population dies. In the wake of the disasters, however, Jesus Christ, only recently risen from the grave on the other side of the world, descends among the people and teaches them for several days. The brief fourth book of Nephi then recounts a long period when the now-united Nephites and Lamanites hold "all things in common." Sadly, it does not last, and Fourth Nephi concludes by describing the decline of egalitarianism and a fresh division between Nephites and Lamanites.

All this political history serves for Mormon$_2$ primarily as the backdrop for a spiritual story he wishes to tell. In his first book, the book of Mosiah, he traces the rise of a totally new religious institution, "the church of God" (unprecedented to that point in the Book of Mormon). Self-consciously distinct from and independent of the monarchical state, the church becomes the locus of a stable Christian community. It is in part the need to protect such an independent organization—against the possible (or even likely) ire of some future sovereign—that pushes the last Nephite king to transform the monarchy into a system of judges. The book of Alma, then, is in many ways, a focused history of how the church of God fares under the reign of the judges. Church leaders quickly find that the law only protects the church, never helping to strengthen it, so that constant revivalism proves necessary to keep the Nephites who make up the church faithful to their Christian convictions. Meanwhile, the church has sent a small group of missionaries among the Lamanites and, apparently because the church presents the gospel of Christ as a universal rather than as a merely Nephite faith, these missionaries have startling success. A major wave of Lamanite converts results, unprecedented in the previous five centuries of Nephite history. Then, in the book of Helaman, this first wave of Lamanite converts gives way to a more or less total conversion of the Lamanite nation to Christ—this at the same time that the Nephites fall into general infidelity (under the influence of the infiltrating robbers). At the end of Helaman, the key prophetic voice is that of a Lamanite, Samuel$_2$, who comes to call the Nephites to repentance in a great reversal of the central event in the book of Alma.

Samuel$_2$ not only calls the Nephites to repentance. He also offers them a set of specific prophecies about what to anticipate regarding the coming of Jesus Christ to the world, and he predicts the climatic disasters that would devastate the New World (occurring, specifically, at the time of Christ's death in the Old World). The third book of Nephi then recounts the arrival of Jesus Christ after his resurrection among the Nephites and the Lamanites, purified by the disasters that occur when Samuel$_2$'s prophecies are fulfilled. Christ replaces the church of God and its rites of anticipatory baptism with a new church of Christ and new rites of fully Christian baptism (in the name of the Father, the Son, and the Holy Ghost). He also predicts, Nephi-like, the future redemption of the Lamanites. Because of the story Mormon$_2$ has just finished telling about the redemption of the Lamanites through the work of the church of God, it suddenly becomes clear that the books of Mosiah, Alma, and Helaman sketch an ancient history that is *typical* of the predicted eschatological story of Lamanite redemption.

Mormon$_2$'s long history, told across several books, provides him plenty of grist for the ethical and moral mill. There are questions about good versus bad governance, good versus bad religion, good versus bad relationships with enemies, good versus bad approaches to warfare, good versus bad ways of handling sedition, and good versus bad ways of responding to heresy. There is consistent reflection on or portrayal of the evils of excessive wealth, the unreliability of human convictions, ethnocentrism and even racism, how women fare in clearly patriarchal societies, the effects of protracted war on human sensibilities, and what paternalism looks like in interethnic relations. From King Benjamin's sermon about responding to the beggar to the story of how King Noah$_3$'s priests kidnapped and forced young Lamanite women into marriage, from King Mosiah$_2$'s discourse about the evils of monarchy to high priest Alma$_2$'s decision to give up the judgment seat to focus on his ecclesial responsibilities, from the violence of a dissident Nephite city toward women and children to hints at how one Nephite atheist drew many women into his orbit while preaching about emancipation from the church, from the tactics and strategies reluctantly and yet proudly used by the military captain Moroni$_1$ to the question of whether a chief judge's servant is right to kill an assassin while in disguise, Mormon$_2$'s several books constantly touch on major moral questions.

Some stories from within Mormon$_2$'s long history have frequently received attention from readers of the Book of Mormon with an interest in ethical concerns. These appear especially in the books of Mosiah and Alma. They deserve particular attention because they are the subject of moral commentary in the chapters that make up the present volume. They are also of special interest because, unlike the exhortative discourses that appear frequently in the Book of Mormon and wear their moral commitments on their sleeves, these stories are often understated and morally ambiguous. Mormon$_2$ as often as not simply presents history to his readers and then leaves to them the task of deciding what the stories mean at the ethical level.

The book of Mosiah opens with a long sermon from King Benjamin that addresses the Christian's duty to care for the beggar and, more generally, the poor. In addition, Benjamin oversees the creation of a Christian monarchy as he delivers his throne to his son. But Benjamin's death shortly thereafter is immediately followed by a long digression about a wayward Nephite colony settled in Lamanite territory, far away. The colony is governed by its own kings, with the prominent King Noah$_3$ as a key exemplar of state oppression. The story of the colony, from its founding under Zeniff through its abandonment two generations later under Limhi, is littered with ethically troubling stories. Not only do goings-on in the colony raise moral questions, but the return of the colonists to the main body of the Nephites (united under King Mosiah$_2$) raises other questions as well, especially because the covenanting members of the church of God are among the returning colonists.

The book of Alma is, in turn, filled with ethically fraught stories. Throughout that book, the unstable reign of the judges leads to contention, with the result that Nephite dissenters repeatedly leave their countrymen and persuade the Lamanites to go to war against the Nephites. Key stories in Alma thus focus on delicate preventive preaching among disillusioned and potentially rebellious Nephite groups—most notably the so-called Zoramites—by representatives of the Nephite church of God. Other key stories (especially the missionary preaching of King Mosiah$_2$'s sons) concern attempts to sway Lamanites toward peace through an embrace of the Christian gospel. When missionaries prove successful with the conversion of those who then call themselves the Anti-Nephi-Lehies, further questions arise: Who has the right to decide the meaning of conversion for these former Lamanites? Should they be integrated into Nephite society due to their conversion?

Following this long history—by far the largest portion of the Book of Mormon—Mormon$_2$ sketches a few chapters of autobiography. He introduces his own life and the circumstances of his taking on the task of writing Nephite and Lamanite history. However, he also recounts a series of conflicts and wars between the Nephites and the Lamanites during his lifetime, conflicts and wars in which he plays a major part because early on he assumes the role of being a commander in the Nephite army. The conflicts eventually culminate in a final battle (during which, the reader later learns, Mormon$_2$ himself dies) that results in the total eradication of the Nephites as a nation.

Moroni$_2$

The remainder of the Book of Mormon is the literary work of Moroni$_2$, Mormon$_2$'s son, whom he apparently names after the great Nephite military captain whose story is told late in the book of Alma. Moroni$_2$ announces initially that he plans to write little—really, to do no more than provide a brief epilogue to his father's essentially complete project. He eventually, however, adds two further "books" to the project: the book of Ether and the book of Moroni. The latter of these is a potpourri—a gathering of ecclesial documents, sermons, and letters from Mormon₂ and some exhortations Moroni₂ directs to the volume's readers. Its last chapter, the last chapter of the whole Book of Mormon, contains a promise to readers that they might learn the truth about the volume through earnest prayer.

The book of Ether, originally intended by Moroni₂ to be the capstone of the volume, recounts the history of a third New World people, neither Nephites nor Lamanites. In Mormon₂'s several historical books about Nephite-Lamanite history, he occasionally mentions that the Nephites discovered the ruins of a more ancient civilization in the lands to the north of the traditional Nephite and Lamanite territories. A record found among the ruins circulates among the Nephites at times, and Mormon₂ promises to give an account of the mysterious ruined civilization, but it is actually Moroni₂ who, in the end, provides the account in the form of the book of Ether. The book thus tells the story of the Jaredites, a group that took its departure from the Tower of Babel (the tower's story is told in Genesis 11 in the Bible). Like Nephi₁'s family later, this group leaves the Old World to settle in the New, giving rise to a large but contentious civilization. Organizing themselves from the beginning in an unstable fashion, the Jaredites have a particularly volatile history, their kings more akin to regional warlords pursuing long-standing blood feuds than to settled monarchies. Eventually, the Jaredites divide into two massive armies that slaughter each other entirely—their one survivor wandering alone only to discover, just before his death, the existence of the later settlers arriving in the New World.

What draws Moroni₂ to this history is more than puzzled curiosity or an interest in antiquities. He explicitly connects the Jaredites to Gentiles. (Having come from the Tower of Babel, the Jaredites are pre-Abrahamic and therefore non-Israelite.) Moroni₂ tells their story as a warning to Gentile readers of the Book of Mormon in the latter days. While the Lamanites are preserved according to God's covenant with ancient Israel, so that they might be (as prophesied) redeemed in the end, the Jaredites totally eradicate themselves, lacking any national promise of redemption from God. Their salvation, it seems, depends entirely on their repentance. Moroni₂, in fact, includes at the outset of the book of Ether a long story about a righteous Jaredite figure, the nameless "brother of Jared," who pierces the veil between human beings and God. The story clearly serves as a model for Gentile repentance, just as the self-destruction of the Jaredites serves as a warning to unrepentant Gentiles.

Moroni₂'s contributions to the Book of Mormon are fewer by far than his father's and fewer even than Nephi₁'s. They nonetheless touch on similar moral questions through the telling of the Jaredite history. In addition, Moroni$_2$ directly addresses the Book of Mormon's readers more frequently than his father does, addressing direct moral diatribes to them. He rails prophetically against Gentile cultures that would prevail at the time of the Book of Mormon's translation and circulation. More specifically, he sees in latter-day Gentile churches an obsession with wealth, one that leads them to neglect or "pass . . . by" the vulnerable and impoverished. Moroni$_2$ also frets over latter-day Gentiles' culture of hyper-rationality, dismissive of faith and in denial about God's continued involvement with the world.

Further Reading

For readers interested in developing a closer familiarity with the Book of Mormon, a few recommendations for further reading might be appreciated. Obviously, it is best to begin with a reading of the Book of Mormon itself. There is a recent and mostly very useful *Annotated Book of Mormon* that helps guide the reader through the storyline. It is a very good place to start:

> Hardy, Grant, ed. *The Annotated Book of Mormon*. New York: Oxford University Press, 2023.

For those hoping to develop a sense for the larger scholarly conversation surrounding the Book of Mormon, there is a recent introduction to the field that can be of real help. It is written primarily with an insider audience in mind (aimed at Latter-day Saint college students especially), but it does important work in simply outlining the shape of the field and guiding readers through the major resources:

> Becerra, Daniel, Amy A. Easton-Flake, Nicholas J. Frederick, and Joseph M. Spencer. *Book of Mormon Studies: An Introduction and Guide*. Salt Lake City: Brigham Young University (hereafter, BYU) Religious Studies Center, 2022.

Two particularly useful books outline the basic reception history of the Book of Mormon. They are both excellent:

> Givens, Terryl L. *By the Hand of Mormon: The American Scripture that Launched a New World Religion*. New York: Oxford University Press, 2002.
> Gutjahr, Paul C. *The Book of Mormon: A Biography*. Princeton, NJ: Princeton University Press, 2012.

Two helpful scholarly guides to the basic contents of the Book of Mormon are worth recommending. The first comes from Oxford University

Press's Very Short Introductions series and, as is appropriate to the series, provides the barest sketch of what the Book of Mormon is. The second, by Grant Hardy, is a "reader's guide" to the book, meaning it introduces readers to the three main voices in the Book of Mormon (Nephi, Mormon, and Moroni) through a narratological lens:

> Givens, Terryl L. *The Book of Mormon: A Very Short Introduction.*
> New York: Oxford University Press, 2009.
> Hardy, Grant. *Understanding the Book of Mormon: A Reader's Guide.*
> New York: Oxford University Press, 2010.

Obviously, there is a substantial, and rapidly growing, literature on ethical issues within the Book of Mormon. Much of this is cited in the references of the chapters making up the present volume.

PART I

Ethical Foundations

2

Moral Psychology and the Book of Mormon

DANIEL BECERRA

This chapter seeks to contribute to a fuller understanding of moral formation as it is portrayed in the Book of Mormon. By *moral formation*—also
sometimes referred to in scholarship as moral/spiritual/ethical development—I mean the process by which human moral potential is actualized.
In the words of the Nephite ruler King Benjamin, this entails putting off
the "natural man" and becoming "a saint through the atonement of Christ
the Lord," which I understand to be humanity's *telos* as it relates to morality
in the text (Mosiah 3:19).[1] Specifically, I examine the relationship between
morality and psychology in the Book of Mormon and ask: How is moral
character reflected in a person's cognitive, emotional, and volitional faculties? In this sense, my investigation centers on three issues that are central
to the study of virtue ethics but have not yet been adequately examined as
they relate to the Book of Mormon: human psychology, human morality,
and psychological manifestations of moral development.[2]

In undertaking this study, I recognize that the Book of Mormon is not
a univocal text. As scholars have long recognized, distinct voices, divergent
views, and complex intertextual relationships are discernible in its pages.[3]
Consequently, any claims about what "the Book of Mormon says" must
be tempered with nuance and a recognition of the text's complex literary
features and theological diversity. Thus, while my primary task in this
chapter may be appropriately characterized as "synthetic," meaning attentive to the unity and coherence of the text, I simultaneously make efforts
to be "descriptive" by acknowledging where diversity and development
of thought occurs.[4] These efforts perhaps will be most clearly seen in the
various tables throughout this chapter, as well as in the endnotes. For ease
of analysis, I follow Grant Hardy and adopt "the internal perspective" of

the Book of Mormon by attributing its distinct claims to the authors and narrators said to articulate them in its pages.[5]

Additionally, it is impossible to separate the ethics of the Book of Mormon from the text's theology. For this reason, I attend to the theological assumptions that inform moral discourse, especially as they relate to theological anthropology (i.e., understandings of human nature) and soteriology (i.e., understandings of human salvation). Finally, this chapter concerns itself primarily with the "moral theory" of the Book of Mormon, meaning its claims about what constitutes good character and conduct.[6] This is not to undermine the task of reading the text as a "moral manual"[7]—that is to say, with respect to its practical, ethical applications or their defensibility as moral standards.[8] Rather, it is only to acknowledge that one cannot responsibly do the latter without first clearly communicating the former.

My analysis proceeds in three parts. Part 1 examines how the Book of Mormon conceptualizes human nature. In it, I identify five component parts of the human person and the psychological faculties associated with each of them. I also address the question of whether human beings are considered inherently good. Part 2 examines different forms of moral discourse in the Book of Mormon in order to clarify its claims about moral character. I demonstrate that by analyzing depictions of moral exemplars; figurative descriptions of moral ideals; psychological descriptions of moral people; and descriptions of virtues and vices, one can better construct a comprehensive portrait of moral character, which I define as a disposition to think, feel, desire, and act in virtuous ways. Part 3 then turns to the relationship between psychology and morality and concludes that the Book of Mormon portrays moral persons as possessing psychological faculties that are superior to those of immoral persons. In this way, I argue, morality and psychology cannot be separated in the Book of Mormon. Because God created humanity with psychological potential that can be fully realized only through the cultivation of moral character, moral character is central to becoming a fully functioning human being.

Human Nature

Moral formation involves bridging the gap between human nature and humanity's potential for goodness. It is therefore helpful to start with the question, What is a human? At least two ways of speaking about human nature are discernable in the Book of Mormon. The first centers on human psychology. "Psychology," as the term is typically used today, refers to the study of the human mind and behavior. Unlike some modern notions of the self, however, the Book of Mormon does not view the "mind" as the principal element of a person, nor does it always predicate human behavior to cognitive operations. For this reason, and in keeping with scholarship that attends to more ancient notions of the self,[9] I use the term "psychology" in this chapter to refer more generally to the different parts and faculties of human beings. What I mean by this will become clearer below. Understanding psychology is important because in the Book of Mormon, the human psyche is the landscape of moral formation—where it occurs and is manifest. Determining how humans function psychologically thus enables one to trace psychological changes and trends as they relate to moral development. The second way the Book of Mormon speaks about human nature is with respect to the effects of the fall of Adam and Eve on humanity. Understanding fallen human nature is important because it constitutes humanity's starting point in their journey of moral development.

Parts and Faculties

Authors throughout the Book of Mormon are consistent in their understanding of both the constituent parts of the human being and the psychological faculties associated with them. The five parts of the person noted in the text are the heart, mind, soul, spirit, and body/flesh (two terms that are often used synonymously).[10] In contrast to how such language may be understood in the modern age (i.e., "spirit" and "soul" are sometimes used interchangeably), the Book of Mormon sees these five parts as distinct,[11] even when they overlap with one another functionally. Additionally, the terms "heart" and "mind" rarely appear to describe human anatomy—that is, cardiac tissue or brain matter.[12] Instead, they function literarily as the loci of different psychological functions.[13] This is not to preclude the possibility of "syllepsis" in the text, or using a word in its figurative and literal sense simultaneously; it is only to say that such literal physiological mapping of psychological faculties is never explicit.

Regarding these various faculties, each part of the person possesses what I will refer to as the *general faculties* of cognition, emotion, and volition, as well as numerous more *specific faculties*. Specific faculties include cognitive functions like belief and understanding, emotional functions like joy and sadness, and volitional functions like desire and intent.[14] To be clear, the Book of Mormon authors themselves do not use these categories, but I employ them here heuristically for analysis and in a way that I think is true to the text. The parts of the human person and their multiple attendant faculties are represented in tables 2.1 through 2.5.

Table 2.1. Heart's Faculties

General faculty	Specific faculty	Reference
Cognition	Think	2 Ne. 20:7; Mos. 5:13, 24:12; Alma 12:7, 18:20, 18:32, 21:6, 43:48; Hel. 9:41
	Understand	2 Ne. 16:10; Mos. 2:9, 12:27, 13:32, 26:3; Alma 10:25; 3 Ne. 19:33
	Imagine	1 Ne. 2:11, 17:20; Hel. 16:22; 3 Ne. 2:2, 2:3, 29:3
	Ponder	1 Ne. 11:1; 2 Ne. 4:15–16, 32:1, 32:8; Hel. 10:3; Moro. 10:3
	Believe	1 Ne. 2:16; Alma 31:22; Hel. 16:15; 3 Ne. 1:22, 2:2
	Remember	1 Ne. 15:10–11; Hel. 12:2
	Conceive	3 Ne. 17:17
Emotion	Joy/rejoicing	2 Ne. 4:28, 4:30, 9:52; Jac. 2:22; Mos. 4:20; Alma 2:8, 17:29, 22:8, 26:11, 30:35; 3 Ne. 4:33; Morm. 2:12
	Sorrow	2 Ne. 4:17; Alma 31:2, 31:31, 25:15; Hel. 7:6, 7:14; 3 Ne. 1:10, 28:5; Morm. 2:19, 2:27; Ether 15:2
	Brokenness	2 Ne. 2:7, 4:32; Jac. 2:10, 2:35; 3 Ne. 9:20; Morm. 2:14; Ether 4:15; Moro. 6:2
	Love	1 Ne. 11:22; Mos. 18:21; Alma 13:29; 4 Ne. 1:15; Morm. 3:12
	Delight	2 Ne. 9:49; Alma 26:24; Morm. 4:11
	Gratitude	Jac. 4:3; Alma 37:37, 48:12
	Anger	1 Ne. 16:38; 3 Ne. 11:29–30
	Crying	2 Ne. 4:30; Alma 36:18; Moro. 9:15
	Gladness	1 Ne. 17:19; Alma 51:13
	Pain	1 Ne. 17:47; Alma 13:27
	Grief	Jac. 3:10; Alma 31:24
	Groaning	2 Ne. 4:19
	Weeping	2 Ne. 4:26
	Cheer	2 Ne. 10:23
	Fear*	2 Ne. 17:4
	Sobbing	Jac. 2:35
	Anxiety	Alma 13:27
	Guilt	Alma 24:10
	Depression	Alma 26:27
Volition[A]	Desire*	Jac. 6:5; Mos. 11:2, 12:29, 18:10–11; Alma 1:30, 4:8, 5:53, 7:6, 17:14, 19:33, 31:24, 31:28, 41:3; Hel. 6:17, 7:21, 12:4, 13:20–21, 13:27; Ether 8:7
	Purpose*	1 Ne. 1:5; 2 Ne. 31:13; Jac 6:5; Mos. 7:33, 21:35; Alma 45:7; 3 Ne. 10:6, 12:24, 18:32; Morm. 9:27; Moro. 7:48
	Sincerity*	1 Ne. 1:5; 2 Ne. 31:13; Mos. 4:10, 26:29; Hel. 3:27; Morm. 3:12; Moro. 10:4
	Intent*	1 Ne. 1:5; 2 Ne. 31:13; Mos. 5:13; Alma 12:7, 18:32, 21:6; Moro. 7:9
	Wish	Alma 13:27, 29:1
	Will	Moro. 29:1

* The word chosen to describe a specific faculty is either my own (as opposed to cited from the text) or is not used in all cited references.

A. The heart is never associated with so-called lower-order volitional operations, such as desire for food, drink, sex, or sleep. This suggests that the heart is not understood to be responsible for more involuntary yearnings. The term "lower-order" is used in H. G. Frankfurt, "Freedom of the Will and the Concept of a Person," *Journal of Philosophy* 68, no. 1 (1971): 5–20.

Table 2.2. Mind's Faculties

General faculty	Specific faculty	Reference
Cognition	Understand*	Mos. 2:9; Alma 32:34; 3 Ne. 17:3
	Assent*	Alma 16:16, 39:16, 48:7
	Belief	Alma 19:6; 3 Ne. 2:1; Ether 4:15
	Decide*	Alma 2:5, 47:6
	Think*	Alma 13:1, 36:18
	Concentrate*	1 Ne. 15:27
	Question	Alma 34:5
	Remember	Moro. 9:25
Emotion	Pain/worry*	Alma 15:3, 15:5, 17:5, 22:3, 40:1, 41:1, 42:1
	Pleasure	Alma 30:53
	Ease	Alma 39:17
	Love	Moro. 10:32
Volition	Purpose*	2 Ne. 25:29; Mos. 2:11, 7:11, 7:33; Alma 39:13; Moro. 10:32
	Desire*	Alma 2:5, 11:4, 17:6, 35:5–6
	Intent	Mos. 4:13

* The word chosen to describe a specific faculty is either my own (as opposed to cited from the text) or is not used in all cited references.

Table 2.3. Spirit's Faculties

General faculty	Specific faculty	Reference
Cognition	Understand	2 Ne. 27:35
Emotion	Contrition	2 Ne. 2:7, 4:32; 3 Ne. 9:20, 12:19; Morm. 2:14; Ether 4:15
	Pain/worry*	Mos. 25:10, 25:13
	Depression	Alma 56:16
	Grief	3 Ne. 22:6
Volition	Desire*	Enos 1:10; Alma 8:10, 17:5A

* The word chosen to describe a specific faculty is either my own (as opposed to cited from the text) or is not used in all cited references.
A. Given the context of these passages, the spirit's ardor and effort appear to take the form of a fervent desire to receive blessings from God.

As one can see, while all five parts of the person participate in the general faculties of cognition, emotion, and volition, some parts are more frequently engaged than others. The heart, spirit, soul, and body/flesh, for example, are most often responsible for emotional expressions, whereas the mind is most often engaged in cognition. The heart participates in the highest number of specific faculties and is the part of the person spoken of most often in the Book of Mormon.[15] In this way it is unique. The heart's prominence notwithstanding,[16] there is little to suggest that it is in some way superior to the other parts of the person. Authors, for example, do not depict any

Table 2.4. Soul's Faculties

General faculty	Specific faculty	Reference
Cognition	Consciousness	Mormon 9:3
Emotion	Joy/rejoicing	1 Ne. 1:15, 8:12, 11:23; 2 Ne. 1:21, 4:30; Mos. 4:11; Alma 7:26, 19:6, 36:20, 46:25, 48:11; Hel. 3:35, 7:8; 3 Ne. 17:17
	Pain/worry*	2 Ne. 9:47, 26:10; Jac. 2:8–9; Mos. 25:11, 27:29, 29:33; Alma 14:6, 31:30, 36:12, 36:16, 36:20, 38:8, 39:7; Morm. 5:8
	Anguish	1 Ne. 17:47; 2 Ne. 26:7; Mos. 19:7, 25:11, 28:4; Alma 8:14, 38:8; Morm. 6:16
	Delight	2 Ne. 4:15–16, 9:51, 11:2, 11:4, 11:5–6, 25:4–5, 25:13, 31:3
	Sorrow	2 Ne. 4:26; Alma 46:25; Hel. 7:9
	Grief	2 Ne. 4:17, 26:11; Jac. 2:6; Alma 61:2
	Comfort	Alma 31:31–32; Ether 15:3
	Happiness	Alma 40:15, 40:17, 40:21
	Misery	Alma 40:15, 40:17, 40:21
	Mourning	Alma 4:3; Ether 15:3
	Anxiety	2 Ne. 1:16
	Abhor	2 Ne. 9:49
	Anger	Alma 51:14
	Agony	Hel. 7:6
	Fear	Morm. 6:8
	Guilt	Morm. 9:3
Volition	Purpose*	Enos 1:9; Mos. 14:12, 26:14; Alma 19:14, 34:26, 46:17, 58:10; Hel. 7:11, 7:14; Morm. 3:12
	Hunger/thirst	Enos 1:4; 3 Ne. 20:8
	Long	Alma 36:22

* The word chosen to describe a specific faculty is either my own (as opposed to cited from the text) or is not used in all cited references.

Table 2.5. Body/Flesh's Faculties

General faculty	Specific faculty	Reference
Cognition	Know	Alma 7:12
Emotion	Suffering/pain*	1 Ne. 15:31; 2 Ne. 6:11; Mos. 3:7; Alma 7:13, 17:5; Ether 15:34
	Depression	Alma 56:16
Volition	Will	2 Ne. 2:29, 10:24
	Lust	1 Ne. 22:23

* The word chosen to describe a specific faculty is either my own (as opposed to cited from the text) or is not used in all cited references.

part of the person as inherently good or bad,[17] nor do they present one part's subordination to another—for instance, the heart to the mind—as normative. Because no single part possesses a given general faculty uniquely, the parts of the person are periodically depicted as fungible even as they remain distinct. Nephi$_1$, for example, writes "my soul is rent with anguish because of you, and my heart is pained" (1 Nephi 17:47). In this poetic parallelism, the shared capacity of the heart and soul for emotion (sorrow in this case) make them functionally indistinguishable.

Explicit language relating to any hierarchical structure among the person's various faculties (as opposed to parts) is similarly absent. In other words, the Book of Mormon does not appear to assume the preeminence of the cognitive, emotional, or volitional operations. Authors, therefore, conceptualize the constitutive aspects of the human person within a remarkably egalitarian framework. Unlike Plato, for instance, as well as many post-Enlightenment scholars who view acquiescence to cognitive operations as morally and psychologically normative,[18] in the Book of Mormon no single part or faculty is explicitly depicted as more important or reliable than any other. Because they consistently have overlapping responsibilities, there exists significant redundancy in human psychological operations in the text.

Assumptions relating to human psychology do evolve, albeit in subtle ways, throughout the Book of Mormon. Stated concisely, the books of Mosiah through Moroni typically provide more narrative examples of human psychological operations than the books of 1 Nephi through Omni. The former books also illustrate a wider variety of specific faculties than do the latter. The likely primary reason for this is that Mormon$_2$, the primary editor of former books, merely wrote more words than the other editors and authors in the Book of Mormon—over twice as much as Nephi$_1$ and more than seven times as much as Moroni$_2$.

Fallen Humanity

Having now defined a human being on a psychological level, we are in a better position to address another topic relevant to the conceptualization of moral formation in the Book of Mormon: the inherent (im)morality of humanity. For, as Cheryl Cottine notes, "Where one begins determines the work that virtue does to enable one to reach the desired end."[19] As previously mentioned, I view humanity's desired moral telos in the Book of Mormon to entail putting off the "natural man" and becoming a "saint through the atonement of Christ the Lord" (Mosiah 3:19). Where, then, does one start on this journey? Are humans inherently good, bad, or neither?

The Book of Mormon offers a complex answer to these questions. Authors consistently view human creation as an intentional act of God, and humans as reflecting the imprint of their creator.[20] According to Lehi₁, who offers the first semi-systematic discussion of the subject, at the time of creation Adam and Eve were "in a state of innocence, having no joy, for they knew no misery; doing no good, for they knew no sin" (2 Nephi 2:23). Put a slightly different way, prior to receiving God's law, they existed in a situation in which moral complexity had not yet entered the world. Lehi₁ explains "righteousness could not be brought to pass, neither wickedness, neither holiness . . . neither good nor bad" (2 Nephi 2:11). Morally speaking, then, Adam and Eve were blank slates, blameless but not praiseworthy, neither good nor bad in character and conduct.

Correspondingly, they also possessed unactualized psychological potential. As Lehi₁ further describes it, without an understanding of God's law, Adam and Eve could not discern good from evil, experience happiness or misery, and had not yet been "enticed" (a form of desire) by the choices available to them (2 Nephi 2:16). Their ability to know, feel, and desire were thus limited in their state of innocence. Significantly, Lehi₁ explicitly links their psychological limitations to their moral state. He explains, for example, that "if there be no righteousness there be no happiness" (2 Nephi 2:13). In this passage, experiencing the emotion of happiness is not possible without being righteous. Appealing to the same logic, Lehi₁ also describes "misery" as a product of sin (2 Nephi 2:13). By framing certain psychological experiences as the consequence of particular moral states, Lehi₁ cultivates a theological seed that bears fruit throughout the Book of Mormon: the idea that the human psyche is where moral formation is manifested.

Once Adam and Eve became aware of God's law and chose to disobey it,[21] their nature and status before him changed and the consequences of their decision would extend to all humanity. Only Lehi₁ and Alma₂ appear to acknowledge some positive effects of the "fall," teaching that it allowed the human family to come into existence and to further develop morally and psychologically (2 Nephi 2:4; Alma 42:3–5). As a direct result of Adam and Eve's choice, their posterity could know good and evil, choose God's will over their own will and pleasure, and experience joy and misery.

Most Book of Mormon authors, however, emphasize the fall's negative consequences. Benjamin (quoting an angel) introduces the phrase the "natural man" to describe postlapsarian human nature (Mosiah 3:19).[22] By describing the natural man as an "enemy to God," Benjamin is the first to explicitly frame fallen humanity's relationship to God in polemical terms (Mosiah 3:19). Unlike the words "lost," "fallen," or "cut off," which other authors use and which primarily imply separation, "enemy" implies hostility

Table 2.6. Consequences of the Fall

Speaker	Consequences	References
Lehi₁	Procreation; capacity to experience joy and misery; capacity to do good; capacity to know sin; capacity to die; kept alive to repent; humans become lost and fallen	1 Ne. 10:6; 2 Ne. 2:21, 2:23–24
Jacob₂	Capacity to die; cut off from presence of Lord	2 Ne. 9:6–10
Benjamin	State of natural man; humans become enemies to God	Mos. 3:19
Abinadi	Humans become enemies to God, lost, fallen, carnal, sensual, devilish, subjected to devil	Mos. 16:3–5
Alma₂	Humans become lost, fallen, carnal, sensual, devilish; become like God, knowing good and evil; capacity to die; kept alive to repent; cut off from presence of Lord; become subjects to follow own will and pleasure; become in the grasp of God's justice	Mos. 27:25–26; Alma 12:22, 12:24, 42:3–10, 42:14
Aaron₂	Carnal state; humans cannot merit anything of themselves	Alma 22:13–14
Amulek	Humans become hardened, fallen, lost; humans must perish	Alma 39:4
Samuel₂	Temporal and spiritual death	Hel. 14:16
Moroni₂	Humans separated from presence of Lord	Morm. 9:12–13
Brother of Jared	Human nature becomes evil continually; humans separated from presence of the Lord	Ether 3:13

and antagonism. Subsequent figures denigrate fallen humanity even more explicitly, describing humans as carnal, sensual, devilish, subjected to the devil, unable to merit anything of themselves, and continually evil (see table 2.6). The exceptions to such descriptions are little children, who are considered by some as "blameless before God," "blessed," "whole," "not capable of committing sin," and "alive in Christ."[23] For this reason, as the resurrected Christ teaches, "the curse of Adam is taken from them in me, that it hath no power over them" (Moroni 8:8).

In summary, then, humanity at the time of creation was morally neutral. After the fall, Adam and Eve began to procreate and their children entered the world "lost, because of the transgression of their parents," in "a state of nature" that is "contrary to the nature of God" and "contrary to the nature of happiness" (2 Nephi 2:21; Alma 41:11). In one of the more expansive statements on the subject, Mormon₂ laments the state of fallen humanity, particularly his own wicked people, saying:

And thus we can behold how false, and also the unsteadiness of the hearts of the children of men. . . . O how foolish, and how vain, and how evil, and devilish, and how quick to do iniquity, and how slow to do good, are the children of men; yea, how quick to hearken unto the words of the evil one, and to set their hearts upon the vain things of the world! . . . Yea, how quick to be lifted up in pride; yea, how quick to boast, and do all manner of that which is iniquity and how slow are they to remember the Lord their God. . . . Behold, they do not desire that the Lord their God, who hath created them, should rule and reign over them. . . . O how great is the nothingness of the children of men; yea, even they are less than the dust of the earth. (Helaman 12:1–7)

As in Lehi₁'s discussion of the fall, psychology and morality intersect in Mormon₂'s lament. The wicked are foolish and forget the Lord, their desires are disoriented, and they find emotional fulfillment in all the wrong places.

The Book of Mormon is clear, however, that these moral and psychological deficiencies—that is, the effects of fallenness—are not insurmountable. As King Benjamin explains, they can be presently overcome if one "yields to the enticings of the Holy Spirit, and putteth off the natural man, and becometh a saint through the atonement of Christ the Lord" (Mosiah 3:19). Significantly, the purpose of moral formation in the Book of Mormon is not to regain Eden; it is to become "as a saint," which is an entirely different thing. Eden is never said to represent the pristine state of humanity, nor are Adam and Eve ever framed as moral exemplars—they were innocent in Eden but not saintly. The next question to address, then, is how the Book of Mormon conceptualizes this saintly ideal. What constitutes moral character in the text?

Moral Character

As stated previously, I define moral character in this chapter as a disposition to think, feel, desire, and act virtuously. I define virtues contextually and as "state(s) of character,"[24] or "dispositional excellences," that reflect and contribute to saintliness and putting off the "natural man" (Mosiah 3:19).[25] In the Book of Mormon, virtues are the building blocks of moral character and lead one to a positive state of relation to deity. The Book of Mormon speaks of human moral character in at least four different but related ways.[26] They are depictions of moral exemplars, figurative descriptions of moral ideals, psychological descriptions of moral people, and descriptions of virtues and vices. These modes of discourse, or literary and rhetorical conventions, collectively provide a foundation for defining what it means to be a good person in the text and, by extension, for examining the unique psychological activities of such people, which will be the task of the final section of this chapter.

I do not include in this list more general exhortations to moral conduct because while such behaviors typically follow from moral character, they are not the same thing in the text. One representative example of this is in Moroni 7. Here, Mormon₂ approvingly discusses prayer and gift giving. He also argues, however, that these practices are not inherently good and can in fact merit censure from God if they are not performed with the proper disposition—that is, with "real intent" and ungrudgingly. He explains:

> For behold, God hath said a man being evil cannot do that which is good; for if he offereth a gift, or prayeth unto God, except he shall do it with real intent it profiteth him nothing. For behold, it is not counted unto him for righteousness. For behold, if a man being evil giveth a gift, he doeth it grudgingly; wherefore it is counted unto him the same as if he had retained the gift; wherefore he is counted evil before God. And likewise also is it counted evil unto a man, if he shall pray and not with real intent of heart; yea, and it profiteth him nothing, for God receiveth none such. Wherefore, a man being evil cannot do that which is good. (Moroni 7:6–10)

Similar language can be seen in Jesus's sermon to the Nephites, in which he teaches that alms, prayer, and fasting should not be done vainly or conspicuously.[27]

Several figures in the Book of Mormon thus draw a distinction between character and conduct. One cannot *do* good without first *being* good, which in these passages relates to the motivations and sincerity with which one performs an action.[28] Or put a slightly different way, one is not judged good by God because of good deeds alone but because of good desires and motives for doing good. For this reason, equating moral character with the performance of certain actions that are typically understood as good misrepresents a significant aspect of moral theory in the text.[29]

Exempla

One way in which moral character is discernible in the Book of Mormon is through descriptions of people whose character and conduct are presented as worthy of emulation, or what are more commonly referred to as *exempla*.[30] Being "perfect," Jesus Christ serves as the most reliable paradigm of virtue in the Book of Mormon (3 Nephi 12:48). Jesus is described as possessing such virtues as love, mercy, long-suffering, humility, compassion, and justice. Nephi₁ and Mormon₂ encourage their readers to follow Jesus's example of sincere and properly motivated obedience to God's commandments, and Jesus himself says, "I have set an example for you," "follow me, and do the things which you have seen me do," and "be . . . even as I am" (2 Nephi 31:12; 3 Nephi 18:16, 27:27).[31] In the Book of Mormon, imitating Christ's character and conduct is a mark of having been born of him and leads to salvation.[32]

Other figures are also explicitly presented as moral exemplars in the text, including Lehi₁, Nephi₁, the sons of Mosiah₂, Shiblon₂, and Captain Moroni₁.[33] As Mormon₂ writes of Moroni₁, "If all men had been, and were, and ever would be, like unto Moroni, behold, the very powers of hell would have been shaken forever; yea, the devil would never have power over the hearts of the children of men" (Alma 48:17). He then describes in more detail what makes Moroni₁ worth imitating:

> Moroni was a strong and a mighty man; he was a man of a perfect under-standing; yea, a man that did not delight in bloodshed; a man whose soul did joy in the liberty and the freedom of his country, and his brethren from bondage and slavery; yea, a man whose heart did swell with thanksgiving to his God, for the many privileges and blessings which he bestowed upon his people; a man who did labor exceedingly for the welfare and safety of his people. Yea, and he was a man who was firm in the faith of Christ, and he had sworn with an oath to defend his people, his rights, and his country, and his religion, even to the loss of his blood. (Alma 48:11–13)

In such passages, these moral figures are not just spoken of approvingly, but their character and virtue-informed conduct are rhetorically framed as an ideal toward which to strive.

Figurative Descriptions of Moral Ideals

In contrast to these more literal portrayals of moral persons, figurative imagery is also used to describe moral ideals in the Book of Mormon (see table 2.7). Such images are typically drawn from the natural world—plants, animals, food, bodies of water, and geography. For example, Nephi₁ says of Lehi₁, "When my father saw that the waters of the river emptied into the fountain of the Red Sea, he spake unto Laman, saying: O that thou mightest be like unto this river, continually running into the fountain of all righteousness!" (1 Nephi 2:9). Lehi₁ then switches metaphors and says to his other son, "Lemuel: O that thou mightest be like unto this valley, firm and steadfast, and immovable in keeping the commandments of the Lord!" (1 Nephi 2:10). In these passages, a river and a valley are intended to function as moral ideals. Their orientation, movement, firmness, and steadfastness are characteristics that transcend their instantiations in nature and may be profitably applied to human beings.

Lehi$_1$'s son Nephi$_1$ is more partial to language of animal husbandry, comparing righteous people to calves and sheep.[34] Jesus, Alma$_2$, and Samuel$_2$ likewise employ the image of sheep.[35] Jacob$_2$ favors agricultural language, equating the righteous, at least implicitly, to a tree that produces good fruit,[36] something that is later echoed in the recorded words of Alma$_2$ and Jesus.[37] Applying similar logic but with a different image, Mormon$_2$ compares a good person to a good fountain of water, explaining that "a bitter fountain cannot bring forth good water; neither can a good fountain bring forth bitter water" (Moroni 7:10–11). Here the implication is that one who "follow(s) Christ" will possess the generative characteristics of a good fountain because "that which is of God inviteth and enticeth to do good continually" (Moroni 7:13).

Elsewhere in the Book of Mormon, Jesus describes good people as the "salt of the earth" that retains its "savor" and as a "light" and a "candle" that shine and "giveth light to all that are in the house."[38] They are also like a "city that is set on a hill" and a "wise man, who built his house upon a rock" instead of the sand.[39] In addition to equating virtuous people to the wise man in one passage, Jesus also likens such people to the edifice

Table 2.7. Figurative Moral Ideals

Figurative Ideal	Related Character and Conduct	Reference
River	Oriented to righteousness; peaceful	1 Ne. 2:9, 20:18
Valley	Firm, steadfast, immovable in keeping commandments	1 Ne. 2:10
Calves	Fear God	1 Ne. 22:24; 3 Ne. 25:2
Sheep	Know and follow Jesus Christ	1 Ne. 22:25; Mos. 26:21; Alma 5:60; Hel. 15:13; 3 Ne. 15:24
Good tree	Produce good works (i.e., "good fruit")	Jac. 5:46–6:7; Alma 5:52; 3 Ne. 14:17–19
Good fountain	Produce good works (i.e., "good water")	Moro. 7:11
Salt	Provide "savor" to earth	3 Ne. 12:13, 16:15
Light/candle	Overt discipleship	3 Ne. 12:15
City on a hill	Overt discipleship	3 Ne. 12:14
Wise builder	Hears and applies Jesus's teachings	Hel. 5:15; 3 Ne. 14:24
House on a rock	Hears and applies Jesus's teachings	Hel. 5:12; 3 Ne. 18:12
Elements of the earth and cosmos	Obey God's command	Hel. 12:7–23
Child	Submissive, meek, humble, patient, full of love	Mos. 3:16–19; 3 Ne. 9:22, 11:37–38; Moro. 8:10

itself in another, praising those who are "built upon my rock" and "built upon my gospel."[40] Finally, several authors idealize children in the Book of Mormon. Benjamin teaches that a person must "become as a little child" to be saved, which involves being "submissive, meek, humble, patient, full of love, willing to submit to all things which the Lord seeth fit to inflict upon him, even as a child doth submit to his father" (Mosiah 3:18–19). Jesus and Mormon$_2$ express similar sentiments.[41]

Psychological Descriptions of Moral People

Another way moral character is represented is through psychological descriptions of moral people. By *psychological descriptions*, I refer to the mapping of moral attributes onto the five parts of the human person. The parts of the person and their attendant positive and negative qualities are represented in table 2.8. Positive and negative qualities are psychologically mapped with roughly the same frequency in the Book of Mormon. The most common positive qualities are soft heart,[42] contrite spirit,[43] firm mind,[44] filled soul,[45] and sanctified body/flesh.[46] Common negative qualities include hard heart,[47] evil spirit,[48] blind mind,[49] hungry soul,[50] and a body/flesh that is full of darkness.[51]

Like figurative moral ideals, psychological qualities in the Book of Mormon are abstract and abstruse at first glance. What, for instance, does it

Table 2.8. Psychological Qualities

Part	Positive Qualities	Negative Qualities
Heart	Soft, pure, lowly, broken, poor, one, open, holy, full, great, sanctified	Hard, proud, turned from God, wicked, uncircumcised, stout, fat, stubborn, false, unsteady, corrupt
Spirit	Contrite, firm, strong, unconquerable, noble, poor, good, free	Evil, contentious, wicked, lying, bad
Mind	Firm, spiritual, sober, pure, delicate, diligent, one	Blind, carnal, sore, frenzied, deranged
Soul	Filled, awake, redeemed, spotless, at rest, illuminated, expanded, enlarged, swelled, saved, at peace, sure, steadfast	Hungry, drooped in sin, wounded, damned, corrupt, thirsty[A]
Body/flesh	Sanctified, holy, full of light	Full of darkness

A. In Enos 1:4, a hungry soul does not necessarily seem to be a negative thing. But it is clearly more negative in 3 Nephi 20:8, in which hunger and thirst imply deficiency that needs to be overcome.

mean to have a "soft" heart? Does this imply softness with respect to cognition, emotion, or volition; or perhaps all three of these general faculties simultaneously; or maybe just two of them? How might softness of heart overlap with other virtues or behaviors, such as faith or love? By analyzing psychological qualities in their literary context and, when possible, with respect to their negative counterparts (e.g., a hard heart), the moral character they describe becomes clearer.

For example, Nephi$_1$ writes that the Lord "did visit me, and did soften my heart that I did believe all the words which had been spoken by my father; wherefore, I did not rebel against him" (1 Nephi 2:16). In this passage, softness of heart is associated with a believing, faithful, and submissive disposition and thus has cognitive and volitional components. Correspondingly, hardness of heart is linked to volitional intransigence, as Nephi$_1$ makes clear in his description of his brothers: "Laman and Lemuel would not hearken unto my words . . . because of the hardness of their heart" (1 Nephi 2:18). Elsewhere in the Book of Mormon, however, softness of heart is associated with fear and thus is more emotional in nature.[52] This is merely to say that articulating the nature of psychological qualities requires attention to their discrete manifestations in the varied contexts in which they appear.

Descriptions of Virtues and Vices

A final way moral character is represented in the Book of Mormon is through descriptions of virtues and vices (see table 2.9).[53] The most attested virtues in the Book of Mormon are righteousness, holiness, peacefulness, and wisdom, whereas the most common vices are wickedness, contentiousness, anger, and pride. Like the previously mentioned forms of moral discourse, virtues and vices often appear in the context of larger narratives. This requires the reader to discern the contours of these attributes based on the portrayal of those who possess them. Periodically, however, one sees extended discussions of specific virtues or vices largely independent of the people in whom they might be found. Some examples of this are Alma$_2$'s discourse on humility and faith;[54] Mormon$_2$'s discourse on faith, hope, and charity;[55] and Moroni$_2$'s discourse on faith.[56] These passages are unique in both their extended length and in the sense that they are more attribute-focused than person-focused.

By way of illustration, take the virtue of faith(fulness). Alma$_2$ writes that "faith is not to have a perfect knowledge of things; therefore if ye have faith ye hope for things which are not seen, which are true" (Alma 32:21). Mormon$_2$ adds to this:

I say unto you that he cannot have faith and hope, save he shall be meek, and lowly of heart . . . and if a man be meek and lowly in heart . . . he must needs have charity; for if he have not charity he is nothing; wherefore he must needs have charity. . . . Charity is the pure love of Christ, and it endureth forever; and whoso is found possessed of it at the last day, it shall be well with him. (Moroni 7:43–44, 7:47)

In these passages, the precise nature of faith, its relation to other virtues, and some of its expressions are described. Mormon$_2$ also teaches that some virtues like "exceeding great faith" and love are infused by God as a "gift," demonstrating the need for divine aid in the process of moral formation, which is a consistent theme in the Book of Mormon (Mormon 10:11). Accordingly, regarding love, he exhorts his readers to "pray unto the Father with all the energy of heart, that ye may be filled with this love, which he hath bestowed upon all who are true followers of his Son, Jesus Christ; that ye may become the sons of God; that when he shall appear we shall be like him, for we shall see him as he is . . . we may be purified even as he is pure" (Moroni 10:48).

Having examined four different ways moral character is described in the Book of Mormon, we are now in a better position to articulate what it means to be a moral person according to the text. Such individuals may be described in at least the following ways:

1. Moral people are like Nephi$_1$, the converted sons of Mosiah$_2$, Shiblon$_2$, Alma$_2$, Amulek, Lehi$_3$, Nephi$_2$, Jesus, Jesus's three Nephite disciples, Captain Moroni$_1$, and the brother of Jared when they are behaving in a praiseworthy manner.
2. Moral people are, in certain respects, like a river, valley, calf, sheep, a good tree, a good fountain, salt, light, a candle, a city on a hill, a wise builder, a house on a rock, and a child.

Table 2.9. Prominent Virtues and Vices

Virtues	Vices
Righteousness, holiness, peacefulness, wisdom, mercy, love, justice, diligence, hope, faith (fullness), goodness, perfection, firmness, forgiving, God-fearing, meekness, cleanliness, long-suffering, steadfastness, humility, compassion, immovableness, kindness, fairness	Wickedness, contentiousness, anger, pride, vanity, unbelief, blindness, cunning, foolishness, uncleanliness, hate, hypocrisy, lust, deceit, mischievousness, lasciviousness, perversion, not fearing of God

Note: I have not included in this list some attributes that appear in tables 2.7 and 2.8.

3. The hearts of moral people are soft, pure, lowly, broken, poor, one, open, holy, full, great, and sanctified. Their spirits are contrite, firm, strong, unconquerable, noble, poor, good, and free. Their minds are spiritual, sober, pure, firm, delicate, diligent, and one. Their souls are awake, redeemed, spotless, at rest, illuminated, expanded, enlarged, swelled, filled, saved, at peace, sure, and steadfast. Their bodies/flesh are sanctified, holy, and full of light.
4. Moral people are righteous, holy, peaceful, wise, merciful, loving, just, diligent, hopeful, faithful, good, perfect, firm, forgiving, God-fearing, meek, clean, steadfast, humble, compassionate, immovable, kind, and fair.

It is assumed throughout the Book of Mormon that such character can be achieved only through the proper exercise of will in conformity with God's law, through the aid of God's spirit and grace, and "through the great Mediator of all men," Jesus Christ (2 Nephi 2:27–28).

Moral Psychology

To restate my purpose, examining how moral character is reflected in human psychological operations is what occupies me in this chapter. By analyzing instances of psychologically engaged moral and immoral people (as described in the previous section), it becomes clear that moral people experience expanded cognitive, emotional, and volitional functionality (see table 2.10). Several representative examples of each will suffice to illustrate this phenomenon.

Cognition

With respect to cognition, immorality compromises a person's ability to perceive, understand, know, remember, and believe truth.[57] Amulek, for example, alluding to the deficiencies of his audience's "hearts," reprimands the wicked people of Ammonihah, saying, "O ye wicked and perverse generation, why hath Satan got such great hold upon your hearts? Why will ye yield yourselves unto him that he may have power over you, to blind your eyes, that ye will not understand the words which are spoken, according to their truth?" (Alma 10:25). Alma$_2$ similarly teaches: "It is given unto many to know the mysteries of God. . . . And they that will harden their hearts, to them is given the lesser portion of the word until they know nothing concerning his mysteries" (Alma 12:9, 12:11). Elsewhere in the Book of Mormon, the hardhearted Laman and Lemuel "did not look unto the

Lord" for understanding "as they ought"; the sinful Korihor is deceived into believing false teachings are true; and the Nephites, "because of their iniquity, . . . began to disbelieve in the spirit of prophecy and in the spirit of revelation" (Helaman 4:23).[58] In these passages, sin either limits cognitive functioning (i.e., one's ability is diminished), makes one less disposed to certain cognitive activities (i.e., one's inclination is diminished), or hinders one's access to cognitively attained information (i.e., God withholds truth).

Correspondingly, moral persons are better able to perceive, believe, understand, and remember God/Christ, his words, works, and mysteries.[59] As previously mentioned, Nephi$_1$ attributes his belief in his father's prophetic words to his own soft heart: "The Lord . . . did soften my heart that I did believe" (1 Nephi 2:16). Such belief is then framed as a prerequisite to his viewing and understanding a heavenly vision of the future. He explains, "The Spirit cried with a loud voice, saying . . . blessed art thou, Nephi, because thou believest in the Son of the most high God; wherefore, thou shalt behold the things which thou hast desired" (1 Nephi 11:6). In the book of Mosiah, Abinadi teaches that moral character enables individuals to perceive and understand the Christocentric nature of the Law of Moses—that "all these things were types of things to come and . . . there could not any man be saved except it were through the redemption of God" (Mosiah 13:31–32). By attributing lack of perception of these things to the wickedness of some ancient Israelites, he implies that righteousness would have enabled such cognitive understanding. Morality is also correlated to recollection. Moral people keep Christ active in their working memory, remembering his body, teachings, that he keeps his promises, and other "great things the Lord hath done" (1 Nephi 7:11).[60] These are things that the wicked are inclined to forget or to which they are cognitively oblivious.[61]

Emotion

Like cognition, emotional faculties are also shaped by moral character, producing both positive and negative emotional states of being. By "positive" and "negative" here, I mean merely emotional states of being that correlate to morality (positive) and immorality (negative). Concerning negative states, sin robs the soul of peace; it promotes fear, horror, unhappiness, remorse, misery, anger, guilt, and sorrow.[62] Nephi$_1$, for example, laments his moral imperfections, saying, "O wretched man that I am! Yea, my heart sorroweth . . . my soul grieveth because of mine iniquities" (2 Nephi 4:17). Alma$_2$ recounts that prior to his conversion "I was racked with eternal torment, for my soul was harrowed up to the greatest degree and racked with all my sins" (Alma 36:12). Later speaking to his son, he reiterates a lesson he learned: "Wickedness never was happiness" (Alma 41:10). Although not often made explicit in the Book of Mormon, sin is also shown to compromise one's ability to love. For example, recounting the wickedness of his people, Mormon₂ explains, "For so exceedingly do they anger that it seemeth me that . . . they have lost their love, one towards another" (Moroni 9:5). Finally, in some cases, sin does produce "delight" and "joy," albeit in performing wicked acts.[63] As several authors say of the Lamanites, "They delighted in wars and bloodshed" and "did boast, and did delight in blood, and the shedding of the blood of their brethren" (Jacob 7:47; Mosiah 11:19). Thus, the text highlights how immoral actions and characters are tied to negative and disordered emotional states.

Moral characters, by contrast, often experience positive emotions such as compassion; love for God, neighbor, and enemy; joy, delight, and gratitude at truth and God's word; joy in others' well-being; and delight in righteousness.[64] Nephi₁ writes that his "soul delighteth" in scripture, "in proving unto my people the truth of the coming of Christ," "in the covenants of the Lord," and "in proving unto my people that save Christ should come all men must perish" (2 Nephi 11:2, 11:4–6). Elsewhere, after seeing the faith of the Nephites, Jesus says, "And now, behold, my joy is great, even unto fullness, because of you, and also this generation; yea, and even the Father rejoiceth, and also all the holy angels, because of you" (3 Nephi 27:30). Affectively, moral people also experience sorrow and pain for the sufferings of others, for their own sins and the sins of others, and abhorrence of sin and fear to sin.[65] For instance, Mormon₂ records that "when Nephi, the son of Nephi, saw this wickedness of his people, his heart was exceedingly sorrowful" and that Jesus "groaned within himself" over Israel's wickedness (3 Nephi 1:10, 17:14). In these passages one notices that spiritual maturity implies a kind of emotional sympathy with Christ. Such emotional expressions are not something that occurs among immoral people.

Volition

Finally, wicked persons are frequently portrayed as desiring to engage in acts of violence and moral depravity or as desiring power, riches, and other "vain" things of the world.[66] This can be clearly seen in Nephi₁'s vision of the great and abominable church of the devil: "And the angel spake unto me, saying: Behold the gold, and the silver, and the silks, and the scarlets, and the fine-twined linen, and the precious clothing, and the harlots, are the desires of this great and abominable church. And also for the praise of the world do they destroy the saints of God, and bring them down into captivity" (1 Nephi 13:7–9). According to Nephi₁, wicked persons "seek the lusts of the flesh and the things of the world, and to do all manner of iniquity," a theme that persists throughout the Book of Mormon (1 Nephi 22:23). Toward the end of the Book of Mormon, in one of Mormon₂'s last descriptions of his people, he writes to his son that the wicked Nephites "thirst after blood and revenge continually" (Moroni 9:5).

Moral character, on the other hand, is correlated volitionally with the desire to accept and obey God's teachings, commandments, and servants; with seeking God's glory and the welfare of others; and with sincerity and purposefulness in doing good.[67] Mormon₂ records that the newly converted sons of Mosiah "were desirous that salvation should be declared to every creature, for they could not bear that any human soul should perish; yea, even the very thoughts that any soul should endure endless torment did cause them to quake and tremble" (Mosiah 28:3). In a similar manner, three of Jesus's Nephite disciples are considered "more blessed" than their counterparts for desiring to "bring the souls of men" to Christ (3 Nephi 28:7, 28:9). In such cases, the volitional operations of humans are represented as being in harmony with God's. Moral people don't just do what God wants; they want what God wants: As the Lord says to Nephi₂, "All things shall be done unto thee according to thy word, for thou shalt not ask that which is contrary to my will" (Helaman 10:5). In some cases, God even fills the faithful "with desire," showing the human-divine volitional collaboration that can occur in the process of moral growth (3 Nephi 19:24). Finally, moral people also carry out God's will "with full purpose of heart, acting no hypocrisy and no deception before God, but with real intent" (2 Nephi 31:13).[68]

Conclusion

In summary, this chapter has attempted to demonstrate that morality (right character and conduct) and psychology (human parts and faculties) cannot be separated in the Book of Mormon. God created humanity with psychological potential that can be fully realized only through the cultivation of moral character. Consequently, moral character is central to becoming a fully functioning human being—that is, to "awake" and "arouse" all of the potential "energies," "faculties," and "power" of the human self.[69] The cognitive, emotional, and volitional operations of those who put off the "natural man" and "become a saint through the atonement of Christ the Lord" give them access to experiences that are beyond the reach of those who lack virtue (Mosiah 3:19) (see table 2.10).

Latter-day Saint apostle Parley P. Pratt's description of the Holy Spirit's transformative effect on humanity may be seen as an apt articulation of moral formation as represented in the Book of Mormon:

Table 2.10. Moral Psychology

Faculty	Morality	Immorality
Cognition	Increases ability to perceive, believe, understand, remember God/Christ, his words, works, mysteries	Compromises ability to understand, know, remember, believe truth
Emotion	Increases compassion; love for God, neighbor, and enemy; joy, delight, gratitude in truth/ God's word, others' well-being, and righteousness; sorrow/pain for others' suffering, sins, and own sins; abhorrence of and fear to sin	Robs peace; promotes fear, horror, unhappiness, remorse, misery, anger, guilt, sorrow; compromises ability to love; engenders delight and joy in wickedness
Volition	Increases desire to accept/ obey God's teachings, commandments, and servants; to seek God's glory and others' welfare; sincerity and purposefulness in doing good	Increases desire for wickedness, power, riches, vain things of world

It quickens all the intellectual faculties[;] increases, enlarges, expands, and purifies all the natural passions and affections, and adapts them, by the gift of wisdom, to their lawful use. It inspires, develops, cultivates and matures all the fine-toned sympathies, joys, tastes, kindred feelings, and affections of our nature. It inspires virtue, kindness, goodness, tenderness, gentleness, and charity. It develops beauty of person, form and features. It tends to health, vigor, animation, and social feeling. It invigorates all the faculties of the physical and intellectual man. It strengthens and gives tone to the nerves. In short, it is, as it were, marrow to the bone, joy to the heart, light to the eyes, music to the ears, and life to the whole being.[70]

My intent here has been to start a conversation. Much more descriptive and synthetic work needs to be done to provide a more exhaustive accounting of moral formation in the Book of Mormon. Having focused primarily on its more individualistic and psychological manifestations in this chapter, future inquiry into the subject might also explore in more detail its social implications. How, for example, are moral people represented as functioning in political, economic, and domestic contexts? How does this differ from immoral people? Or put a slightly different way, what does the ideal society look like in the text? What is Mormon$_2$'s *kallipolis*?[71] Another underexplored topic in scholarship is the various means by which moral formation is facilitated. What practices, or "spiritual exercises," are most conducive to the cultivation and maintenance of virtue?[72] And how might one characterize the relational dynamics of these exercises, such as with respect to human and divine agency? Attending at least to these issues will further contribute to bringing the moral theory and resources of the Book of Mormon to light.

Notes

1. In the Book of Mormon, human beings are also said to exist for the purpose of possessing the earth, experiencing joy, keeping God's commandments, and glorifying him forever. See 1 Nephi 17:36; 2 Nephi 2:25; Jacob 2:21. Mosiah 3:19 reads in full: "For the natural man is an enemy to God, and has been from the fall of Adam, and will be, forever and ever, unless he yields to the enticings of the Holy Spirit, and putteth off the natural man and becometh a saint through the atonement of Christ the Lord, and becometh as a child, submissive, meek, humble, patient, full of love, willing to submit to all things which the Lord seeth fit to inflict upon him, even as a child doth submit to his father." I interpret this passage to mean that yielding to the Holy Spirit is the same as putting off the natural man, and that becoming a saint is equivalent to becoming as a child.

2. For a concise summary of scholarship on ethics and the Book of Mormon, see Daniel Becerra, "Ethical Approaches to the Book of Mormon," *Journal of Book of Mormon Studies* 32 (2023): 97–116. For a brief introduction to contemporary articulations of virtue and virtue ethics, see Cheryl Cottine, "Virtue and Virtue Ethics," in *Encyclopedia of Religious Ethics*, vol. 1, ed. William Schweiker and Maria Antonaccio, 162–69 (Hoboken, NJ: Wiley Blackwell, 2022).

3. See, for example, Grant Hardy, *Understanding the Book of Mormon: A Reader's Guide* (New York: Oxford University Press, 2010); Nicholas Frederick, *The Bible, Mormon Scripture, and the Rhetoric of Allusivity* (Lanham, MD: Fairleigh Dickinson Press, 2016); and Daniel Becerra, Amy Easton-Flake, Nicholas Fredrick, and Joseph M. Spencer, *Book of Mormon Studies: An Introduction and Guide* (Provo, UT: BYU Religious Studies Center, 2022), 40–50.

4. I am borrowing these terms from Richard Hays, which he uses in the context of his work on New Testament ethics. See *The Moral Vision of the New Testament: A Contemporary Introduction to New Testament Ethics* (New York: HarperOne, 1996), 3–4.

5. Hardy, Understanding the Book of Mormon, xvi.

6. Amy Olberding distinguishes between reading text as "moral theory" versus "moral manual." See her *Moral Exemplars in the Analects: The Good Person Is That* (Oxfordshire: Routledge Press, 2011), 1–7.

7. Hardy, Understanding the Book of Mormon, xvi.

8. Within the Latter-day Saint tradition, the Book of Mormon's religious significance is tied in part to its role as a moral manual, or as one church authority figure describes it, a "handbook of instructions as we travel the pathway from bad to good to better and to have our hearts changed." See David A. Bednar, "The Atonement and Journey of Mortality," *Liahona* (April 2012): 40.

9. See, for example, A. A. Long, *Greek Models of the Mind and Self* (Cambridge: Harvard University Press, 2015).

10. Daniel Becerra, *3rd, 4th Nephi: A Brief Theological Introduction* (Provo, UT: Neal A. Maxwell Institute for Religious Scholarship, Brigham Young University, 2020), 25–27. I do not include "bowels," which appears eight times in the Book of Mormon. Bowels are the locus of some emotional expressions, like mercy and compassion (Mosiah 15:9; Alma 7:12, 26:37, 34:15; 3 Nephi 17:6–7). However, this is only the case for Christ's bowels. No other human's bowels appear to perform psychological functions. See also John Peters, "Bowels of Mercy," *BYU Studies* 38, no. 4 (1999): 27–41.

11. One possible exception to this is Alma 40:15.

12. Some exceptions are Alma 47:24, 47:26, and Helaman 2:9, in which the heart is spoken of as a literal organ.

13. In other words, when Nephi₁ says, "I sat pondering in my heart," I do not think he understood his cardiac muscle to be doing the "pondering" (1 Nephi 11:1). On the possible physiological relationship between the heart and cognitive activity, see Robert A. Rees, "The Heart in Alma 12 and 13," in *A Preparatory Redemption: Reading Alma 12–13*, ed. Matthew Bowman and Rosemary Demos (Provo, UT: Neal A. Maxwell Institute for Religious Scholarship, BYU, 2018), 44–53.

14. For more on emotions in the Latter-day Saint tradition, see Mauro Properzi, *Mormonism and the Emotions: An Analysis of LDS Scriptural Texts* (Lanham, MD: Fairleigh Dickinson University Press, 2015).

15. The word "heart" appears in every book of the Book of Mormon except Omni and Words of Mormon. It is most common in Alma (142 occurrences), 2 Nephi (54 occurrences), Helaman (53 occurrences), 1 Nephi (43 occurrences), Mosiah (41 occurrences), and 3 Nephi (38 occurrences). The division of the remaining attestations are as follows: Jacob (22 occurrences), Ether (18 occurrences), Mormon (17 occurrences), Moroni (15 occurrences), 3 Nephi (5 occurrences), Jarom (2 occurrences), and Enos (1 occurrence). On the heart in Alma 12 and 13, see Rees, "Heart in Alma 12 and 13," 44–53.

16. On the prominence of the heart in other Christian moral literature, see Harriet Luckman and Linda Kulzer, eds., *Purity of Heart in Early Ascetic and Monastic Literature* (Collegeville, MN: Liturgical Press, 1999).

17. It is true that language of physicality (e.g., "flesh," "body," "carnal") often takes on a negative connotation in the Book of Mormon, whereas psychical language takes on a positive one—e.g., "to be carnally-minded is death, and to be spiritually-minded is life eternal" (2 Nephi 9:39). Both parts of the self, however, are just as often portrayed as morally neutral. Only Lehi₁, Nephi₁, and Jacob₂ explicitly associate the "flesh" with sin and sinful inclinations. See 2 Nephi 2:29, 4:17, 10:24.

18. Lisa Sowle Cahill, "Love and Compassion," in Schweiker and Antonaccio, *Encyclopedia of Religious Ethics*, 150.

19. Cottine, "Virtue and Virtue Ethics," 163.

20. E.g., 1 Nephi 17:36; 2 Nephi 2:25; Jacob 2:21; Mosiah 7:27.

21. Lehi$_1$, Jacob$_2$, Benjamin, Alma$_2$, and Aaron$_2$ describe this act as a transgression. See 2 Nephi 2:21–22, 9:6; Mosiah 3:11; Alma 12:31, 22:12.

22. The phrase "natural man" appears in one other place in the Book of Mormon, in Alma 26:21. However, it is unclear whether Ammon$_2$ understands the term in the same way as Benjamin. Robert Millet discusses this concept in light of the broader Latter-day Saint scriptural and prophetic tradition in "The Natural Man: An Enemy to God," in *The Book of Mormon: Mosiah, Salvation Only through Christ*, ed. Monte S. Nyman and Charles D. Tate Jr. (Provo, UT: BYU Religious Studies Center, 1991), 139–59.

23. Mosiah 3:16; Moroni 8:8, 22.

24. For a helpful introduction to the differences and evolution of objectivistic and relativistic approaches to morality, see William M. Kurtines and Jacob L. Gewirtz, "Certainty and Morality: Objectivistic versus Relativistic Approaches," in *Morality, Moral Behavior, and Moral Development*, ed. William M. Kurtines and Jacob L. Gewirtz, 3–23 (New York: Wiley, 1984).

25. Cottine, "Virtue and Virtue Ethics," 163; Daniel Lapsey, Timothy Reilly, and Darcia Narvaez, "Moral Self-Identity and Character Development," in *The Oxford Handbook of Moral Development*, ed. Lene Arnett Jesen (New York: Oxford University Press, 2020), 691.

26. Becerra, *3rd, 4th Nephi*, 54–55.

27. 3 Nephi 13:1–18.

28. For more on sincerity and proper motivations for obedience, see Becerra, *3rd, 4th Nephi*, 47–53.

29. On this idea in more modern Latter-day Saint discourse, see Dallin Oaks, "Why Do We Serve?" *Ensign* (Oct. 1984): 12–15.

30. For a concise summary of exempla as a literary form, see Abraham Malherbe, *Moral Exhortation: A Greco-Roman Sourcebook* (Philadelphia: Westminster Press, 1986), 135–36.

31. 2 Nephi 31:16; Mormon 7:10.

32. 2 Nephi 31:10–16; Moroni 7:48.

33. 1 Nephi 7:8; Alma 17:11, 39:1, 48:17; Helaman 5:6–7. Others include Alma$_2$, Amulek, Lehi$_3$, Nephi$_2$, Jesus's three Nephite disciples, and the brother of Jared. See Ether 12:13–21, 12:30.

34. 1 Nephi 22:24–26.

35. Mosiah 26:20–21; 3 Nephi 15:17, 15:21, 15:24, 16:1, 16:3, 18:31.

36. Jacob 5:46–6:7.

37. Alma 4:34–36, 4:52; 3 Nephi 14:16–20.

38. 3 Nephi 12:13–16, 16:15.

39. 3 Nephi 12:14, 14:24.

40. 3 Nephi 18:12–13, 27:8–11. Cf. 1 Nephi 28:28. Helaman$_3$ appears to compare the faithful to the builder and building in the same verse, saying, "Remember that it is upon the rock of our Redeemer . . . that ye must build your foundation; that when the devil shall send forth his mighty winds . . . it

shall have no power over you to drag you down to the gulf of misery and endless woe, because of the rock upon which ye are built, which is a sure foundation" (Helaman 5:12).

41. 3 Nephi 9:22, 11:37–38; Moroni 8:10.

42. 1 Nephi 2:16, 7:5, 7:19, 18:19, 18:20; 2 Nephi 10:18; Mosiah 21:15, 23:28, 23:29; Alma 24:8; Helaman 12:2.

43. 2 Nephi 2:7, 4:32; Helaman 8:15; 3 Nephi 9:20; Mormon 2:14; Ether 4:15; Moroni 6:2.

44. Jacob 3:1, 3:2; Alma 57:27; Moroni 7:30.

45. 1 Nephi 8:12; Alma 5:18, 36:20, 51:14; Helaman 7:9; 3 Nephi 20:8; Mormon 6:8.

46. 3 Nephi 28:39; Moroni 4:3.

47. 1 Nephi 2:18; 7:8, 12:17, 13:27, 14:2, 14:6, 14:7, 15:3, 15:4, 15:10, 15:11, 16:22, 17:19, 17:30, 17:41, 17:42, 17:46, 17:47, 22:5, 22:18; 2 Nephi 1:17, 5:21, 6:10, 25:10, 25:12, 25:27, 33:2; Jacob 1:15, 6:4, 6:5, 6:6; Jarom 1:3; Mosiah 3:15, 10:14, 11:29, 12:1, 13:32, 26:3; Alma 1:24, 8:11, 9:5, 9:30, 9:31, 10:6, 12:10, 12:11, 12:13, 12:33, 12:34, 12: 35, 12:36, 12:37, 13:4, 13:5, 14:11, 15:15, 21:3, 21:12, 22:22, 23:14, 30:29, 30:46, 33:20, 33:21, 34:31, 35:15, 37:10, 48:3; Helaman 6:35, 7:18, 10:13, 10:15, 12:2, 13:8, 13:12, 16:15, 16:22; 3 Nephi 1:22, 2:1, 7:16, 20:28, 21:6, 21:22; 4 Nephi 1:31, 1:34; Mormon 1:17, 3:3, 3:12, 4:11; Ether 4:15, 8:25, 11:13, 15:19; Moroni 9:4, 9:10.

48. 2 Nephi 32:8; Mosiah 2:32, 3:6, 4:14.

49. 1 Nephi 7:8, 17:30; Alma 48:3; 3 Nephi 2:1.

50. 2 Nephi 27:3; Enos 1:4.

51. 3 Nephi 13:23.

52. E.g., 1 Nephi 18:20.

53. I define "virtues" above in the "Exempla" section of this chapter. For some relatively recent treatment of individual virtues and vices in the Book of Mormon, see Kirk Weeden, "'Lifted up in the pride of their eyes': Pride and Cultural Distinction in the Book of Mormon," *Journal of Book of Mormon Studies* 28, no. 1 (2019): 291–300; Jason Kerr, "'Virtue' in Moroni 9:9," *Journal of Book of Mormon Studies* 26, no. 1 (2017): 260–65; and Richard Draper, "*Hubris* and *Atē*: A Latter-day Warning from the Book of Mormon," *Journal of Book of Mormon Studies* 2, no. 3 (1994): 12–33.

54. Alma 32:7–43.

55. Moroni 7:20–44.

56. Ether 12:6–21.

57. For some examples not cited, see 1 Nephi 7:8–12, 15:3, 15:11, 16:2; Mosiah 13:32, 3:15; Alma 33:20; Helaman 12:2, 16:20–22; 3 Nephi 2:1–2, 15:18–20. See also Becerra, *3rd, 4th Nephi*, 60–61.

58. 1 Nephi 15:3; Alma 30:53; Helaman 4:23

59. For some examples not cited, see 1 Nephi 2:16; 3 Nephi 20:11.

60. See also 3 Nephi 15:1, 18:7, 18:11, 20:11, 27:12.

61. E.g., 1 Nephi 7:10–12; Helaman 12:2.

62. For some examples not cited, see Mosiah 28:4; Alma 36:14–15, 41:11, 42:18; Helaman 5:12; 3 Nephi 1:18; Mormon 2:13, 9:3–4; Ether 15:3, 15:22. Good people also experience some of these emotions in the Book of Mormon but typically for different reasons and with different responses.

63. E.g., Mosiah 24:7; Alma 17:14, 17:35; 3 Nephi 27:11; Mormon 4:11; Moroni 9:13.

64. For some examples not cited, see 2 Nephi 4:15–16, 9:49, 25:4–5, 25:13; Mosiah 23:14, 24:21–22; Alma 8:22, 19:14, 26:37, 48:12; 3 Nephi 12:44, 17:20, 27:30.

65. E.g., 1 Nephi 2:18, 7:8, 4:17; 2 Nephi 9:49; Mosiah 8:7; Alma 4:7, 13:12, 27:28, 30:46, 31:24, 61:2; 3 Nephi 1:10, 7:16, 17:14, 27:32, 28:9, 28:38.

66. For some examples not cited, see 1 Nephi 1:20, 2:13, 4:11, 4:28, 7:14, 7:16, 7:19, 10:21, 17:44; 2 Nephi 2:17–28, 5:19; Mosiah 10:15, 11:26; Alma 3:7, 9:23, 10:14, 17:14, 17:39, 18:2, 48:2, 51:8; Helaman 1:8, 2:5; 4 Nephi 1:31; Ether 8:15–16, 9:5, 10:33, 11:2, 13:15–16, 13:22.

67. For some examples not cited, see 2 Nephi 1:25; 3 Nephi 11:23, 17:8, 19:9, 28:2, 28:29.

68. See also Jacob 6:5; Mosiah 7:33; 3 Nephi 10:6, 12:23–24, 18:32; Moroni 7:6, 7:9, 10:4.

69. Jacob 3:11; Mosiah 29:14; Alma 32:27.

70. Parley P. Pratt, *Key to the Science of Theology*, 9th ed. (Salt Lake City: Deseret Book), 100–101.

71. The term *kallipolis* refers to the ideal city imagined by Plato in the *Republic*. See especially books 2–8.

72. On the concept of spiritual exercises, see Pierre Hadot, *Philosophy as a Way of Life* (Oxford: Blackwell, 1995), 81–144.

3

The Moral Reality
of the Book of Mormon

COURTNEY S. CAMPBELL

A moral vision of the relationship of ethics and the scriptural witness of religious truth known as the Book of Mormon must account for several features of how religion and theology inform ethics and morality. Scripture is necessarily a source for ethical reflection and moral teaching in a religious community that has been formed by the book. However, scripture is never an exclusive or sufficient source; there is no *sola scriptura* ethic. The moral tradition of a religious community supplements scripture with interpretive models, ecclesiastical and prophetic teaching, exemplary narratives, communal norms and practices, personal experience and moral agency, and inspiration attributable to a divine source, such as an "inner light" or a conscience. Scripture rarely dictates a moral conclusion about a specific issue, question, or choice without the intermediation of these other moral authorities internal to the faith community, but it is indispensable for ethical perception and moral deliberation—that is, scripture informs how persons within the community both envision or "see" moral situations and issues and reason about moral choices.

The sources for ethics internal to a religious community—scripture, interpretive and ecclesiastic tradition, narratives, communal practice, personal experience, inspiration—are necessarily tested for coherence relative to broader questions that go beyond the specific community, including philosophical, scientific, and theological views of the world; interpretations of the nature of moral agents (or moral anthropology); the conditions for acquiring moral knowledge (or moral epistemology); constructions or models of normative ethical theory; and conceptions of situations and conflicts requiring moral deliberation and choice.[1] These tests or base points external to the faith tradition provide insight into the consistency, coherence, clarity, and comprehensiveness of an ethic of a religious community. That is to say that the moral cogency and persuasiveness of an ethic derived from or implied by scripture must function at three different levels: interpreting the human condition and the reality of the moral world, identifying and justifying moral norms (in the form of principles and rules) and virtues to guide and direct actions and the cultivation of moral character, and formulating processes to resolve practical situations of moral choice and decision making.

These tests also expect that the ethical significance of scripture is not limited to cultivating the moral culture of a particular religious community; scriptural narratives and texts can shape the character and responsibilities of diverse professions, civic communities, and the broader society. A central conviction in the American founding was that the moral teachings of religious traditions were necessary pillars for democratic political governance.[2] Notwithstanding increasing patterns of secularization, a 2022 Pew Research Center survey disclosed that one in three Americans concurred with the view that religious convictions are necessary for being a moral person.[3] While it seems indisputable that historically in the West, the Abrahamic religions bequeathed a moral legacy to contemporary societies, this does not mean that the characteristics of virtuous persons, professional or civic responsibilities, or social morality are necessarily or logically dependent on religious belief. Such a position presents the problematic implications that religion has priority over and is immune from ethical judgments and implies an exclusionary morality. The scope and breadth of a religious scriptural text, however, can illuminate the ethical vision of moral communities beyond the religious community even when it is not prescriptive or normative.

My claim in this chapter is that the Book of Mormon presents not only a witness to religious and ultimate truths but also, among such ultimate matters, a deeply profound moral reality and witness. Relying on methods of moral philosophy, moral theology, and ethical analysis, I interpret and explore this moral reality through four core contexts and questions about the relationship of religion and morality, epistemic claims regarding knowledge required for moral agency, normative moral content, and constructs of moral situations. These moral contexts correspond to the three levels of moral discourse—interpretations of the moral world, norms and virtues for conduct and character, and practical decision-making processes—identified in the preceding overview of the general issues raised by the relationship of scripture and ethics, and they help situate the Book of Mormon within the sources for ethics of the religious community. My interpretive endeavor is complemented by a constructive proposal that the embedded moralities in the text have relevance for ethical discourse beyond the religious community. As a text that aspires to universality, the Book of Mormon is not only a testimony of what to believe but also about how to live, be, and act in the world.

Religion and Morality

Ethics within a religious community relies on a more-or-less coherent cluster of pre-moral understandings about the world, moral agents, and moral situations—that is, a pervasive *moral reality*.[4] The Book of Mormon presents and is embedded within narratives about a divine ordaining and engagement with the world and a story of human salvation that are suffused with moral concepts, including justice, mercy, love, promise, and accountability, in the absence of which "God would cease to be God" (Alma 42:13–15, 42:22–26). These narratives disclose that the ultimate powers that bear upon and influence human interactions and relationships are creative, nurturing, and transforming, and are disposed to human joy and happiness rather than as arbitrary and indifferent or cruel and hostile to human welfare.

An implicit aspect of this moral reality is a necessary interrelationship of religion and morality. For purposes of this exposition, I understand "religion" to refer to a person's quest within a community for a divine presence and revelation of the sacred in human experience, which is cultivated by various spiritual disciplines, such as faith, prayer, fasting, worship, contemplation, scripture study, and so on. The concept of "morality" involves an orientating regard of a person and community toward the material welfare of other persons and an assumption of some degree of responsibility for promoting their good.[5] The religious and moral dimensions of human experience are interrelated and intertwined in the narratives, precepts, and teachings of the Book of Mormon (and in most sacred literature in other religious traditions). In the moral reality portrayed in the text, it would not make sense to affirm a post-Enlightenment project of establishing nonreligious foundations for morality or to compartmentalize religion and morality from public life.[6]

I offer four brief illustrations of this intertwining moral reality embedded in textual narratives. The story of Enos is centered on his lengthy petitionary prayer for his "own soul" (a religious motivation) that seamlessly expands into a prayer for the "welfare of [his] brethren" (a moral motivation) (Enos 5–12). The narrative of the preaching of Alma$_2$ and Amulek to dissenting Zoramites concludes with Amulek's call to prospective believers for continuous prayer (a spiritual practice) that must, at the peril of hypocrisy, be accompanied by works of charity manifested through care for the needy and sick and "impart[ing] of your substance" to the poor (moral practices) (Alma 34:17–29). Notably, the text invokes the metaphor "impart" to refer both to preaching the gospel and to providing material support for the vulnerable, implying a conceptual equivalency.[7] The Nephite king Benjamin grounds this communal commitment of care for the vulnerable in a theological anthropology that affirms the radical dependence of human beings on God; furthermore, enacting this responsibility is necessary for "retaining a remission of . . . sins" (Mosiah 2:21, 4:16–21, 4:27). Religious belief (radical dependence) is framed as vital for moral responsibility (care for the vulnerable) and the moral practice in turn is essential to religious hopes for divine forgiveness.

It is then possible to interpret the moral reality disclosed in the Book of Mormon through a series of relationships about religion and morality. There is a clear *ontological* relationship of religion and morality: the character and the creating and redeeming activity of God in offering human salvation is integrally moral in nature. There is an evident *psychological or motivational* relationship between religion and morality: Moral practice is invariably portrayed in the narratives as motivationally dependent on religious conviction even as religious integrity requires moral action. The interrelationship is well framed by Daniel Becerra, who persuasively argues in his textual commentary that cultivating moral potential by "selflessly seeking the welfare of others" necessarily contributes to "spiritual development."[8] Alternatively, this symmetry of the religious and the moral is manifested when corruption in belief or in moral intention culminates in hypocrisy and prophetic calls to repentance. Furthermore, the text manifests a pronounced *sociological or communal* relationship between religion and morality. Communities that receive the promised blessings of liberty and prosperity as part of their covenant of obedience to divine commands are necessarily communities that treat others as equals, manifest unity and solidarity, and care for the vulnerable and poor. This is epitomized in the community established in the wake of the ministry of the resurrected Christ, within which "all were converted unto the Lord," social contention ceased because of "the love of God," possessions were held in common, "every man did deal justly one with another," and unity prevailed in a culture of peace (4 Nephi). The contrasting social models of pride, disbelief, self-possessiveness, strife and war, and neglect of the poor that culminate in the apocalyptic endings of the Nephite community (Mormon 5–7) and the Jaredite community are likewise illustrative of the necessary integration of religion with morality in a flourishing culture. Finally, it is possible to propose an *epistemological* relationship of religion and morality—that is, that knowledge of or belief in God bestows knowledge of the morally good or right, either as a matter of general norms for conduct and character or of right actions in specific situations. However, I want to contest this particular interpretation through closer scrutiny.

Moral Epistemology

The issues of moral epistemology have implications for four central parameters for moral choice: agency, knowledge, judgment, and accountability. The principal epistemic question is the relationship between learning and knowing certain truths that pertain to the realm of religiosity, such as the textual witness to the salvific atonement of Christ, and discerning knowledge of moral values, norms, and actions. The text gives evidence that "good" is sourced ontologically in God and Christ, that there is no *concept* of "good" outside the divine will and character.[9] Furthermore, *knowledge* of good and evil, a minimal criterion for the exercise of moral agency, is depicted frequently as possessing a universal scope: "Good and evil have come before all men" who have been "instructed sufficiently that they know good from evil."[10] The moral epistemic question, then, fundamentally concerns whether knowledge of moral good requires knowledge of religious truths. Put another way, the issue of epistemic dependence of morality on religion addresses whether acquiring moral knowledge presumes revelation and belief convictions in salvational truths or whether knowing the good is possible even in the absence of belief. Is morality the exclusive possession of a faith community, or is morality embedded in a more encompassing scope of human experience?

My "either/or" juxtaposition demands a "both/and" affirmation: Within a particular religious community, teachings of religious truth and moral knowledge are necessarily intertwined, but when religious teaching is not communally contextualized, it does not mean that interactions between strangers outside the community lack moral dimensions and content. The first textual narrator, Nephi₁, presents in his concluding witness multiple interrelated purposes of his teachings for his own people: "It persuadeth them to do good; it maketh known unto them of their fathers; and it speaketh of Jesus" (2 Nephi 33:4). The prospect of "doing good," which presumes "knowing good," seems distinguishable from, although certainly related to, words that witness to Christ. Nephi₁ subsequently expands his audience to an inclusive "all": "The words of Christ . . . teach all men that they should do good" (2 Nephi 33:10). The religion-morality relationship seems motivational rather than epistemic: A religious conviction about Christ offers clarifying instruction on moral goodness and enabling grace to enact it within specific communities; however, a lack of knowledge or faith in Christ does not preclude moral knowledge or even enacting the good. Such a distinction between religious and moral knowledge likewise seems so embedded in the claim of Nephi₁'s successor, Jacob₂, that those in the Lamanite community, despite following different teachings and traditions, are nonetheless "more righteous" than the Nephites because of their observance of precepts of marital love and fidelity (Jacob 3:5–9).

The issue of moral epistemology likewise emerges, if inchoately, in a sermon of the primary anthologizer, Mormon₂, to "peaceable followers of Christ"—that is, to a particular religious community. Mormon₂ instructs this community about their ability for righteous judgment, which is attainable through a universalized capacity identified as "the Spirit of Christ" (or "light of Christ"). This spiritualized capacity is bestowed on every person, not just the peaceable followers, so that they may "know good from evil." All persons, then, have a capacity to make judgments that differentiate what "inviteth to do good, and to persuade to believe in Christ" from what "persuadeth men to do evil, and believe not in Christ" (Moroni 7:12–19). The parallelism in the text suggests that discerning what is good from evil is a separate, if related, process from judgments about matters of religious conviction. One plausible way of interpreting the epistemology of judgment is to claim that knowing the difference between good and evil is inherent in *human* experience and knowing the difference between correct and incorrect beliefs, and cultivating "perfect" knowledge, is more specific to the life of a believer and their *particular* religious faith community. Knowing the good may, in a communal context of religious teaching and worship, be embedded in and perfected by the moral reality of belief, but the text does not seem to make a case that moral knowledge resides solely in the realm of life organized by a religious community's witness to salvific truth. It is conceptually and theologically possible for a person to cultivate moral character and enact right action without explicit religious conviction.

My interpretation of the epistemic relation of religion and morality and its correlate proposition of generally accessible knowledge of good and evil have important implications for the nature of moral agency and the scope of morality. First, all persons have an inherent capacity for moral agency— that is, a capacity to reflect on choices and actions in light of their moral knowledge, discern and "judge" between good and evil, and then enact their choice. This assessment coheres with scripture, ecclesiastical teaching about moral agency and accountability, philosophical discussion of conscience, and personal lived experience in the moral world. Furthermore, the claim that every person has a divine-based moral capacity to discern foundational moral knowledge assumes that all moral agents are accountable to live by the good that they know. The universalistic scope of accountability is a presupposition for the possibility of prophetic moral teaching and criticism, which would otherwise be incoherent in the absence of generally accessible moral knowledge. The epistemic matter of *knowing* the good, however, is a separable question from the sources of cultivating resolution and motivation to *live* by knowledge of good. Religious teaching, enabling grace, moral exemplars, and a moral culture can all influence moral formation and motivation.[11]

Normative Conduct and Character

The moral narratives of the Book of Mormon evince numerous communal and motivational reasons for claiming that moral conduct and character is best cultivated within the setting of a particular religious community. It does not follow, however, that interactions and relationships outside the community fall into the realm of the amoral or immoral; rather, they are guided and constrained by the universalized capacity for judgment and choice of good from evil, or what I have framed as generally accessible moral knowledge. My argument is that the text presents two related but differentiated forms of morality: (1) a thin and *minimalist morality* structured by a core of moral prohibitions ("refrain from *x*") that are necessary conditions for personal moral agency and for communal cohesion and sustainability, and (2) a thick and *covenantal morality* structured by affirmative responsibilities ("perform *x*") that are necessary conditions for a *moral* community and communal flourishing.[12] In this interpretation, the common minimalist morality of prohibitions comprises a generally accessible morality for which all moral agents and communities, regardless of belief, are accountable. This minimalist morality is integral to the moral infrastructure of moral communities; however, the responsibilities of covenantal morality comprise "a more excellent way" of being and doing in *particular* communities and relationships.[13]

The minimalist and common morality is constituted by a core cluster of prohibitions and traits of character that reflect the persisting moral legacy of the Decalogue and the Deuteronomic moral code for these diasporic communities. The first leaders of the Nephite community, Nephi₁ and Jacob₂, give voice to this common code that is reiterated throughout the text, often as not through its violation: "The Lord God hath commanded that men should not murder; that they should not lie; that they should not steal; that they should not take the name of the Lord their God in vain; that they should not envy; that they should not have malice; that they should not contend one with another; that they should not commit whoredoms; and that they should do none of these things; for whoso doeth them shall perish" (2 Nephi 26:32; cf. 2 Nephi 9:28–37). The minimalist morality prohibits actions that harm and injure others as well as dispositions and vices, such as malice, envy, and greed, that reflect corruption in moral character. The specific prohibitions (some of which may be legally enforced) establish a standard of minimal moral decency necessary for the exercise of agency and for social cohesion. Communal violations of these interrelated moral boundaries on actions and character constitute not merely discrete wrongs but a form of structural and communal corruption that is represented in the text by the language of "iniquity," "abomination," and "wickedness."[14] A pattern of pervasive moral corruption means the community—be it Jerusalem, Ammonihah, Zarahemla, or eventually the entire Nephite civilization—is on a path toward dissolution, notwithstanding prophetic calls to accountability, because moral agency can no longer be meaningfully exercised.

This minimalistic moral core is expressed in various forms at least twenty-five times in the text and is applied as a standard of accountability for predecessor communities, contemporary communities, and communities in future generations.[15] Table 3.1 summarizes these core prohibitions and their correlative traits of character or vices.

A community can sustain itself cohesively through adherence to the morality of prohibition, but a minimalist morality does not make it a moral community. A moral community is created or renewed by prophetic invitation to a covenantal way of life to persons and communities whose commitments expand beyond responsibilities of not harming others to responsibilities of assisting, benefiting, and doing good for others. A thick covenantal morality is illustrated most clearly in the moral narratives of Nephite king Benjamin's covenantal invitation to his people, the formation of Alma$_1$'s community of exiles, the covenants of the converted Lamanites who form the Anti-Nephi-Lehies, and the peaceable community of unity and love created by the ministry of the resurrected Christ. The commitments

Table 3.1. Minimalistic Moral Core

Prohibited Action	Variations of Prohibition	Prohibited Character Traits (Vices)
Murder	Shedding innocent blood	Anger
Whoredoms	Adultery, Fornication	Lasciviousness, Lust
Stealing	Theft, Robbery, Plunder	Envy
Lying	Deceit, False witness	Malice
Contention	Strife, Quarreling, Tumult	Pride, Anger
Riches for worldly gain	Costly apparel, Neglecting poor	Pride, Greed
Idolatry*	Worldly treasures	Hardened heart, Stiff neck
Persecution	Reviling, Mockery, Priestcraft	Pride, Hatred

* The pursuit of riches to advance self-interest can become a form of idolatry. See 2 Nephi 9:30; Helaman 13:21–22. Notably, both avarice and idolatry are associated with neglect of the poor and vulnerable.

of these four moral communities to a covenantal morality involve several shared processes: (1) The creation of the community is preceded by an experience of deliverance from evil, suffering, bondage, oppression or sin and by conversion through the salvific atonement of Christ. (2) The conversion experience is represented as a "mighty change of heart" that transforms the interiority of the religious and moral self from dispositions of malice, anger, greed, and harm to virtues of submissiveness, meekness, humility, patience, and love. (3) This transformation of moral interiority is experienced by a collective people and is a catalyst for cultivating a fundamental moral "disposition . . . to do good continually" (Mosiah 5:2; Alma 5:12–14). (4) The moral virtues and dispositions are developed in concert with a change in moral perception—namely, esteem for and treatment of other persons as "like unto yourselves" (Jacob 2:17–21; Mosiah 23:7, 27:4). This analogy of other as self, a form of empathic imagination, opens the self to morally expansive capacities in personal character and in communal actions of caring, presence, witnessing, and service.

The covenantal foundation of these moral communities cultivates a moral culture that is neglected and not sustained by the common morality of minimal decency. The characteristics of this covenantal culture encompass (1) a moral logic that shifts from not harming others to assisting others with their human needs for material and spiritual welfare; (2) a shift in moral focus from (prohibited) actions or ways of *doing* to moral intentionality, character, and integrity, or ways of *being*; (3) the practical primacy of the coordinating virtues of faith, hope, and love that channel enabling grace for actions of "doing good";[16] (4) reliance and trust in the covenantal promise that binds members of the community to one another in unity and love; (5) the presence of moral exemplars, such as a just leader, a child, or Christ; and (6) a communal moral purpose that aspires to the peace, love, and material equality experienced by a unified community following the ministry of the resurrected Christ.[17]

The most definitive expression of this capacious moral culture is a redirection of material wealth and prosperity from self-serving materialism to a covenantal commitment to "do good—to clothe the naked, and to feed the hungry, and to liberate the captive, and administer relief to the sick and the afflicted"; conversely, neglecting the poor and vulnerable symbolizes a dissolution of the moral character of a covenantal community (Jacob 2:13; Alma 4:12–13). Notably, the prophetic invitations to covenantal relationship intertwine moral responsibilities with redemptive ends. Benjamin's admonition to the covenanted community that "retaining a remission of your sins" requires a commitment to "impart of your substance to the poor" is echoed in the dual covenantal commitment of baptism among

Alma₁'s newly formed community: A moral covenant of sharing burdens and providing solace to those who are burdened, mourning, and in need of comfort is inextricably intertwined with a religious covenant to be a witness of God in all things. It follows that bearing witness to the redemptive grace of Christ without caring for the vulnerable manifests the moral corruption of hypocrisy.[18]

Table 3.2 draws on the narratives of these moral communities to organize core elements of a covenantal morality through both constitutive virtues that express covenantal moral character and defining actions that sustain the relationships and flourishing of a moral community. That is, life in a moral community inculcates interrelated ways of being and ways of doing that comprise a "more excellent" way of communal life.

My claim is that the narratives and teachings in the Book of Mormon display a minimalistic morality of prohibitions that is generally accessible and provides a shared standard of moral accountability for any community and a more demanding morality of covenantal relationship applicable to

Table 3.2. Covenantal Morality

Transforming Virtues	Coordinating Virtues	Covenantal Virtues	Covenantal Actions
Diligence	Faith	Disposition to do good	Non-injury, refrain from unjust killing
Gentleness/ Kindness	Hope	Equality, Reciprocity	Esteem others as self
Gratitude	Love	Unity, Love	Peaceable community (avoiding contention)
Humility		Chastity, Purity of heart	Marital fidelity
Long-suffering		Patience, Love	Parental care
Love		Humility, Empathy	Service
Meekness		Presence, Love	Works of charity (care for the vulnerable)
Moderation/ Temperate		Justice, Mercy	Justice, Forgiveness
Patience		Gratitude, Empathy	Impart substance to the needy
Submissiveness		Liberality, Equality	Common possessions (consecration)
		Core References	
Mosiah 3:19; Alma 7:23, 13:28, 24:7-10	2 Nephi 31:20; Alma 7:24, 13:29; Moroni 7	2 Nephi 1:21; Jacob 2:27-28; Mosiah 4:13-16, 4:27-28, 5:3, 18:21, 27:3-4; Alma 1:30; 4 Nephi 4	Jacob 2; Mosiah 2:16-19, 2:4-5, 2:18, 27:3-4; Alma 1, 4, 7, 24, 4 Nephi 1-15

particular prophetically formed moral communities. This normative moral content provides a setting within which moral agents in the text experience various forms of moral conflicts.

The Nature of Moral Conflict

The preceding discussions of moral epistemology and moral content have highlighted four parameters—the capacity for moral agency, moral knowledge of norms of conduct and character, judgment in accordance with moral knowledge, and accountability—for experiencing what philosopher E. J. Lemmon designates as "moral situations."[19] While Lemmon highlights three principal moral situations, the moral narratives of the text enable the construction of a more complex and richer typology of different moral situations and conflicts; this more expansive account of moral situations can illuminate the nature of moral experience generally. (1) A situation of *moral integrity* occurs when a moral agent possessing knowledge about the good accepts accountability and acts in accord with that knowledge. Moral integrity is displayed in the "I will go and do" commitment of Nephi$_1$, in narrative portrayals of various persons as exemplars, and in the unified peaceable community created by the ministry of the resurrected Christ (see 1 Nephi 3:7; Mosiah 2; Alma 48:11–13, 17–19; 3 Nephi 27:27; 4 Nephi 1:19). (2) The choices that comprise moral integrity can be contrasted with situations of *moral weakness*, which emerge as persons in their familial or religious communities have knowledge of good action but lack the courage, resolution, motivation, or desire to perform such actions, for which they are held accountable by prophetic teachers. As exemplified in Jacob$_2$'s or Alma$_2$'s admonitions to different Nephite communities (Jacob 2; Alma 5), moral admonitions from ecclesiastical leaders consistently seek to cultivate the resolution and moral culture that moves persons from weakness to integrity and moral wholeness—that is, a congruence between external action and internal disposition and character. The moral situations of integrity and weakness affirm the criteria for moral experience in contrast to (3) situations of *moral ignorance* in which agency, knowledge, and judgment are attenuated and moral accountability is thereby inapplicable. This moral situation is emphasized most particularly for younger children, who lack knowledge of good and evil and have not developed a capacity for agency and therefore are held to be "blameless" or lack accountability.[20] The ethics of the family and the community necessarily require providing the moral instruction and examples so that children can develop the capacities necessary to be moral agents (Mosiah 4:14–15).

The text discloses four related types of moral situations that call into question the underlying moral coherence of the world for persons and communities that aspire to moral integrity. Communities can experience (4) situations of *moral uncertainty*, in which there is some, but inconclusive, evidence of a responsibility to engage in an action but likewise some, but inconclusive, evidence of a responsibility to refrain from the action. A circumstance of moral uncertainty presumes moral knowledge and conviction to act morally but requires deliberation and discerning judgment about the primacy of the responsibilities in conflict. A relevant illustration is the consideration given by the Anti-Nephi-Lehies as to whether they should assume a responsibility to participate in war efforts when the Nephite nation was imperiled both by external enemies and internal dissension even at the expense of violating their covenant to refrain from shedding blood (Alma 53:10–15). Moral uncertainty is distinguishable from (5) a situation of a *moral dilemma*, in which a person has a responsibility to both perform and not perform an action, and one responsibility will be violated no matter which course of action is undertaken. The primary, and perhaps exclusive, textual illustration of a moral dilemma is Nephi$_1$'s conflict about killing the priestly record holder Laban (1 Nephi 4).[21] A life of discipleship and moral integrity also does not immunize a person from experiencing situations of (6) *moral complicity* and (7) *moral distress*. Moral complicity reflects a person's judgment that to perform or participate in a particular action would cooperate with and lend credibility to wrong and evil and thereby compromise their own integrity. The posture of non-cooperation with evil is best exemplified in Mormon$_2$'s refusal to lead his community's armies in battle because of their pervasive evil, bloodlust, and oaths of revenge (Mormon 3:11–16). A situation of moral distress emerges when a person of moral integrity is witness to an immoral action or unjust condition but is incapable or powerless to intervene. The circumstance of moral distress informs the anguish of prophetic teachers: Alma$_2$ and Amulek are spiritually constrained from intervening when witnessing the moral atrocity of the fiery martyrdom of numerous women and children in Ammonihah, while Mormon$_2$'s rejection of moral complicity generates his self-designation as an "idle witness" to the "abominations" and evil of his community and soldiers.[22]

In contrast to these foregoing moral situations that presume a basic moral disposition to do good, even if constrained in particular ways, numerous narratives give ample evidence of (8) situations of *moral rebellion*—that is, stories of individuals and communities who received moral instruction and knowledge of the good and the divine commandments and not only fail to enact the good but also act contrary to it. Such communities display a deficiency in moral character, which the text morally maps through the embodied metaphors of "hardness of heart" and "stiffneckedness," and a corrupt moral epistemology: Instead of exercising judgment of good from evil, they are characterized as "knowing evil from good" (Mosiah 16:3).[23] When communities act persistently contrary to the good, especially the minimal common morality, they risk a kind of moral amnesia in which knowledge of the good is forgotten or withheld (Alma 12:10–11). Moral rebellion is an inflection point that summons not merely communal instruction or admonitions to reform and repent but the sharp witness of prophetic criticism as the community, typified by the people of Noah, the community of Ammonihah, and the endings of both the Nephite and Jaredite civilizations, is in peril of dissolution.

The context of rebellion is characteristically correlated with (9) situations of *moral self-deception*, which occurs when persons and communities tell and live by a misguided or false narrative that sanctions wrong conduct as right. Self-deception manifests agency, but mistaken or erroneous judgment is invariably accompanied by a self-serving claim of innocence and an evasion of accountability, as illustrated in the rhetorical response by the people of King Noah to the prophetic criticism of Abinadi: "What great evil hast thou done, or what sins have thy people committed? . . . We are guiltless, and thou, O king, has not sinned" (Mosiah 12:13–14). When embedded in flattering priestcraft that "calls evil good and good evil" (2 Nephi 15:20, quoting Isaiah 5:20), self-deception is notably pervasive among and benefits privileged classes at the expense of the poor and vulnerable, thereby providing a rationalization for social stratification and hierarchy.

The evasion of accountability characteristic of narrative self-deception can evolve into (10) situations of *moral excuse* wherein moral agents acknowledge acting contrary to received communal moral practice but offer reasons as claims for exemptions from accountability. One compelling illustration of moral excuse is the patriarchal pretensions exhibited by the adult males in an early Nephite community: They reasoned that, although deviating from marital fidelity that historically had been understood by the community to comprise the "abominations" of adultery and whoredoms, as concubinage was practiced by historical Israelite exemplars, they were exempt from accountability for their own concubinage practice (Jacob 2:23–35). The connection between self-deception and moral excuses is exemplified in Jacob$_2$'s critique of the self-serving narratives of the rich. The community of privilege has told themselves a story that their own actions have brought their prosperity, and Jacob$_2$ counters that the accumulation of riches is attributable to the reality that "the hand of providence hath smiled upon you most pleasingly" (Jacob 2:13). The false communal narrative has moral consequences of pride and class differentiation and underlies the moral excuse for concubinage. The Lamanite prophet Samuel$_2$ similarly calls a subsequent Nephite community to accountability for failing to remember that prosperity is attributable to divine blessings (Helaman 13:21–22).

A community that is in peril of dissolution attributable to continuous patterns of rebellion, moral deception, and excuse is ultimately called to accountability by prophetic witnesses such as Abinadi, Alma$_2$, Samuel$_2$, Mormon$_2$, and Ether. A rejection of prophetic accountability and subsequent persistence in moral rebellion invariably brings the false community into a (11) situation of *moral callousness*. The core moral capacities, especially including agency and judgment, atrophy and moral atrocities occur (Mormon 2:13–18; Moroni 9:19). A morally incorrigible community is on a course to its own apocalyptic ending.

Norms and Contexts

These textured moral situations presume or require judgments, deliberation, and moral choice. The relative silence of the text regarding narratives of personal moral judgment and its emphasis on decisions by ecclesiastical, political, and prophetic leadership makes it difficult to assess just how the norms of character and conduct of the minimal or covenantal morality were retrieved and applied to inform specific moral judgments and choices. However, some patterns and methods for moral formation and decision making emerge in textual narratives that merit attention. There is a pronounced and encouraged usage of the *analogical imagination* by which the moral legacy of the past, of the traditions and examples of the "fathers" of the community, are retrieved and offered as frameworks for seeing and guiding actions in the present. The Exodus narrative, for example, provides a way of seeing a situation of oppression within a narrative of deliverance and a community creation by a covenantal morality. A community that may be perplexed about their responsibilities to the poor can have their moral vision expanded by analogies that invite reflection about a common relationship with God (Mosiah 4). The analogical imagination embedded in community narratives is extended to readers who are invited to "liken" the teachings and precepts of the text to their own situations and relationships. This propels the religious and moral meanings of the text from the time of its authorship into the similarly hypocritical and callous worlds of modernity and postmodernity (Mormon 8).

The textual narratives also highlight *exemplary practices* of trusted leaders and moral mentors who live with integrity. These practices include the fundamentals for organizing communities around principles of equity, care, unity, and liberty. They reflect the responsibilities of community leaders to emulate Christ-likeness by serving rather than exploiting their communities

(Mosiah 2, 29). These practices highlight the importance of seeking counsel on perplexing questions of civic or church discipline from persons who possess experience and credibility because of the manner in which they have lived. The exemplary practices offer patterns for moral emulation.

Moral communities, including families and the church, are likewise indispensable as sources for judgments about what is true and good and for moral guidance. The family and the church are entrusted with responsibilities for religious and moral education of what is termed the "rising generation," who can find themselves divided between the paths of integrity and rebellion. The text is replete with examples of the life-changing legacy of teachings of fathers, whose words can penetrate the very souls of children (Enos 3; Alma 36:17), and the life-saving legacy of the teachings of mothers (Helaman 56:48, 57:21). The church cultivates spiritual practices of prayer, fasting, and scripture study and of necessity becomes a school for the practice of the covenantal morality.

The primary textual authors—Nephi$_1$, Jacob$_2$, Mormon$_2$, and Moroni$_2$,—give a unified witness about the personal and communal necessity of reliance on God and Christ for *personalized inspiration*. Nephi$_1$ tells his community (and his readers) very explicitly that "the words of Christ will tell you all things what ye should do," and the Holy Ghost "will show unto you all things what ye should do" (2 Nephi 32:3, 32:5). Nephi$_1$'s language seems all-encompassing, although the context for discerning "what ye should do" pertains to following the doctrine of Christ to receive salvation and eternal life (2 Nephi 31). Moreover, Nephi$_1$'s admonitions are somewhat ironic in that in the narrative of the killing of Laban, he experienced a *conflict* between "the words of Christ" to refrain from killing and the prompting of the Spirit to "slay him." Such conflicts highlight the necessity for right judgment, which, as discussed previously, is portrayed by Mormon$_2$ as a universalized capacity for knowing the good and believing Christ. The inner "light" for judgment also reflects a personalized resource for moral guidance and religious understanding that must be ingrained in moral character through processes of habituation and moral formation. At the same time, its universalized applicability to "all [persons]" opens the very distinct prospect of shared and common, if minimal, morality.

Conclusion

I have argued that the Book of Mormon not only is a repository of religious truths for believers but that it also manifests and conveys a thoroughgoing moral reality. This is of no small importance for a religious tradition that often conceptualizes the "moral" as pertinent primarily to matters of sexual relationships, chastity, and virtuous thought. This constricts the realm of the moral to the intimate and interpersonal in private life. However, it makes little sense to ecclesiastically lament moral decline in society when professional, communal, and social interactions are conceptualized as amoral. My argument, by contrast, is that the formative text of the religious community has an expansive moral voice that is intertwined with its witness to religious truths. It is not a moral "answer book" and does not dictate specific choices in concrete moral situations; rather, its narrative framing and invitation to analogical application aids moral vision and perception and cultivates empathic imagination. The Book of Mormon is *morally revelatory* of the necessary contours of moral choice—agency, moral knowledge, judgment, and accountability—and of the complexity and diversity of moral experience and situations.

These capacities are exercised in relation to a minimalist morality and a covenantal morality that provide norms of character and conduct for personal life, community sustainability, and communal flourishing. In this way, for religious communities that were formed by the narratives and teachings of the book, sacred texts can be understood to expand moral vision and perception, helping persons "see" this moral reality in a new way, and perhaps for the first time. Insofar as the Book of Mormon is represented as a testimony and witness of religious truth for all peoples, it has meaning, including generally accessible and applicable moral meaning, for all communities. The moral ways of being, acting, and living portrayed in the book are not incidental but integral to its religious witness.

Notes

1. James M. Gustafson, *Protestant and Roman Catholic Ethics: Prospects for Rapprochement* (Chicago: University of Chicago Press, 1978), 138–59; Martin Benjamin, *Philosophy and This Actual World* (Lanham, MD: Rowman and Littlefield), 2003.

2. See, e.g., George Washington, "Farewell Address," in *The Sacred Rights of Conscience*, ed. Daniel L. Dreisbach and Mark David Hall (Indianapolis: Liberty Fund, 2009), 468–70; Steven Waldman, *Founding Faith* (New York: Random House, 2009).

3. Pew Research Center, "Many People in U.S., Other Advanced Economies, Say It's Not Necessary to Believe in God to Be Moral," April 20, 2023, https://www.pewresearch.org/short-reads/2023/04/20/many-people-in-u-s-other-advanced-economies-say-its-not-necessary-to-believe-in-god-to-be-moral/.

4. Courtney S. Campbell, *Mormonism, Medicine, and Bioethics* (New York: Oxford University Press, 2021), 1–34.

5. See David Little and Sumner B. Twiss, *Comparative Religious Ethics: A New Method* (New York: Harper and Row, 1978).

6. See Richard Rorty, "Religion as Conversation Stopper," in *Philosophy and Social Hope* (New York: Penguin Books, 1999), 168–74.

7. The conceptual equivalency is very direct in Mosiah 18:29 and in Alma 1:20, 1:27. Illustrations of "imparting substance" include Mosiah 4:21, 4:26; Alma 1:27–28, 4:15, 34:28. Illustrations of "imparting the word of God" include Mosiah 28:1; Alma 12:9, 24:15, 32:23.

8. Daniel Becerra, *3rd, 4th Nephi: A Brief Theological Introduction* (Provo, UT: Neal A. Maxwell Institute for Religious Scholarship, BYU, 2021), 44–66.

9. See Alma 5:40; Ether 4:11–12; Moroni 7:12–13. My interpretation benefits from Joseph M. Spencer's chapter in the present text, "What Is the Good and How Does One Know It? Ethics and the Book of Mormon."

10. See 2 Nephi 2:5, 2:16; Alma 12:31, 13:3, 29:5.

11. The issue of moral psychology is insightfully developed in Daniel Becerra's chapter in the present text, "Moral Psychology and the Book of Mormon."

12. Michael Walzer, *Thick and Thin: Moral Argument at Home and Abroad* (Notre Dame, IN: University of Notre Dame Press, 1994); Richard B. Miller, *Terror, Religion, and Liberal Thought* (New York: Columbia University Press, 2016), 121–28.

13. I have adapted the phrasing "a more excellent way" from Ether 12:11.

14. This language is pervasive. "Iniquity" is used 227 times, "wickedness" 167 times, and "abominations" 115 times. See "Word Frequency in the Book of Mormon," *Gospel Cougar*, December 23, 2007 (reformatted May 1, 2021), https://gospelcougar.blogspot.com/2007/12.

15. See 2 Nephi 9:28–42, 26:32; Mosiah 2:13, 2:12–13, 29:14, 29:36; Alma 1:17–18, 1:32, 4:8, 16:18, 17:14, 23:3, 30:10, 50:21; Helaman 4:12, 6:17, 6:21, 8:26, 13:22; 3 Nephi 16:10, 21:19, 24:5, 30:2; 4 Nephi 16; Ether 8:16; Mormon 8:31, 8:36. While statements of the morality of prohibitions are primarily directed to the Nephites, the common code is applied to the Jaredites in Alma 37:29 and Ether 8:16; to the Lamanites in Jacob 3:5–9, Mosiah 10:17, and Alma 17:14, 23:3; and to future communities in 3 Nephi 16:18 and Mormon 8:31, 8:36.

16. I designate faith, hope, and love as "coordinating virtues" for a moral life based on the several textual references where religious and moral teaching converge, as exemplified in Alma$_2$'s admonition "see that ye have faith, hope, and charity, and *then* ye will always abound in good works" (Alma 7:24; my italics) and in Mormon's discourse on the process of acquiring these virtues in answering the question "How is it that ye can lay hold on *every* good thing?" (Moroni 7:20–48). See also 2 Nephi 31:20 and Alma 13:29.

17. See Mosiah 2:11–18, Mosiah 3:19, and 3 Nephi 27:27 for implicit illustrations of moral exemplars and 4 Nephi 2–3 and 2:15–17 for the realization of the peaceable community.

18. The text provides compelling examples of "walking the talk" of covenantal care for the vulnerable and needy, as when Amulek provides hospitality to a famished Alma$_2$ (Alma 8:20–26), the Nephites give the land of Jershon to the Anti-Nephi-Lehies (Alma 27:21–30), and the Anti-Nephi-Lehies welcome the persecuted refugees of the Zoramites (Alma 35:6–9). The principle in general is

illustrated in Mosiah 4:16–26, 18:8–11, Alma 1:27–30, 4:12–13, 5:53–55, 34:28; Helaman 4:12.

19. E. J. Lemmon, "Moral Dilemmas," *Philosophical Review* 71, no. 2 (1962): 139–58.

20. The theology of the fall presented by Lehi₁ ascribes this situation to Adam and Eve before their transgression (2 Nephi 2:22–23). The absence of accountability is applied to little children (Mosiah 3:16–21) as well as those who "knoweth not good from evil" (Alma 29:5). Mormon₂ considers the two categories of persons salvationally equivalent: "All little children are alive in Christ, and also all they that are without the law" (Moroni 8:22).

21. There is substantial literature on this narrative. For some recent treatments, see Charles Swift, "'The Lord Slayeth the Wicked': Coming to Terms with Nephi Killing Laban," *Journal of Book of Mormon Studies* 28 (2019): 137–69; Patrick Q. Mason and J. David Pulsipher, *Proclaim Peace: The Restoration's Answer to an Age of Conflict* (Provo, UT: Neal A. Maxwell Institute for Religious Scholarship, BYU, 2021), 46–53.

22. The concept of moral distress originated with philosopher Andrew Jameton in his book *Nursing Practice: The Ethical Issues* (Englewood Cliffs, NJ: Prentice-Hall, 1984), 6. For relevant examples, see Alma 8:16, 13:37, 14:9–13; Mormon 3:16.

23. Amulek attests to the core feature of rebellion: "I did harden my heart, for I was called many times and I would not hear; therefore, I knew concerning these things, yet I would not know" (Alma 10:6). See also the language of rebellion in Jacob 1:8; Mosiah 2:36–37, 3:19, 15:26, 16:5; Alma 41:1; 3 Nephi 6:18; 4 Nephi 38; Mormon 1:16.

4

What Is the Good, and How Does One Know It?

Ethics and the Book of Mormon

JOSEPH M. SPENCER

It is often observed that much of what has been written about the Book of Mormon divides along well-established lines. As Grant Hardy sums up the situation, "Most studies tend to mine the text for evidence in larger arguments about the nature of Mormonism as a religious movement or the credibility of its first prophet."[1] What this means is that, generally speaking, scholarly study of the Book of Mormon has traditionally followed an itinerary established by those who exhibit skepticism about the book. While much or even most of what has been written on the Book of Mormon in an academic vein is the work of the book's devotees, they have largely taken up the tools of the academy principally in order to respond to (often less-than-scholarly) criticisms of the book's value. For the most part, then, Thomas O'Dea's famous statement that "the *Book of Mormon* has not been universally considered . . . as one of those books that must be read in order to have an opinion of it" has proven true.[2] The book has been read within the walls of the academy mostly because one already has an opinion regarding the Book of Mormon for which one seeks intellectual backing.

The principal issue in all this writing—whether in criticizing or in defending the Book of Mormon—has traditionally been history. Because influential critics of the Book of Mormon early in the twentieth century questioned the volume's historical reliability,[3] believing scholars took up the tools of history to defend the book's credibility. Others naturally responded in kind, addressing historical questions but drawing different conclusions. Recently, however, this situation has begun to change in important ways.[4] Over the past two decades, a style of Book of Mormon scholarship has emerged that *assumes* the value—or, depending on the author, at least the relevance and the importance—of the book. Accordingly, such work has begun to outline a set of new itineraries for the scholarly study of the Book of Mormon. The question of historical origins has come to play a far less dominant role in the conversation. Literary and theological questions, as well as questions about influence and impact, have become prominent.

For the purposes and interests of the academy, this development is an important and welcome one.[5] There is a sense in which the Book of Mormon is becoming a richer object of academic inquiry. In one key dimension, however, the Book of Mormon's critics continue to determine the shape of scholarly writing about the volume—and thus arguably keep it from receiving (ideally) serious and balanced academic attention. This dimension concerns ethics. Where the relationship between the Book of Mormon and ethical matters comes into question, the book's scholarly interpreters still seem to divide into those who criticize and those who defend.[6]

It has to be admitted that there are reasons for this situation: Women are astonishingly less represented in the volume than men; the book seems to say a good deal about race in ways that need explaining; violence appears to be approved by God at various points in the volume; and the book seems to draw exclusivist conclusions regarding religious matters. After the #MeToo movement, the rise of Black Lives Matter, widespread concern about religiously motivated violence, and rapidly spreading secularity, these are issues that readers (scholarly or not) naturally wish to see explained, for better or for worse.[7] That said, a genuinely honest—and certainly any thorough—treatment of even these ethical issues in the Book of Mormon requires contextualization. Does the Book of Mormon have its own larger moral vision? If so, how does it inform, modify, or stand in tension with the apparent moral issues often identified in the text?

In this chapter, I address just one of the many tasks required for elaborating the moral vision immanent to the Book of Mormon. Taking up the most basic question of ethics ("What is the good?"), I attempt to sketch a tension within the Book of Mormon between two irreducibly distinct answers to it. As it turns out, the most useful passages for developing such a sketch are ones that *assume* rather than *argue for* their respective conceptions of the good. This is because the stated subject of the relevant passages is not the *nature* of the good but rather *the means of intellectual access to it*. In other words, they ask not "What is the good?" but "How does one know the good?" Consequently, in this chapter I sketch not only the tension between two distinct Book of Mormon conceptions of the good but also each conception's relevant epistemology. The Book of Mormon, in sum, sets forth two different ethical ontologies and two different ethical epistemologies.

Two Sermons on Knowing the Good

The Book of Mormon is a sprawling work. Its main narrative traverses more than a thousand years of history, with many important twists and turns in the story it sets forth. Its many pages include a good deal of self-consciously sermonic material, moments where the larger narrative slows in order to allow one Book of Mormon character or another to deliver an extended discourse on some theological subject or another. It is to such discourses one most naturally turns to find anything approaching a direct treatment of the ethical. While the stories that fill the Book of Mormon touch in numerous ways on a wide range of ethical issues, at least two sermons in the volume go right to the heart of the ethical as such, raising the question (somewhat indirectly) of what the good is and (very directly) of how it can be known. It is in investigating these two sermons that a basic account of the Book of Mormon's two conceptions of the good and its knowability become visible.

Separated by more than 250 pages (in the first printed edition) and more than four hundred years (according to the narrative), the two sermons in question appear in dramatically distinct contexts, each with its own textually local motivations. The first is a missionizing sermon delivered by a priestly figure named Alma$_2$ to a group of impoverished inquirers. It takes place outdoors in a city that is largely antagonistic to Alma$_2$ and his companions.[8] The second is a pastoral sermon by a military leader named Mormon$_2$, a man who also holds some kind of churchly authority, delivered to a group of seasoned believers. It takes place in "the synagogue,"[9] among friends and co-religionists, but in a time of intense conflict—a protracted war that in fact culminates in the eradication of Mormon$_2$'s people.[10] What rather plainly motivates Alma$_2$'s sermon, beyond the immediate pursuit of converts, is the recent appearance in the narrative of a full-blooded skeptic, Korihor, who ridicules Alma$_2$'s religious convictions as "foolish" because of what he alleges is their epistemological groundlessness.[11] Alma$_2$ (somewhat belatedly) labors to counteract Korihor's skepticism with an extended sermon on how one comes to know the goodness of the word he preaches. What is supposed to have motivated Mormon$_2$'s sermon is left unclear in the text, but the reason for its inclusion in the volume is relatively clear. It is inserted into the book by Mormon$_2$'s son, Moroni$_2$, who often and openly frets about how the Book of Mormon will be received upon its latter-day emergence.[12] For this anxious compiler, it seems, the sermon obliquely explains to latter-day readers how they might come to know the goodness of the volume they are reading.

Alma$_2$'s sermon begins by laying out concepts in relatively abstract terms, but he eventually—and rather famously for believers in the Book of Mormon—concretizes his message by couching it in an extended parable about planting a seed and watching to see whether it grows into a tree of life. The seed, he says, is the word he preaches (concerning Jesus Christ). The question for the hearer of Alma$_2$'s preaching, then, is, What happens when, in faith, she plants such a word/seed in her heart? Does it swell, sprout, and begin to grow? And if so, what effect does that have on her relationship to the planted seed? At what point can the planter of a seed—and, by analogy, the hearer of a word—say that she knows the goodness of what she has received? And what happens to her faith at the point when knowledge arises, whether one speaks of planted seeds or of heard words? For Alma$_2$, it is in cashing out this parable's implications that a satisfactory answer to Korihor's skepticism emerges.[13]

The text initially presents Mormon$_2$'s much later sermon as if its chief subject were "faith, hope, and charity."[14] As the sermon itself unfolds, however, it becomes clear that its chief subject is faith. Of the sermon's nearly 2,000 words, just 137 are concerned with hope and 232 with charity. Most of the remaining words, nearly three-quarters of the sermon's totality, either set the stage for discussing faith or directly concern faith. For Mormon$_2$, the question of faith is at bottom a question of laying hold of good things, but this means he has to explain how it is that one can discern good things from evil things. His basic explanation is that such knowledge depends deeply on a peculiar—and perhaps even metaphysical—epistemic relationship with Jesus Christ. It is because "the Spirit of Christ is given to every man," he says, that it is possible to judge good from evil; it is only in "the light of Christ" that one might "not judge wrongfully."[15] Leaning on this theological elaboration, Mormon$_2$ pleads with his listeners and co-religionists to "lay hold upon every good thing and condemn it not,"[16] something Mormon$_2$'s son, Moroni$_2$, seems to repurpose to warn latter-day readers of the Book of Mormon not to reject the Book of Mormon and its good word about Christ.[17]

In the next two sections of this chapter, I will treat these two sermons—Alma$_2$'s and Mormon$_2$'s—separately, riddling out their respective conceptions of the good and its knowability. Before doing so, however, it is important to note that the two sermons are related to one another. Unmistakable allusions to Alma$_2$'s sermon within Mormon$_2$'s sermon are clearly meant to suggest dependence to the alert reader. That is, readers are expected to understand that Mormon$_2$ has read and is in some way responding to Alma$_2$. I have already noted that both sermons concern themselves with faith and knowledge, as well as with the knowability of the good. Further, however, there are subtler allusions in certain key phrases and specific theological ideas that appear in these two sermons. For example, Alma$_2$'s sermon speaks four times and Mormon$_2$'s sermon three times of "a perfect knowledge."[18] Or to take another example, both sermons—uniquely within the Book of Mormon—explicitly set forth a notion of faith as trust in a specifically *angelic* message.[19]

More textual work needs to be done on the relationship between Mormon₂'s later sermon and Alma₂'s earlier one. The relationship is apparent enough already, however, to see that the two ask to be read in light of each other—that Mormon₂'s sermon is meant to be read as in some ways confirming but as in other ways either contesting or recontextualizing Alma₂'s sermon. The tension I will sketch in this chapter is, one might say, *canonically immanent* to the Book of Mormon.[20] In other words, it is something to which the canonical shape of the volume seems to mean to draw attention rather than something to be seen only by the skeptic. The whole problematic of what I have above called the basic problem of ethics is, arguably, native to the Book of Mormon. It is time, therefore, to take up these two sermons in turn, coming afterward to the task of drawing some conclusions.

A First Model

There is talk of good things from the moment Alma₂ begins to deploy his comparison of the preached word (of Christ) with a seed. "Now," Alma₂ says, "we will compare the word unto a seed. Now, if ye give place that a seed may be planted in your heart, behold, if it be a true seed or a good seed—if ye do not cast it out by your unbelief, that ye will resist the Spirit of the Lord—behold, it will begin to swell within your breasts."[21] What is good here—or at least what is *potentially* good here—is the seed itself. Although this does not initially help to clarify how Alma₂ understands the good, that the seed is what is good is unsurprising. As I have already noted, the question Alma₂ addresses (because he understands his hearers to be asking this question) is how one can decide whether the word that Alma₂ and his companions preach is a good one. He recommends an experiment ("an experiment upon my words"),[22] and he predicts the response of the experimenter who yields a positive result. Upon encountering the first promising data, he claims, "Ye will begin to say within yourselves, 'It must needs be that this is a good seed.'"[23] And as further data accumulate, he adds, "Ye will say, 'I know that this is a good seed.'"[24]

It is important that nowhere in these passages does Alma₂ speak of what the positive data prove *objectively*; he speaks consistently instead of what the data prove *to someone in particular*—that is, what the data *lead the experimenter to say*. What interests him, according to the text, is the process involved in a concrete individual's growth into conviction rather than some imagined process of establishing universally intelligible facts.

(He speaks at several points of the sense of taste, as if to underscore the irreducibly personal nature of the experience.[25]) This is not to say, however, that everything Alma$_2$ speaks of is subjective. What is objective (or universal), for Alma$_2$, is not the goodness of the seed or word but rather the kind of reaction the goodness of the seed or word provokes. The experience is unique to the experimenter, but given a certain sort of experience, Alma$_2$ assumes that every human being will react in the same way. It is only on the grounds of such an assumption that Alma$_2$ can reliably predict the very words of those who experiment on his (good) word.

Why is Alma$_2$ confident that a positive experience with the seed will produce conviction (knowledge) about the goodness of the seed for the experimenter? It is in answering this question that one might begin to discern the (implicit) definition of the good in Alma$_2$'s sermon. Alma$_2$ himself explains his confidence in prediction by asking and answering a question: "And now, behold, are ye sure that this is a good seed? I say unto you, yea, for every seed bringeth forth unto its own likeness. Therefore, if a seed groweth, it is good; but if it groweth not, behold, it is not good. Therefore it is cast away."[26] Here, Alma$_2$ anticipates experimenters reacting in the predicted way for very specific *reasons*. In other words, he imagines them doing a bit of reasoning, developing their convictions regarding the goodness of the seed or word on specifiable rational grounds. Alma$_2$'s prediction about his experimenters, in the end, is based on the rational nature of the world, which he takes to be accessible to human beings. This is an important point. One could ground Alma$_2$'s predictions on universal human nature (human beings just are the sort of creatures who respond to a certain sort of experience in a certain way). What is objective for Alma$_2$, however, is apparently not human nature but the rational nature of the world, on which an honest and reasonable being can reflect and come to predictable conclusions.

The reasoning Alma$_2$ attributes to his experimenters after their first experiences deserves some unpacking. It unfolds over the course of several dense lines (quoted just above), but two of these lines ("if a seed groweth, it is good; but if it groweth not, behold, it is not good") seem to form the key premise in the reasoning Alma envisions.[27] Together, they establish a strict logical equivalence. On the right in what follows, there are logical formalizations, where capitalized words are predicates, "x" is a variable, "(x)" means "for all x," "c" is a constant (i.e., some particular), → means "implies that," and ≡ means "if and only."

A seed is good if and only if it grows.	$(x) (\text{Seed}_x \rightarrow (\text{Good}_x \equiv \text{Grows}_x))$

This equivalence between growth and goodness apparently forms a first premise in an (implicit) argument. The whole argument would have the following form:

Premise: A seed is good if and only if it grows. $(x)\,(Seed_x \rightarrow (Good_x \equiv Grows_x))$

Premise: This seed grows. $Seed_c\ \&\ Grows_c$

Conclusion: This seed is good. $Good_c$

This is a classically valid argument, logically speaking. It is worth spelling it out formally because it makes clear, for the first time, what Alma understands the good to be—or at least understands good seeds to be. For a seed, it seems, goodness is a matter of growth. Good seeds grow, and growing seeds are good. Speaking slightly more broadly, then, what defines goodness for seeds seems to be a kind of alignment of what actually happens with what is meant to happen. Seeds are meant to grow. Seeds that do what they are meant to do—seeds that grow—are good seeds. This equivalence, in the form of a premise in an argument, seems to form a hard kernel for the reasoning at issue.

It is difficult to avoid the impression that there is something Aristotelian about the reasoning Alma$_2$ attributes to his experimenters. What decides the goodness of a seed is its *physis* or *natura*.[28] I take it that such an idea underpins the fact that Alma$_2$, at one point in his sermon, rhetorically equates goodness and truth—or at least the goodness and the truth of a seed. At the outset of his parable, that is, he states as one of the conditions for the accumulation of positive experimental data that the seed being planted "be a true seed or a good seed."[29] This phrase can be glossed in various ways, but if, as seems likely, "or" in the phrase signals equivalence, Alma$_2$ collapses truth and goodness into a single category. The most obvious philosophical reason for doing so would be an Aristotelian-like conception of essence (that is, of a thing's nature). A seed's goodness, it seems, just is its being true to its nature.[30] One could gloss the first premise in the argument Alma$_2$ envisions his experimenters making within themselves as follows:

Premise: A seed is good if and only if it's true to its nature. $(x)\,(Seed_x \rightarrow (Good_x \equiv True_x))$[31]

This philosophically weighty premise seems to lie at the foundation of the argument Alma$_2$ imagines his hearers making when they undergo the right experiences.

For the above formally valid argument to work convincingly on Alma$_2$'s imagined experimenters, two further things would have to be the case. That is to say there are two further things that Alma$_2$'s prediction implicitly presupposes. First, it presupposes that his would-be experimenters, before undertaking the bit of reasoning he spells out, must already know what makes a seed good or true (must already know the nature of seeds). If they were to lack this knowledge, they would be unable to acknowledge the propositional truth of the first premise or to recognize the relevance of the second premise's truth to the argument. Hence, Alma$_2$'s prediction presupposes *the knowability of the good* (or at least the good with regard to seeds). Second, Alma$_2$'s prediction presupposes that his would-be experimenters naturally feel the compulsory force of valid reasoning. It might seem pedantic to point out this second presupposition, but it seems to me essential to make it explicit. It makes clear that Alma$_2$ grants value to reason as such and that he assumes his hearers and imagined experimenters do so as well. For Alma$_2$, *nature* (or at least the nature of seeds) *is rationally available to rational human beings.*

Alma$_2$'s picture again looks Aristotelian in spirit. Nature is rationally available to rational human beings, in such a way that the good (of at least certain things) is inherently knowable. It is, at any rate, because the measure of a seed's goodness is knowable that Alma$_2$ can set forth a reliable experiment; those who know what seeds are meant to do and then attempt to prove the goodness of some particular seed by experiment will inevitably do a bit of valid reasoning to draw a wholly rational—in fact, a wholly natural—conclusion. The good here concerns the alignment between a thing's nature or essence and its actual state in the world.[32] The knowability of the good involves both the knowability of a thing's nature or essence and the knowability of its actual alignment with that nature or essence. Such knowability, Alma$_2$ appears to assume, is inherent to the world as it stands before (rational) human beings. That world Alma$_2$ elsewhere presents as organized and governed by "a supreme creator," a divine being who suffices to explain "the earth and all things that is [*sic*] upon the face of it—yea, and its motion, yea, and also all the planets which move in their regular form."[33] Presumably, the good *and* its knowability are functions of God's intentions with the world, as among so many of Aristotle's late-medieval Christian heirs.

Of course, it has to be pointed out that Alma$_2$'s Aristotelian-like conception of things appears within the framework of a parable, where seeds stand for words and harvests for eternal life. The word on which Alma$_2$ hopes his hearers will experiment is the (angelic) word regarding "the Son of God."[34] It is, he says, "this word" that he hopes they will plant in their hearts, "and as it beginneth to swell, even so nourish it by your faith, and behold, it will become a tree springing up in you unto everlasting life."[35] As Alma$_2$'s words here make clear, however, he assumes that the word regarding the Son of God has a knowable nature of its own—something, in short, that it is intended to do and that allows for the measurement of its actual goodness when received in faith. Even as the parable is, as it were, demystified, the nature of the good seems to remain the same, as does the means of its being known.[36]

A Second Model

The matter of knowing the good arises much earlier in Mormon$_2$'s (later) sermon than it does in Alma$_2$'s (earlier) sermon, preceding everything he has to say about the ostensible themes of the discourse: faith, hope, and charity. In fact, the theme of the good appears as early as Mormon$_2$'s opening address. Speaking to people gathered for worship, Mormon$_2$ begins by calling them "the peaceable followers of Christ" and then explains his reason for believing them to be such. "I judge these things of you," he says, "because of your peaceable walk with the children of men."[37] Mormon$_2$ immediately goes on to ground this judgment on a still more fundamental conviction, one drawn from the divine word: "For I remember the word of God which saith, 'By their works ye shall know them'—for if their works be good, then they are good also."[38] It is not difficult to see how this "word of God," along with what seems to be a supplementary explanation of it, is supposed to justify Mormon$_2$'s judgment.[39] It is even harder, though, to know why he is supposed to feel that his judgment needs justification in the first place.

Mormon$_2$ pursues this point at length, however, developing the justification for his judgment into a kind of extended prologue for the sermon. He comes to faith, hope, and charity only after fully clarifying what he has to say by way of justifying his knowledge of his hearers' goodness. When he finally comes to the topic of faith, in fact, he calls it "the way whereby ye may lay hold on every good thing."[40] At first, the kinds of things Mormon$_2$ calls potentially good are gifts and prayers, and the aim at that early point in the discourse is apparently to undercut the idea that human beings have the capacity to give good gifts or to offer good prayers at all. "A man, being evil, cannot do that which is good," Mormon$_2$ says; "neither will he give a good gift."[41] Here, then, the central issue is arguably less whether the good can be *known* than whether the good can be *done*. And this concern continues for fully half of the prologue to the sermon, exhausting itself before Mormon$_2$ eventually turns from the doability to the knowability of the good.

A threshold passage appears at the point where the knowability of the good begins to come into focus—a passage that can be read as being about either the doability or the knowability of the good. "Wherefore," Mormon$_2$ says, "all things which are good cometh of God, and that which is evil cometh of the devil."[42] Does this explain, in the fashion of Saint

Paul, that any good that a human being *does* is ultimately the effect of God acting in that person, or does it begin to articulate the criterion by which to discern and therefore to *know* whether a thing is good? The latter is a real possibility because, after just one more sentence, Mormon₂ issues a warning about right judgment: "Wherefore, take heed, my beloved brethren, that ye do not judge that which is evil to be of God, or that which is good and of God to be of the devil."[43] At any rate, from that point forward in (the prologue to) the sermon, the knowability of the good fully displaces the doability of the good. Mormon₂ consistently addresses next what it means to avoid misconstruing good things as evil and evil things as good.

As the threshold passage appears that separates questions about the good's doability from those about its knowability, the prologue to Mormon₂'s sermon begins to be organized by a significant textual structure that is key to understanding what is said about the knowability of the good. The structure is plainly chiastic,[44] and it deserves being laid out in full:

A For the devil is an enemy to God and fighteth against him continually, and inviteth and enticeth to sin and to do that which is evil continually.

B But behold, that which is of God inviteth and enticeth to do good continually—wherefore, everything which inviteth and enticeth to do good and to love God and to serve him is inspired of God.

C Wherefore, take heed, my beloved brethren, that ye do not judge that which is evil to be of God, or that which is good and of God to be of the devil.

D For behold, my brethren, it is given unto you to judge, that ye may know good from evil.

E And the way to judge is as plain—that ye may know with a perfect knowledge—as the daylight is from the dark night.

D' For the Spirit of Christ is given to every man, that he may know good from evil.

C' Wherefore, I show unto you the way to judge.

B' For everything which inviteth to do good and to persuade to believe in Christ is sent forth by the power and gift of Christ—wherefore ye may know with a perfect knowledge it is of God.

A' But whatsoever thing persuadeth men to do evil and believe not in Christ and deny him and serve not God, then ye may know with a perfect knowledge is of the devil.[45]

At a glance, one sees how this long passage opens and closes in A and A' with statements about what the devil invites, entices, or persuades human beings to do. Stepping inward, one finds in B and B' clarifications of the contrasting idea of divine invitations, enticements, or persuadings to do good. Then, in C and C' comes a warning about judging wrongly and a promise of instruction about how to judge rightly. Coming to D and D', one notes parallel uses of "is given unto"/"is given to" and "that ye may know good from evil"/"that he may know good from evil." Finally, at the heart of the chiasm, at E, is a statement about the plainness of judgment; this makes "a perfect knowledge" the focal point of this whole sequence of the text. The chiasm here, it is evident, is rather tightly organized.

This chiastic structure in the text reveals the logic of this part of Mormon₂'s sermon because it is in the differences between elements in the chiasm's first half and their parallel counterparts in the chiasm's second half that the progress of the argument is marked. In C and C', for instance, there is a clear sense of progress from Mormon₂'s blunt placement of the burden of discerning good from evil on his hearers (C) to Mormon₂'s promise to provide assistance to those hoping to judge rightly (C'). Indeed, the whole pathway from A to E, moving toward the chiasm's center, is taken up with placing the burden of judging on Mormon₂'s hearers, while the pathway from E to A', moving away from the chiasm's center, finds Mormon₂ giving his hearers the help he seems to know they would need. The chiasm's center at E thus marks a rather strong transition.[46]

Digging deeper into this sense of progress from burden to assistance, it is important to highlight two places where the shift is particularly theologically salient. The first concerns D and D', where parallel uses of "is given unto"/"is given to" and "that ye may know good from evil"/"that he may know good from evil" appear. What is found at D in the first, burden-focused half of the chiasm is, precisely, the burden of judgment: "For behold, my brethren, it is given unto you to judge, that ye may know good from evil."[47] The purposive clause here, "that ye may know good from evil," not only introduces the theme of knowing good (which replaces the earlier theme of doing good), but it also seems rhetorically meant to explain the value of shouldering the burden of judgment. Apparently, for Mormon₂, carrying the weight of having to decide between good and evil is essential to developing any real knowledge of good and evil; one cannot really knowingly disentangle good from evil without having some kind of direct responsibility to judge such a matter. Crucially, however, the two phrases from D that appear anew in D' do very different work in their second iteration: "For the Spirit of Christ is given to every man, that he may know good from evil."[48] Here, in D', in the lighter and more hopeful half of the chiasm, "is given to" concerns the source of assistance rather than the assignment of responsibility, while "that he may know good from evil" marks not the motivation for assuming responsibility but an ability to succeed that comes with the promised assistance. Thanks, it seems, to the introduction of "the Spirit of Christ,"[49] purposive burden gives way to real possibility; the good becomes genuinely knowable.

Second, it is important to consider the A and B, and then the B' and A', moments in the chiasm. It is in the crucial but subtle difference between these extremes of the chiastic structure that the significance of the hinge-like promise of E is decided. First, it must be noticed just how similar A and A' are to each other, as are B and B' in turn. The devil invites and entices to sin in A, just as he persuades to do evil and avoid serving God in A'. Similarly, everything that invites one to do good is of God in B, just as it is again in B'. Are A and A', like B and B', then, just the same? If they were, all talk of plainness in E would ring hollow, and the promise of C' would feel cheap. Closer reading, though, reveals a key difference between A and A', as well as between B and B'. The whole chiasm ends where it began, with a restatement of the claim that good comes from God and evil from the devil. The crucial difference between the opening and the closing of the whole larger chiasm, however, is that references to Jesus Christ show up *only* in the second half of the structure. That is, A and B speak only of God, but B' and A' speak of God *and of Christ*. Because, as just noticed above, D' introduces "the Spirit of Christ" as what creates the knowability of the good—this right before C' offers its word of promise and right after E marks the central point of transition from burden to assistance—progress toward talk of Christ in B' and A' is essential to Mormon$_2$'s theological purposes.

In light of these points of analysis, the progress in the second half of the chiasm gains in coherence. Each step in the chiasm from E to A' serves as a crucial link in a strong logical chain: (1) The turning point in the chiasm comes in E, which insists on the plainness of the difference between good and evil; (2) D' then introduces "the Spirit of Christ," which for Mormon$_2$ makes the good knowable by human beings; (3) next, C' issues a clear promise, in which Mormon$_2$ commits himself to providing help to his hearers as they execute their responsibility to judge good from evil; and, finally, (4) the restatements of the chiasm's opening in B' and A' recast the relationships that good and evil things have to supernatural beings, the good testifying of and the evil denying Jesus Christ. The upshot of the argument is that it is not enough to know that good things come from God and evil things from the devil. Promisingly dichotomous as that idea sounds at first, Mormon$_2$ insists that it is insufficient, because any would-be judge of good and evil must know the *criterion* by which to decide between them. And that criterion is, it seems, its relationship specifically to Jesus Christ.

In Mormon$_2$'s sermon, it is apparently whether or not any given thing aligns with Christ—in other words, persuades people to believe in Christ—that is the crucial question. Christ is the criterion, something that becomes perfectly clear as Mormon$_2$ continues. "And now my brethren," he says after the close of the chiasm, "seeing that ye know the light by which ye may judge—which light is the light of Christ—see that ye do not judge wrongfully."[50] Mormon$_2$ here circles back to his warning against misjudging good things and evil things (element C in the first half of the chiasm), but he adds Christ to it (from the second half of the chiasm). Christ has become the light that has to be shone onto things to see them well enough to judge aright.[51] So it is that Mormon$_2$ enjoins, "Wherefore I beseech of you, brethren, that ye should search diligently in the light of Christ."[52] With Christ as the light, as the criterion for judging between good and evil, the diligent search for the good can begin in earnest.

With this, the prologue of sorts to Mormon$_2$'s sermon comes to a close, and Mormon$_2$'s talk of the good and its knowability give way to reflections directly on faith, hope, and charity. At this point, then, it is possible to take stock of Mormon$_2$'s conception not only of the good as such but also of its knowability. Mormon$_2$, it has to be said, is less forthcoming than Alma$_2$ about exactly what the goodness of a thing consists of. It is clear, of course, that for him all good things come from God, but what their goodness consists of remains unclear. He speaks of good gifts and prayers and says that these are gifts and prayers offered "with real intent,"[53] but he never sets forth anything so clear or metaphysically freighted as Alma$_2$ does when speaking of the goodness of seeds. By contrast, though, Mormon$_2$ has much to say about what constitutes the knowability of the good and so about the criterion by which one might discern good things from evil things. The good is knowable in its goodness, thanks only to "the Spirit of Christ," which is "given to every man."[54] By asking about a thing's relationship to Christ, its ontological rootedness in God is supposed to become clear.

Two Models in Tension

With the above summary treatments of Alma$_2$'s and Mormon$_2$'s sermons complete, it is possible to ask how their respective conceptions of the good and its knowability compare. The most forceful way to come at the theological differences between the two sermons, however, might be to emphasize first the place that each grants to Jesus Christ. In Alma$_2$'s sermon, Christ is the *question*. In Mormon₂'s sermon, Christ is the *criterion*. That is, in Alma₂'s sermon, the question that drives the parable is whether Christ (announced in the word that Alma₂ figures as a seed) is good. Alma₂ challenges his hearers to try an experiment to know whether the word announcing Christ—and therefore whether Christ himself—is good. Mormon₂ recommends Christ to his hearers, however, as the criterion by which to decide whether anything at all is good. The difference here might be put as follows: For Alma₂, the criterion by which the goodness of a thing is known is a *natural* matter, an issue of whether a thing (a seed, a word, Christ himself) is true to its nature (that is, to what it is intended to do). For Mormon₂, though, the criterion by which the goodness of a thing is known is a *Christological* issue, a matter solely of whether or how a thing persuades one to believe in Christ. If there is a controversy between Alma₂ and Mormon₂, it seems it is a function of whether Christ is the thing that might be known to be good (by, explicitly, some *non*-Christic means) or whether Christ is the thing that allows good things to be known as good (things that would not obviously include Christ).

This first difference opens onto differences between conceptions of the good and its knowability. As I argued above, Alma₂ does not specify where the knowability of the good comes from, except to intimate that it is in some sense natural.[55] Human beings can know the nature of things, and, reasoning their way from what they know of nature and whether experience confirms a particular thing's conformity to its nature, they can decide on its goodness. The good concerns nature, human reason is crucial to knowing, and the "great question" is whether Christ,[56] or the word of Christ, is good. Things are rather different in Mormon₂'s sermon. Mormon₂ never calls into question—perhaps because the "peaceable followers of Christ" in his congregation setting do not themselves call into question[57]—whether Christ or the word of Christ is good. He asks instead about the goodness of everything *but* Christ. For Mormon₂, Christ is the means by which the goodness of things is knowable.[58]

In each of these two sermons, there is something mysterious about the knowability of something relevant to the good. However, what exactly registers as mysterious in each case is distinct. What is mysteriously knowable for Alma₂ is nature, but what is mysteriously knowable for Mormon₂ is Christ himself. Alma₂'s hearers would have to wonder whether and how their knowledge of the natures of things might prove adequate enough to allow them to decide on the goodness of Christ. Mormon₂'s hearers would have to wonder whether and how their knowledge of Christ might prove adequate enough to allow them to decide on the goodness of all other things. One could say that the two sermons, between themselves, raise the question of whether it is knowing Christ that allows for the knowability of good things as good, or whether it is knowing the goodness of things that allows for the knowability of the goodness of Christ. Alma$_2$ and Mormon$_2$ seem to answer this question in diametrically opposed ways.[59]

Can these two sermons be reconciled? It is a question well worth asking, especially in light of the apparent connections between them, the only somewhat subtle allusions that suggest to the reader that Mormon$_2$'s sermon is dependent on Alma$_2$'s. Can Alma$_2$ be read as suggesting that, however rational nature is, it remains inaccessible through reason in some way?[60] Can Mormon$_2$ be read as holding that although the knowability of the good always hinges on the revelation of Christ, there is no sense in which the revealed is beyond rationality?[61] Or as I have argued here, are the two sermons ultimately distinct in their philosophical and theological orientations?[62]

The work of fully developing the moral assumptions native to the Book of Mormon—the ethical baseline by which the ethical implications of its various teachings and stories must be measured and contextualized—has only just begun. The tension between the volume's two most explicit reflections on the good and its knowability suggests that the task is a substantial one. Before the Book of Mormon can be brought up for trial on moral or ethical grounds, this task deserves a good deal more attention. That it will have to be worked out in conversation with potentially varying positions on the most basic of ethical questions is, I think, clear. Despite the challenge, however, the task is worth pursuing. A religious text that guides the moralities of millions of believers, the Book of Mormon begs for closer and more responsible readings, even and especially when it comes to its ethical bearings.

Notes

1. Grant Hardy, *Understanding the Book of Mormon: A Reader's Guide* (New York: Oxford University Press, 2010), xii.

2. Thomas F. O'Dea, *The Mormons* (Chicago: University of Chicago Press, 1957), 26.

3. Especially important in this regard was the treatment of the Book of Mormon in Fawn M. Brodie, *No Man Knows My History: The Life of Joseph Smith, the Mormon Prophet* (New York: Alfred A. Knopf, 1945).

4. Dramatic changes in the field of Book of Mormon studies can largely be dated to the 2002 appearance of Terryl Givens's *By the Hand of Mormon: The American Scripture That Launched a New World Religion* (New York: Oxford University Press, 2002). For some discussion, see Joseph M. Spencer, "On Signifiers and Signifieds: Terryl Givens and Twenty-First-Century Book of Mormon Studies," *Journal of Book of Mormon Studies* 31 (2022): 56–74.

5. It is important to underscore "for the purposes and interests of the academy." Naturally, the purposes and interests of the churches that embrace the Book of Mormon and scripture are distinct from those of scholars writing as scholars.

6. A vast literature of morally focused writing on the Book of Mormon exists in a noncritical vein, of course, but very little of it is scholarly. Much devotional and pastoral writing on the Book of Mormon takes as its aim to form the moral life of believers.

7. Because there are defenders as much as critics in this regard, it is important to underscore that there is a substantial literature—and a growing one—that makes the case that the Book of Mormon can be exonerated on most or all ethical charges. For a basic survey of the literature in an introductory fashion, see Daniel Becerra, Amy Easton-Flake, Nicholas J. Frederick, and Joseph M. Spencer, *Book of Mormon Studies: An Introduction and Guide* (Provo, UT: BYU Religious Studies Center, 2022).

8. This sermon is found in the original Chapter XVI of the book of Alma, within the Book of Mormon. It is today's chapter 32 in Latter-day Saint editions of the Book of Mormon.

9. Moroni 7:1. All quotations of the Book of Mormon come from Royal Skousen, ed., *The Book of Mormon: The Earliest Text* (New Haven, CT: Yale University Press, 2009), although I have taken the liberty of replacing Skousen's punctuation with my own wherever it seems appropriate.

10. This is found in the original Chapter VII of the book of Moroni of the Book of Mormon, and it remains chapter 7 in both Latter-day Saint and Community of Christ editions.

11. Alma 30:13–14.

12. For a helpful introduction to Moroni$_2$ as editor in the Book of Mormon, see Hardy, *Understanding the Book of Mormon*, 215–67.

13. For important recent treatments of the parable, see Mark A. Wrathall, *Alma 30–63: A Brief Theological Introduction* (Provo, UT: Neal A. Maxwell Institute for Religious Scholarship, BYU, 2020), 46–68; Joseph M. Spencer, "Is Not This Real?" *BYU Studies Quarterly* 58, no. 2 (2019): 87–104.

14. Moroni 7:1.

15. Moroni 7:16, 7:18.

16. Moroni 7:19.

17. For an important recent treatment of the sermon, see Charles Swift, "'After This Manner Did He Speak': Mormon's Discourse on Faith, Hope, and Charity," *Religious Educator: Perspectives on the Restored Gospel* 19, no. 2 (2018): 278–89.

18. In Alma$_2$'s sermon, see Alma 32:21, 32:26, 32:29. In Mormon$_2$'s sermon, see Moroni 7:15, 7:16, 7:17.

19. See Alma 32:21–23; Moroni 7:21–25.

20. For helpful elaboration of this idea of canonically immanent tension within a book of scripture, see Brevard Childs's work on the New Testament's four gospels. Brevard S. Childs, *The New Testament as Canon: An Introduction* (Philadelphia: Fortress Press, 1984), 55–209.

21. Alma 32:28.

22. Alma 32:27.

23. Alma 32:28.

24. Alma 32:30. Note that at certain points (even in this very passage, in fact), Alma$_2$ uses not only the modal verb "will" in such predictions but also "must."

25. See, especially, Alma 32:28, 32:35.

26. Alma 32:31–32.

27. Given the use of "therefore" at the beginning of these two lines, they seem to be an explication of the deeply ambiguous earlier line "every seed bringeth forth unto its own likeness." In other words, the equivalence relation (a seed is good if and only if it grows) seems to be, for Alma$_2$, the meaning of "every seed bringeth forth unto its own likeness." At any rate, the equivalence relation is the apparent anchor for the reasoning Alma$_2$ attributes to his experimenters.

28. The roots of the larger philosophical view that the goodness of a thing concerns the actualization of what its nature assigns to it potentially are thoroughly Aristotelian, although the long history of this view is labyrinthine. For an introduction to the basic philosophical underpinnings of the view, see R. J. Hankinson, "Philosophy of Science," in *The Cambridge Companion to Aristotle*, ed. Jonathan Barnes, 109–139 (New York: Cambridge University Press, 1995). It is necessary to underscore that I do not mean to suggest that there is any direct—or even largely indirect—historical line of influence traceable from Aristotle or Aristotelianism to the Book of Mormon.

29. Alma 32:28. This passage is all the more striking for the fact that it marks the only moment in the whole of the Book of Mormon where truth and goodness are obviously conflated. (That is not to say that other passages in the Book of Mormon do not acknowledge some kind of moral valence in the notion of truth—see, for instance, the somewhat regular coupling of "just" and "true" [1 Nephi 14:23; Mosiah 2:35, 4:12; Alma 18:34, 29:8; 3 Nephi 5:18, 8:1; Moroni 10:6.]) No other passage in the volume, though, seems to equate the good and the true.)

30. It is worth noting that the Book of Mormon elsewhere attributes to Alma$_2$ a rather strong idea of things having a nature—in fact, a nature to which they must ultimately be restored (according to justice). See especially Alma 41:12. It should be noted also that the apparent equivalence between "true" and "good" here ("if it be a true seed or a good seed") distances Alma$_2$ from any conception in which truth is especially applicable to propositional content. Again, truth here is true to something-ness rather than the truth of propositions.

31. For the full validity of the formal argument to continue to hold, the second premise would be glossed as follows: *Premise*: This seed is true to its nature. (Seed$_c$ & True$_c$)

32. Again, elsewhere in the Book of Mormon Alma$_2$ seems to define the bad as occurring when "a thing of a natural state" is placed "in an unnatural state" or "in a state opposite to its nature" (Alma 41:12).

33. Alma 30:44.

34. That the question for Alma$_2$ is whether the word regarding Christ is good—rather than, say, whether Christ is the Son of God—reflects the staging

of the stories in the Book of Mormon. Never in the Book of Mormon is there a question of whether the Jesus of history is in fact the Christ of faith, and this seems to be because the peoples whose stories are told in the book lived on the other side of the world, far from Israel and the locales the Jesus of history knew.

35. Alma 33:22–23.

36. There remain difficulties, at the end of Alma₂'s parable, about exactly what a good word is supposed to do once it is planted in one's heart. A good seed, Alma₂ says, "swelleth and sprouteth and beginneth to grow" (Alma 32:30), but what is the parallel series of promising occurrences for a good word? Alma₂ does not provide an answer to this question within the boundaries of the sermon in question, but he arguably does spell out an answer in later preaching. For some discussion, see Spencer, "Is Not This Real?"

37. Moroni 7:3–4.

38. Moroni 7:5.

39. The Book of Mormon as originally dictated by Joseph Smith lacked punctuation, so it remains a question of interpretive judgment to decide where "the word of God" quoted by Mormon₂ is supposed to end. I suspect that the quoted "word" is short, such that the conditional ("if their works be good, then they are good also") is intended to be understood as Mormon₂'s explanation of the divine word (rather than his further quotation of the divine word). No scriptural "word of God" in the Book of Mormon or the Bible matches what Mormon₂ quotes, although the repeating refrain of Matthew 7:16, 20—"By their fruits ye shall know them"—(quoted in the Book of Mormon in 3 Nephi 14:16, 14:20) may be the intended "word of God."

40. Moroni 7:20.

41. Moroni 7:10. It might be noted that Mormon₂ seems to borrow here from Matthew 7:11 (a passage in close proximity to the apparent source for the "word of God" Mormon₂ cites just prior to this), a passage quoted in the Book of Mormon at 3 Nephi 14:11.

42. Moroni 7:12.

43. Moroni 7:14.

44. For more than half a century, scholars have given attention to the use of chiasmus (and other parallelistic structures) in the Book of Mormon, often in attempts to demonstrate the book's antiquity. Regardless of what the presence of such structures in the volume means about its historicity, they unquestionably appear on occasion, as in the present passage.

45. Moroni 7:12–17. In his full formatting of parallelistic structures in the Book of Mormon, Donald Parry does not find chiasmus in this passage, although he finds a few smaller structures. See Donald W. Parry, *Poetic Parallelisms in the Book of Mormon: The Complete Text Reformatted* (Provo, UT: Neal A. Maxwell Institute for Religious Scholarship, BYU, 2007), 554.

46. It is perhaps no surprise that the central E element of the chiasm speaks directly of stark contrasts, as stark as the difference between day and night.

E materially as much as formally marks a key change in the direction of the discourse.

47. Moroni 7:15.

48. Moroni 7:16.

49. The interpretive history of this passage's reference to "the Spirit of Christ" has been overdetermined in the Latter-day Saint tradition by one mid-twentieth-century systematization of various nineteenth-century theological models of the divine spirit. For a sketch of the relevant history, see Terryl L. Givens, *Wrestling the Angel: The Foundations of Mormon Thought: Cosmos, God, Humanity* (New York: Oxford University Press, 2015), 124–29. For the dominant mid-twentieth-century picture, see Joseph Fielding Smith, *Doctrines of Salvation*, 3 vols. (Salt Lake City: Bookcraft, 1954), 1:38–55.

50. Moroni 7:18.

51. Where the interpretive history of "the Spirit of Christ" has been overdetermined by one mid-twentieth-century attempt at systematizing earlier Latter-day Saint theologies of the divine spirit, the phrase "the light of Christ" in Moroni 7 has been—in the Latter-day Saint context—entirely dominated by it. The standard interpretation is that Mormon refers to a divine influence, akin or maybe equivalent to the moral conscience, that divinely operates on all human beings and alerts them to what is good or evil among moral options. While something like that theological picture is possibly on display in other Latter-day Saint scriptural texts (outside the Book of Mormon), it actually seems more natural to read the reference to "the light of Christ" in Mormon's sermon as deploying a simple metaphor (rather than a metaphysical principle): It is *in light of Christ* (that is, by asking what relationship something sustains with Christ) that one knows the goodness of something.

52. Moroni 7:19.

53. Moroni 7:6.

54. Moroni 7:16.

55. It must be stressed that "natural" here does not mean that the knowability of the good is not, for Alma$_2$, something created or set in order by God. The contrast class for "natural" here is not "supernatural" but specifically "Christological."

56. Alma 34:5.

57. Moroni 7:3.

58. This controversy between Alma$_2$ and Mormon$_2$ (if it *is*, in fact, a controversy) smacks of the Euthyphro dilemma, the question posed by Socrates about whether the (Greek) gods are good because they are pious or whether the gods are pious because they are good. (See Plato, *Euthyphro*, 10a.) One way to cash out the Euthyphro dilemma is in terms of reason and revelation. If the gods are good because they are pious, then they presumably follow the rational order of things toward goodness like any human being (albeit perhaps with divine aid) might do. But if the gods are pious because they are good, then to know of the gods' piety is to have their goodness unveiled or revealed.

59. In a handful of articles over recent years, Robert Couch has argued for a quasi-Aristotelian (or perhaps quasi-Thomist) reading of the Book of Mormon. His works, it seems to me, are essential reading for anyone wishing to pursue Alma$_2$'s ethical vision. See especially Robert Couch, "On Zeezrom's Conversion: Rationality, Tradition, and Money," *Journal of Book of Mormon Studies* 29 (2020): 120–51; and Robert Couch, "Desiring Riches: A Radical-Practical Critique of Modern Business," in *Reapproaching Zion*, ed. Nathan B. Oman and Samuel D. Brunson, 35–61 (Salt Lake City: BCC Press, 2020).

60. Even if the goodness of the word is rationally knowable for Alma$_2$, it has to be noted that he presents the word as angelic in origin (see Alma 32:23). At the same time, Alma$_2$ ventures at least once in the Book of Mormon something like the cosmological argument for God's existence, which arguably trades on a conception of revelation that is rational at its base (see Alma 30:44).

61. After Mormon$_2$, in another text, receives a revelation regarding whether infant baptism is good (he learns in the revelation that it is evil), he does not hesitate to offer thoroughly rational arguments for the position he presents as revealed—rational enough that he proves willing to condemn those who conclude otherwise on rational grounds (see Moroni 8:9–23). At the same time, Mormon$_2$ clearly predicates the three classically "theological virtues" (of faith, hope, and love) on the revelation of Christ, apparently distinguishing them from the merely rational and locating their goodness solely within Christ (see Moroni 7:21–48).

62. One speculative solution to the dilemma would be to argue that Christ is the (revealed) means to (rationally) knowing the goodness of the word about Christ. What if Christ is the criterion by which the question about the goodness of Christ is decided? If Alma$_2$'s and Mormon$_2$'s positions were fused in this peculiar way, coming to know the goodness of Christ would be something like the making explicit of the life one has always lived in Christ unknowingly—as in, for instance, the famous opening paragraphs of Saint Augustine's *Confessions* (I.1–5).

5

Do Values Depend on Other Persons?

The Book of Mormon's Apocalyptic Solitude

RYAN W. DAVIS

How much do other people matter to the meaning of your life? In his *Death and the Afterlife*, philosopher Samuel Scheffler develops an argument aimed to show that others in our community matter much more to us and our ability to find value in the world than we typically suppose.[1] Scheffler argues from a contrast between two cases. First, imagine discovering that shortly after your natural death, your entire social world would come to an end. Scheffler holds that for many people such a discovery would attenuate or even destroy the meaning they find in life. Nevertheless, many are still fully able to find meaning in their own life, notwithstanding the lack of a belief that they personally will survive their death. Scheffler infers that the persistence of our community after our death matters more to our values than our own individual persistence after death. Scheffler concludes that even our seemingly individual values depend significantly on the presence of other persons. Call this the *communal value thesis*.[2]

Scheffler's account finds perhaps a surprising test in the Book of Mormon. Facing the imminent end of their civilization, Mormon[2] and Moroni[2]—the book's final prophetic writers—anticipate both the end of their social world and their own individual persistence after death.[3] Even before the outset of Nephite society, the Book of Mormon's first writer, Nephi[1], also foresees his people's apocalyptic end. The communal value thesis would anticipate that their individual values would be undermined by these discoveries. But that is not how the story unfolds. Although they are deeply affected, neither Nephi[1] nor Mormon[2] and Moroni[2] interpret the complete destruction of their society as a challenge to the values guiding their lives. On the contrary, they see that destruction as evidence *supporting* their values. Their accounts provide a puzzle for the communal value thesis.

As Scheffler would anticipate, Nephi$_1$, Mormon$_2$, and Moroni$_2$ are far from indifferent to the coming apocalypse—just not in a way that compromises their commitment to, or confidence in, their values. Why not? My answer will be controversial, both as a normative thesis and as a reading of the Book of Mormon. Near the end of the Book of Mormon, Moroni$_2$ surveys the extraordinary achievements of the prophetic figures chronicled in the book's nearly thousand-year history. He comes to despair over his own "weakness" and pleads with God on behalf of his own future readers. The answer he receives is striking: The choices of other persons do not matter to his own salvation. Among the Book of Mormon's final lessons is that redemption does not depend on the actions (or even the presence) of anyone else. The entire arc of the Book of Mormon's grand narrative, culminating in a single person outliving their civilizational context, is a story about that person's salvation. Moroni$_2$'s parting lesson is that living a redeemed life—a life "perfected" in Christ—is a matter between the individual who is living that life and God.

That is not to say that love for those around us is irrelevant. But, I will suggest, Mormon$_2$ and Moroni$_2$ do learn something about love: Loving another person does not consist in wanting them to be saved; it doesn't consist in any particular aim at all.[4]

My hope in this chapter is to think about the Book of Mormon's concluding chapters as a case for Scheffler and to think about Scheffler's puzzle as a frame for interpreting the Book of Mormon. This chapter is in six sections. Section 1 develops Scheffler's communal value thesis. Section 2 presents a challenge to Scheffler's thesis. Sections 3 and 4 consider two Book of Mormon prophets, Nephi$_1$ and Moroni$_2$. Section 5 explores a lesson for the concept of charity. Section 6 defends the revisionist reading of the Book of Mormon.

Apocalypse and Communal Value

Scheffler poses two central cases in his *Death and the Afterlife*. Here is the first:

> Suppose you knew that, although you yourself would live a normal life span, the earth would be completely destroyed thirty days after your death in a collision with a giant asteroid. How would this knowledge affect your attitudes during the remainder of your life?[5]

The second case is drawn from P. D. James's *Children of Men*.[6] The novel takes place in a dystopian future in which humanity has become infertile. There have been no births in twenty-five years. As the last generation ages, people must confront the possibility of human extinction. As in the asteroid scenario, an individual living in this world must reckon with the prospect that none of their personal values will continue much beyond their own individual life. However, the novel's world differs in that it is fully compatible with each individual person living out the natural course of their life. Once again, Scheffler wonders how knowledge of the oncoming end of the social world will affect one's individual valuing attitudes.

In both cases, Scheffler's answer is that the coming apocalypse will likely undermine one's values in the present. First, consider personal values or projects that are other-regarding or future-regarding in their motivation. A scientist working on a cure for cancer will have little reason to continue their research if the world will end in a few years anyway. A composer laboring over their score will have little reason to continue if they know it will never reach an audience.

Second, consider activities that are based on a tradition or community. Scheffler holds that much of what infuses our lives with normative significance derives from our participation in ongoing traditions. Traditions help answer a vexing problem: How can we understand ourselves as beings moving across time?

According to Scheffler, we face a common problem.[7] For example, it is not possible to return to cherished times in the past in the same way that we can return to cherished places. We can go back to locations that have a special meaning in our lives. We can walk the hallways of our old school, revisit the house where we grew up, or plan a return trip to a past vacation spot. But we cannot go back and revisit *times* from the past.[8] In Scheffler's telling, we are all threatened with a kind of temporal homelessness. Traditions, by Scheffler's account, provide at least a second-best kind of solution. By participating in the same activities or performing the same actions, sometimes in company with the same people, at the same point in a week or a year, we can approximate the feeling of returning to the past. Traditions allow us to stake out a home in time. The feelings associated with home—comfort, security, peace, and so on—can also be present in the performance of traditions.

Now, however, consider participating in a tradition when you know that your way of life will soon come to an end. Scheffler anticipates that under these circumstances, the tradition would ring hollow.[9] We would lose our reasons to continue the tradition if we anticipated it would shortly come to an end regardless of what we do now. This is especially true in the asteroid scenario, but Scheffler thinks the infertility scenario would also attenuate our commitment to standing traditions. If we knew it was futile to pass the tradition down to future generations, that would already compromise the value of maintaining it.

Next, Scheffler considers cases of actions to maintain a "communal or national group." We might, for example, cheer on a sports team, participate in a religious faith, or engage in civic or political activity aimed at improving our nation. All these activities, likewise, would be threatened by an imminent apocalyptic event. Like temporally extended activities, other-regarding activities, and activities situated within traditions, they would lose meaning in either the asteroid scenario or the infertility scenario.[10] What good is group membership when the group is about to end?

Even actions not immediately connected to any of these categories might be deprived of meaning. Take game playing, for example. Scheffler conjectures that the appeal of games stems in part from a kind of artifice of seriousness. We can take a game seriously—absorbing ourselves in its rules—as an escape from the very real seriousness of our own lives. But if deprived of central sources of meaning in our real lives, we might also find that the pretense of meaning offered by games is no longer a pleasant diversion.[11] At worst, it might even underscore the lack of meaning otherwise available. So it might even be the case that in the asteroid or infertility scenarios, we would lose our appreciation for the pleasures afforded by games (and perhaps other recreational activities as well). In James's novel, humans confront overwhelming boredom as many people give up on all the activities that once had enriched their lives.

Let's suppose that Scheffler is right about the consequences of the asteroid and infertility scenarios for individual values. What would we learn from this about the nature of valuing? Scheffler argues that we would centrally learn that valuing has a distinctively collective aspect. The presence of other people, including those who will continue our own valuing practices, deeply informs our appreciation of what we care about. Even if we pursue our values in a solitary way, our own valuing attitudes may depend on unrecognized social facts.

The surprising conclusion from this line of argument is that the continuity of our society or social world may be of greater importance to our valuing practices than our own individual continuity. Although many people are distressed by the prospect of their future death, imagining a world in which we no longer exist does little to compromise our own practices of valuing.[12] Many people who do not believe in a personal afterlife nevertheless have no difficulty in filling their present mortal existence with meaningful activity. What is centrally important, Scheffler concludes, is that we remain confident in the ongoing existence of a social world in the future when our values will be at home. This confidence is compatible with going out of existence and perhaps even being entirely forgotten. Scheffler writes, "[Even if] the survival of the group does not mean that one will personally be remembered, it nevertheless gives one license to imagine oneself as retaining a social identity in the world of the future."[13] With this identity intact, the reasons that follow from it—including from our individual values—can continue to motivate us to action.

We're now in position to reconstruct Scheffler's argument for the conclusion that the existence of our social world after our death—what Scheffler calls the *collective afterlife*—is more important to our individual values than is our own persistence after death, or what we might call the *personal afterlife*. The argument proceeds something like this:

1. The lack of a personal afterlife does not diminish our tendency to invest activities with meaning.
2. The lack of a collective afterlife does diminish our tendency to invest activities with meaning.
3. The best explanation for (1 and 2) is that the failure to believe in a personal afterlife is much less likely to erode people's confidence in the meaning of their activities.
4. A belief is more important than another belief if lacking that belief has a greater effect on our confidence in the meaning of our activities.
5. So belief in a collective afterlife is more important than belief in a personal afterlife.

I've rehearsed already the reasons to accept (1) and (2). Scheffler accepts (3) because he thinks that is the simplest way of accounting for both the fact that lacking confidence in a collective afterlife would undermine our values and the fact that lacking confidence in a personal afterlife does not. In the next section, I question whether there are other possible explanations for the conjunction of (1) and (2).

A Challenge for Scheffler

Let's grant all of Scheffler's data. That gives us:

a. We do engage in robust valuing even if we don't anticipate our individual afterlife.
b. Many people (including those skeptical of a personal afterlife) would not engage in robust valuing if they did not believe in a collective afterlife.

Scheffler is contrasting an imagined person who does believe in a collective afterlife but does not believe in a personal afterlife with a person who believes in neither the collective afterlife nor the personal afterlife. So we're comparing the belief sets {believes in collective afterlife; does not believe in personal afterlife} and {does not believe in collective afterlife; does not believe in personal afterlife}. We can represent this space with a typology (table 5.1). Scheffler agrees the best case would be if *both* we and our social world continued after our individual physical death (cell 1). The worst case, by contrast, is where we anticipate both our individual nonexistence and the end of our social world (cell 4).

There are two reasons to resist inferring that a collective afterlife is more important than an individual afterlife—at least from the data we have in the table so far. First, Scheffler's two scenarios compare cell 2 (in which an agent does not believe in a personal afterlife but does believe in a collective afterlife) with cell 4 (in which neither afterlife obtains). We cannot infer that a collective afterlife is more important than an individual afterlife from this comparison, even if we grant Scheffler's intuitions about the cases. For all we know, it might be that the only cell in which people would abandon their valuing commitments is in cell 4—if they lose faith in *any* afterlife. That is, perhaps faith in *either* an individual or a collective afterlife would be sufficient to maintain valuing attitudes. And if that might—for all we know—be true, then we have no evidence about whether one is more important than the other.

A second explanation is that it isn't the news that there won't be a collective afterlife that undermines our values but rather the news that there won't be the particular kind of afterlife in which we previously believed. So for all Scheffler says, his cases may be compatible with a personal afterlife being just as (or more) important than a collective afterlife.

To see this point, consider that Scheffler's two cases involve moving from a belief in the collective afterlife to a belief in no afterlife (table 5.2). The two scenarios Scheffler considers involve not only comparing cells but also the movement between cells. It might be that it is the movement from one belief state to another that explains the undermining of value. Perhaps, for example, if someone has long held the belief that there is no personal afterlife but has believed in a collective afterlife, then they will have adopted

Table 5.1. Personal vs. Collective Afterlife

	Believes in a personal afterlife	Does not believe in a personal afterlife
Believes in a collective afterlife	(1) Best case	(2) Atheist in the actual world
Does not believe in a collective afterlife	(3) Theist in the asteroid scenario	(4) Worst case

Table 5.2. Asteroid Scenario

	Believes in a personal afterlife	Does not believe in a personal afterlife
Believes in a collective afterlife	(1) Best case	(2) Atheist in the actual world
Does not believe in a collective afterlife	(3) Theist in the asteroid scenario	(4) Worst case

projects that are achievable, given that belief set. If I believe in a collective afterlife only, then I might take up projects that future generations could continue or complete, and then I may find meaning in contributing my share. Discovering that there will be no collective afterlife would disrupt those projects. Likewise, if I believe in a personal afterlife only, then I might adopt projects that will promote the well-being of my post-mortal self. Discovering I will not continue after my death would, in expectation, then disrupt those particular projects. If belief change is what matters, then which form of afterlife is more important will depend on what kind of afterlife one *previously* believed in.

So far, I've tried to show how Scheffler's data is insufficient to abductively infer the truth of his conclusion. We don't yet know whether his premise (3) is true, simply because we haven't compared his favored explanation against other candidates. To do this, we would need to compare the world in which one believes in a collective afterlife but no personal afterlife against a world in which one believes in a personal afterlife but no collective afterlife (see table 5.3). Given that we have granted that cell (4) does undermine value and cell (2) does not, the question left is to consider cases of cell (3). If someone who believes in a personal afterlife but comes to disbelieve in a collective afterlife would lose confidence in their values, then that would be evidence that belief in the collective afterlife is more important to our valuing than belief in the personal afterlife. The next section will turn to this question.

Table 5.3. Cases for Comparison

	Believes in a personal afterlife	Does not believe in a personal afterlife
Believes in a collective afterlife	(1) Best case	*(2) Atheist in the actual world*
Does not believe in a collective afterlife	*(3) Theist in the asteroid scenario*	(4) Worst case

Nephi₁

The Book of Mormon tells the story of a family who flees Jerusalem after receiving divine warning of its imminent destruction at the hands of Nebuchadnezzar's army.[14] Nephi₁, the book's first author, narrates his family's flight into the wilderness and divinely guided journey to the American continent. There, the family divides into two great nations—Nephites and Lamanites—who will inhabit the continent for a millennium. Having scarcely left Jerusalem, before any division, Nephi₁ sees in a vision that his own descendants will be completely destroyed by his brothers' descendants (1 Nephi 12:19–20). The image is one he revisits throughout his life, imagining their violent end in a heavenly display of power—"thunderings and lightnings, and earthquakes, and all manner of destructions" (2 Nephi 26:6). His prophetic vision affects him deeply: "O the pain, and the anguish of my soul for the loss of the slain of my people! For I, Nephi, have seen it, and it well nigh consumeth me before the presence of the Lord; but I must cry unto my God: Thy ways are just" (2 Nephi 26:7). Writing these words a millennium in advance of the events, Nephi₁ still sees the apocalypse as temporally proximate: "And when these things have passed away a speedy destruction cometh unto my people" (2 Nephi 26:10). Grant Hardy has written in his commentary that by this point in his life, Nephi₁ has spent so much time in the prophetic future that he may feel more at home there than in his own age: "Indeed, the concept of time itself can become slippery for someone who is more sure of the future than the present."[15]

Nephi₁ is living in a kind of extreme version of the asteroid scenario.[16] His own life will proceed normally—or at least as normally as a life can unfold when the person living it knows the distant future in high-resolution detail. However, he knows of the end of his own social world—in fact, he knows its demise before he even knows its creation. And as Scheffler predicts, this knowledge is unsettling. It poses a challenge to Nephi₁'s values. As his brothers leave to form their own, separate familial group—setting in motion the historical narrative whose eventual destination is already known to Nephi₁—he despairs over his failures within his family (2 Nephi 4). At the same time, Nephi₁ gives no indication that he ever doubts the meaning of his life. Rather, he recenters his life's meaning around the Book of Mormon itself, coming to see the impact of his life's work as centered among his future readers. Nephi₁ reports that he had secured a promise from God that his writing would be "kept and preserved" and that one day his words would "go from generation to generation as long as the earth shall stand" (2 Nephi 25:22). His words would have authority in the future, providing a basis for God's judgment of the nations who have access to them.

Nephi$_1$'s prophetic success provides a frame through which he interprets the future Nephite apocalypse. After his descendants' annihilation, the writing of the Book of Mormon, including his own words, will still speak: "And after they have been brought low to the dust, even that they are not, yet the words of the righteous shall be written. . . . For those who shall be destroyed shall speak unto them out of the ground, and their voice shall be as one that hath a familiar spirit" (2 Nephi 26:15–16). Nephi$_1$ interprets the Nephites' scripture as a fulfilment of Isaiah 29's prophecy of a "voice that whispers out from the dust" (Isa. 29:4). In his final farewell, Nephi$_1$ casts himself directly in the role of Isaiah's voice. To his future readers, Nephi$_1$ writes, "I speak to you as the voice of one crying from the dust" (2 Nephi 33:14). Nephi$_1$ has no doubts about the value of his work, the completion of which he regards explicitly as "of great worth" (2 Nephi 33:2).

Let's return to Scheffler's theory. Nephi$_1$ lives out a version of the asteroid scenario, albeit at great temporal remove (though not by his own accounting). As Scheffler would anticipate, Nephi$_1$ is distressed by the destruction of his society. However, he pivots from focusing on his immediate surroundings to considering the impact of his life from a grander, transhistorical perspective. From that vantage point, he finds that his life still has great value, perhaps even greater than it might have otherwise had. As Hardy observes, his distress over his people's downfall finds solace in "the consolation of prophecy."[17]

Nephi$_1$'s account poses a challenge for Scheffler because Nephi$_1$'s sense of meaning is not compromised by the loss of his (imagined) social world. In a sense, his sadness fortifies his commitment to his life's divinely appointed purposes. At the same time, the meaning Nephi$_1$ locates in his later life is not independent of other persons. Rather, it is exactly his work's value to a foreseen future readership that redeems his sacrifices. He is confident that his voice from the dust will be heard and that it will have authority in God's interactions with future nations. So while Nephi$_1$ is able to recover the meaning of his life from the destruction of his social world, his recovery depends less on his own post-mortal vindication by God's judgment and more on his continuing influence in a reconstituted social world of his own prophetic imagining.

Moroni$_2$

Moroni$_2$ is the Book of Mormon's final author. After the destruction of the Nephite people foreseen from the foundations of their society, Moroni$_2$ is divinely directed to complete the text and bury the plates on which the book is written. Almost all of Moroni$_2$'s narration is carried out in postapocalyptic solitude. He introduces himself to the reader by repeatedly pointing out that he is alone (Mormon 8:3, 8:5). His writing is understandably shaken by the destruction around him: "My father hath been slain in battle, and all my kinsfolk, and I have not friends nor whither to go; and how long the Lord will suffer that I may live I know not" (Mormon 8:5).

Moroni$_2$ writes in the wake of the complete destruction of his social world. He has no one left. That he is affected by these facts is obvious. However, after his brief opening remarks, Moroni$_2$ sets about completing the commandments from God, given to him by his father before Mormon$_2$'s own death. Among Moroni$_2$'s tasks is to include an account of a separate people, the Jaredites, before concluding the Book of Mormon as a whole. This people lived long before the Nephites ever arrived in the promised land, but their civilization followed the same historical arc. Eventually, the Jaredites destroyed themselves in a series of pitched battles, concluding with a single observer of their annihilation. In recounting the life of Ether, the final, solitary prophet among the Jaredites, Moroni$_2$ pauses to reflect on his counterpart's faith. Though Ether prophesied "great and marvelous things," he was not accepted by the people.

Moroni$_2$'s consideration of Ether's faith prompts him to reflect on a series of paradigm cases of faith taken from the Bible as well as the Book of Mormon's own extensive chronology. Moroni$_2$'s examples include God's giving Moses the law as well as the fulfillment of the law in Christ (Ether 12:11). He notes that Book of Mormon prophets Alma$_2$ and Amulek were delivered from a prison by faith, with God causing the prison to collapse around them (Ether 12:13; cf. Alma 14:27). Another pair of Book of Mormon missionaries, Nephi$_2$ and Lehi$_4$, converted the Lamanites to Christ through faith (Ether 12:14; cf. Helaman 5:50). Ammon$_2$, another missionary, exercised similar proselytizing power (Ether 12:15; cf. Alma 17–26). Moroni$_2$ mentions the brother of Jared, a prophet at the outset of Jaredite society whose faith enabled him to see God and then to see the world from God's vista (Ether 12:20–22). Finally, Moroni$_2$ says that it is by faith that his "fathers" secured the promise that the Book of Mormon would be conveyed to the Gentiles. That promise, first made to Nephi$_1$ at the outset of Nephite civilization, is now one that, Moroni$_2$ realizes, has fallen to him to make good on (Ether 12:22).

Moroni$_2$'s ruminations on faith lead him into a more personal reflection. In the midst of summarizing the Jaredite record for inclusion in the Book of Mormon, Moroni$_2$ compares his own writing unfavorably with the works he is reading. He regards the brother of Jared's writing as conveying God's own voice "unto the overpowering of man to read them" (Ether 12:24).[18] Moroni$_2$ petitions God in prayer, fearful that the Gentiles will mock the imperfections of his language. What follows is a dialogue between Moroni$_2$ and God. Moroni$_2$ first receives reassurance that if the Gentiles do mock his work, it will be to their own damnation. Second, he is assured that weaknesses, once recognized, will be made strong by God. Moroni$_2$ is comforted and moved to reflect further on God's love for his children. He then prays on behalf of the Gentiles that they will receive grace from God to have charity. God answers Moroni$_2$ again, and his message is remarkable:

> And it came to pass that the Lord said unto me: If they have not charity it mattereth not unto thee, thou hast been faithful; wherefore, thy garments shall be made clean. And because thou hast seen thy weakness thou shalt be made strong, even unto the sitting down in the place which I have prepared in the mansions of my Father. (Ether 12:37)

In this continuation of the dialogue, God offers a corrective to Moroni$_2$'s petition.[19] In his prayer, Moroni$_2$ had reasoned that God loved the world "even unto the laying down of thy life for the world," and then identifying God's love as charity (12:33–34). Moroni$_2$ next observes in his prayer that if men do not have charity, they "cannot inherit that place which thou hast prepared in the mansions of thy Father" (Ether 12:34). It's easy to see how Moroni$_2$ could reason from there to his own petition that God grant the Gentiles charity. If he was right about salvation, then the Gentiles could not be saved without it. And, perhaps more urgently, it might also seem that if all of his suppositions are correct, he himself could not be saved without adopting something like this attitude toward his fellow persons. Consider formulating the reasoning this way:

1. Charity is the love of God.
2. If you have the love of God, you should hope for the salvation of other persons.
3. If persons do not have charity, they cannot receive salvation.
4. So if you have charity, then you should hope that other persons have charity.

Moroni$_2$ states (1) explicitly (Ether 12:34), if we identify "the place [Christ] has prepared in his Father's mansions" with salvation, then Moroni$_2$ also clearly accepts (3). He seems to believe that he ought to pray for the Gentiles to have charity, that doing so comports with his understanding of the normative status of God's love. That means he should also accept (2), and although he is less explicit about it, it seems like he does, in fact, believe (2) as well. Moroni$_2$ gives the atonement of Christ as the illustrative case of God's love, and he understands the atonement as sacrificing one's own life for others' salvation. If the love of God is so powerful that it provides reasons for Christ to lay down his own life for others, then for us to possess that love, we should at least hope (and pray) for others to meet the conditions for salvation. One of those conditions is that they themselves have charity, so we ought to hope and pray that they will have charity.

This interpretation of Moroni$_2$'s thought is a reconstruction, but I think it is only a slight reconstruction. Moroni$_2$ very nearly gives each premise directly, so his moving directly to a petition to God for the Gentiles to have charity feels very natural. What is remarkable, then, is that God's answer apparently takes exception to Moroni$_2$'s reasoning: "If they have not charity it mattereth not unto thee." What matters instead is that Moroni$_2$ has seen his own weakness and thereby met the qualification for weakness to be "made strong." It is this strengthening that appears to constitute the reception of salvation. God's assurance is that he will be made strong "unto" the sitting down in the Father's mansions.

What's noteworthy in this is that Moroni$_2$'s meeting the conditions for salvation requires his own self-perfection and appears not to depend on any other person. It doesn't even matter to Moroni$_2$, the divine answer insists, whether others have charity (and thereby meet the conditions for salvation) or not. *Salvation for Moroni$_2$ is just about the strengthening of what is weak in Moroni$_2$.*

Where did Moroni$_2$'s own reasoning go wrong? He had assumed, based on his understanding of the atonement of Christ, that there was an obligation to promote, or at least hope for, others to have charity. But on this point, God redirects his attention. If we take this dialogue seriously, then it seems that God's answer entails that there is no obligation to promote (or even to hope) for others to gain charity. Read most literally, there may not even be reason to hope for that. "It mattereth not unto thee," Moroni$_2$ is told.

Charity and Communal Value

Let's go back to Scheffler's communal value thesis. In the first sections, we established the need for cases in which a person remains confident of their personal afterlife but not in the collective afterlife of their society. Nephi$_1$ seemed to provide one such case, but it turned out that he could be interpreted as maintaining his values by relocating himself within a different social world—that of his future readers.[20] So although Nephi$_1$ foresaw the end of his social world in one sense, and was affected deeply by that imagined end, his prophetic status enabled him to imaginatively immigrate to a much distant future society. Or in his preferred terminology, he was able to "liken the scriptures" to himself in a way that staked out a new, meaningful identity for him as a figure in his own interpretation of scripture.

We then turned to Moroni$_2$, who saw (as opposed to foresaw) the apocalyptic end of his whole society. He explicitly tells us that he is without any human relationship. And yet Moroni$_2$ presses on in compliance with God's (and his own father's) plans. He does not doubt the value of his projects. And he reasons his way into thinking, like Nephi$_1$, that he ought to understand his role in God's plan as promoting, or at least hoping for, the salvation of the imagined future readers of his life's work. If it were left there, Moroni$_2$'s case would read ambiguously, as Nephi's does. However, that is not where it ends. God intervenes to offer a corrective to Moroni$_2$'s interpretation. Whether the Gentiles have charity is, for Moroni, a matter of indifference. What matters is Moroni$_2$'s personal growth or strengthening, which is, if not constitutive of, at least very closely tied to his assurance for salvation.

Here I will take for granted that God's promise to Moroni$_2$ of his salvation is sufficient to confer meaning to his life and activity. Moroni$_2$ has lost all of his human relationships, and God's word has severed any connection between the meaning of Moroni$_2$'s projects and an imagined future community of readers.[21] In its place, the inserted condition for salvation insists not on a kind of other-regardingness but instead on a kind of self-understanding.[22]

In effect, this case provides the most extreme version of the asteroid scenario. Moroni$_2$ lives through the apocalypse to find himself completely alone on the other side. More than that, the dialogue between Moroni$_2$ and God cancels what we might otherwise infer: that the continued meaning of his life was tied to the future reception of his work and so connected him prophetically to a future social world. Despite all this, Moroni$_2$'s life is a meaningful one, and we have a clear explanation of why: He can be confident of salvation in his personal afterlife. Contrary to Scheffler's hypothesis, vividly considering a case of a personal afterlife with no collective afterlife reveals it to be open to the possibility of meaning and value. This does not show that a personal afterlife is more important than the collective afterlife, but it does cut against Scheffler's suggestion that the collective afterlife is more important than a personal afterlife.

Objections

One might counter that I'm making way too much of a single passage of text near the end of the Book of Mormon.[23] My objector might contend that much of the narrative force of the book goes in the opposite direction, insisting that some version of the communal value thesis is correct. "After all," the objector might say, "isn't the Book of Mormon full of stories of prophets caring deeply about bringing salvation to others?"

I believe this objection misunderstands what may be the Book of Mormon's most central message. To start, consider that the reasoning in this objection runs very close to the reasoning Moroni₂ followed to his initial conclusion, the one with which God differed. Moroni₂'s heroes of faith were the ones who got things done. They were the prophets who famously converted hundreds, or thousands, entire cities or kingdoms. They were the heroes doing the most obviously, paradigmatically heroic things. Starting with those cases, it would be natural to assume that the calling card of faith is to act as those exemplars did—namely, in exactly those ways that promoted or at least facilitated the acquisition of salvific virtues among other humans.

Notice that in this way, Moroni₂'s heroes of faith narrative parts company with the corresponding chapter from the Letter to the Hebrews. In Hebrews 11 the famous list of faith's exemplars also famously selects figures and actions that are in some way puzzling or surprising. The list mostly avoids giving the stereotypically "greatest" actions of the heroes as the ones modeling the virtue of faith.[24] Abraham sets out for a place commanded by God, despite "not knowing where he was going" (Hebrews 11:8). Moses is praised for refusing to be called a son of Pharoah's daughter (Hebrews 11:23). The faithful have suffered "mocking and flogging, even chains and imprisonment" (Hebrews 11:36). The faithful wander in mountains and deserts (Hebrews 11:38). For the author of Hebrews, faith is less about manifest triumph and more about seeing what is invisible to an ordinarily rational standpoint.

It appears, then, that Moroni₂'s list stands in a slight, implicit tension with the list from Hebrews 11. But this is before we had considered the dialogic revelation subverting Moroni₂'s initial interpretation. Moroni₂ had drawn the *initial* lesson that, like his selected exemplars, we ought to promote the salvation of others. However, if Moroni₂ was drawing the wrong lesson, then perhaps he might have fared better by focusing on some other set of actions as paradigmatic of faith. Aware of how Moroni₂ got the interpretation slightly amiss, we should be wary of deploying the Book of Mormon's heroically successful missions as the dispositive model for faithful discipleship. However tempting, that would reproduce his same mistake.

Moroni₂ had proposed to understand charity as a hope or effort on behalf of others' acquisition of virtue. The dialogue challenges that interpretation, but it does not insert another in its place. Is there, then, any other model for understanding the virtue of charity?

I will suggest that the text does provide an alternative. There isn't space in this chapter to consider it in detail, but I will gesture at it here to at least parry the objection. In his own life, Moroni₂'s father, Mormon₂, describes his experience of seeing an apocalypse among his people. On one occasion,

Mormon$_2$ recounts that he had "poured out" his soul in prayer of them "all the day long," notwithstanding that it was "without faith, because of the hardness of their hearts" (Mormon 3:12). Later, he notes that even after he resumed his role in leading the Nephite society, he was "without hope," in the sense that he regarded their destruction as a foregone conclusion (Mormon 5:2). As the shadow of destruction loomed closer, Mormon$_2$ gave up faith in his people, in the sense that he had no expectation of their temporal deliverance from their enemies. He also gave up hope for his people, in the sense that he did not think there was any chance they could enter into the rest of God (cf. Moroni 7:3).

Finally, he comes close to giving up his love for his people.[25] For a while, he decides to dissociate from them entirely. In that bleak moment, he says, "I *had* loved them, according to the love of God which was in me, with all my heart" (Mormon 3:2; italics added). Mormon$_2$ then believed that his leaving his people was what God wanted (Mormon 3:15). Later, however, his people beseech him to come back, and, seeing the looks on their faces, he does (Mormon 5:1). He also must have come to think that his earlier judgment about God's will was mistaken, as he says he repents of his former commitment to "stand as an idle witness" (Mormon 5:1). Mormon$_2$ never gives any indication that he has resumed faith in or hope for his people. Sometimes it is simply true that faith and hope are not fitting. When Mormon$_2$ reverses course, he changes his mind about something. What he learns, I'm conjecturing, is that it is never the case that love is unfitting. At some point, Mormon$_2$ composes a letter to this effect to his son. He tells Moroni$_2$ that charity—the love of God—is the greatest of the theological virtues (faith, hope, charity), because only charity is always appropriate. He says, "Charity never faileth. Wherefore, cleave unto charity, which is the greatest of all, for all things must fail" (Moroni 7:46). Faith and hope can fail.[26] Charity is something you can hold on to, no matter what.

We're now in a position to see both what was wrong with Moroni$_2$'s claims about charity and also what was plausible about it. Recall that Moroni$_2$ held that if you have the love of God, you should hope (and work) for the salvation of other persons. However, hope is not always a fitting response. There are conditions when hope is inappropriate, including when there is no reason to believe that the object of one's hope could possibly be realized. Mormon$_2$'s lived experience in the impending apocalypse provides one such a case. Mormon$_2$ first seems to think that not only are there cases when faith and hope are not appropriate, but there are also cases when love is not appropriate. But in this, he later concludes, he was wrong. In his letter to his son, he insists on his own hard-won lesson: You should never give up on love.

If we take all this for granted, then we can diagnose the error in Moroni$_2$'s premise.[27] Moroni$_2$ had thought that if you love someone, you should hope for their salvation. However, if there are times when it makes no sense to hope for someone's salvation, then (on that premise) it would follow that you don't love them. Except that doesn't follow. There are cases when we ought not hope for another's salvation, but there are no cases when we ought not love them. So it is not true that if we love someone, we should hope for their salvation.

Conclusion

This chapter started with a puzzle about which is more important: one's personal afterlife or the collective afterlife of one's society. According to the communal value thesis, the continued existence of other persons matters more to our own values than our own personal post-mortal existence. I have not argued that this thesis is false, but I have argued against Scheffler's abductive inference to reach it as a conclusion.

Thinking about the communal value thesis has also raised a question about how to understand the love of God in the Book of Mormon. One possibility is that the love of God consists in hoping for, praying for, and working to achieve the salvation of other persons. I've attributed this view to Moroni$_2$ as he read and interpreted his prophetic predecessors in the millennium of Lehite society preceding him. However, Moroni$_2$'s dialogue with God in Ether 12 challenges this conception of God's love. What Moroni$_2$ learns in that exchange is that his view was mistaken. Moroni$_2$'s father, Mormon$_2$, has his own struggle over how to come to terms with the impending apocalypse. The lesson he learns in his struggle, which he then shares with his son, provides a different view of love. Love is not about aiming to bring about some state of affairs in which another person has some virtue or another. Instead, love can mean letting go of any aims one has to bring about some state of affairs in the life of another person, however righteous those aims might be. The communal value thesis is false, but that is good news for the importance of love for others. Love can remain—love *is what remains*—after the aspiration to change someone has been abandoned.

Notes

1. Samuel Scheffler, *Death and the Afterlife*, ed. Niko Kolodny (New York: Oxford University Press, 2016).

2. Scheffler's provocative case has been taken up in the philosophical literature. See, for example, Roman Altshuler, "Bootstrapping the Afterlife," *Journal of Moral*

Philosophy 14, no. 2 (Feb. 25, 2017): 201–216, https://doi.org/10.1163/17455243–46810049; Michael Cholbi, "Time, Value, and Collective Immortality," *Journal of Ethics* 19, no. 2 (June 1, 2015): 97–211, https://doi.org/10.1007/s10892–015–9198–1; Ben Bradley, "Existential Terror," *Journal of Ethics* 19, no. 3 (Dec. 1, 2015): 409–418, https://doi.org/10.1007/s10892–015–9204–7; Jens Johansson, "The Importance of a Good Ending: Some Reflections on Samuel Scheffler's Death and the Afterlife," *Journal of Ethics* 19, no. 2 (June 1, 2015): 185–95, https://doi.org/10.1007/s10892–015–9197–2; Toby Handfield, "A Good Exit: What to Do about the End of Our Species?" *Journal of Moral Philosophy* 15, no. 3 (June 19, 2018): 272–97, https://doi.org/10.1163/17455243–20170010; Travis Timmerman, "Doomsday Needn't Be So Bad," *Dialectica* 72, no. 2 (2018): 275–96, https://doi.org/10.1111/1746–8361.12227.

3. The Book of Mormon's apocalyptic themes have been explored before. For important contributions, see Heather Hardy, "'Saving Christianity': The Nephite Fulfillment of Jesus's Eschatological Prophecies," *Journal of Book of Mormon Studies* 23, no. 1 (Jan. 1, 2014), https://scholarsarchive.byu.edu/jbms/vol23/iss1/4; Adam S. Miller, *Mormon: A Brief Theological Introduction* (Provo, UT: Neal A. Maxwell Institute for Religious Scholarship, BYU, 2020); Jared Hickman, "The *Book of Mormon* as Amerindian Apocalypse," *American Literature* 86, no. 3 (Sept. 1, 2014): 429–61, https://doi.org/10.1215/00029831–2717371.

4. Compare J. David Velleman, "Love as a Moral Emotion," *Ethics* 109, no. 2 (Jan. 1999): 338–74, https://doi.org/10.1086/233898; Kieran Setiya, "Love and the Value of a Life," *Philosophical Review* 123, no. 3 (July 1, 2014): 251–80, https://doi.org/10.1215/00318108–2683522.

5. Scheffler, *Death and the Afterlife*, 18.

6. P. D. James, *The Children of Men* (New York: Vintage, 2006).

7. See "The Normativity of Tradition," in Samuel Scheffler, *Equality and Tradition: Questions of Value in Moral and Political Theory*, 1st ed. (New York: Oxford University Press, 2012). For an excellent discussion of losing a way of life, see Jonathan Lear, *Radical Hope: Ethics in the Face of Cultural Devastation* (Cambridge: Harvard University Press, 2008).

8. Adam Miller makes the related point that a physical resurrection doesn't recover events from the past and so does not solve the problem of time's passage: "Resurrection is the promise that, in Christ, life can continue to pass, not that it will finally stop passing." See Miller, *Mormon: A Brief Theological Introduction*, 15.

9. Scheffler, *Death and the Afterlife*, 33.

10. Scheffler, *Death and the Afterlife*, 34–35.

11. Scheffler, *Death and the Afterlife*, 56–58.

12. On confronting one's own death, see Bradley, "Existential Terror."

13. Scheffler, *Death and the Afterlife*, 34.

14. One might wonder if the Book of Mormon is really a suitable test case for Scheffler's theory. However, Scheffler's own use of a novel to develop his view invites the use of literary resources. On the use of literary cases, see Antonia

Peacocke, "How Literature Expands Your Imagination," *Philosophy and Phenomenological Research* 103, no. 2 (2021): 298–319, https://doi.org/10.1111/phpr.12716.

15. Grant Hardy, *Understanding the Book of Mormon: A Reader's Guide*, 1st ed. (Oxford: New York: Oxford University Press, 2010), 82.

16. As Terryl Givens points out, Nephi is living between two apocalypses. The first volume of Nephi's contributions concludes not with his family's arrival in the promised land but with their learning that Jerusalem has been destroyed. Terryl Givens, *2nd Nephi: A Brief Theological Introduction* (Provo, UT: Neal A. Maxwell Institute for Religious Scholarship, BYU, 2020).

17. Hardy, *Understanding the Book of Mormon*, 82.

18. On the importance of language in the Jaredite account, see Samuel Morris Brown, *Joseph Smith's Translation: The Words and Worlds of Early Mormonism* (New York: Oxford University Press, 2020).

19. On revelation as dialogue, see Terryl L. Givens, *By the Hand of Mormon: The American Scripture That Launched a New World Religion* (Oxford: Oxford University Press, 2002).

20. Another way of reading the Book of Mormon's apocalypse is as fulfillment of Jesus's own prophecies of imminent destruction. Hardy describes how the Book of Mormon counters the "apparent nonfulfillment of Jesus's eschatological prophecies." Hardy, "Saving Christianity," 25.

21. I talk more about individualism in the early Latter-day Saint tradition in Ryan W. Davis, "Frontier Kantianism: Autonomy and Authority in Ralph Waldo Emerson and Joseph Smith," *Journal of Religious Ethics* 46, no. 2 (2018): 332–59, https://doi.org/10.1111/jore.12220.

22. Cf. J. David Velleman, "Motivation by Ideal," in *Self to Self: Selected Essays*, ed. J. David Velleman (Ann Arbor: Michigan Publishing Services, 2020), 415–36.

23. For a compelling presentation of the value of society in Lehite life, see Daniel Becerra, *3rd, 4th Nephi: A Brief Theological Introduction* (Provo, UT: Neal A. Maxwell Institute for Religious Scholarship, BYU, 2021).

24. I think this is a fairly conventional reading, but for discussion, see Matthew C. Easter, *Faith and the Faithfulness of Jesus in Hebrews* (Cambridge: Cambridge University Press, 2014), ch. 3.

25. Miller offers an extended discussion of Mormon$_2$'s love of his people. Miller describes "Mormon's book as a beginner's guide to the end of world." Miller, *Mormon: A Brief Theological Introduction*, 14.

26. Cf. Miller, *Mormon: A Brief Theological Introduction*, ch. 7.

27. My own view is that Moroni$_2$'s reading of the Book of Mormon provides a criterion for how we ought to read it. Compare, for example, with how Crossan thinks that the historical Jesus provides a criterion for interpreting differing messages about violence in the Bible. See John Dominic Crossan, *How to Read the Bible and Still Be a Christian: Is God Violent? An Exploration from Genesis to Revelation* (New York: HarperOne, 2016).

6

Epic History, Ethical Pedagogy

The Book of Mormon's Scene of Instruction

KIMBERLY MATHESON

Joseph Smith's 1830 publication of the Book of Mormon—the product, he claimed, of a divine gift to translate an ancient gold record retrieved from a hillside near his family farm—fomented a minor scandal in upstate New York in the early to mid-nineteenth century. The book mobilized a variety of responses. From some, it drew satirical commentary in newspapers or full-length discrediting monographs. From others, it sparked social derision and economic isolation and even physical assault aimed at Smith and his followers.[1] Along with scornful attention, however, the Book of Mormon also generated converts and missionaries, galvanizing a small religious movement that eventually built cities in Ohio and Illinois and (most famously) crossed the plains to establish a protest government in what would eventually become the state of Utah. The Book of Mormon is a text that moves bodies, and it has been doing so from the very beginning of its history: bodies that get baptized and bodies that pen scathing opinion articles, bodies that build temples and bodies that burn them. The corporeal configurations left in its wake mark the Book of Mormon as a powerful piece of moral instruction—the kind of instruction that incites strong reactions both for and against its teaching and that leaps off the page to effect real change in the world. This chapter asks about that moral instruction. It asks about the ethical claims the book makes on its readers and the techniques (rhetorical and otherwise) it employs in order to make them. Given that the Book of Mormon moves readers' bodies, this chapter investigates how it does so.

Thus, when I speak of "ethics" in what follows, I do not mean a list of political(ly) sensitive issues or concerns nor a collection of normative claims. I mean to gesture to the effects of the book's ethos or climate more than any set of rules that one might derive from it. I mean the book's *Sittlichkeit* rather than its *Moralität*, its subject-shaping techniques rather than a quasi-Kantian extraction of principles.[2] I am asking, in short, about the persuasive forces that the Book of Mormon exerts on its imagined audience, forces that capture imaginations and impel bodies to behave in particular ways. This is ethics as an investigation of rhetorical performance more than it is any kind of prescription for how readers ought to behave with respect to this book. In this, my use of the term "ethics" will hew closer to its classical sense. *Ethos* referred anciently to moral character inculcated through subject formation in a philosophical school rather than to a body of normative principles instilled through rational argument. It was, as Pierre Hadot put it, a question of one's "way of life."[3] Ancient ethics was transmitted less by intellectual debate or moral imperative and more through literary and rhetorical configurations that transformed disciples' mode of living. Ethics was about the formation of human subjects, about changing how a person acts by changing who they are.[4]

When I use terms like "ethics" or "morality," then, I will be referring to a body of persuasive forces, rhetorical techniques, and subject-forming investments displayed in the text of the Book of Mormon. The book's "ethic" is the set of values that govern its internal worldview and, further downstream, the set of hoped-for behaviors coaxed out of readers due to the value-laden pressures exerted on them by the book. Its "morality," similarly, refers to the mold in which it hopes to fashion its readers, including the ideals and conduct it wishes to instill. Human action is always a consequence of human subject formation. For this reason, examining *how* a text shapes its readers is just as urgent an ethical task as examining *what* behaviors that text enjoins on them.

Because this investigation focuses on what we might call the Book of Mormon's conditional investments (how it *might* be received, what it *hopes* to achieve, what it *attempts*), it is important to note that I situate myself in what follows at some distance from history. I mean neither to wager claims on the book's origins nor to evaluate the book's successes or failures in producing the subjects for which it hoped. Where I suggest persuasions active in the nineteenth century, this is only because the book clearly imagines itself to speak (only in part, but certainly first) to an audience of nineteenth-century Protestants. Where I comment on the book's aims to convict readers of its divine reality or to inculcate largesse toward native peoples, I do so fully cognizant of the fact that these are not the readers produced by the book in every case. My method, in short, hews away from actual readers toward imagined readers, away from questions about history and historicity to the book's salvation-historical self-image and the prophetic voice of its self-stylings. It goes without saying that the historical realities surrounding the Book of Mormon were much messier than those the book imagined for itself. Nonetheless, we stand to learn a great deal about the Book of Mormon through its imagined idealizations, so I will focus my efforts there.

In so doing, I hope to put my finger on the book's rhetorical persuasions—that is, how the Book of Mormon works to capture the desires and mold the subjectivities of its readers. And the unit by which I propose to investigate the book's ethical teaching is what Mark Jordan calls a "scene of instruction." Here, Jordan names a text's imagined sites and methods of readerly formation, including things like its genre, pacing, and literary tics. A reader is formed by stepping into the place conjured by a text ("the place addresses important questions: Is the teaching public or private? . . . How does the scene connect to the sites of daily life—the kitchen or bedroom or bath, the marketplace, the temple?") and submitting themself to the text's prescribed temporal unfolding ("How much time will the scene's pedagogy consume—fifty minutes, a year of late adolescence, more than a lifetime?").[5] Indeed, reading well means more than simply analyzing these textual features; reading well, for Jordan, means being able to "reactivate" their formative ethical powers:

> Finding effective meaning in an old text, you do more than repeat its words. You gather new words to reperform its persuasion in the changed languages and historical circumstances of your present. More robust remaking is required to inherit ethical texts. . . . Most of all, I must appreciate and perhaps imitate the sound of the voice that makes precepts or patterns ethically attractive, persuasive in the more sustained way that ethics requires. . . . A scene of instruction is a ritual occasion for revivifying language.[6]

Ethical reading, following this model, looks like investigating the persuasive registers already operative in a text before asking how and where that text's propositional content bumps up against contemporary politics. It is to prioritize a text's performative register above its constative register, to attend first to *how* it shapes readers and only secondarily to *what* it hopes those newly formed readers might do. Here I wish to lay groundwork for that kind of examination of the Book of Mormon by attuning to the ethical speech in which the book already traffics and the subject-formative work it already employs as it enflames the desires and enlivens the imaginations of its readers.

Two final methodological caveats are in order. First, no text is ever fully separable from its paratext, and this is especially true of the Book of Mormon, which arrives in readers' hands together with insistent claims about its supernatural origin. These claims had and continue to have a profound place in the moral formation of the book's readers. Although most readers will likely associate the book either with believers' claims about angels and gold plates, on the one hand, or critics' talk of origins within nineteenth-century frontier life, on the other, I am constrained by space limitations and so purport to look at only some features of what lies between the covers of the book itself. I do so, however, fully acknowledging that the Book of Mormon's scene of instruction bleeds out beyond those covers in particularly dramatic ways. Second, and relatedly, the Book of Mormon is large and complex. To give even a representative sketch of the book's scene of instruction is daunting; any attempt to be exhaustive is laughable. Many, many points will, of necessity, be left out. In this chapter I take a macroscopic approach, knowing as I do so that I inevitably lose the fine grain of individual passages. My hope, nonetheless, is that we might find the affordances of a macro lens worthwhile for scoping the Book of Mormon's capacious moral ambitions.

Failing to be comprehensive, then, the instructional elements I *will* cover in this chapter include, first, the Book of Mormon's status as a book, together with its para-biblical resonances. As a printed text, the Book of Mormon cannot be read except as intending to join the culture of literacy already operative in nineteenth-century America, and as pseudo-biblical, it presents itself as a Hebrew Bible made rationally compelling for its intended audience of "latter-day" Protestants. Next, I'll discuss the persuasive charms of the Book of Mormon's genre as an epic history of a lost civilization and how this envisioning of the American past both scratches readers' itch to be knowing subjects and imports moral stakes by recontextualizing present behavior. The book's double audience (Gentile and Israelite) will then be addressed—specifically in terms of how it allows for a universalism without abstraction—followed by sections on the Book of Mormon's self-styling as itinerant and fragmentary. Finally, en route to a conclusion, I will examine the book's self-conscious anxiety about the success of its persuasive project and what kinds of persuasion might reside even there, in the book's worries about its potential failure to connect with intended readers.

The Book of Mormon stages an extended argument that what modernity most lacks is a supplemental history of sacred American beginnings; it performs a pretension to the insufficiency of the Bible and to the re-enchantment of Western society at the dawn of secularity by restaging, over and over again, the drama and persuasion of reading sacred writ; it professes that divine covenants are not past relics but also extend into the present (although their extension is made precarious by the passage of time and the passage between hands); and it asserts that if Christian eschatological hopes have yet to be fulfilled, it is only for a lack of subjects and bodies that have been adequately (in)formed to do what is millennially required. In these, as in its other claims (both performed and stated outright), the Book of Mormon serves as a reminder that a text is best deployed for contemporary ethical conversations when we can hear the ethical register in which it already speaks, and that the Book of Mormon's moral power lies less in being rendered applicable to contemporary sociopolitical conversations and more in the persuasive charms it exerted on its earliest readers and continues to exert in the twenty-first century.

A (Biblical) Book

The Book of Mormon's first and most obvious scene of instruction is, naturally, that of book.[7] It bears a cover and provides pages for readers to turn. It comes packaged in all manner of bookish apparatus (copyright, page numbering, authorial credit); it seeks ingestion through the privacy of interiorization; and it appears to nonreading viewers through the distinctly literary assemblages it creates with its human points of transit: a book *plus* reading body, curled up in a chair; a book *plus* itinerant preacher, proffering it for sale across fences and doorways. The Book of Mormon requires passage through a printing press, sits comfortably on a bookshelf, submits itself to grubby fingers and coffee stains and marginalia. It instructs, for the vast majority of its audience, through the act of reading.

By presenting itself as a book, the Book of Mormon announced its intention to join the culture of literacy already operative in nineteenth-century New York. Books were, of course, familiar technology by 1830 and a culture of literacy was already well established. The Book of Mormon thus presented as an iteration in an already available category and aimed to take part in the established conventions of literate life, including the morally formative effects of those conventions. Indeed, the volume predicts the circulation of other books—especially of the Bible—in the context of its appearance (2 Nephi 29). In order to grab hold of potential disciples, the book demands both a certain pace of reading (the time that it takes to ingest a five-hundred-page narrative) and a certain space (all the sites where one is most likely to read). Its scene of instruction comprehends several months of evenings next to a fireside, four weeks of the sunrise hour between milking and breakfast, or a week of feverish late nights spent reading in bed, candles burning low on the bedside table.[8] Its status as a book prescribes a certain timetable for its rhetorical effects, just as its portability allows it to pass hands, be stored in saddlebags, or infiltrate a variety of scenes within everyday life.

This is moral formation through reading, made possible by the Book of Mormon's status as a book. Nor is its bookishness benign. Somewhat famously, the Book of Mormon obsesses over its own production and circulation as a written object; the corollary, then, is that it also implicitly obsesses over scenes of reading. Indeed, many such scenes are staged within its pages. The book's first prophet, Lehi$_1$, reads a book from heaven (1 Nephi 1:11–12) followed by a set of Bible-like brass plates (1 Nephi 5:10). His son, Nephi$_1$, so fully bodies forth a reading of Isaiah that whole swaths of it are reproduced within the Book of Mormon (2 Nephi 12–24). The late narrator Mormon$_2$ is imagined poring over the small plates (Words of Mormon 1:3–4), newly reunited Nephite colonies investigate each other's records (Mosiah 25:5–7), the king Mosiah$_2$ studies the Jaredite documents in the course of their translation (Mosiah 28:10–18), and the book's last narrated compiler (and proto-angel to Joseph Smith in 1830), Moroni$_2$, examines the letters of his father (Moroni 8–9). Even Jesus himself is not spared this obsessive restaging; the risen Christ takes time out of his transcendent visitation to inspect Nephite records for their comprehensive accuracy (3 Nephi 23:6–13).

Reading is both method and content for the Book of Mormon. Portraying people in the act of reading, the book stages exempla for what it hopes readers' own literary encounter will produce. Those who read books, in the Book of Mormon, journey into the wilderness in the face of imminent destruction at the hand of empire (1 Nephi 1–2), revisit biblical prophecy in search of contemporary fulfillment (2 Nephi 12–24), start new churches (Mosiah 17:1–4, 17:18), or reform their governmental norms (Mosiah 29).[9] The Book of Mormon moves the bodies of its readers in part by describing bodies in (reading-induced) motion. It delivers ethical speech about what bodies are supposed to do in and after an encounter with a sacred book.

The sites of that encounter are also worth reflection. The Book of Mormon's reading is necessarily distributed across scenes of everyday living. A five-hundred-page book is rarely consumed in a single sitting; as such, the Book of Mormon metes itself out in measured doses across a stretch of time that is simultaneously occupied by lived life, thus weaving itself together with a reader's normal routines. Because it virtually demands engagement across a long stretch of time, the Book of Mormon is usually studied privately by the literate in punctual moments between work, chores, and mealtimes. The book weaves itself into one's routines until, before you know it, your bedroom and your field and your commute and your reading nook and your kitchen table are colonized by the Book of Mormon. Who does not associate particularly formative books with the season or smells proximate to the time of their reading? The Book of Mormon hopes to be sufficiently impactful to indelibly brand the times and places through which it moves.[10]

Here again, the book's operation at the level of individual encounter echoes in miniature what the book's content hopes to portray on a much grander scale. Just as the Book of Mormon hybridizes itself with the everyday life of its readers, so too it takes familiar American geography and freights it with the sacrality of ancient Palestine or takes Indigenous Amerindians and overlays them with Israelite pedigree. The Book of Mormon's persuasive mechanics operate, in part, by elevating the familiar, at scales both lived (individual readers, feeling their everyday lives shot through with new revelation) and epic (all of America, elevated to biblical status). As Eran Shalev writes, there's a certain "frisson gained through invoking language still seen as quasi-sacred to describe contemporary reality."[11] The Book of Mormon wagers its persuasive and subject-shaping powers on the gambit of that frisson.

Of course, the Book of Mormon presented itself not just as any book in general (thus inserting itself only into expectations about literacy, the tempo of reading, or the symbiosis of life with especially impactful texts). It presented itself as a deliberate echo of one book in particular: the Bible. Beginning with its earliest editions, the Book of Mormon was made to look and sound like the Bible, from its Elizabethan English and the "-ites" suffix of its tribal naming conventions to its book and chapter divisions, later columns and versification and footnotes, and even bindings that seemed deliberately to mirror 1829 and 1830 American Bible Society editions.[12] Apart from formal considerations such as printing, binding, and diction, the Book of Mormon also stakes its claim to biblical status through extensive quotation from the Hebrew Bible and New Testament, as well as commenting directly on the Bible in order to position itself as the Bible's supplement, solution, and natural successor.[13] In all this, it is easy to see the Book of Mormon's self-conscious biblicism as laying claim to a certain kind of legitimacy.

Even more, however, the Book of Mormon's selection of the Bible as its contrast space and conversation partner also lays claim to an ethical terrain already mapped out by Christianity. The book arrived in the hands of its first readers bound in brown leather with two horizontal gold stripes on the spine, as if to say "This, too, is divine and authoritative." It bore chapter and verse divisions and spoke in King James English, as if to say "You should respond to this book as you do to the Bible: credulously, faithfully, and by translating its moral imperatives into action." By styling itself like the Bible, the Book of Mormon activates already-laid tracks of persuasion and moral formation in its reader. It anticipates an audience previously habituated in relation to the Bible, already deferent and inclined to assent to biblical language. In something like the same way that Augustine traded on the power of the Christian virtues when he wrote his *Enchiridion*, or the way that Nietzsche traded on readers' relationships with the New Testament gospels in *Thus Spake Zarathustra*, the Book of Mormon's biblicism hopes to lay new wiring alongside already-active Protestant circuits.[14]

This willingness to work with the biblical wiring of the nineteenth-century American imaginary calculates a path of least resistance to the Book of Mormon's first anticipated readers. Rather than shaping its readers by fundamentally reorganizing their imaginaries, the Book of Mormon instead simply runs a new program on already-existing hardware. Because it anticipates an American mind organized biblically, it trusts that readers will hear biblical-sounding language as the ethical register of veracity. Elizabethan English was, in the words of Eran Shalev, "a language through which Americans regularly revealed truths, either scriptural or political"; by hearing it spoken to them through the Book of Mormon, readers were "condition[ed] . . . to perceive their history and construct their . . . expectations in scriptural categories."[15] The Book of Mormon's use of biblical language anticipates a reader who is already initiated into frontier Christianity, able to appreciate canonical references and feel at home in theological grammar. It trades, too, on an audience primed to respond to this language in acquiescent ways. The Book of Mormon chooses not to attempt a full-scale rewrite of the American Protestant operating system because, in part, it hopes to trade on the persuasive satisfactions of effortlessly functional software. The book presents itself to readers as a piece to their biblical puzzle, hoping to thrill them with the gratification of watching it fit seamlessly with what they already know and how they already think. It is true, of course, that the Book of Mormon often failed spectacularly in this regard. For very many first readers, extra-biblical scripture was too far beyond the pale. It challenged the peerlessness of the Bible. In a good many cases, then, the text of the book—replete with as many persuasive charms as it could muster—couldn't reach the escape velocity required to evade the gravity of its own extravagance. As we will see in the later section on the Book of Mormon's anxiety, this is a possibility of which the book is keenly aware.[16]

The Book of Mormon's biblicism did more, however, than render it familiar and thereby authoritative. It also made claims to improve upon the Bible. As Grant Hardy explains, the Book of Mormon remedied the gaps in the Bible by restoring lost prophecies from Joseph in Egypt and otherwise unknown Hebrew prophets. . . . And where the Bible seemed vulnerable—on matters of authorship, transmission, and translation—*The Book of Mormon* presented impeccable credentials: written and edited by named prophets, with the original documents being miraculously preserved on metal plates, and translated by divine assistance.[17]

But perhaps the biggest "improvement" of all came from the book's projection of Christianity onto the Old World. Hardy continues: "*The Book of Mormon* offered a plainer version of the Christian gospel than the New Testament itself."[18] Anticipatory prophecies mention Christ by name, identify his mother, designate his hometown, and outline in exquisite detail the events of his life and ministry, including the precise redemptive import of his death and resurrection—and all this from a narrative setting contemporary with the biblical prophets Isaiah and Jeremiah, some six hundred years before Christ's birth.[19] The Book of Mormon functions, in effect, like a bible that says outright what Protestants had only limned implicitly in the Hebrew prophets or Mosaic law. Part of the book's persuasive charm, then, would have been its recognizable Christianity, which, rather than having to be cobbled together piecemeal from an anachronistic New Testament hermeneutic, spoke directly and overtly from the Book of Mormon's opening pages. Protestant Christians could thus feel soothed by the clarity of a theological picture that they already held to be true. The book enacted, in other words, a harmony between Hebrew Bible and New Testament that would have been rationally compelling to a nineteenth-century Christian audience, as if to say "You were right all along—the Old Testament world was Christian, too."

In some ways, then—especially given all that the Book of Mormon hoped to accomplish—it couldn't help *but* be a book, and a biblical one at that. How else to insert itself into the routines of modern life while simultaneously trading on the moral terrain already explored by the Bible? How else to weave its scripturalizing epistemic modes with the everyday life it hoped to elevate? How else to simultaneously inform and soothe, challenge and reassure, surprise and mollify? As a biblically consonant book, the Book of Mormon could import a full history under the imprimatur of heaven.

History of a Lost Civilization

The contents of this book-length chronicle are just as notable as its biblical style and packaging. Performatively speaking, the Book of Mormon professes that what late-modern readers require for their moral reform is—of all things—a *history*. This is already an audacious claim about the moral power of retelling the past, but it appears even more striking when compared to other texts that more readily code as ethical. As Laurie Maffly-Kipp explains, "*The Book of Mormon* does not dictate lifestyle traits or health codes, nor does it educate readers about priesthood hierarchy, ordinances for the dead, esoteric rites, or eternal marriages. *The Book of Mormon* is, first of all, a story of ancient peoples."[20] Or as Nancy Bentley puts it, "In *The Book of Mormon* the keys to securing a place in the afterlife are not spells or incantations but—as befits a modern people—a true knowledge of American history."[21] The book is clearly a religious text of some sort, but it is not a catechetical manual, a set of procedural norms for ecclesiastical governance, a code of morals, a devotional handbook, or a table of monastic hours.[22] Its chosen genre for persuading nineteenth-century readers and reshaping subjectivities such that they might launch a new religion is, instead, history—and a long history, at that: The book's narrative spans roughly one thousand years. We need to ask, then, not only about the ethical formation wagered by the genre of history but also about the moral effects of such a *lengthy* history, in particular. What does the book hope to achieve by subjecting its readers to a full millennium's worth of American chronicle?

One suspects, in part, that the Book of Mormon's thousand-year scale is meant to convey a certain verity. History operates on the scale of centuries, so, wanting to impress its authenticity on readers, the book abridges the records of an entire millennial dispensation. Moreover, there is a certain pedigree that comes only with long stretches of time. This would have been especially compelling to the book's earliest readers, who felt themselves occupying a new world, almost unbearably young when compared to the storied institutions and aged buildings of Europe. By imbuing the American landscape with centuries of additional history—and a sacred, quasi-biblical history at that—the Book of Mormon enticed readers with its offer of temporal dignity for a fledgling nation and its self-conscious world-historical adolescence.

But the book operates not only through the force of millennial history presented all at once in a synchronic mass. This is history rendered through the performance of time's diachronic transience as well. As Jillian Sayre puts it, "The text is marked by an aggressive chronological structure that foregrounds the passage of time. The phrase 'and it came to pass' overwhelms . . . the text."[23] Not just history, then, but also history's *passage* proves crucial to the book's scene of instruction. Here we might imagine a kind of cogent momentum toward the present, the Book of Mormon's repeated iterations of elapsing time as propulsion of ever-accumulating narrative stakes into the reader's present. "Time passed and passed and passed—and now here you are!" it seems to say. Time's passage gathers up America's past eras and concentrates them on the critical necessities of the reading present—a present that grows all the more fateful with each anticipatory century that gets piled onto the narrative.

Readers thus find themselves presented with a one-thousand-year history that names them, in their present reading, as its culmination. The Book of Mormon hopes to charge readers with eschatological urgency by the book's injection of a millennium's worth of prophecy and providence into their lives. This "eschatological prism," as some have called it, contextualizes the present of the book's reading with stakes, pedigree, and high drama, all by constellating the eyes of every Book of Mormon prophet on you, the reader.[24] This eschatological urgency is well calculated for ethical motivation. The book hopes that by amassing enough chronological detail and enough millennial import, it can crash all that historical gravity into the reader's present and move them by sheer dint of its narrative tonnage. The longer the history, the weightier its implication, the more mass it has for moving bodies.

What modernity urgently needs, then, according to the Book of Mormon, is not new forms of government adequate to a rational age, Enlightenment warrant to untether modern man from tradition, or even new religious movements (though, of course, its earliest readers created just that). Modernity suffers, rather, from a deficit of history, and the Book of Mormon's first tactic for shaping its anticipated readers was to situate them within an elaborate saga taking place on the very soil under their feet. Modernity will be best served, the book claims, not by jettisoning history but instead by ramifying it. The Book of Mormon agrees with its modern readers on the necessity of challenging the authoritarian past, but rather than negating outright that past tradition's authoritative status, it reacts obliquely against its singularity. Rather than cutting off history altogether, it asks, Why not multiply it? Why not attend to more peoples, more divine interactions, more sacred books? Modernity suffers from a deficit of history, for the Book of Mormon, because the history jettisoned by the Enlightenment had not been fully exhausted. What's needed is novelty, to be sure, but novelty by way of multiplicity rather than by way of detachment.

Telling history as a mode of moral instruction, the Book of Mormon also creates a past that it can backfill with moral stakes and valuations to recontextualize the present behavior of its readers. Nineteenth-century treasure hunting, for instance, looks different when it's contextualized by a past world of buried objects, whether the hidden treasures of ancient robber bands (Helaman 11:10, 13:34–35) or the sacred records interred by ancient prophets (1 Nephi 13:35; 4 Nephi 1:48–49; Mormon 5:12).[25] Living at a distance from Christ (the modern situation par excellence) looks different when set in the context of Nephite messianism, which was imagined to be a form of Christianity *always* at a distance from Christ (both temporally and geographically) for most of the Nephite story.[26] The Book of Mormon thus provides readers a supplemental history as moral framework for present action. This recontextualization hopes to change imagined readers' dispositions and, thereby, their bodily orientation in the world. If Indigenous Native Americans are, in fact, the Israelite remnant of God's covenant people, you will feel increased pressure to relate to them more generously in spoken interactions, trade relations, and land disputes.[27] If the Rocky Mountains are the hideouts of bygone robber bands, you move through their slot canyons more timidly.[28] And if the Book of Mormon is a true book, you get baptized in frigid lakes and attend services in the Whitmer family home and build temples and drag handcarts westward. Here again, the ethical power of the text cashes out less as a normative to-do list and more as a moral map that frames the register of a subject's possible behavior in the first place. The history provided by the Book of Mormon layers a fresh atlas over the familiar terrain of everyday life, providing readers with new departure points, new destinations, and new landmarks for orientation along the way.

These ethical contexts and dispositions are made more likely to take hold, moreover, because of what the book purports to be a history *of*: a lost civilization. So lost, in fact, that the book's earliest readers had never heard of it. Unlike the lost tribes of Israel, of whom the Book of Mormon's earliest readers were unquestionably aware, the peoples described in the Book of Mormon were not mentioned in the Protestant canon and were never marked by the Bible as missing.[29] With this plot device, the Book of Mormon trades on a certain mystique. To move modern readers, the book must first capture their imagination and inflame their desire, and the promise of hidden knowledge about a vanished civilization seems especially well calculated to achieve these aims. Readers are caught by their own yearning to be knowing subjects, to have part in something larger than life, and (perhaps) to inveigh against the dawn of secularism by importing the anciently enchanted. They are caught, furthermore, by the desire to avoid civilizational ruin for themselves. Both aspirations—to know the fate of the nation recounted within the book's pages and to avoid sharing that fate—are a function of history: history as (synchronic) knowledge of a bygone era and (diachronic) stage on which that era's downfall plays out. Indeed, the book is so insistent on the importance of lost civilizations to its rhetorical effect that it doubles down by containing a *second* lost civilization in the

Jaredites. The specter of civilizational decay must hover over the volume at every moment, it seems, even when its main protagonists have not yet fallen into ruin.

The Book of Mormon's chosen genre of history thus aims to contextualize and reorder dispositions, with readers inclined to assent to that subject formation only because the history has first been experienced as mysteriously compelling. Owing to its mystique, the book's imagined history rewrites modern readers' relationship to the past, leading them to understand antiquity as an era of decline and tragedy such that the present is then figured as an era of possibility and regeneration by contrast. In addition to all the other rhetorical effects of its historical genre—verity, dignifying the American project, and pressing time's weight on the reader—the Book of Mormon also hopes to win assent by inflating the redemptive possibilities of the present. This, then, turns us to the book's task as well as the curiously split register in which that task is articulated.

Two Nations, Two Audiences

Another curious feature of the Book of Mormon is how—in both its narrative content and its implied audience—the book speaks in double. It speaks *about* two different nations, on the one hand, and it is *addressed* to two different audiences, on the other. At every point of its narration, the Book of Mormon operates on two levels simultaneously. Indeed, the book's main plot is not about one lost civilization but, more precisely, about two—and two that are lost in distinct ways. (If one includes the Jaredites, the Book of Mormon technically includes three lost civilizations. I leave the Jaredite plot out of this accounting, however, because the Jaredites, while unquestionably important to the Book of Mormon, nevertheless play only a minority role in the book's main narrative.)

Nephite civilization is lost through their eventual extinction (with no hope for future recovery), while Lamanite civilization is lost through their scattering (though the book anticipates their future regathering). The Book of Mormon is always the story of two nations, never just one, and even this basic observation reveals a handful of techniques for the book's moral persuasion of readers.

For starters, the juxtaposition of Lamanites and Nephites builds moral contrast right into the narrative, with either nation's righteousness pointed up as an example by the contrasting spiritual failures of the other. Thus, when the Nephites are shown to be righteous and prospering, their goodness is sharpened by contrast with Lamanite degeneracy. And when the Lamanites instead become the moral exemplars of the book, their superiority is rendered all the more dramatic by way of contrast with the then-depraved Nephites. Focusing narrative content on two nations rather than one allows the Book of Mormon to specify the full range of its ethical imaginary by illustrating both its poles.

The presence of two nations additionally serves the book's rhetorical aims by training readers' attention on divine covenant. The narrative as a whole traces a multigenerational covenant that extends from the beginning of the book (when divine promise is extended to Lehi₁, the patriarch of the nuclear family that inaugurates the book's storyline) all the way into the readers' present (through imagining that covenant's tenure for Lehi₁'s descendants).[30] Of course, as readers learn over the course of the Book of Mormon, those descendants do not include the Nephite protagonists, who forfeit their covenant inheritance through moral decline and eventual extinction. Thus, the "remnant of the house of Israel," which the Book of Mormon intends to address in its late-modern coming-forth refers instead to the modern-day Lamanite descendants who persist somewhere in the Americas. The fortunes of this multigenerational covenant serve as the macro structure that governs the Book of Mormon across the vagaries of its millennium-length history. Narrating the fortunes of these *two* nations rather than one is calculated to train readers' attention on that covenant because, as the book is at pains to show, what ultimately marks the difference between Nephite annihilation and Lamanite preservation is the extension of this covenant. The Lamanites secure a promise of future redemption on condition of their fidelity to certain founding commandments (Jacob 3:6) and their unwavering devotion when eventually converted (Helaman 15:10–12). The Nephites, however, forfeit their covenant incorporation over the course of the book through a series of domestic and moral failures. The juxtaposition of Nephites and Lamanites, then, results not just in local moral lessons but also in structural distinctions that focus readers on the comprehensive logic of the book as a whole. By contrasting Nephite destruction with Lamanite preservation, the Book of Mormon contends that divine covenant is weighty enough to regulate the extinction of entire ancient peoples—that covenant commands both divine favor and national fortunes. The Book of Mormon moves readers by performing covenantal mandate over the extinction of some bodies and the conservation of others.

The book purports, then, to address itself primarily to these Lamanite descendants, alerting them to the reality of the covenant. But just as the book's contents are spoken in a split register (an account of both Lamanites and Nephites), so too its anticipated audience bifurcates along covenant lines. The book addresses itself primarily "to the Lamanites, who are a remnant of the house of Israel," but it also speaks at times to the latter-day

"Gentiles," who are tasked with delivering the book to its primary audience. The Book of Mormon addresses itself directly to latter-day Israelites, but it also speaks out of the corner of its mouth to the European settlers it anticipates as its secondary audience. In this way, the book extends a high-stakes framing device right into the situation of its modern readers. Not only did a covenant govern the *past* fortunes of two interrelated nations, but that same covenant persists into the present, where it governs once again the fortunes of two correlated peoples—except that, this time, one of those peoples may well include you, the reader. To the lost Israelites among its audience, the Book of Mormon urges reidentification with the dormant covenant that is already theirs. To modern-day Gentiles, the book urges an alliance that may eventually be rewarded by covenant incorporation. The book's double audience represents the eschatological inheritance of the book's double nations.

These two audiences, moreover, are reminded of their status throughout the text, often through direct address. The book's early prophet Nephi₁ addresses himself to both "all those who are of the house of Israel" *and* "all ye ends of the earth" (2 Nephi 33:13). The later prophet Mormon₂ speaks directly to the Lamanites, inviting them to recognize their covenant status ("know ye that ye are of the house of Israel" [Mormon 7:2]) and act accordingly ("therefore repent, and be baptized" [Mormon 7:8]). The book's final narrator, Moroni₂, makes frequent appeals to latter-day Gentiles (Mormon 8:35, 9:1, 9:30) and closes the last chapter of the book with a split appeal—the first half addressed to Lamanites (Moroni 10:1–23) and the second half addressed to "all the ends of the earth" (Moroni 10:24). As one commentator puts it, "The text's frequent invocation of the reader gives him material space on the page . . . and inscribes upon him a future accounting." The reader is "spoken into the text by its prophets."[31] Within a genre as classically third-person and expository as history, these moments of second-person speech are especially arresting. Here is yet another of the Book of Mormon's techniques for gripping the reader and exerting subject-formative power.

This double-speak universalizes the book's anticipated audience without forfeiting its particularity. With respect to this divine covenant, readers might be "in" or they might be "out," but anyone who picks up the book will stand in one of these two relations to the Israelite remnant. In this way, the Book of Mormon covers the full spread of possible relationships to the covenant it describes without thereby sacrificing the particularities of covenant relationship in an abstract universalism. What's more, the particularity of each audience's respective identity gives way to the particular tasks that the book wishes to enjoin upon them. Gentiles are charged with delivering the Book of Mormon to the Lamanite remnant, while the Lamanite audience is tasked with circulating the record among themselves and then, in response, gathering together as the lost Israelite remnant that they are. The book moves bodies, here, by figuring particularized flesh as a point of transit—Gentile flesh as messengers bearing a book, Israelite flesh as the collective body that mobilizes in response. Here again, the particularity of each responsibility is meant to be more compelling than, say, an abstractly universal set of ethico-religious norms. The Book of Mormon moves bodies by arguing, with self-conscious urgency, that if you *don't* move—and move in the particular configurations assigned to you by these covenant identities—all will be lost.

The Book of Mormon's split audience also creates certain ambiguities of identity that work to instill desire in its imagined readers. No matter which kind of reader one happens to be—whether Gentile or long-lost Israelite—certain modal ambiguities attend his or her identity. The Gentile, for instance, is told that she might become an honorary member of the Israelite covenant. In this way, her present identity is determinate (she *is* a Gentile) but her future identity is conditional (she *might become* a member of the covenant). To the Lamanite remnant, however, the book affixes a present indeterminacy: any individual presently encountered only *might* be an Israelite. In this way, the reader's present identity is conditional (you *might* be a Lamanite) while his future identity is determinate (if so, you *are already* within the scope of covenant redemption, and so your covenant future is secured). Where the determinacies work to encode moral value, the ambiguities serve to instill desire. To be (determinately) a Gentile is to be valued among the secular wicked of the last days, while to be (conditionally) a potential Israelite is to hold out the hope of—and thus instill desire for—joining with the redeemed. In a similar way, to be (determinately) an Israelite is to be valued among the Book of Mormon's primary audience and one of God's chosen people, while to be only (conditionally) potentially locatable in this or that fleshy instantiation is to instill desire around the work of location and identification. Gentile bodies are thus moved by being interpolated as points of transit for the record, while Lamanite bodies are moved by the moral freight of a newly remembered identity.

The doubled content of the Book of Mormon's narrative ensures that the inscriptions of and promises to the reader are particular enough to seem authentic, and the book's doubled audience renders the reader's tasks distinct and specific. The book wagers that readers will be more forcefully moved by sharp imperatives with precise parameters than by general moral vagaries. Speaking to a doubled audience, the Book of Mormon speaks with particularity, even as it speaks to everyone.

Itinerant and Incomplete

These ambitions for broad reach and imperatives around gathering speak to another element of the Book of Mormon's scene of instruction: The book presents itself as deeply itinerant. It passes through countless hands on its way to its Lamanite audience and then imagines itself passing *among* those Lamanite hands as a mechanism for Israelite restoration. From the book's several narrators and its drama of intergenerational transmission, to the handful of scribes involved in its translation, and right on down through the long history of the Mormon missionary apparatus, the Book of Mormon is unquestionably a traveling book. This itineracy even extends to an expectation of what will happen after the book *leaves* readers' hands. The Book of Mormon promises that, once it is passed along through the individual purveyance of missionary work, other books will come to replace it. The book names an eschatological urgency that, it hopes, will mobilize its circulation but also tenders supplemental assurances about its absence giving way to other records. The Book of Mormon is itinerant in the sense of both its own internal tendency toward transmission as well as its role within an entire system of mobile, nomadic texts.

This anticipation is constructed primarily through the narrative drama of records being passed from father to son, an intergenerational chain of narrators extending from Nephi$_1$ to Amaleki$_1$, and from Benjamin to Mormon$_2$.[32] The text is littered with scenes of record transmission, from briefer reports, such as Jacob$_2$'s admission that "Nephi gave me . . . a commandment concerning the small plates, . . . that I should write upon these plates a few . . . things" (Jacob 1:1–2), or Omni's felt pressure to "write somewhat upon these plates to preserve our genealogy" (Omni 1:1), to the much longer sermon between Alma$_2$ and his son Helaman$_2$, in which the new custodian of the record is admonished to "take the records," provide an account of the people, carefully guard certain contents that are not fit for public consumption, and even polish the plates to prevent tarnishing (Alma 37:1–2, 37:5–6, 37:21, 37:27–29). The Book of Mormon is itinerant, first, in its self-invested portrayal of all the moments it anciently passed hands.

This internal itineracy serves a dual rhetorical function. On the one hand, it adds moral weight to the book's production. The Book of Mormon does not present itself as the work of just one long-lost prophet. It purports, rather, to be a record produced by many hands over the course of nearly one thousand years. The resulting historical pedigree and cumulative authority renders the book a much more powerful artifact. Because it has performatively garnered the assent of so many people, it exerts a persuasive bid on the reader: "All *these* people have been convinced; why not you too?" The Book of Mormon's itineracy also serves, then, to distribute the book's messianism among several people—up to and including readers.[33] The intergenerational passage by hand that constructs the book's historical verity also draws attention to readers' hands as they grip the book and turn its pages. Its central drama, we might say, is not just the inscription of divine words on metal but the further hope that the typographic force of that inscription will shock the record into motion. Modeling its own nomadic quality, the book hopes to generate enough narrative momentum that it will impel physical motion on the part of its audience.

Of course, for a text to be mobile, it also needs to meet certain criteria of transmissibility. In this regard, it is important that the Book of Mormon presents itself as only a fragment of the time and place it represents. It is a kind of message in a bottle, a scrap of ancient American history made portable across millennia precisely by leaving so much out. For all that it numbers over 500 pages, the book presents itself as dramatically incomplete—an abridgement of a much larger history (of which "even a hundredth part" cannot be written[34]) studded with gaps and lacunae, from the 116 lost pages to other records and other prophecies, some of which it purports to incorporate, others of which it does not, and still others of which are promised at a future date.[35] This book is transmissible, in part, because it is fragmentary.

The book's incompleteness leverages certain rhetorical effects around what *is* contained in the book as well as what is left out. On the one hand, its performed incompleteness shores up the significance of what one finds included in the text; highlighting what is missing authorizes what is present. The import of the Book of Mormon's contents is thus underscored by the halo of the 99 percent that didn't make the cut. At the same time, however, the book's constant profession of omissions renders its gaps as sites of readerly desire. Here again, proclaiming absence is calculated to urge readers' libidinal investments in the possibility of filling lacunae. The Book of Mormon names its own incompleteness, gestures to readers' potential access to that missing knowledge in future records and prophecies, and makes that access contingent on moral reform—all of this fashioning a potent cocktail for ethical formation. Longing to fill the gaps and know what is lost, readers are encouraged to engage in the behaviors that will result in future revelation and the retrieval of further records. In this way, the book's incompleteness delineates its own reward. If readers accept the book in faith and submit to its moral formation, they will be rewarded with more found manuscripts, other histories of unknown ancient nations, more Israelite sagas, and (as a result) ever greater status as knowing subjects. They will be rewarded, that is, with more of what the Book of Mormon offers. Rhetorically speaking, the book functions with the lucrative predictability of an online advertising algorithm: You've expressed interest in the Book of Mormon before; might we interest you in another Book of Mormon?

The book's professed incompleteness and its anticipation of future records not only lassoes readers' desire for future revelation; it also stages moral change in a community over time. Built into the claim of future records' emergence is a kind of progress through different levels of initiation. One begins with the Book of Mormon, but if they hold faithful, they will advance to other and still other records and knowledges. Holding faithful to the Book of Mormon will eventually yield access to its sealed portion; holding faithful to *that* record will then grant access to the chronicles of some other and as-yet-unknown tribe of Israel, and on and on through the never-ending chain of God's similar dealings with other peoples. In the string of promised records lies an implicit road map of moral progress as well as admittance into varying ranks of esoteric knowledge. The Book of Mormon knows what every piano teacher and karate sensei knows: Disciples are amply motivated by a sense of progress, clearly defined levels of attainment, and the rewards that attend those levels. By way of future records, the book engenders a clear sense of where the reader is headed, what lies that way, and a motivating desire to achieve it.

Gesturing to other records also incorporates into the text a reassurance of future verification. Professing itself to be new scripture, the Book of Mormon risks generating skepticism and resistance in the very Christian audience it hopes to persuade. By holding out the hope of future records (some related directly to the Book of Mormon and some not), the book stages a commitment to the positive valuation of previously unknown scripture. "New divine books you've never heard of before are not a bad thing," it seems to say. "They are, in fact, something to which *this* new book also looks forward." Assenting to new scripture allows the imagined modern reader to rationally verify her inherited religious tradition (see also Mormon 7:8–9). Future records also allow the initial charisma of the Book of Mormon to proliferate. Once the early magnetism of the book wears off—that is, once the reader sates their curiosity about new scripture and an unknown account of ancient American inhabitants precisely *through* its reading—what is to impel their continued allegiance to this book? If so much of the book's appeal is concentrated in its initial encounter, how can it provoke the longer-term commitments that are required for the reader's ethical formation? Here again, the promise of future records serves a vital function. It promises a redeployment of the very same intrigue that brought the reader to the Book of Mormon in the first place. Flush in the success of its being read at all, the book hopes to redeploy, over and over again, the power of encountering other sacred texts.

In this respect, the role of the twenty-four Jaredite plates within the narrative is key. With this embedded story, the Book of Mormon stages the discovery, emergence, and translation of another set of ancient records, themselves tied to the fate of a destroyed nation whose intrigue spans the majority of the book's plot. Even if the other future records promised by the Book of Mormon remain as yet hidden and inaccessible, right here in *this* book there's another set of records, access to which can be gained only by reading the Book of Mormon to its end. (The book of Ether, which recounts the contents of this embedded record, comes only at the tail end of the Book of Mormon.)

Here again, access to future records is ensured only by reading in faith the text one already has. And if reading only the opening pages of the Book of Mormon has already slaked readers' thirst for the novelty and mystique promised by Joseph Smith's gold bible, the Jaredite story offers a similarly keyed incentive to carry through with the reading all the way to the end.

The Book of Mormon is itself, then, a deeply itinerant book, but it also gestures to a broader itinerancy: There are *lots* of books proliferating around the periphery of God's workings with ancient peoples, and those books are always in motion. The book promises that even if the nomadism of the Book of Mormon were ever to be exhausted, rest assured, dear reader, that other books are always on their way.

Anxiety

Anyone who makes it to the end of the Book of Mormon will find themselves faced not only with the finally unveiled narrative of the Jaredites but also with the marked fretfulness of the narratorial voice in which that story is couched. The last editorial personality in the Book of Mormon is Moroni$_2$, a character who gilds the entire project with a late-stage anxiety. Moroni$_2$ worries over the quality of the writing, apologizes for "imperfections" in the record, and wrings his hands over Gentile responses to this book.[36] Of this handwringing tone, Laura Scales remarks, "It is an unusual scripture that anticipates such trouble with its readership."[37] Unusual scripture, perhaps, but not unusual ethical writing. Morally invested texts always wrestle to varying degrees with the specter of their misfire. Ethical persuasion is never guaranteed and high-stakes teaching must also grapple with the possibility of its failure. On this score, the Book of Mormon agonizes loudly. In addition to Moroni$_2$'s editorial worries, the early prophet Nephi$_1$

foresees the book's rejection among latter-day skeptics, the narrative stages various scenes of disbelief among "rising generation[s]," and the prophet Alma$_2$ must represent the book's prophetic tradition against an acute strain of secular rationalism.[38] The prophet-narrator Mormon$_2$ experiences the wholesale failure of moral reform among his people, ultimately witnessing Nephite extinction at the end of the book, and Moroni$_2$ is then left to hurl the Book of Mormon straight into the very modernity he worries will thwart its aims. To some extent, we can measure the Book of Mormon's moral investments by the volume at which it worries that those investments will fail to take hold of readers.

This anxiety is tied, in part, to the book's genre. As already noted above, the Book of Mormon presents itself as history, trading thereby on a bevy of rhetorical and persuasive benefits—elevating the readers' present by way of past pedigree, newly contextualizing present action, addressing modern readers in the very idiom at stake in nineteenth-century negotiations of national and racial identity, and so on. But history's evocation of vast stretches of time also introduces risks in ethical formation. Against the backdrop of a millennium's worth of Nephite and Lamanite saga, there emerges an anxiety about holding moral reform through time (something that both the Nephites and the Lamanites fail to do). Although performing historical itineracy bestows several rhetorical benefits, the Book of Mormon also worries about the dangers of that itineracy—in particular, the possibility that the persuasive charms that worked in earlier generations may fail to lay hold in later ones. In some ways, the book stages the very problem at issue in modernity: the persuasive fractures between old and new cohorts, between inherited tradition and an age that is no longer inclined to inherit. Although heavily invested in its own itineracy and its passage between generations—so invested, in fact, that it repeatedly stages ancient fathers tendering records to sons—the Book of Mormon also anticipates its own failure residing in the same moment; it imagines its persuasions to founder in the seams when the record trades hands.[39]

Of course, self-professed anxiety still exerts a rhetorical effect on the reader. How might the Book of Mormon's self-conscious disquiet redound to shore up its own aims? What kinds of ethical speech might reside even here? The book's anxiety could be imagined, for instance, to call forth a kind of disarmed pity from readers (something akin to "don't worry, little guy—you're doing better than you think"). More likely, they seem meant to invoke pique ("I'm not one of *those* Gentiles"). Either way, by worrying about its reception among a diffuse and abstract "many," the Book of Mormon issues an ethical call for a kind of readerly authenticity, the courage to step forward and wager faith in a book that most people will pass by. It attempts, we might say, to tap into the anticipated reader's desire for exceptionalism.

This anxiety also tells us a great deal about the book's imagined scene of instruction. The Book of Mormon worries most, it seems, about its initial encounter. Knowing that it makes audacious claims (to be new scripture, to catalog a one-thousand-year history on the American continent, to emerge from the ground on gold plates at the words of an angel and be translated by a farm-boy prophet), the book frets over whether the shock of that encounter will prove a bit *too* audacious for a first-time reader. The book's narrators do not, for instance, express anxiety over readers' long-term stamina through an arduous course of religious reform. The Book of Mormon is not presented as a handbook of spiritual exercises that then worries over readers' discipline, or an ascetic regimen that then worries about demons charming disciples away with visions of sumptuous feasts and plump young women. The text seems to worry, rather, that someone will sit down to read the book and shut the cover in disgust after a few hours or even a few pages. Its imagined failure is embodied in Mark Twain more than in the lapsed initiate.[40]

The Book of Mormon attempts to resolve these neuroses through redoubled calls to faith. In the same chapter where Moroni$_2$ famously frets that "the Gentiles will mock at these things" (Ether 12:23), the Lord responds with a formula for alchemizing the text's weakness into an asset: "If they humble themselves before me, and have faith in me, then will I make weak things become strong unto them" (Ether 12:27). Relying on both the language and logic of Pauline theology ("my strength is made perfect in weakness," 2 Corinthians 12:9), the Book of Mormon here transmutes its worries into a hermeneutic claim: This book cannot wear its message on its sleeve. It must, instead, be written in weakness so that only those disposed to remain with the book in faith will be able to uncover its message. It is the kind of text that one must sit with seriously, read slowly, and to which one must extend the benefit of the doubt—all long enough that its more subtle persuasive charms can begin to take hold. The book's anxiety thus redounds to a call for faith. Against the worry that an initial encounter will prove too audacious, the book counters with a theology of weakness and appeals to fidelity, encouraging readers to hang on just a little bit longer—trusting all the while that its more delicate subject formations will take hold if the reader can just hold skepticism at bay for a moment or two more.

In part, then, the Book of Mormon tracks the fading fortunes of traditional forms of Christian moral persuasion. It styles itself as a bible, but a bible that is curiously anxious about its reception in the modern Western world—anxious, we might imagine, because it knows that biblical forms of persuasion are losing hold. The very cracks in traditional persuasive forms that allow an opening for the Book of Mormon in the first place also threaten the book's ability to persuade its readers over the long term. It breaks through the weak points of biblical tradition, in other words, but then worries about its own reliance on some of those formative techniques. It is this anxiety, perhaps more than anything, that styles the Book of Mormon as ethical speech. Scenes of instruction often fail. Worrying *about* that failure is one of the things that morally invested texts do best.

Conclusion

Scenes of instruction operate by managing flows of desire in their pupils. In a classroom setting, desire is motivated by the promise of good grades, successful mastery of material, and display of that mastery relative to one's peers. In a monastic setting, desire is motivated by the example of one's mentor, by the promise of divine control over the passions, and by the display of achieved holiness that sparks a yearning for emulation. The Book of Mormon, too, works to form subjects by instilling in them certain desires—desires for grand narrative and incorporation within an epic and sacred history, desires for the collapse of distance between the era of Christian beginnings and modernity. And it also instills desire in its readers through the ambiguities that surround their identity vis-à-vis the book. Whether Gentile or Lamanite, readers watch as the Book of Mormon casts a certain mystique over the flesh that sits across from its pages. With these fundamental desires in place, the book imagines that its moral imperatives can begin to take hold.

Ethics, on this reading, is a way of hearing the persuasive claims made by a text, how it activates and interacts with readers' desires, and the voice with which it lays claim to the formation of readers' subjectivity. The Book of Mormon works its moral persuasion through registers as varied as a book, biblicism, telling the history of a lost civilization, and distributing that history across two registers. It is itinerant, fragmentary, and deeply anxious. But across all these qualities and conventions, the Book of Mormon is, most fundamentally, attempting to form its readers and exercising persuasive charms in the hope of readerly consent to that formative work. Deploying this text as ethical speech, then, cannot be a question solely of its propositional content. The strongest moral registers of the Book of Mormon lie elsewhere than its calls to Christian living or its recitations of particular commandments or even its sophisticated development of varied moral themes. Ethics is the art of changing behavior by changing subjects, and the Book of Mormon will be most available for contemporary ethical redeployment when scholars are as attentive to the subject-formative techniques of the text as they are to its recommended behaviors.

Summarizing precisely that subject-formative work, Grant Shreve calls attention to the way the Book of Mormon enchants readers with its self-referential performance.[41] Referring to one of the characteristic genres within the book, Shreve lingers over a "class of prophecies . . . that seem to be fulfilled by the book's sheer existence rather than by its mere content."[42] Here he cites references to Joseph Smith in 2 Nephi 3, or anticipations of skepticism at the idea of a sealed book, as in 2 Nephi 27. Moments like these, he says, "sacralize . . . the book in its reading" because they attempt to constellate the reader into the performance of fulfilled prophecy that is enacted by sheer dint of the book's existence. The Book of Mormon prophesies of its own existence and its own future emergence such that readers are effectively forced to play a role in the drama of prophetic fulfillment simply by undergoing the task of reading it.

In addition to neatly summarizing one of the book's most potent persuasive tactics, Shreve also encapsulates many of the points explored in this chapter. By speaking of readers, he invokes the book's status *as* a book; in the text's "self-scripturalization," he gestures to the Book of Mormon's biblicism; with these "prophetic loops" we might think of the diachronic temporality made possible by the book's historical genre; and as the book projects prophetic fulfillment off its pages and into the readers' present, we are reminded of the fragmentary incompletion that hovers constantly around the text. The moral persuasions of the Book of Mormon are concentrated in moments of readerly encounter precisely because the book is a morally invested text. It is invested in enthralling its readers because it is invested in shaping them. "Given this aspect of the book," Shreve concludes, "it should come as no surprise that one of the LDS Church's primary methods of winning converts is to urge them to read *The Book of Mormon* and, ideally, to experience the sensation of revelation."[43] The book can function so effectively simply through its enacted reading because everything about the text has been calibrated to do so. The Book of Mormon—before and quite apart from contemporary "ethical" deployments—is already ethical speech.

To hear the register of moral persuasion that is operative within the Book of Mormon means translating its persuasive tactics into contemporary language—"reactivating" the text, as Mark Jordan put it at the beginning of this chapter. Perhaps more than any other contemporary scripture, the Book of Mormon endorses translation. I conclude, then, with one attempt at ventriloquy. We might—and should—generate many more:

Dear reader, you suffer from a deficit of history. Modernity has taught you to sever yourself from past religious tradition, but you have jettisoned the wrong thing. What you need in late modernity to bring you to God is the epic history of a long-lost civilization—because, in fact, this civilization has everything to do with you.

I contain that history. As a book, I will operate like other texts you know, but I also stand apart from them. I am like the Bible. I speak of Jesus, and Christianity, and virtues you already hold dear. For all that, however, you will likely not be impressed by this book. That is by divine design, so that you might learn faith.

Think of me like a message in a bottle—a fragmented scrap from a mysterious past, sent to you across time and space. Around its torn edges, feel the promise of additional documents and deeper histories.

And whoever you are, please know that this is a story about you. You might well be a Lamanite and, if so, your present is connected to this past by the covenant that God has been extending to you across centuries; please engage in the moral reform that will enable you to access it. As for you Gentiles, God's covenant plan depends on you; please engage in the moral reform needed to deliver this record to the Lamanite remnant.

Whatever your position with respect to this book, you will find truth within its pages. Take it up and read.

Notes

1. For examples of critical newspaper reception, see Abner Cole's acerbic commentary (published under the pseudonym "Obadiah Dogberry") in his newspaper, the *Reflector*, Sept. 3, 1829, Sept. 16, 1829, Sept. 23, 1829, Oct. 7, 1829. An especially famous instance of monograph-length censure was Alexander Campbell, *Delusions: An Analysis of the Book of Mormon; with an Examination of Its Internal and External Evidences, and a Refutation of Its Pretences to Divine Authority* (Boston: Benjamin H. Greene, 1832). For introductions to the history of The Book of Mormon with an eye to its reception, see Terryl L. Givens, *By the Hand of Mormon: The American Scripture That Launched a New World Religion* (New York: Oxford University Press, 2002); Paul C. Gutjahr, *The Book of Mormon: A Biography* (Princeton, NJ: Princeton University Press, 2012); Michael Hubbard McKay and Gerrit J. Dirkmaat, *From Darkness unto Light: Joseph Smith's Translation and Publication of the Book of Mormon* (Provo, UT: BYU Religious Studies Center, 2015); and Richard Lyman Bushman, *Joseph Smith's Gold Plates: A Cultural History* (New York: Oxford University Press, 2023). For a good history on the broader phenomenon of anti-Mormonism, see J. Spencer Fluhman, *"A Peculiar People": Anti-Mormonism and the Making of Religion in Nineteenth-Century America* (Chapel Hill: University of North Carolina Press, 2012).

2. The distinction between *Sittlichkeit* and *Moralität* is drawn from the political philosophy of G.W.F. Hegel (in particular, from *The Philosophy of Right*), but readers wishing to be spared the density of Hegel's prose might also look to chapters 6 and 7 of David Rose, *Hegel's Philosophy of Right: A Reader's Guide* (New York: Bloomsbury Academic, 2007).

3. Pierre Hadot, *Philosophy as a Way of Life*, trans. Michael Chase (Malden, MA.: Blackwell Publishers, 1995).

4. This approach to ethics—that is, ethics as moral formation—is exemplified especially in literature on the rhetorical and moral techniques operative in early Christian teaching. See, for example, Paul R. Kolbet, *Augustine and the Cure of Souls: Revising a Classical Ideal* (Notre Dame, IN.: University of Notre Dame Press, 2010); Derek Krueger, *Liturgical Subjects: Christian Ritual, Biblical Narrative, and the Formation of the Self in Byzantium* (Philadelphia: University of Pennsylvania Press, 2014); Paul C. Dilley, *Monasteries and the Care of Souls in Late Antique Christianity: Cognition and Discipline* (New York: Cambridge University Press, 2017); Mark D. Jordan, *Teaching Bodies: Moral Formation in the* Summa *of Thomas Aquinas* (New York: Fordham University Press, 2017). Of course, the usefulness of these methods extends far beyond the field of Christian theological rhetoric. As a representative example of a similar approach to the study of rabbinic Judaism, see Jonathan Wyn Schofer, *Confronting Vulnerability: The Body and the Divine in Rabbinic Ethics* (Chicago: University of Chicago Press, 2010).

5. Mark D. Jordan, *Transforming Fire: Imagining Christian Teaching* (Grand Rapids, MI: Eerdmans, 2021), 17–18.

6. Jordan, *Transforming Fire*, 23–24.

7. I say "obvious" but I should note that there are some who would contest this claim on the grounds that the Book of Mormon's earliest scene was, in fact, oral rather than written. Here, however, the persuasive effects of its orality operated for only a few: Smith's earliest scribes (Emma Smith, Martin Harris, Oliver Cowdery, and John Whitmer) and, perhaps, Smith himself. For treatments of the Book of Mormon that view its oral delivery as the original text, see Royal Skousen's critical text, *The Book of Mormon: The Earliest Text* (New Haven, CT: Yale University Press, 2009), as well as his accompanying six-volume *Analysis of Textual Variants of the Book of Mormon*, 2nd ed. (Provo, UT: BYU Studies; FARMS, 2017). See also William L. Davis, *Visions in a Seer Stone: Joseph Smith and the Making of the Book of Mormon* (Chapel Hill: University of North Carolina Press, 2020); and Ann Taves, *Revelatory Events: Three Case Studies in the Emergence of New Spiritual Paths* (Princeton, NJ: Princeton University Press, 2016).

8. Though here, as elsewhere, I mean only to conjure the book's potential or imagined readers, we do have some limited data about the reading habits of the Book of Mormon's earliest devotees. See Janiece Johnson, "Becoming a People of the Books: Toward an Understanding of Early Mormon Converts and the New Word of the Lord," *Journal of Book of Mormon Studies* 27 (2018): 1–43.

9. Here again, historical data suggest that these hopes and imaginations took hold. These are all things that the book's earliest adherents went on to do.

Numerous studies confirm early Mormonism's millenarianism, biblicism, and political theology; for just one especially good source that combines these themes into a single investigation, see Christopher James Blythe, *Terrible Revolution: Latter-day Saints and the American Apocalypse* (New York: Oxford University Press, 2020).

10. Indeed, the insistence with which the Book of Mormon seeks to supplement daily life can be fruitfully thought alongside the Derridean supplement. For a wonderful investigation of Joseph Smith's theology of books that briefly takes up this theme, see John Durham Peters, "Recording beyond the Grave: Joseph Smith's Celestial Bookkeeping," *Critical Inquiry* 42, no. 4 (2016): 842–64.

11. Eran Shalev, *American Zion: The Old Testament as a Political Text from the Revolution to the Civil War* (New Haven, CT: Yale University Press, 2013), 91.

12. Paul C. Gutjahr, "The Golden Bible in the Bible's Golden Age," *American Transcendental Quarterly* 12, no. 4 (1998): 275–93.

13. The most prominent examples of extensive biblical quotation within the Book of Mormon are 2 Nephi 12–24 (echoing Isaiah 2–14) and 3 Nephi 12–14 (echoing Matthew 5–7), but numerous other borrowings and parallels exist at the level of individual verses and phrases. For overt instances of the Book of Mormon's commentary on the Bible, see 1 Nephi 13:23–29, 13:38–41; 2 Nephi 29:1–10; Mormon 7:8–9. The available literature on the Book of Mormon's relationship to the Bible is vast. For a general introduction to the conversation, see Grant Hardy, *Understanding the Book of Mormon: A Reader's Guide* (New York: Oxford University Press, 2010). Two further introductory texts, focusing on the Bible in Mormonism more broadly, and then on the Bible in Latter-day Saint scripture, are Philip L. Barlow, *Mormons and the Bible: The Place of the Latter-day Saints in American Religion* (New York: Oxford University Press, 2013); and Nicholas J. Frederick, *The Bible, Mormon Scripture, and the Rhetoric of Allusivity* (Lanham, MD: Farleigh Dickinson University Press, 2016). For the most precise exegetical examination produced to date of the role of a single biblical book within the Book of Mormon, see Joseph M. Spencer, *A Word in Season: Isaiah's Reception in the Book of Mormon* (Champaign: University of Illinois Press, 2023).

14. Here again it is worthwhile to note that the Book of Mormon anticipates the Bible being in circulation before the Book of Mormon's appearance. See 1 Nephi 13:20–42; 2 Nephi 29:3–14.

15. Shalev, *American Zion*, 108, 114.

16. For more on the canonical affronts posed by the book, see David F. Holland, *Sacred Borders: Continuing Revelation and Canonical Restraint in Early America* (New York: Oxford University Press, 2011).

17. Grant Hardy, "*The Book of Mormon* and the Bible," in Fenton and Hickman, *Americanist Approaches to the Book of Mormon*, 112.

18. Hardy, "*The Book of Mormon* and the Bible," 112.

19. See 1 Nephi 11:13, 11:24–34; 2 Nephi 9:4–17; Mosiah 3:8, 15:5–7; Alma 7:10.

20. Laurie Maffly-Kipp, Introduction to the Penguin edition of *The Book of Mormon* (New York: Penguin Books, 2008), vii.

21. Nancy Bentley, "Kinship, *The Book of Mormon*, and Modern Revelation," in Fenton and Hickman, *Americanist Approaches to the Book of Mormon*, 236.

22. The tail end of the Book of Mormon does contain contrasting genres of this sort, but they are explicitly included as both an afterthought and an appendix. See Moroni 1–6.

23. Jillian Sayre, "Books Buried in the Earth: *The Book of Mormon*, Revelation, and the Humic Foundations of the Nation," in Fenton and Hickman, *Americanist Approaches to the Book of Mormon*, 34–35.

24. Elizabeth Fenton and Jared Hickman, Introduction to *Americanist Approaches to the Book of Mormon*, ed. Fenton and Hickman (New York: Oxford University Press, 2019), 9–10: "*The Book of Mormon* articulates and embodies a strong reading of Joseph Smith's America as an eschatological prism through which the past can be seen to be seeking its fulfillment in the present and the present finding its fulfillment in the past."

25. The classic text on early Mormonism in the context of nineteenth-century New England folk magic remains D. Michael Quinn, *Early Mormonism and the Magic World View*, 2nd ed. (Salt Lake City: Signature Books, 1998).

26. For a sophisticated and explicitly philosophical take on the Book of Mormon's messianism, see Adam S. Miller, *Rube Goldberg Machines: Essays in Mormon Theology* (Draper, UT: Greg Kofford Books, 2012), 21–35.

27. As the history of early Mormon settler-colonialism shows, however, the moral suasion attempted by the Book of Mormon on this point proved tragically and dramatically unreliable. See Jared Farmer, *On Zion's Mount: Mormons, Indians, and the American Landscape* (Cambridge: Harvard University Press, 2008). On the shifting allegiances and identifications between Mormons and Amerindians, see Peter Coviello, *Make Yourselves Gods: Mormons and the Unfinished Business of American Secularism* (Chicago: University of Chicago Press, 2019). For a further look at the Book of Mormon and its racializing logics vis-à-vis Indigenous Americans, see Jared Hickman, "*The Book of Mormon* as Amerindian Apocalypse," *American Literature* 86, no. 3 (2014): 429–61.

28. See Blythe, *Terrible Revolution*, 98–129; and W. Paul Reeve, "'As Ugly as Evil' and 'as Wicked as Hell': Gadianton Robbers and the Legend Process among the Mormons," *Journal of Mormon History* 27, no. 2 (2001): 125–49.

29. For more on the Book of Mormon's account of lost peoples and how they diverge from related nineteenth-century literary conventions, see chapter 4 of Elizabeth Fenton, *Old Canaan in a New World: Native Americans and the Lost Tribes of Israel* (New York: New York University Press, 2020).

30. See the Book of Mormon's title page, as well as 1 Nephi 15:12–20; Enos 1:13–18; 3 Nephi 20–21; Mormon 5:8–24.

31. Sayre, "Books Buried in the Earth," 36–37.

32. I say "father to son" but in truth there are a few scenes of transmission that pass between brothers or between nonrelated persons. The majority of the scenes, however, are filial.

33. As Laura Scales puts it, the Book of Mormon's "system of mediation and shared prophecy opens the messianic role to multiple people." Scales, "Writing of the Fruit of Thy Loins," 203.

34. The book insists so fully on its incompleteness that this refrain is repeated several times: Jacob 3:13; Words of Mormon 1:5; Helaman 3:14; 3 Nephi 5:8, 26:6; Ether 15:33.

35. The 116 lost pages reference a segment of the early translation that Smith allowed Martin Harris, the project's initial scribe and financier, to take home and display to a select few relatives. Several weeks later, Harris reported the pages missing, their fate unknown. For the Book of Mormon's internal references to the 116 lost pages, see 1 Nephi 9:5; Words of Mormon 1:7. For incorporated external prophecies, see 1 Nephi 19:12, 19:16; Jacob 5; Alma 33:3, 33:13–15; Helaman 8:19, 15:11; 3 Nephi 10:16. For the promise of future records, see 1 Nephi 14:26; 2 Nephi 27:11, 29:12–13; Ether 1:1–4, 4:16.

36. Mormon 8–9; Ether 12:23–25.

37. Scales, "Writing of the Fruit of Thy Loins," 193.

38. 2 Nephi 29:1–9; Mosiah 26:1; Alma 30. On this last confrontation, see especially Joseph M. Spencer, "Is Not This Real?" *BYU Studies Quarterly* 58, no. 2 (2019): 87–104.

39. For an exploration of temporal and spatial distance as they are reflected in Joseph Smith's larger translation project, see Samuel Morris Brown, *Joseph Smith's Translation: The Words and Worlds of Early Mormonism* (New York: Oxford University Press, 2020).

40. In an enduringly famous quip, Twain described the Book of Mormon as "chloroform in print." He went on: "If Joseph Smith composed this book, the act was a miracle—keeping awake while he did it was, at any rate." Mark Twain, *Roughing It* (Hartford, CT: American Publishing Company, 1872), 127.

41. Jan Shipps had already drawn attention to this feature of the Book of Mormon some thirty-five years earlier; see Shipps, *Mormonism: The Story of a New Religious Tradition* (Urbana: University of Illinois Press, 1985), 37.

42. Grant Shreve, "Nephite Secularization; or, Picking and Choosing in *The Book of Mormon*," in Fenton and Hickman, *Americanist Approaches to the Book of Mormon*, 224.

43. Shreve, "Nephite Secularization," 226.

7

The Moral Visions
of the Book of Mormon

Ethics and the Gospel of Agency

KELLY SORENSEN

In a famous moment in the Book of Mormon, even more important than it first appears, a person asks God to light up some rocks. The moment tells us how to read the Book of Mormon's moral and ethical vision—or, more accurately, moral and ethical *visions*. I will say more about those rocks soon. But here is where I am going in this chapter: On my reading, what the Book of Mormon offers is an agentic and participatory ethics—an ethics that is neither algorithmic nor necessarily particularistic, one that asks the reader both to notice what it looks like when God extends an individual's agency and, simultaneously, to notice what the reader herself aims to do with the book. The Book of Mormon offers a gospel of agency.

By "agency," I mean a person's capability to make choices among multiple options for thought and action. (I have no particular metaphysics about choice in mind; various metaphysical views will work with the account below.) By saying that God "extends an individual's agency," I mean a variety of ways that God responds to human choice by enhancing it, encouraging it, assisting it, expanding it, or adding to it. For example, if a person decides to try to make a certain outcome happen, then God makes that outcome more likely to happen, or simply happen, or helps the person enter circumstances in which she can make the outcome happen, or something similar. Then God wants the choosing person (and the choosing community and readers too) to reflect about that choice—its consequences, its nature, and its motivational wellsprings—and, by reflecting, to make even better choices in the future. On my reading of the Book of Mormon, in this way God is acting to develop human agency: God wants individuals and communities, across time, to become more capable of choice and, importantly, more capable of morally better choice. God aims at the moral development of human choice-making through interacting with human choices. That is what I am calling a "gospel of agency."

This interpretation yields a non-consequentialist ethic, since God is willing to extend and enhance morally permissible but non-optimal and non-maximizing human choice. And it is a non-consequentialist ethic because there is no indication that God views the morally best choices as choices that maximize the good. Consequences matter in the book, as they do in most philosophical ethical theories, but action types and virtues are also part of the ethics of the Book or Mormon. Most generally, the question about the morally right thing to do becomes a question humans answer participatorily with God through choice and reflection.

Here is an outline of the chapter. First, I want to look at those lit rocks. Second, I will turn to two parallel cases of types of escape from oppressive regimes. The third case is about defensive violence. A fourth case is about how individuals and communities respond to three of the Book of Mormon's most famous antagonists. From these and a few other brief cases,[1] I will argue that the Book of Mormon offers a gospel of agency: The book is full of instances where God extends people's choices with the expectation that they (and readers) will see and learn whether those choices are morally good and whether they could be even morally better.[2]

Example One: Providing Light

The famous moment in the Book of Mormon occurs when Jared's (otherwise unnamed) brother presents God with a problem: a specific problem about lighting a dark enclosed vessel. God says in reply, "What will ye that I should do?" (Ether 2:23). The next verses and the story of the lit stones suggest that God's question is best understood as "What will ye that I should do as a way to extend your agency?" or "What do you want me to do to assist your choices?" Jared's brother has made choices with a trajectory, and God then joins in and extends those choices and their trajectory. God in the Book of Mormon will actually participate in and extend many kinds of agency, or at least not block many kinds of agency. Sometimes the book will make it explicit and clear that God is extending a specific form of human agency but other times it is left implicit, and in a fugue-like way this puts demands on our own agency as the book's readers about the agency use of others.

It is worth noting what precedes the event with the lit stones. Under the worry of confusion and a looming loss of language and culture, Jared and his brother resolve to petition God for help and a place to go. God responds to this exercise of agency with compassion, travel instructions, and an intended land of promise (Ether 1:38–43, 2:7, 2:12). But at a water obstacle the small Jaredite community stops and stays indefinitely. And the community's meaningful use of agency also apparently stops, a stoppage that after four years results in God's chastening (Ether 2:14). God seems to be expecting more and better human agency. A repentant Jared's brother is told to build barges to cross the sea, and he does so to God's specifications. But God has left some problems for Jared's brother to puzzle over—a breathing problem and a light problem. The breathing problem comes from the tight, sealed nature of the barges, and once Jared's brother asks about the problem, God rewards the agency of the question with a solution: holes in the top and bottom that can be sealed (Ether 2:18–21). Yet the light problem remains, and God waits for more agency here. God notes that neither windows nor fire will work. And then God asks, "Therefore what will ye that I should prepare for you that ye may have light when ye are swallowed up in the depths of the sea?" (Ether 2:25). God is asking for participation and agency, with an expression of willingness to honor and extend that agency. God seems to be teaching a model of agentic divine/human interaction here.

Jared's brother goes to work on what seems to be his own idea, not God's. He prepares sixteen small clear stones. (One wonders what God would have done with other forms of agency besides clear stones.) Jared's brother then requests—and this can seem brazen, even though he prefaces the request with humility and faith—that God touch the stones with his finger and "prepare them that they may shine forth in darkness." In fact, God honors this agency directly and immediately. God does touch and light the stones with his finger. Jared's brother goes on to receive more than lit stones; he receives an exceptional visual experience of the body of Jesus Christ (Ether 3:1–16). The details of the narrative are remarkable.

As various readers have noted, God wants engagement from Jared's brother. I want to broaden that observation below in the following ways: (1) God wants not just engagement but also to *extend* the agency manifest in the engagement, and (2) God invites us to read the Book of Mormon as offering instances of human/divine interaction so that we can observe and interpret God's extensions of human agency. Seen in this way, the Book of Mormon is a distributed version of God's invitation to Jared's brother: The Book of Mormon asks to each reader, "What will ye that I should" do to extend your agency—what will *you petition the book's resources to do for you?*

Example Two: Parallel Escapes

Let us turn to a second and straightforward example. There are two parallel escapes by oppressed communities in the book of Mosiah.[3] In the first escape, Limhi's community is in bondage to the Lamanites. Previous violent uprisings aimed at resisting this bondage have failed (Mosiah 7:18, 21:7–12). Limhi says that God has not yet rewarded the agency of these struggles because the people have transgressed, but he also says that God still stands ready to offer deliverance (Mosiah 7:29–33). Left open for consideration in the text is what explains God's withholding of aid: the people's transgressions, or their violent *means* of resisting bondage as a category or type of agency, or both.[4] In any case, a community member named Gideon proposes a new, nonviolent means of escaping the captivity: getting the guards drunk and sleepy such that the community can sneak out of enemy territory (Mosiah 22:1–6). The plan works, but the text attributes to God little direct aid or agency extension in the execution of the escape plan. The Lamanites send an army in pursuit of the community of Limhi, but the army gets lost in the pursuit. One might make the case that God helped the community by influencing Gideon, the originator of the plan to get the guards drunk, but the text is vague about the nature of God's influence through Gideon (Alma 1:8), and God's extension of the community's agency seems small (and mentioned only in a later editorial afterthought) in comparison to the second escape story that immediately follows in the Book of Mormon.

That second escape concerns the community of $Alma_1$.[5] This group is also in bondage to a group of Lamanites—in fact, in bondage to the very lost army that had pursued the community of Limhi (Mosiah 23:30). The backstory of this community matters: $Alma_1$, formerly one of a cohort of corrupt priests of an oppressive king, repents and becomes a transformed believer. He teaches other new believers in secret and meets with them in the wilderness to organize a church. Warned by God that the oppressive king now knows about the wilderness church, $Alma_1$ leads his fellow believers away to a new settlement. It is this settlement that the lost Lamanite army pursuing Limhi discovers and captures. $Alma_1$'s people are paradigmatically faithful and devoted, and $Mormon_2$, the editor of both accounts, is eager for readers to know that God repeatedly extends the agency of $Alma_1$'s people—first, by warning them to leave the oppressive king's city (Mosiah 23:1–2) and, second, in an escape that parallels the escape of Limhi's people, but with an important difference: God himself puts the guards to sleep (Mosiah 24:17–25). Throughout the narration, $Alma_1$'s people choose and act well, helping each other and twice uprooting their settled lives; God extends that agency directly and clearly in a way that is absent in the case of Limhi's people.

Mormon$_2$ seems to narrate the two proximate escapes with a lesson about agency and devotion in mind: I believe that Mormon$_2$ wants careful readers to notice God's direct enhancement of human agency in the second case and its contrasting indirectness and smaller scope in the first case. A heavyhanded and didactic narrator in some cases (pronouncing "and thus we see" about some of what he considers historical lessons), here Mormon$_2$ holds back and trusts readers to see what is clear by juxtaposition.

Also worth noting is that Alma$_1$'s people face no easy path: God responds to their growing goodness and agency with help, but he does not stop the lost Lamanite army from capturing them. The God of the Book of Mormon extends human agency, but that same God allows burdensome challenges to come to even those he most helps. One might argue that these new challenges, in this case and elsewhere in the book, set the conditions and opportunities for more agency. If so, the Book of Mormon does not offer a simple prosperity gospel, some stepwise recipe for obtaining God's comprehensive aid; instead, it offers what we might call a gospel of agency.

Example Three: Defensive Violence

The parallel escapes in the second example exhibit differences in the *scope* and *directness* of God's extension of human agency—different responses from God to human agency. A third example is less straightforward but very important. The third example, defensive violence, offers the opportunity to distinguish among actions on a spectrum from merely *morally adequate* to *morally higher and preferable*. That is, defensive violence in the Book of Mormon offers the opportunity to compare cases that are merely above some minimal threshold of moral adequacy with cases that are more admirable and well above that moral threshold.

The Book of Mormon portrays many varieties of instances of violence, with considerable work left to the reader to determine when violence is permitted and even whether the specific subclass of *defensive* violence is permitted—that is, violence to protect oneself or one's community in response to violence initiated by another party. I will discuss two interpretations of defensive violence in the Book of Mormon, one by Duane Boyce and a second, more careful interpretation by David Pulsipher.

Boyce's interpretation is that the Book of Mormon not only permits but actively *requires* defensive violence. In Boyce's view, a community is morally required to fight against an unjust aggressor, and a community that does not do so is morally deficient. Boyce thinks the Book of Mormon matches everyday American morality in this way: He notes that many people think that killing to defend loved ones from violence "is not only permissible, but morally *obligatory*."[6] Boyce points to a number of instances of defensive violence in the Book of Mormon, including Captain Moroni$_1$'s spirited leadership of the Nephite armies to fend off enemy attacks. And he notes that Mormon$_2$, the editor of the largest segment of the book, himself leads people in cases of defensive violence and that Mormon$_2$ celebrates his predecessor Captain Moroni$_1$ as "firm in the faith of Christ" (Alma 48:13). Boyce might claim, using my terms, that God extends the agency of those, and only those, who are willing to defend themselves with violence.

Boyce's interpretation about defensive violence matches the sense that some readers get from the book. In Boyce's interpretation, people who forego defensive violence either make a moral mistake by failing to fulfill a moral obligation or they constitute some sort of rare exception instance. But Boyce's view is all trees and no forest. His monotonic interpretation does not sufficiently address the book's nonviolent elements—first, the multiple occasions on which communities in the Book of Mormon flee from violent aggression instead of responding with violence and, second, the case of the Anti-Nephi-Lehies. In a superior interpretation, the Book of Mormon morally *permits* (and does not morally *require or obligate*) defensive violence, but it simultaneously signals that nonviolence is morally *better*.

David Pulsipher makes the case for this superior interpretation.[7] Key to Pulsipher's argument are these explanatory verses written by Mormon$_2$: "Now the Nephites were taught to defend themselves against their enemies, even to the shedding of blood if it were necessary; yea, and they were also taught never to give an offense, yea, and never to raise the sword except it were against an enemy, except it were to preserve their lives" (Alma 48:14). But, Pulsipher notes, Mormon$_2$ does not stop at this descriptive statement of justified self-defense. Mormon$_2$ says next that for the faithful people, God would "warn them to flee, or to prepare for war, according to their danger; and also, that God would make it known unto them whither they should go to defend themselves against their enemies, and by so doing, the Lord would deliver them" (Alma 48:15–16). Next, Pulsipher invites us to look at the text for instances of God telling people either to use defensive violence or simply to flee. Importantly, there are *no* instances in the Book of Mormon of God advising people to prepare for a war of defensive violence; when asked, God never tells a group to respond to an attack with violence. Instead, there are only—and many—instances of God telling people to flee (1 Nephi 2:1–2; 2 Nephi 5:5; Omni 1:12; Mosiah 23:1–2; Mosiah 24:16–17—the last two instances are the examples of parallel escapes just above). Pulsipher notes that "when it comes to strategies for preserving his children, the narrative describes an Eternal Father (of *all* sides in any given conflict) who explicitly directs only nonviolent options, such as flight, at least when given a chance to weigh in beforehand."[8] In the Book of Mormon, there is no Olympian Greek god urging people to initiate violence and aiding them in it, and there is no attribution to God of a command that one group of people should "utterly destroy" another (Deuteronomy 20:17; 1 Samuel 15:3). In the Book of Mormon, when asked for counsel, God only tells people to flee from violence.

Readers like Boyce who believe that defensive violence is morally required note the following passage in the Book of Mormon that describes a group of people who choose to fight against unjust aggressors: "Inasmuch as ye are not guilty of the first offense, neither the second, ye shall not suffer yourselves to be slain by the hands of your enemies. And again, the Lord has said that: Ye shall defend your families even unto bloodshed" (Alma 43:46–47). Boyce leans on the prescriptive construction of the last sentence to argue for a moral obligation to violently protect others: You *shall* use violence to defend your families. But Pulsipher reads the passage with more care: The sentence says that you shall defend your families *even unto*, or on Pulsipher's reading, *up to and including (but not only with)* violence. "The exact method for defense," Pulsipher says, "is left to the discretion of individuals and communities. It might involve bloodshed. Then again, it might not."[9] When people in the Book of Mormon do choose defensive violence, God sometimes extends their agency. But the text itself gives us numerous examples of people choosing to flee instead of fight—and God extends their agency even more powerfully. If people who choose defensive violence are blessed by God with help and extension of their agency, then those who choose nonviolence are (to use a phrase relatively common in the Book of Mormon) even "more blessed."[10] God encourages this "more blessed" and morally "more excellent way" (Ether 12:11). To put it all another way, God will stick with us in a variety of non-ideal choices, such as violent self-defense, but this does not imply that God thinks violent self-defense is best, and it is compatible with the view that God hopes we will grow into better uses of agency.

I said above that in Boyce's monotonic view, nonviolent people in the Book of Mormon either make a moral mistake by failing to fulfill a moral obligation, or they constitute some sort of rare exception to his view. We have seen that the book, in fact, does not defend a moral requirement or obligation to engage in defensive violence; let us turn now to the most stunning case of nonviolence in the Book of Mormon: the case of the Anti-Nephi-Lehies.

This group of people chose to respond to a violent attack with intentional, highly active nonviolence. When the Anti-Nephi-Lehies saw violent attackers approaching, they actively and agentically "went out to meet them," lay down on the ground, and began addressing God as the attackers arrived (Alma 24:21). Over a thousand of the nonviolent Anti-Nephi-Lehies were killed in the attack, maybe fewer than would have died responding with defensive violence. But even more remarkably, this communal nonviolent intentional action transformed many of the attackers themselves—the attackers, filled with remorse, gave up on violence. More than a thousand attackers changed sides and actually joined the nonviolent Anti-Nephi-Lehi community (Alma 24:22–27).

The case makes trouble for Boyce's view, since it morally valorizes nonviolence. Boyce has to attempt to say that there is nothing morally generalizable about this transformative nonviolence: He seems to hope that the narrative says nothing to call into question his claim that defensive violence is morally obligatory. Boyce thinks it is crucial that the Anti-Nephi-Lehies have a morally compromised past: They have committed wartime violence in the past, and it is this past that, in his view, puts them under a unique and rare obligation to *not* commit violence again, even defensive violence. Put another way, Boyce believes defensive violence is morally obligatory for everyone but former killers (and presumably not many of them; there are other former killers in the Book of Mormon that Boyce selectively and inexplicably does not worry about in the same way). Boyce seems revealingly urgent to treat the case of the Anti-Nephi-Lehies as exceptional and irrelevant to his view that defensive violence is obligatory. And it is no wonder he works so hard to dismiss the case: It is one of the most morally compelling narratives in the book, and it anticipates the twentieth-century moral breakthroughs of Gandhi and Martin Luther King Jr., who also advocated nonviolent action both to stop aggressive violence and to transform the hearts of the aggressors.

So the Book of Mormon offers cases of both defensive violence and nonviolence—cases where God assists with both. Which does the book favor? The answer is nonviolence. We have already seen that when people begin by using their agency to ask God, God consistently responds to that agency by recommending flight and escape and never commands a group to prepare for defensive violence. Pulsipher notes additional evidence. Captain Moroni$_1$, celebrated for his leadership in an intense campaign of defensive violence, brings about only five years of peace. A contrasting nonviolent endeavor has better results: Four brothers, sons of Mosiah, non-aggressively enter enemy territory and win the trust and renunciation of violence by thousands of people there.[11] Later, two brothers take a similar nonviolent strategy and win over eight thousand enemies, a period that is followed by centuries of peace between the Book of Mormon's two dominant warring factions; God extends the brothers' agency by intervening with miracles, an earthquake, and God's direct but mild voice (Helaman 5:18–34). Also important is that valorized figures in the book who use defensive violence earlier in their lives often foreswear it later. Pulsipher summarizes these and many other examples from the text: "Nonviolent strategies . . . are depicted as more efficacious, redemptive, accompanied by even greater miracles, and effective in achieving enduring peace."[12] In the Book of Mormon's narrative high point, the resurrected Jesus visits the book's people and re-emphasizes that loving one's enemies is a "more blessed" moral code. To use a modern example, the God of the Book of Mormon may help people violently resist the Nazis when they choose to, but what he wants is more of the active, nonviolent protection of the people of Le Chambon.[13]

In sum, God in the Book of Mormon honors the agency of people, provided they are choosing somewhere within the range of morally permissible actions, even when they do not make morally preferable choices. Intriguingly, the text explicitly says in multiple places that God "granteth unto men according to their desire" (Alma 29:1–4; see Jacob 4:14; 3 Nephi 28:1). God expects us to think about and learn from God's extension of people's agency and desires, to think and learn about their downstream consequences and the upstream character and desires from which human agency proceeds.[14]

How far can we take this reading of the Book of Mormon as a gospel of agency? I am not sure. Maybe we should even consider reading it this way from an instance of violence in its very first pages. In those first pages, Nephi₁ and his family flee from threatened violence. When Nephi₁ stumbles at night across a drunk and seemingly unconscious Laban, the first thing Nephi₁ notices is Laban's sword, and the first thing Nephi₁ does is draw it out and look at it—at its gold, at its craftsmanship, at its hard blade (1 Nephi 4:9). Does what happens next indicate God's extension of Nephi₁'s desires—Nephi₁'s desires about gold and blades and his gut response to Laban's theft and death threat (1 Nephi 3:13, 3:24–27)? We might wonder what would have happened for the thousand years after had Nephi₁ not had these desires and gut responses. We might wonder, and be asked by the book to wonder, what other agency God would have extended, and extended more eagerly. On a reading of the Book of Mormon as a gospel of agency, maybe God expects us to interpret its thousand years of human experience, saturated with Nephite wealth seeking and violence—gold and blades—as too insufficient a response to God's original call to Nephi₁'s family. God's original call is to flee from violence, and the family does. But Nephi₁ is not ready to leave all violence behind, so in that dark night with Laban, God aids Nephi₁'s defensive violence agency but leaves it to the reader to see its insufficiency. In the book's first pages, this first family heads in a good direction but is not fully on the best moral rails; and what happens in the rest of the Book of Mormon, immediately and then over a thousand years, reflects a first family that is already partly off the best moral rails.

Example Four: Responses to Three Antagonists

Next, consider differences among the narratives of three antagonists often grouped together as the Book of Mormon's "Anti-Christs": Sherem, Nehor, and Korihor. All three promote views at odds with the book's favored moral and spiritual leaders (Jacob₂ in the first case and Alma₂ in the second two cases[15]). Those leaders and the community respond variously to moral and spiritual threats. Paying attention to those responses yields important insights that match my claim that the Book of Mormon offers a gospel of agency.[16]

Korihor, explicitly called an "Anti-Christ" in the text, denies that Jesus Christ will come for the remission of human sins. Instead, he argues that society should function as a bald and unforgiving meritocracy, that there is no afterlife, and that no human action is really any sort of crime (Alma 30:6, 30:15–18). Korihor is "bound up" more than once because of these teachings and finally brought to the high priest Alma₂ (Alma 30:29). The text makes clear at the beginning of the narrative that the Nephite law of this period had "no law against a man's belief" and instead punished only actions like murder and other physical actions (Alma 30:7–11). So the binding of Korihor—something like an arrest—presents Alma₂ with a choice to make: a choice about whether there should be any punishment of Korihor at all and, if so, whether the punishment should come from the human political community or from God. The dialogue between Korihor and Alma₂ includes challenges about truth claims, and Alma₂ says that Korihor is actually lying about his unbelief. Korihor asks for a sign, and Alma₂ pronounces that the sign will be a silencing of Korihor by God. The text says that "when Alma had said these words, Korihor was struck dumb, that he could not have utterance, according to the words of Alma" (Alma 30:50). A natural reading here is that this silencing marks God's extension of Alma₂'s brisk agency. Alma₂ has chosen the form of response itself and claims no particular revelation in the text about what that form should be, but God carries it out collaboratively anyway.

What happens to Korihor after the silencing? Korihor confesses (in writing) that he was lying about his unbelief to promote his own success and eventually became convinced by his own lies (Alma 30:52–53). But as Deidre Nicole Green notes, there is no indication in the narrative that Korihor's confession is made public.[17] After confessing, Korihor requests a reversal of the silencing, but Alma$_2$ denies Korihor's request, and here God honors Alma$_2$'s agency again: Korihor still cannot speak. With his career as a moneymaking sophist at an end, a silenced Korihor must resort to begging for food, and he dies by some sort of trampling (Alma 30:58–60).

What happens more broadly in the community after the silencing? There's relatively little to celebrate. In the next verse following Korihor's death, Alma$_2$ is sickened by the continuing "iniquity of the people" (Alma 31:1) and struggles to address it in the subsequent chapters. In the decades after Korihor's death, Alma$_2$'s community faces protracted wars involving "great slaughter," arriving at no more than a shaky peace. The community lives "in great fear, lest they should be overpowered, and trodden down, and slain, and destroyed" (Helaman 4:20). So in sum, the silencing of Korihor does not correlate with good consequences for the community.

The story of Nehor, a second antagonist, has some similarities to Korihor's: Nehor is a popular teacher with a lucrative set of false claims. Nehor does not stop merely at teaching moral and spiritual falsehoods: He commits a clear social crime when he kills a man (the same Gideon who enacted nonviolent escape for Limhi's community) for speaking out against him. Nehor's subsequent legal punishment and death are not followed by good consequences for the community (Alma 1:16). As Green observes, the text suggests that the success of Nehor's specific teachings and lucrative false claims represent "a failing of a society of people who crave false doctrine rather than a problem traceable solely to the false teachers themselves."[18] The silencing of Korihor and Nehor leads to little or no transformation toward a better life for the people in these communities. The silencing of Korihor and Nehor does little for either community's well-being or moral development.

For a case of a treatment of an antagonist that *does* result in the community's well-being and positive moral development, Green points to intriguing details about Sherem, a third antagonist (Jacob 7:1–23). Green thinks it is telling in the first place that Jacob$_2$, a religious leader of Sherem's day, does not himself use the boldly accusatory term "Anti-Christ" for Sherem. Instead and remarkably, Jacob$_2$ gives Sherem something like the last word in Jacob$_2$'s brief writings. Sherem's teachings share content with the teachings of Korihor and Nehor, the other smooth-talking sophists. But Jacob$_2$'s agency and specific responses in an encounter with Sherem are notably different from Alma$_2$'s—and so are the encounter's consequences.

Sherem, like Korihor, demands a sign from God that Jacob$_2$'s claims about the future coming of Christ and his atonement are true. But unlike

Alma$_2$, Jacob$_2$ does not pronounce a silencing from God on Sherem. Jacob$_2$'s agency is more modest. "What am I that I should tempt God to show unto thee a sign?" he says. Jacob$_2$ chooses to leave it to God whether there is to be any sign at all (Jacob 7:14). God honors Jacob$_2$'s choice with a sign that does not silence Sherem. The sign arrives in a form of physical weakness that preserves Sherem's capacity to speak. Physically weakened but finally resolving to speak the truth, Sherem asks for the community to gather, and "he spake plainly unto them and denied the things which he had taught them, and confessed the Christ" (Jacob 7:17). Even the end of Sherem's life is described in less severe and more voluntarist language than Korihor's and Nehor's: Sherem "gave up the ghost" (Jacob 7:20).

What happens more broadly in the community after the non-silenced Sherem speaks both his original teachings and then later his retraction? The answer is that "peace and the love of God was restored again among the people, and they searched the scriptures" (Jacob 7:23). Not everything becomes perfect and external threats remain (Jacob 7:24–25), but the community becomes better. In this flowering of peace and the love of God, the text notes a special extension of another instance of Jacob$_2$'s agency. When the people are listening to Sherem's retraction, Jacob$_2$ says that he prayed for God's help for what he thought he could not achieve on his own—help such that the people would come to realize that Sherem's teachings were false (Jacob 7:22). Green notes that Jacob$_2$ is humble and brave enough to let the work of moral transformation occur not through Jacob$_2$'s own voice and testimony but instead through the voice of Sherem, his unsilenced former antagonist. Green says, "Jacob's humility before Sherem and the Nephites eventually elicits their humility, which allows reconversion."[19]

The observation here is not that Alma$_2$ did the wrong thing to Korihor or Nehor—God honored both Alma$_2$'s agency and Jacob$_2$'s agency, just like God honors different responses to violence. The observation is rather the compelling—and in some ways frightening and challenging—point that God is prepared to honor a broad range of human agency in this book of scripture and, further, that God honors our agency by asking for readers' hard work and perceptiveness in watching the various ways God cooperates with human agency.

More broadly, note that the Book of Mormon itself does not silence these three antagonists. The book ensures that we readers know details about what the three antagonists taught and why they were persuasive. In that way, the text is non-paternalistic—it does not hide these dangerous ideas from us—and, accordingly, it opens up space for our own thinking and agency. In noting these dangerous ideas, and in offering us different human agentic responses to dangerous ideas and the antagonists who promote them, the Book of Mormon offers a gospel of agency.

Additional Examples

There are many other instances of God extending agency in the Book of Mormon. Consider several additional brief examples.

The Liahona is an intriguing material instance. Early in the Book of Mormon, when the book's first family is leaving Jerusalem, they discover outside a tent door an unusual brass ball (named the "Liahona" later in the text) that can provide geographical directions and apparently other kinds of guidance (1 Nephi 16). The Liahona, a gift from God, successfully operates only once the family exercises righteous agency, and then it responds to that agency by pointing the way to resources and better circumstances. Like the stones God lit for Jared's brother, here God extends human agency through a material object, handed over for human use—perhaps like the material object of the Book of Mormon itself.[20]

For another example, Alma$_2$ invites his listeners to "experiment" with his words—to "awake and arouse your faculties," to "experiment," to "exercise a particle of faith," and "even if ye can no more than desire to believe, let this desire work in you" (Alma 32:27). Alma$_2$ promises that God imparts experiment-worthy words to everyone—men, women, and children—and that the agency of performing this "experiment" leads to increased faith, an enlightened understanding, and "fruit" that is sweet and satisfying (Alma 32:22–43). The promise is that God will extend the agency of human experiments with faith, knowledge, and truth, and will help fill human hearts with new and better desires.[21]

Most important of all, as an honoring of the agency of countless people across the book's first six hundred years, Jesus Christ himself comes to visit (3 Nephi 11–27). In response to his teachings, the people choose and act well. And God in turn extends that agency by helping the people achieve two hundred years of peace, justice, egalitarian prosperity, and the absence of racial and ethnic tensions (4 Nephi 1:1–23). There may be no more stunning evidence in the book for the power of good moral action than these two hundred years.

A Non-Consequentialist Moral Vision

Morality and ethics in the Book of Mormon includes all three classic factors in philosophical ethics: consequences, but also action types and virtuous motives and character. In the cases above I have drawn attention to the *consequences* of different choices and God's extension of those choices. I have pointed to downstream consequences as a way to consider what we can learn from the Book of Mormon about morally adequate versus morally preferable ways of choosing and acting. I have done this for two reasons. The first reason is simplicity: Consequences are not the only factor, and often not the most important factor, relevant to morality and ethics, but they are straightforward. The second reason is that the authors themselves in the book often use consequentialist locutions, from "it came to pass" to "and thus we see" followed by some didactic observation. But the ethics of the Book of Mormon is not fundamentally consequentialist. There are other factors in the book besides consequences that are relevant to morality and ethics.

One way to see this is to notice cases where God does *nothing* to participate in cases of human agency: There are cases where human agency is used so abhorrently that God does not honor it by contributing to its extension in any way. Most obvious is the end of the book, when two factions fight a war of attempted annihilation against one another (Mormon 6). The action types in this final war are overwhelmingly abhorrent. The atrocities include rape, murder, and cannibalism (Moroni 9). Mormon$_2$ notes in a letter to his son that he fears that "the Spirit of the Lord hath ceased striving with them" (Moroni 9:4). And for a period of time, Mormon$_2$ follows God's example and withdraws his own extension of his people's agency: Mormon$_2$ withdraws from helping with their wartime actions (Mormon 3:11). Where God does not extend agency, there is a reason (even if it is a defeasible reason) to ask whether the chosen action type is simply morally wrong, simply morally impermissible—too wrong (if we can think of wrongness as having degrees) for God to help human beings progress toward better agency by extending it. Even if the consequences and outcomes of these action types were somehow beneficial, the action types would themselves remain impermissible and wrong.

There are also cases where God recommends *against* human action types that would seem to promote better consequences and outcomes. In Alma 14, God's Spirit tells Alma$_2$ to refrain from attempting to rescue innocents from mass violence. The story is disturbing. But however else readers should think about the case, the reasons behind the Spirit's recommended non-intervention seem more about longitudinal justice, a more deontological and theological matter, than consequences and outcomes.

Other examples are common. In the Book of Mormon, God does not honor non-defensive violence or political power grabs or various other action types, even if these action types were to somehow lead to better consequences. And the book is often concerned with justice in ways that are hard to read in consequentialist terms. To summarize the last three paragraphs in the jargon of contemporary philosophical ethics, in the Book of Mormon there are moral "deontological" constraints against maximizing good consequences: Certain action types are simply morally wrong, no matter what the consequences are.

So consequences and deontological action types are two separable factors in the Book of Mormon's moral vision—morality is about more than consequences. A third factor is the moral goodness of the motives and character of people exercising agency—the motivational wellsprings of both consequences and action types. The book worries about the impact on people's character of certain action types.[22] For instance, we saw above that an important part of the case of the Anti-Nephi-Lehies was not just the outcome of the number of lives saved through nonviolence but the upstream positive moral transformation in the desires and character of the original aggressors. The moral character of the victims also matters: Mormon$_2$ recounts the case in consequentialist terms, with more individuals saved than slain (Alma 24:21–27). But even if the numbers had gone the other way, what makes the victims' actions morally admirable is their faithfulness to their covenantal and promissory commitment to not commit violence. In sum, moral formation, motive and character transformation, and virtuous faithfulness define the case of the Anti-Nephi-Lehies beyond and beside the numbers and consequences.

As another instance of moral character, the Book of Mormon even hypothetically (if only hypothetically) entertains the striking idea that were God to support injustice, or were God to be broadly inconsistent in his relations with human beings, God would "cease to be God" (Alma 42:13, 42:22–25; Mormon 9:19). The book's moral vision attends not just to downstream consequences but also to the upstream virtues and character traits of human agents and divine agents.

So the Book of Mormon's ethical visions include consequences, deontological action types, and virtuous character: all three of the standard set of elements of contemporary philosophical ethics. The book indicates that for God to extend one's agency, one must be acting morally permissibly—that is, acting above some baseline threshold of moral rightness and decency. This threshold of moral rightness is not determined by the consequences of the action type alone. One's action type need not be supererogatory (that is, beyond mere morality obligation) in order for God to extend one's agency, but one's action type must be above a minimal moral threshold.

A Gospel of Agency

Terryl Givens says the Book of Mormon has been taken as important more for its existence than its content.[23] Few of the doctrines associated with the Nauvoo era of LDS history are present in the text. Instead of doctrines of premortal existence (barely there), deification, and vicarious work for the dead, we find human experience and agency and God working with experience and agency. But I believe that those narratives of human experience and agency and God working with them—and our engagement and discovery of this key point and purpose of the Book of Mormon—give the book a particular ethical strength. I have been revealing a reading of the Book of Mormon as a gospel of agency—a book that talks about agency (2 Nephi 2) but, importantly, a book that also walks its own talk.[24] In this reading, the book invites our attentiveness to the ways God interacts with human choices—abjuring some human choices, directly honoring others, and extending some choices more than others. Through this invitation—and this is crucial—the book develops and builds the reader's own agency and choice-making capacities. In an introduction to the Book of Mormon, Joseph Smith is quoted as saying that it is "the most correct of any book on earth."[25] Maybe among the reasons it is the most correct of any book is its gospel of agency and its specific initiation of readers into exercising their own moral interpretive agency.

This approach to reading the Book of Mormon may not be obvious at first. But examples in the text that support it are plentiful. The book whispers the gospel of agency from the dust of its challenging length and prose (2 Nephi 26:16)—it certainly does not scream—and maybe this is because the book wants us to exercise *our* agency in reading it as well. The book needs us to make interpretive choices before it—and God—can work on and extend our interpretive agency.

An entailment of this approach is that the Book of Mormon does not therefore offer a single, unified view about the moral issues it takes up. There exists not *one* Book of Mormon view on a given moral issue but instead a plurality of views, some bad and some permissible and some better, and this plurality is a guided invitation for readers to exercise their own agency in determining what to do. When Richard Hays published a book called *The Moral Vision of the New Testament* in 1996,[26] I wondered what a similar project about the Book of Mormon should look like and began thinking about writing a similarly titled book (although with different priorities than Hays) about the Book of Mormon. I thought that the title would have to turn plural; it would need to be called *The Moral Visions of the Book of Mormon*.

So the Book of Mormon is a distributed version of God's invitation to Jared's brother that we encountered above in the case of the lit stones: The Book of Mormon asks each reader, "What will ye that I should do" to extend your agency—what will *you petition this book's resources to do?* The Book of Mormon does not allow *any and all* reader interpretations, and among those it permits, it favors some over others. But it does actively, if gently, invite its use toward a constrained set of good (and better than merely good) endeavors. My interpreting allies and opponents all put the Book of Mormon to work. I mean this about Grant Hardy, about Duane Boyce and David Pulsipher, about Deidre Nicole Green, and I mean it about myself. What views and choices do we want the book and God to honor and extend? Why do we want the Book of Mormon to be doing the work we think it is doing? The things we want from the text, the things you want from the text—what do these things say about us as interpreters and about our own moral character? As the saying goes, a good book reads you.[27]

Notes

1. I characterize the methodology of the chapter as an instance of Rawlsian reflective equilibrium.

2. My interpretive aim is in line with this observation from Elder Dale G. Renlund, a member of the LDS Quorum of the Twelve Apostles: God's "goal in parenting is not to have His children *do* what is right; it is to have His children *choose* to do what is right and ultimately become like him." Dale G. Renlund, "Choose You This Day," https://www.churchofjesuschrist.org/study/general-conference/2018/10/choose-you-this-day.p9?lang=eng#p9.

3. Noting the similarities and differences between the two escapes has been popular in various commentaries on the Book of Mormon. For one example, see Grant Hardy, *Understanding the Book of Mormon: A Reader's Guide* (New York: Oxford University Press, 2010).

4. Are the transgressions sufficient for God not extending the people of Limhi's agency? Or is it the combination of the people's transgressions and their violent means that is sufficient? Some evidence that it is not the violent means alone that are sufficient for God not extending the people of Limhi's agency appears in the discussion of defensive violence.

5. Often referred to outside the text as "Alma the Elder" but here simply "Alma$_1$."

6. Duane Boyce, *Even unto Bloodshed: An LDS Perspective on War* (Salt Lake City: Greg Kofford Books, 2015), 1.

7. J. David Pulsipher, "Defend Your Families and Love Your Enemies: A New Look at the Book of Mormon's Patterns of Protection," *Brigham Young University Studies Quarterly* 60, no. 2 (2021): 163–83. I thank David Pulsipher for this paper's significant influence on my reading of violence in the Book of Mormon and on God's extension of agency more broadly. An early influence on my view that God works with human beings to move them toward increasingly better moral views is Eugene England, *Making Peace: Personal Essays* (Salt Lake City: Signature Books, 1995).

8. Pulsipher, "Defend Your Families," 172.

9. Pulsipher, "Defend Your Families," 173.

10. Pulsipher ("Defend Your Families," 172) notes these instances of the term "more blessed": Alma 32:12–16; 3 Nephi 12:1–2, 28:1–11.

11. The four brothers enter enemy territory nonviolently, but complicating the story in an intriguing way is one brother's violence to defend the property of an enemy leader (Alma 17).

12. Pulsipher, "Defend Your Families," 177, 174–81.

13. For more on Le Chambon, see Philip Hallie, *Lest Innocent Blood Be Shed* (New York: Harper & Row, 1979).

14. Pulsipher, "Defend Your Families," 179–83.

15. Often referred to outside the text as "Alma the Younger" but here simply "Alma$_2$."

16. This reading of the Book of Mormon's three anti-Christs draws directly and heavily from Deidre Nicole Green. See Green, *Jacob: A Brief Theological Introduction* (Provo, UT: Neal A. Maxwell Institute for Religious Scholarship, BYU, 2020), 49–59.

17. See Green, *Jacob*, 54, carefully reading Alma 30:57.

18. Green, *Jacob*, 55, reading Alma 1:16.

19. Green, *Jacob*, 53.

20. Kimberly Matheson notes that, unlike the brother of Jared's lit stones, the Liahona is a material object that is more like the Book of Mormon itself. The brother of Jared came to God with a problem and some unlit stones, but in the case of the Liahona and the Book of Mormon itself, God lands a material object in human hands and asks (if only implicitly), "What will you do with that?" See Matheson's chapter, "Epic History, Ethical Pedagogy: The Book of Mormon's Scene of Instruction," for more on the ethical challenge that the Book of Mormon as a material object offers to its readers.

21. Joseph Spencer, "Is Not This Real?" *BYU Studies Quarterly* 58, no. 2 (2019): 87–104.

22. Relatedly, the book seems to worry about the character of its readers and its potential for and role in cultivating that character.

23. Terryl L. Givens, *By the Hand of Mormon: The American Scripture That Launched a New World Religion* (New York: Oxford University Press, 2002), 62–88.

24. I thank Meghan Busse for this locution.

25. This comment is reported by Wilford Woodruff in B. H. Roberts, ed., *History of the Church* (Salt Lake City: Deseret News, 1902) 4:461.

26. Richard B. Hays, *The Moral Vision of the New Testament: A Contemporary Introduction to New Testament Ethics* (New York: HarperOne, 1996).

27. Along with those already cited above, I thank Jim Faulconer, my Missionary Training Center president, for opening me up to an especially serious and close reading of the Book of Mormon. I also thank Joseph Spencer for his work and Courtney Campbell for very helpful comments on the whole chapter, and for pointing out specific additional cases of non-consequentialism. I also thank Apryl Martin, Thomas Sorensen, and Meghan Busse for helpful comments.

PART II

Practical Applications

8

Moral Agency, Resistance, and Resilience in the Story of the People of Anti-Nephi-Lehi

RACHEL ESPLIN ODELL

Any effort to establish a field of Book of Mormon ethics must grapple with the fraught moral relationship of the text to Indigenous peoples, given the book's nature as a text published by settler-colonialist Euro-Americans in nineteenth-century North America that claims to be an account of events and spiritual teachings in ancient America written by ancient Native Americans. Many scholars and activists in the Mormon studies field, such as Hokulani K. Aikau, Angelo Baca, Moroni Benally, Elise Boxer, Joanna Brooks, Gina Colvin, P. Jane Hafen, Michael Ing (a contributor to this volume), Farina Noelani King, Thomas Murphy, Sarah Newcomb, and Stanley Thayne, are engaged in that work, illuminating how the Book of Mormon functions as a settler-colonialist text and how Lamanite identity has been both a tool of erasure and a source of resistance for Indigenous peoples.[1] These efforts have been led by Indigenous scholars and activists, with contributions from some Euro-Americans who have performed ethnographic work centering the voices of Indigenous peoples. Their efforts to decolonize the Book of Mormon must be treated as foundational to the field of Book of Mormon ethics. This chapter—a close reading of how dynamics of moral agency, assimilation, and cultural resilience operate in the story of the people of Anti-Nephi-Lehi—is informed and inspired by their work and seeks to contribute to that foundational project.

I argue that, ironically, the dynamics of agency, resistance, and resilience in the story of the people of Anti-Nephi-Lehi subvert the Book of Mormon's frequent employment as an assimilation tool in modern Mormonism. I find that the people of Anti-Nephi-Lehi espouse a moral logic akin to that of contemporary revisionist war ethics, condemning killing in an unjust war as murder but permitting killing in a just war. This is juxtaposed against the Nephite narrators' more traditional just war ethic, which separates the justice of acts of killing in war from the justice of the war. Furthermore, the Nephite narrators superimpose an ethic of strict promissory obligation on the people of Anti-Nephi-Lehi that fails to reflect the people's confidence in the power of repentance and redemption. Despite these assimilating moves, the moral logic of the Anti-Nephi-Lehies, inculcated within families across generations, persists and becomes a source of community resilience, integrity, and resistance for future Lamanites.

My metaethical argument is that Euro-American Latter-day Saints (such as myself) whose ancestors colonized native lands and worked to assimilate Indigenous peoples, and who themselves have been inculcated in and perpetuated colonialist mind-sets and strategies, have a moral obligation to grapple with how the Book of Mormon has been and still is used as an assimilationist tool. This is especially true when Euro-American Latter-day Saints engage in analysis of how the Book of Mormon text deals with issues of indigeneity, Lamanite identity, and cultural or racial difference, as I do in this chapter. As a foundation for this metaethical argument, I have learned from Indigenous scholars the importance of stating my own positionality vis-à-vis the subject of my scholarship up front. I thus begin by acknowledging that I am deeply implicated in the history of Mormon settler colonialism by both inheritance and personal life experience. I am a multigenerational Euro-American Mormon, descended primarily from early Latter-day Saint converts who colonized Ute, Paiute, Goshute, Diné (Navajo), and Shoshone lands in the Great Basin, Rocky Mountains, and Colorado Plateau. My fourth great-grandfather, John Somers Higbee, was the president of the first Mormon colony in the Utah Valley in the territory of the Timpanogos band of Utes. He oversaw the building of Fort Utah in 1849, and his successor as bishop and brother, Isaac Higbee, co-orchestrated the massacre and enslavement of the Timpanogos band in 1850. My fourth great-grandfather, Isaac Chauncey Haight, was the LDS stake president who ordered the Mountain Meadows Massacre in 1857 and conspired in efforts to blame it on Paiutes. Rachel Staley Worthington, my third great-grandmother and one of my namesakes, together with her husband, James, was among the first Mormon missionaries to the Goshute tribe at Ibapah in western Utah in 1860, with their son and my great-great-grandfather, Stephen, operating freight and mail routes, including the Pony Express, and building stage and train routes from Salt Lake through Goshute lands to California.[2] Some of my ancestors were members of the Hole-in-the-Rock expedition that colonized the San Juan River Valley in the 1880s, a site of ongoing efforts by white Latter-day Saints to disenfranchise Diné and other Native American voters and shrink the Bears Ears National Monument in order to exploit the natural resources of ancestral Native lands.[3] My family participated in the LDS Church's Indian Student Placement Program in its waning years when I was preschool-age, hosting a Shoshone-Bannock teenager in our home from the nearby Fort Hall Indian Reservation. As a child, I was also an avid consumer of the Book of Mormon and the associated cultural products and discourse surrounding it, including those that speculatively linked Book of Mormon peoples and places to Native American peoples and places with little regard for the intrinsic value of Indigenous peoples' own inherited origin stories.

Through experiences in adulthood living in diverse places and engaging with diverse people, studying and researching the history of colonialism, critically analyzing my assumptions and biases, and advocating for ethics in government and society, I have been motivated to reckon with my personal and inherited identity as a colonizer and to begin to participate in the decolonization of my faith tradition. This is why I have elected to engage in a close reading of the Book of Mormon's story of the people of Anti-Nephi-Lehi, synthesizing my academic work on war and peace in international relations with my commitment to decolonizing Mormonism and the Book of Mormon as a form of intergenerational reparation. I preface this analysis with a reflection on the metaethics of Book of Mormon study as it relates to indigeneity, situating my analysis within that metaethical context.

Narrative Interpretation as a Metaethical Mode of Decolonizing the Book of Mormon

As implied in the preceding introduction, I engage in narrative interpretation of the Book of Mormon text in the vein of Grant Hardy.[4] As Hardy notes, unlike the Hebrew Bible, the Book of Mormon is a text with narrators (self-identified in the text as Nephi₁, Mormon₂, and Moroni₂), who claim to be summarizing and at times quoting from primary materials such as previously written histories, letters, sermons, and speech transcripts. Hardy observes, "Under close scrutiny, [the Book of Mormon] appears to be a carefully crafted, integrated work, with multiple narrative levels, an intricate organization, and extensive intratextual phrasal allusion and borrowings." This "multilayered" quality of the Book of Mormon opens up abundant possibilities for complex interpretation of how the different voices in the text relate to one another and adopt varying beliefs, worldviews, and modes of moral reasoning.

I will treat the text as a multilayered narrative work in order to uncover messages about cultural assimilation, resistance, and resilience that are unexpectedly embedded in the text, visible underneath the narrators' (or Joseph Smith's) own prejudices and paternalism. This approach is compatible with a plurality of beliefs about the text's origins; for example, one could believe it to be a record of ancient peoples in the Americas that was transmitted and translated through supernatural power, or a narrative manifestation of the cultural ideas and norms of nineteenth-century America as they took shape in the mind of Joseph Smith and his social network.

That is not to say the Book of Mormon's historicity is not an important question. In fact, since the book's claim to historicity has itself been used as a tool by white Euro-Americans for assimilating Indigenous peoples by supplanting their own origin stories, this is an essential question. Bracketing the Book of Mormon's historicity too completely risks perpetuating a contemporary assimilation dynamic similar to the one I identify in the book's own narrative. However, many stories in the Book of Mormon, including that of the people of Anti-Nephi-Lehi, depict marginalized people exercising moral agency to resist erasure by dominant groups, thereby subverting the Book of Mormon's use as an assimilation tool in modern Mormonism and illustrating how distinctive moral frameworks provide a resource for group identity preservation across generations. Identifying these dynamics of agency, resilience, and resistance within the Book of Mormon can be an important means of grappling with the fraught metaethical history of the Book of Mormon. At the same time, this is only one such method and to insist upon this approach to the text would itself be a form of colonial oppression.[5]

Rather, Indigenous scholars and activists have highlighted that there are many ways to decolonize the Book of Mormon, and they are not all mutually exclusive. One line of effort is to research and explain the evidence for the Book of Mormon being a nineteenth-century Euro-American text in order to render its nature as a settler-colonialist artifact clear.[6] This effort can involve illustrating how the external imposition or internal adoption of Book of Mormon narratives and identities has caused harm, while creating space for centering the origin stories of Indigenous peoples.[7] Another approach is to recount ways that Book of Mormon narratives and identities such as Lamanites, children of "Father Lehi," or descendants of the House of Israel have been used as a source of power, solidarity, and resistance by Indigenous Mormon converts whose own native traditions and origin stories had already been violently repressed by prior colonizers, as a source of solidarity across different groups of Indigenous Mormons, or as a source of resistance against the assimilating pressures of Euro-American Latter-day

Saint Church leadership.[8] This approach can involve tracing how contemporary LDS Indigenous communities have created syncretic traditions to integrate their own peoples' origin stories with LDS and Christian concepts, including those found in the Book of Mormon.[9] Another approach is to highlight possible influences by Native Americans in early nineteenth-century upstate New York on Joseph Smith and on the stories and ideas in the Book of Mormon itself, recognizing the earlier role of Indigenous peoples in crafting forms of Christian-Indigenous syncretic traditions that were echoed in the Book of Mormon.[10] A potential related line of effort is to press the Church of Jesus Christ of Latter-day Saints leadership to recognize that to the extent the Book of Mormon claims to be an ancient American text, it ought to be recognized as the intellectual property of the Seneca Nation and the Iroquois Confederacy, from whose land it purports to have come, and to repatriate artifacts that allegedly accompanied the golden plates on which the Book of Mormon was inscribed to the Seneca Nation.[11]

Yet another approach is to de-literalize the Book of Mormon, recognizing that the potential value of the text—much like many cultures' origin stories—does not lie in whether its events actually occurred.[12] This lattermost approach can be coupled with an effort to deconstruct the text itself, separating the Book of Mormon from its paratext and the narrative that Smith and subsequent primarily white, Euro-American church leaders have told about it, in order to search for and center the voices of marginalized peoples in the text itself. Such an exercise surfaces how the Book of Mormon's more racist, sexist, and colonialist narratives are unsettled by the text's own subaltern dynamics.[13] This chapter operates in such a mode.

In a final interpretive move, this approach can then be linked back to efforts to illustrate the nineteenth-century origins of the text by demonstrating how the colonialist, racist, and sexist oppression in the text and the subaltern's means of resisting that oppression echo similar dynamics in nineteenth-century America. Angelo Baca's imagining of Samuel₂ the Lamanite and Eduardo Pagan's analysis of the evidence for a segregated society in the Book of Mormon operate in this mode, demonstrating that these various methods of decolonization are not mutually exclusive. Other commentators engage in this process of deconstruction while avoiding that final move of linking the text's power dynamics to nineteenth-century America attitudes. This avoidance is sometimes overt, at other times evident though unstated. In all cases it is likely deliberate, whether out of genuine belief in the text's ancient status or out of a desire to make the analysis legible and accessible to believers; to avoid imposing any one way of belief, including on Indigenous Latter-day Saints who embrace the text's historicity and their identity as Lamanites, children of Father Lehi, or descendants of the House of Israel; and in some cases, to render the text acceptable to the LDS Church's official publishing and educational institutions.

In this chapter, I devote most of my attention to narrative interpretation, but in the conclusion, I make an initial, partial effort to link that interpretation back to its nineteenth-century context. A more complete effort would seek to identify debates about the ethics of war in Joseph Smith's own time and prevailing perceptions among Euro-American settlers in upstate New York of how Native Americans thought about war and peace. It would be especially important to analyze the ethical teachings and stories of the Haudenosaunee (and the Seneca specifically) as the Indigenous peoples whose land the Smith family occupied and who still lived and traveled in the area at the time of Smith's upbringing—a time when, according to his mother, Smith often shared tales about "Indians" even before dictating the Book of Mormon text.[14] Foundational stories of the Haudenosaunee include tales of Hiawatha and the Peacemaker, of warring groups who set aside violent ways—signified by literally burying their weapons—which could have served as an inspiration for the story of the people of Anti-Nephi-Lehi.[15]

The Story of the People of Anti-Nephi-Lehi and Debates about Its Ethic of Nonviolence

The story of the people of Anti-Nephi-Lehi is one of the more dramatic tales in the Book of Mormon. Mormon$_2$, the book's titular military and religious leader, who narrates events that took place among groups of people called Lamanites and Nephites hundreds of years before his day, tells of a group of Lamanites who convert to the gospel of Jesus Christ after hearing the preaching of a group of Nephite missionaries, who happen to be the sons of a Nephite king. As a sign of their conversion, they rename themselves the people of Anti-Nephi-Lehi and bury their weapons of war rather than use them against a different group of Lamanites that, incited by dissident Nephites, is poised to attack them. The people of Anti-Nephi-Lehi do not fight back against the attack, and over one thousand of them are killed before the attackers stand down. Later, those same converts want to take up arms to help defend the Nephites against attack, but they are compelled not to by Nephite leaders who do not want the converts to break their covenant. Instead, the Nephite leaders accept two thousand sons of that group to form a special band under the command of the Nephite prophet-general Helaman$_1$ to fight in their defense, reasoning that those sons had not made the same covenant. The sons have faith they will be protected by

God according to the teachings of their mothers, and, miraculously, none of them are killed in subsequent battles.

The story of the people of Anti-Nephi-Lehi has often been cited—and debated—as an example of pacifism in the Book of Mormon. Many commentators have hailed the people of Anti-Nephi-Lehi as the text's shining exemplars, standing as a rebuke to others, Nephites and Lamanites alike, who participate in and perpetuate endless cycles of violence.[16] In rebuttal, Duane Boyce has argued that the Anti-Nephi-Lehies were not actually pacifists—as evident in their willingness to take up arms to defend their Nephite allies—and in any case are the exception that proves the rule, demonstrating that the supreme moral principle related to war in the Book of Mormon is not pacifism but the state of the heart.[17] By this account, as long as one's heart is right before God and one does not glory in the shedding of blood, then war in defense of one's land and family is not only morally justified but required.

David Pulsipher argues that both pacifist and just war approaches to the story of Anti-Nephi-Lehi fail to adequately account for the moral bravery of the sons (in the case of pacifist interpretations) and the fathers (in the case of anti-pacifist or just war interpretations). He dubs this the "Ammonite Conundrum" (after the Nephite missionary who visited the people).[18] He argues that this conundrum can be resolved by rejecting a binary approach: that a range of different responses to violence can be morally acceptable, with "some partial and others more fully divine." Pulsipher's view is that the stance of the fathers represents that more fully divine approach, as they employed "weapons of love" akin to Gandhi's strategy of *satyagraha*. Patrick Mason and Pulsipher develop this idea more fully, citing other Latter-day Saint scripture published by Joseph Smith that clearly articulates a distinction between morally *justified* defensive violence under certain strict conditions and the morally superior, *sanctifying* stance of nonviolent forbearance.[19]

Angelo Baca, a Diné (Navajo) and Hopi scholar and activist, has critiqued the metaethical implications of the discourse about the people of Anti-Nephi-Lehi and their successor Samuel$_2$ the Lamanite, observing that "The 'good' Lamanite, in Mormon eyes, is the one who is a pacifist."[20] Baca's critique suggests that simplistic interpretations of the story of Anti-Nephi-Lehi facilitate the Book of Mormon's use as a tool to assimilate Indigenous peoples. The efforts by some Euro-American Mormon studies scholars to pedestalize the people of Anti-Nephi-Lehi as the ethical paragons of the Book of Mormon risk perpetuating these narratives, even if unintentionally. Such a narrative renders the Anti-Nephi-Lehies as objects constructed statically around the remarkable choices they made at one point in time—to bury their weapons of war and lay down their lives rather than to kill in self-defense—instead of seeing them as moral agents who continued to grapple with thorny ethical dilemmas throughout their lives. Although more recent scholarship, such as that of Boyce, Pulsipher, and Mason, has acknowledged the complex evolution of their choices, these authors have not critically interrogated the text's presentation of the story itself, much less grappled with how this story relates to the metaethical uses of the text in Mormon and Native American history.

In this chapter, inspired by Baca's metaethical critique, I seek to adopt a different approach to this story than preceding accounts. I do not use the example of the people of Anti-Nephi-Lehi to develop or refute a normative theory of pacifism or just war. Rather, I conduct a close reading of the moral agency and moral reasoning employed by the different people and groups in the Book of Mormon's story of the people of Anti-Nephi-Lehi as a lens through which to view intergroup dynamics of paternalism, resistance, assimilation, syncretism, and resilience. I do so by focusing on voice and narration, distinguishing between the voices of the Anti-Nephi-Lehies themselves and the voices of contemporary Nephites and later Nephite narrators. This does not require viewing the text as a historical account; this close reading is compatible with a literary interpretation of the narrative as fictional storytelling with different characters using distinct voices. At the same time, such a close reading is also compatible with a more historical interpretation. Indeed, seen from a devotional perspective, since the Book of Mormon narrators themselves warn that the record contains "the mistakes of men," an ethical approach to the Book of Mormon must seek to surface and center the voices of the marginalized in the text by identifying direct quotation of those voices whenever possible. When those quotations are not available—and even when they are—it is important to analyze how the text's Nephite scribes and narrators may have imputed Nephite ways of thinking or introduced anti-Lamanite bias into their descriptions of Lamanite behavior and motivations and even through their selective compilation of quoted material. The analyst must read between the lines and engage in a degree of context-based imagination to identify the possible motivations and perspectives of the Lamanites or Anti-Nephi-Lehies that are implied or unstated in the text.

Whereas previous interpretations of this account fail to disentangle the moral reasoning of Mormon$_2$ and Helaman$_1$ as narrators from that of the people of Anti-Nephi-Lehi themselves, I find that a close reading reveals that these two groups exhibit distinct modes of moral reasoning. Viewing their moral reasoning through the lens of contemporary debates on the ethics of killing in war, I argue that the people of Anti-Nephi-Lehi follow a moral logic akin to that of the revisionist or Oxford school of war ethics, in juxtaposition to a more traditional just war ethic espoused by Mormon$_2$ and Helaman$_1$. Moreover, I argue that Mormon$_2$ and Helaman$_1$ superimpose an ethic of strict promissory obligation on the people of Anti-Nephi-Lehi that those people never themselves articulate or endorse.

I also illustrate how both Mormon$_2$'s narration and Helaman$_1$'s contemporary account of the people of Anti-Nephi-Lehi reveal an attitude of paternalism and anti-Lamanite prejudice that leads them to ignore or misunderstand the moral reasoning and discount the moral agency of the people of Anti-Nephi-Lehi. Helaman$_1$ actively subordinates that moral agency in real time, while Mormon$_2$ does so more subtly in his retelling of the story. Helaman$_1$'s rejection of the people of Anti-Nephi-Lehi's moral reasoning and forceful denial of their moral agency transforms the fathers in that group from subjects to objects and renders the mothers' moral teachings to their sons superficially admirable but essentially misunderstood. Helaman$_1$'s substitutive paternalism toward the sons *appears*, by his and Mormon$_2$'s telling, to result in the assimilation of that second generation into the dominant Nephite cultural-ethnic group, signified when they begin to call themselves Nephites and ascribe to Helaman$_1$'s promissory moral logic.

However, a careful reading of the text also reveals that these dynamics of assimilation are neither so Nephite-controlled nor so complete as Mormon$_2$ and Helaman$_1$ would have us believe. The early Lamanites who convert to the gospel of Christ exercise their agency to embrace and construct a syncretic belief system that is deliberately independent and distinct from that of the Nephites. Moreover, despite the apparent assimilation of the so-called stripling warriors, the sons of the converted Lamanites, later generations of Lamanite converts to the gospel of Christ embrace the ethical commitments of the original people of Anti-Nephi-Lehi. This suggests that either the assimilation of the two thousand sons had not been complete or the unmentioned *daughters* of the people of Anti-Nephi-Lehi had remained unassimilated and continued to teach their children the same ethical commitments that their mothers had likely taught them alongside their brothers. Notably, those future generations reassert their identities as Lamanites, even while maintaining the syncretic belief systems of the Anti-Nephi-Lehies.

Seen in this light, the story of the people of Anti-Nephi-Lehi is not necessarily a tale of relations between pacifists living a higher law and more violent people living a lower law. Rather, it is a tale of a group of people that exercises moral agency to choose a new way of living and acting upon contact with a missionizing Other, while deliberately maintaining a distinct cultural identity. Central to their cultural resistance and resilience is the Anti-Nephi-Lehies' crafting of a syncretic moral code that selectively draws from and creatively adapts the Other's moral-cultural resources, integrating them with their own moral logics and transforming them through revelatory and agentic innovation. Meanwhile, the prejudicial and paternalistic mind-set of Nephite leaders both at the time of the Anti-Nephi-Lehies and hundreds of years later leads them to misunderstand or ignore the internal moral reasoning of another social group and discount their moral agency. The Nephites attempt a form of assimilation by exploiting a separation of the children of that group from their parents—a common tool used by colonizers to assimilate Indigenous peoples, including by Euro-American settlers toward native peoples of the Americas. And yet even in the Nephites' partial historical narrative, evidence emerges that this assimilation was ultimately unsuccessful as the Anti-Nephi-Lehies' syncretic faith and moral reasoning proves more resilient and is transmitted by Samuel$_2$ the Lamanite to the disbelieving and erring Nephites, reversing the missional direction.

In turn, these observations can be recursively applied to interpretations of the Book of Mormon itself. The story of the Anti-Nephi-Lehies reveals possibilities for how Indigenous and antiracist interpretations of the Book of Mormon text (and Mormon teachings more generally) can challenge dominant interpretations of the Book of Mormon text among Euro-American Mormons in the geographic core area of the Church of Jesus Christ of Latter-day Saints. While those dominant interpretations may glorify violence, embrace Christian nationalism, laud a prosperity gospel, or perpetuate racist paternalism, subaltern interpretations that disrupt those narratives and highlight ethical alternatives in the text have the potential to persist across generations, acting as the prophetic voice of warning to the dominant group.

Moral Agency, Cultural Resistance, and Intergenerational Resilience

The story of the people of Anti-Nephi Lehi is recounted in several chapters of the Book of Alma, the largest section of the Book of Mormon, with echoes in the words of Samuel$_2$ the Lamanite, a later Lamanite prophet, to the Nephites (Helaman 15). The books of Alma and Helaman are both narrated by Mormon$_2$, who the text describes as a prophet and general who lived and worked four centuries after the events in the account unfold, based on a body of historical texts and letters that he has become the steward of and seeks to abridge and summarize. Much of the account of the people of Anti-Nephi-Lehi is Mormon$_2$'s paraphrasing of the story. However, Mormon$_2$ directly quotes the words of two Lamanite kings and a Lamanite queen during their conversions (in Alma 18–20 and Alma 22), before they renamed themselves Anti-Nephi-Lehies, and also cites some primary texts, including a speech given by a subsequent king of the people of Anti-Nephi-Lehi (in Alma 24) and an epistle written by the Nephite general Helaman$_1$ to Moroni$_1$ (in Alma 56). Helaman$_1$'s epistle further quotes the words of the sons of the people of Anti-Nephi-Lehi (Alma 56:46, 56:48). Later, Mormon$_2$ quotes the words of Samuel$_2$ the Lamanite from a record of his preaching to the city of Zarahemla—one that may have been inscribed at the express order of the resurrected Christ when he visited the Americas and chastised the people for not recording Samuel$_2$'s words. These are the sources that I will closely examine below.

Several key elements of cultural resistance and resilience emerge in the story of the people of Anti-Nephi-Lehi, including moral agency, syncretism, identity, education (as an intergenerational and cross-gender endeavor), and iterative adaptation. These elements counteract the operation of the forces of assimilation, which include paternalism, refusing to use others' chosen names, family separation and parental erasure, denial of agency through refusing the right to choose, and imputing false motivations to others' acts through control of narrative history.

Throughout the story, the people of Anti-Nephi-Lehi and their forerunners and descendants demonstrate agency—in particular, moral agency—by choosing to take or not take certain actions based on ideas about right and wrong. A cursory reading of the story might suggest that those moral ideas are derived from the proselytizing message of the sons of the Nephite king Mosiah. Mormon$_2$ himself tells us that "thousands were brought to believe in the traditions of the Nephites" (Alma 23:5). However, a closer examination reveals that the Anti-Nephi-Lehies craft a moral reasoning that is distinct from that of their Nephite counterparts, a syncretic set of beliefs drawn from elements of their preexisting faith tradition, from critical reflection on their past and present, from Nephite teachings about redemption through Christ, and from direct ecstatic spiritual experience and divine revelation. Not only is their moral reasoning distinct, but also the Nephite narrator of their story (Mormon$_2$) and at least some of their contemporary Nephite interlocutors do not fully understand the Anti-Nephi-Lehies' moral reasoning, which—especially in the case of Helaman$_1$—contributes to the way the Nephites at times discount the moral agency of the Anti-Nephi-Lehies.

Agency Asserted: King and Queen Lamoni, Ammon, and Early Lamanite Conversions

The active role of the Lamanites in choosing their conversion to the gospel of redemption is evident from before the first encounter between the Lamanite king Lamoni and the Nephite missionary Ammon$_2$ even occurs. Lamoni already believes in the Great Spirit and perceives his people to be guilty of "murders," fearing they merit "great punishments" and that he also may have done wrong in slaying his servants (Alma 18:2–5). When Ammon$_2$ analogizes the Great Spirit to God and preaches that God created all things and knows the intents of the heart, Lamoni is quoted as saying, "I believe all these things which thou hast spoken." The immediacy of Lamoni's affirmation and the lack of any apparent struggle with dissonance could suggest that Ammon$_2$'s words resonate with Lamoni's previous conception of the Great Spirit. Thereafter, Ammon$_2$ shares additional teachings in three main categories: (1) the biblical origin story of creation, Adam and the fall, and the teachings of the prophets to the people of Israel until the time their shared ancestor Lehi left Jerusalem (Alma 18:36); (2) the Nephite narrative of the "journeyings of their fathers in the wilderness" since Lehi fled Jerusalem—including an account of "the rebellions of Laman and Lemuel, and the sons of Ishamel" and "all the records and scriptures" since that time—presumably all Nephite records (Alma 18:37–38); and (3) the plan of redemption and the prophesied coming of Christ (Alma 18:39).

After summarizing Ammon$_2$'s words in these areas to King Lamoni, Mormon$_2$ as narrator tells us that "the king believed all his words" (Alma 18:40)—but notably without directly quoting Lamoni. In other words, we do not know from Lamoni himself how he viewed everything that Ammon$_2$ taught, especially his narration of the Nephite version of their shared Lehite history. When the king later arises from his ecstatic stupor to testify in his own words of his divine vision, he declares that he has seen his Redeemer and affirms the Christian elements of Ammon$_2$'s teachings. However, we never see evidence that Lamoni embraced and then promulgated *all* of Ammon$_2$'s teachings, including the Nephites' biblical origin stories and their versions of Lehite history. Mormon$_2$ states that Lamoni began to teach his people "the words which he had heard from the mouth of Ammon," without specifying which words specifically (Alma 19:31). The only direct quotations of Lamoni's words do not include any reference to Ammon$_2$'s teachings at all but rather refer to his own direct personal divine encounter.

Likewise, when the queen later arises from her own ecstatic vision, she too testifies of Jesus's salvation and speaks "many words which were not understood." Mormon$_2$ does not tell us *who* did not understand them. The queen could have been speaking in tongues unintelligible to anyone present, but it is also possible she was speaking in a Lamanite tongue unintelligible to Ammon₂ but edifying to her fellow Lamanites, perhaps as a deliberate form of code-switching designed to attest to her independent agentic revelation unmediated by the Nephite other. The narrative introduces Abish, a "Lamanitish" woman who was a servant to the queen and had been converted without any intervention from Ammon₂ at all, years before his arrival, "on account of a remarkable vision of her father." When the king, queen, and Ammon₂ are all unconscious, overcome by their spiritual ecstasy, Abish takes the initiative to proclaim the working of God throughout her community (Alma 19:17); when the people quarrel over the meaning of the scene, she exercises the agency to rouse the queen to resolve the crisis (Alma 19:29). Thereafter, King Lamoni himself and other converts among Lamoni's household do the bulk of the early proselytizing in Lamoni's lands, testifying of their own direct experiences with the divine (Alma 19:31–36).

Although Ammon₂ continues to preach among King Lamoni's people, the text makes clear that Lamoni maintains the leading role among his people in governing the political and religious order. Lamoni orders the building of synagogues and the organizing of a church among his people; he "did teach them many things" and declare that they were "a free people" with the "liberty of worshiping the Lord their God according to their desires" (Alma 21:20–23). He also refuses to allow Ammon₂ to continue as his servant (Alma 21:19). The text does not tell us why Lamoni makes this choice. He may have been motivated by his genuine esteem for Ammon₂'s prophethood (Alma 20:15), but he also could have been aiming to introduce some respectful distance in his relationship with Ammon₂ to emphasize Lamoni's authority in teaching and governing his own people independent from Ammon₂.

In sum, Ammon₂'s role in the conversion of the Lamanites is less fundamental than it appears at first glance, in Ammon₂'s own account (discussed further below), or in the surface of Mormon₂'s narrative, which was based primarily on an inherited collection of Nephite records. Although Mormon₂ tells us that Ammon₂, "being wise, yet harmless," essentially tricked Lamoni into agreeing to believe all of his words, such that the king was "caught with guile" (Alma 18:22–23), Lamoni's exercise of such robust autonomy and agency before, during, and after his conversion renders this explanation implausible. This explanation is better understood as a Mormon/Nephite interpretation, one that emphasized the control and influence of Ammon₂ as a proselytizer and subtly discounted Lamoni's agency as a proselyte. It instead seems likely that Lamoni was the one who was wise in navigating this encounter, engaging with Ammon₂ to obtain the knowledge and activate the divine encounter for which he was yearning, even while carefully affirming his own independent spiritual and secular authority and ensuring indigenous ownership of the Redeemer-oriented spiritual awakening among his people.

Lamoni's Father, Aaron$_2$'s Greater Cultural Sensitivity, and the Choice of a New Name

A similar pattern bears out in the conversion of Lamoni's father, who is king over all the Lamanites, with some crucial differences that suggest possible learning among the Nephite missionaries or differences between Ammon$_2$ and his brother Aaron$_2$. After a dramatic encounter where the king nearly slays Lamoni and Ammon$_2$ after Lamoni tells his father of his conversion, and Ammon$_2$ fights the king in defense of Lamoni, the king is deeply impressed with Ammon$_2$'s love for Lamoni and with both Ammon$_2$'s and Lamoni's words (Alma 20:8–27). He rejects the offer of Ammon$_2$'s brothers to be his servants and instead insists that they expand on Ammon$_2$'s words (Alma 21:1–3). In reply, Ammon$_2$'s brother Aaron$_2$ delivers a catechism that partially resembles the one Ammon$_2$ delivered to Lamoni but differs in a crucial respect. Aaron$_2$ preaches of the creation and fall of Adam and the promised redemption through Christ, but he omits Ammon$_2$'s discourse on the Nephite version of their shared Lehite origin story. This could be a practical accommodation to Lamoni's father's particularly strong sense of grievance against the Nephites (Alma 20:10, 13). But considering how the Nephite historical narrative did not seem to have been embraced by Lamoni in his own preaching, it could also suggest that Ammon$_2$, Aaron$_2$, and their brothers had realized that this part of their message was culturally tone-deaf and had fallen flat among Lamoni's people and other Lamanites and Ama-lekites. Perhaps they realized that such a biased historical narrative was not fundamental to the gospel of redemption and would serve only to alienate the Lamanites. They may have even begun to learn from their Lamanite and Amalekite interlocutors in a process of mutual exchange, listening to their differing origin stories and historical narratives and awakening to their own inherited biases. For example, King Lamoni, who was sensitive to the potential to give offense to his father (Alma 20:11), may have advised Ammon$_2$ and his brothers to jettison those Nephite-centric messages.

Evidence for this interpretation may be found in Ammon$_2$'s discussion with his brothers in Alma 26. Although Ammon$_2$'s self-congratulatory paternalism is on full display (Alma 26:9, 26, 31), his brothers appear to be somewhat more self-aware as they gently chastise him for taking too much credit for the Lamanites' conversions (Alma 26:10). Ammon$_2$ also seems to have engaged in some learning, illustrated as he remembers how their fellow Nephites had mocked them prior to their missionary journey. He describes how the language of those naysayers had included several negative stereotypes about the Lamanites as being "stiffnecked," "delighting in the shedding of blood," spending their days "in the grossest iniquity," and how their "ways have been the ways of a transgressor from the beginning" (Alma 26:24). He cites how the Nephites had used those stereotypes to argue that instead of preaching to them, they should destroy them with force. Ammon₂ then professes that he and his brothers had a more enlightened view, desiring to save souls rather than destroy life (Alma 26:26), which forms the basis of his continued self-centered narrative of the privations they suffered through in their missionary journeys in pursuit of that enlightened goal. Finally, when Ammon₂ arrives at the point of describing the "fruits of our labors," he pivots to focus on the "sincerity" of those who converted and their "great love" and sacrifice. In so doing, he grants some credit to the people themselves, even though he simultaneously pedestalizes them to some extent, avowing that there has never been such "great love in all the land . . . even among the Nephites" (Alma 26:33). In using the word "even," Ammon₂ reflects his own implicit bias in his surprise that Lamanite righteousness could surpass that of the Nephites. This reveals some degree of learning by Ammon₂ as he realizes his previous assumptions were incorrect but also demonstrates that he is continuing to pedestalize the Anti-Nephi-Lehies.

Indeed, Ammon₂ never directly refutes the negative stereotypes that he attributed to his fellow Nephites, instead just expressing his belief in the need to convert rather than destroy. This suggests that some of those stereotypes may have appeared in his discourse to King Lamoni about Lehite history, which could explain why King Lamoni was so careful to maintain his own authority as his people's principal spiritual teacher and leader rather than ceding that ground to Ammon₂. Conversely, Aaron₂'s relative cultural humility and sensitivity could have been why Lamoni's father was more willing to place Aaron₂ and his brothers in a more prominent preaching role after his own conversion (Alma 22:26). This also may explain why Lamoni's father chose to counsel with Aaron₂, along with Lamanite priests, about choosing a new name for the people who had chosen to embrace the gospel of Christ (Alma 23:16).

As a result of that process, the people choose a new name for themselves—the Anti-Nephi-Lehies—that symbolizes their syncretism, neither Lamanite nor Nephite but something new, perhaps something against or prior to the distinctions that emerged among Lehi's sons and their descendants.[21] Whatever the meaning of the specific term, which is not explained in the text—possibly a motivated omission from this Nephite record if the name reflects negatively in some way on the Nephites—choosing this new name ensures the distinctness of their identity. It signals not only their desire to distinguish themselves from other Lamanites who have not converted to the redemption gospel but also their lack of intention to assimilate with the Nephites despite embracing some shared beliefs about redemption through Christ. This is underscored in the following verse, which notes that the people of Anti-Nephi-Lehi "were friendly with the Nephites" and "did open a correspondence with them" (Alma 23:18), phrasing that makes clear the groups remained separate despite establishing warmer relations.

Strategic Rhetoric and Moral Reasoning among King Anti-Nephi-Lehi and His People

Soon after the converts choose their new name, the king over all the Lamanites (i.e., Lamoni's father) prior to his death bestows the overall kingship on Lamoni's brother, whom he names King Anti-Nephi-Lehi. This succession takes place in a time of crisis, as the unconverted Amalekites, Amulonites, and Lamanites are staging a rebellion against the king and preparing to wage war against the Anti-Nephi-Lehies (Alma 24:1–4). Ammon$_2$ and his brothers request a council with King Lamoni and his brother, King Anti-Nephi-Lehi, to discuss how they might defend themselves against the imminent attack (Alma 24:5). It does not appear that such a council is actually granted. Instead, the Anti-Nephi-Lehies reject the premise of the requested council as they make clear to Ammon$_2$ and his brothers that "not one soul" among them intends to fight against "their brethren," the attackers, and that their king has, in fact, commanded them not to do so (Alma 24:6).

The narrative then includes a lengthy speech by King Anti-Nephi-Lehi justifying this commandment. This speech exhibits both strategic rhetoric and the unique moral reasoning underpinning this exercise of agency. The introduction in King Anti-Nephi-Lehi's speech contains language that, at a surface level, appears to place the Anti-Nephi-Lehies in a position of moral subordination or indebtedness to the Nephite missionaries:

> I thank my God, my beloved people, that our great God has in goodness sent these our brethren, the Nephites, unto us to preach unto us, and to convince us of the traditions of our wicked fathers. And behold, I thank my great God that he has given us a portion of his Spirit to soften our hearts, that we have opened a correspondence with these brethren, the Nephites. (Alma 24:7–8)

Considering the dynamics described above between Lamoni and Ammon$_2$ and Lamoni's father and Aaron$_2$, the people's deliberate choice of a name distinct from the Nephites (possibly one that connoted a rejection of the group divisions the Nephites embraced), and King Anti-Nephi-Lehi and Lamoni's apparent rejection of a war council with Ammon₂ and his brothers, this prefatory statement should be read critically. There had previously been references in this story to the sons of Mosiah₂ setting out with the objective, in part, of convincing the Lamanites of the "baseness" of the "traditions of their fathers" (Alma 17:9) and of the Lamanites supposedly being convinced of "the wicked traditions of their fathers" (Alma 19:14, 21:17, 23:3). This phrase and the mentality it represented had long been entrenched in prejudiced Nephite views of the Lamanites (see, for example, Enos 1:20; Mosiah 1:5; and Mosiah 10:11–17). Notably, the previous uses of this term in the story of the conversion of the Anti-Nephi-Lehies were not in direct quotations from Lamanite sources but rather in Mormon₂'s framing of events, which itself was heavily informed by Nephite records and Nephite biases (more on this below).

However, there had not previously been instances of Lamanite converts such as King Lamoni or his father directly decrying the "traditions" of their fathers using this same formulation (though they had acknowledged the sins of themselves and their people). King Anti-Nephi-Lehi's use of this term is thus unique. Why did he resort to this language? King Anti-Nephi-Lehi had no doubt been trained in the art of diplomacy. Thus, this may have been diplomatic language calculated to keep the sons of Mosiah₂ at bay and maintain their autonomy amid the sons' request for a council or, conversely, to obtain future assistance from or alliance with the Nephites by appealing to Ammon₂'s vanity. His fawning praise for the Nephites' role in "convincing" his people of the wicked traditions of their fathers was likely a ritualistic or strategic move, designed to do honor to the Nephite missionaries (who were also the sons of the Nephite king Mosiah₂) or gratify their pride. It is possible that King Anti-Nephi-Lehi knew something about Ammon₂'s attitudes toward his missionary efforts (evident in Ammon₂'s words to Lamoni in Alma 18:34–35 and in his discussion with his brothers in Alma 26, as described above). This in turn could have led him to appeal to Ammon₂'s sense of self-importance as God's instrument, recognizing that Ammon₂ was the leader of the sons of Mosiah₂ (Alma 17:18) and thus possessed power among them and potential political power among the Nephites as well. Of course, Lamoni at least did seem to hold Ammon₂ and his brothers in genuine esteem (Alma 20:15), so some expression of gratitude and love from his brother toward these men would not be unexpected. Rather than a strategic calculation, this could have been a cultural form among the Anti-Nephi-Lehies simply intended to bestow honor. At a minimum, however, there is no evidence that the king's reference to "wicked traditions" constitutes a wholesale rejection of their inherited origin stories, much less an embrace of the Nephite origin story. (Of course, despite being king over all the Lamanites, King Anti-Nephi-Lehi's views are not necessarily representative of those of all his people. In particular, he may simply have had a different mind-set than King Lamoni or their father and a different attitude toward the Nephite missionaries.)

At the same time, this introduction and the speech that follows do exhibit critical self-reflection on the Anti-Nephi-Lehies' past sins and that of their forebearers, especially the "many murders" they committed (a phrase the king repeats three times). This self-reflection echoes that expressed by King Lamoni prior to meeting Ammon$_2$ and by King and Queen Lamoni and Lamoni's father during their conversion processes (Alma 18:2, 18:5, 19:29, 22:15, 22:18). This critical self-reflection did not involve a wholesale embrace of the Nephites' moral reasoning, however. On the contrary, a close reading of King Anti-Nephi-Lehi's address compared to Mormon$_2$'s and later Helaman$_1$'s framing of the Anti-Nephi-Lehies' actions suggests that the moral reasoning King Anti-Nephi-Lehi espouses—particularly his ideas on violence and killing in war—differs from the moral logic of not only the Nephites but also from the logic that these Nephite military leaders ascribe to the Anti-Nephi-Lehies. In the context of their conversion to a gospel of redemption, which was the central message embraced by King and Queen Lamoni and Lamoni's father, the people of Anti-Nephi-Lehi embrace a moral logic that views their past violence (including in times of war) as sin, that embraces repentance in order to access atonement and redemption, and that commits to refrain from further killing as a testament or signifier of their repentance and redemption (Alma 24:10–16). This concern about the sinfulness of violence had been the central concern of Lamoni from before he met Ammon$_2$ and continues to manifest itself in his brother's moral logic. By contrast, Mormon$_2$ characterizes their moral logic as one of strict promissory obligation—a mechanistic covenant rather than a symbolic testament.

These alternate forms of moral reasoning also have implications for how they view the morality of killing in war. To cite distinctions in modern debates over the ethics of killing in war, the reasoning of King Anti-Nephi-Lehi in Alma 24 is more aligned with the revisionist critique of just war theory, which argues that killing in an unjust war cannot be morally justified. By contrast, the frame imposed on this speech by Mormon$_2$ in that same chapter, as well as the discussion of the stripling warriors by Helaman$_1$ and Mormon$_2$ later in the book of Alma, exhibits a more traditional just war ethic, which treats the morality of war separately from the justice of the war's cause.[22]

King Anti-Nephi-Lehi repeatedly refers to the killing that he and his people had enacted previously as "murders." In previous chapters in Alma, these same Lamanites had engaged in wars with the Nephites; moreover, Anti-Nephi-Lehi refers to weapons of war—large quantities of swords—rather than to knives or poisons more often used in individual homicides. To be sure, the king likely has in mind such individual murders, along with political executions—for example, of King Lamoni's servants at the waters of Sebus—as violence that must be foresworn. However, he also is clearly repudiating the past killings they conducted in war, dubbing them "murders." Framed using concepts from just war theory, this view of their past killing in war as murders represents a rejection of the moral equality of combatants. This idea, also repudiated in the revisionist critique of just war theory, holds that soldiers on all sides of a war are generally not individually liable for killing opposing soldiers, regardless of the justice of their side's cause for fighting the war. Moreover, King Anti-Nephi-Lehi refers to his people as a group, not excusing any of them (whether women, children, or otherwise) as innocents, but instead describing a collective guilt. Like the revisionist critique, this challenges the idea of noncombatant immunity in just war theory, which draws distinctions between armed forces that directly participate in violence and civilians that support the armed forces.

By contrast, Mormon₂, in his narration of and commentary on the story, never uses the word "murders" to describe the previous wars and killings of the converted Lamanites. The only time he uses the word "murders" is when the Lamanites kill 1,005 of the people of Anti-Nephi-Lehi, who at that point were enacting a nonviolent witness to God (Alma 24:25). Nor does Helaman₁ use this term. As hardened generals, weary of killing and—particularly in Mormon₂'s case—nihilistically unconvinced of the justice of any of the killing surrounding him and even, presumably, perpetrated by his own hand, they do not discriminate between just and unjust killing in war in the same way that Anti-Nephi-Lehi and his people do.

Instead of espousing the same ethical reasoning that King Anti-Nephi-Lehi articulates, these Nephite leaders frame the commitments of the Anti-Nephi-Lehies not to take up arms in terms of a strict sense of promissory obligation grounded in a natural law sensibility, which may in turn be distinguishable from a more utilitarian or conventional view of promissory obligation among the people of Anti-Nephi-Lehi, as evident in their later willingness to take up arms in defense of their Nephite allies (see further discussion below). For example, after quoting the speech of King Anti-Nephi-Lehi, Mormon₂ interpolates his own interpretation of the king's explanation for why they were burying their swords:

And this they did, it being in their view a testimony to God, and also to men, that they never would use weapons again for the shedding of man's blood; and this they did, vouching and covenanting with God, that rather than shed the blood of their brethren they would give up their own lives; and rather than take away from a brother they would give unto him; and rather than spend their days in idleness they would labor abundantly with their hands. (Alma 24:18)

Mormon₂'s refusal to acknowledge the essence of the reasoning used by King Anti-Nephi Lehi reflects his failure to ascribe them full moral agency and moral reasoning powers. He attributes their choice not to take up arms to the oath they had taken rather than to their desire to avoid murder. He reduces their moral reasoning—which was grounded in a logic of sin, repentance, redemption, and testament—to one of promissory obligation. Mormon₂'s interpretive comment also reveals the paternalistic prejudice of Mormon₂ toward Lamanites generally, including the people of Anti-Nephi-Lehi, by ascribing to them a preexisting tendency toward idleness. This more general anti-Lamanite prejudice manifests itself repeatedly throughout the Book of Mormon text, including in Alma 17:14–15 when Mormon₂ first introduces the mission of the sons of Mosiah₂ to the Lamanites.[23]

Despite Mormon₂'s failure to fully comprehend King Anti-Nephi-Lehi's strategic rhetoric and moral reasoning, there is evidence that the king's strategic rhetoric bears fruit in diplomatic success with the Nephites and that the moral reasoning he employs is recognized by Ammon₂ and his Nephite contemporaries. After the initial attack on the Anti-Nephi-Lehies by the Lamanites—instigated and led by Amalekites and Amulonites, dissident former Nephites who lived among the Lamanites—loses momentum, the Lamanites redirect their ire against the Nephites in battle (Alma 24–25). When they fail to make significant ground in that effort, the Amalekites again foment violence against the Anti-Nephi-Lehies, who again refuse to use violence in self-defense (Alma 27:1–3). Ammon₂ and his brothers then implore King Anti-Nephi-Lehi to flee with his people to Zarahemla, the land of the Nephites, where their father, Mosiah₂, is king. Although Mormon₂ presents this offer as the unilateral and altruistic idea of Ammon₂ and his brothers, seen from the perspective of King Anti-Nephi-Lehi and in light of his strategic rhetoric described above, it could also represent the fruition of Anti-Nephi-Lehi's careful diplomatic efforts. His exchange with Ammon₂ in Alma 27:4–13 can thus be seen as a skillful diplomatic negotiation. The king's initial protest of Ammon₂'s offer, due to fear that the Nephites will destroy the Anti-Nephi-Lehies because of the "many murders" they had formerly committed against the Nephites in war, and his offer for his people to serve as slaves to the Nephites to repair those murders, may have been strategically calculated to appeal to Ammon$_2$'s sense of paternalism and lead Ammon$_2$ toward a strategy of seeking buy-in from his fellow Nephites to ensure the viability and sustainability of their migration.

When the sons of Mosiah$_2$ return to Zarahemla and speak with the chief judge about their desire to admit the people of Anti-Nephi-Lehi to their lands, the chief judge solicits the voice of the people. Mormon$_2$ quotes the response of the people, who agree to grant the land of Jershon to the Anti-Nephi-Lehies and defend them militarily in exchange for financial and material support of their armies. They agree to do so "that we may protect our brethren . . . on account of their fear to take up arms lest they should commit sin; and this their great fear came because of their sore repentance which they had, on account of their many murders and their awful wickedness" (Alma 27:23). This proclamation partially echoes the words of King Anti-Nephi-Lehi, demonstrating the effectiveness of the king's words in eliciting eventual support from the Nephites in preserving his people's lives while upholding their moral commitments.[24] This also suggests that although the narrator Mormon$_2$, far removed in time and cultural context, had failed to appreciate the moral logic of the Anti-Nephi-Lehies, their Nephite contemporaries, informed by the sons of Mosiah$_2$, who had labored alongside the Anti-Nephi-Lehies as they established their own indigenous Christian church, were better informed.

Agency Denied: Helaman$_1$ and the Fathers/Mothers/Sons/Daughters of Anti-Nephi-Lehi

Despite the Nephites' initial comprehension of the Anti-Nephi-Lehies' moral reasoning, their paternalistic mind-set also results in gradual assimilationist dynamics that impede mutual understanding and threaten the heretofore carefully protected cultural integrity of the Anti-Nephi-Lehies. The seeds of this dynamic are evident from the time the people of Anti-Nephi-Lehi arrive in the land of Jershon, when the Nephites call them the "people of Ammon" instead of their chosen name of Anti-Nephi-Lehies and view them as "among the people of Nephi" (Alma 27:26–27). This alternate name reflects a colonialist and assimilationist mind-set and may have been particularly galling considering Ammon$_2$'s own sometimes culturally insensitive teachings and the care that King Lamoni took to emphasize his own independent spiritual authority, the agency of his people, and the indigeneity of their Christian faith.

This assimilationist dynamic reaches its apex during the time of the Nephite general Helaman$_1$, after more than a decade of ongoing warfare between the Nephites and Lamanites. Over the course of those years, the people of Anti-Nephi-Lehi had witnessed the losses incurred by the Nephites in their defense, including during an initial "tremendous battle" in which the Nephites defeated the Lamanites who were chasing the Anti-Nephi-Lehies fleeing to Jershon, which Mormon$_2$ tells us was without precedent in Lehite history (Alma 28). A decade later, as the Lamanites, in tandem with dissident Nephites, gain significant ground in battle against the Nephites, seizing several Nephite cities, Mormon$_2$'s narrative returns for the first time to the people of Anti-Nephi-Lehi. In reintroducing them, he attributes their conversion and their protection in ways that diminish the Anti-Nephi-Lehies' agency. He calls them the "people of Ammon" rather than by their chosen name (Alma 53:10) and states that they had been converted "by Ammon and his brethren, or rather by the power and word of God," language in which Mormon$_2$ seems to check his initial inclination to grant credit to the sons of Mosiah$_2$ rather than God but still fails to acknowledge the people's role in their own conversion and establishment of their church. He also attributes their protection to the "pity and love" of Ammon$_2$ and his brethren and to the Nephites (Alma 53:11–12). By contrast, the people of Anti-Nephi-Lehi ascribe credit to God as their protector (Alma 56:47).

In this context, Mormon$_2$ recounts the following:

> But it came to pass that when they saw the danger, and the many afflictions and tribulations which the Nephites bore for them, they were moved with compassion and were desirous to take up arms in the defence of their country. But behold, as they were about to take their weapons of war, they were overpowered by the persuasions of Helaman and his brethren, for they were about to break the oath which they had made. And Helaman feared lest by so doing they should lose their souls; therefore all those who had entered into this covenant were compelled to behold their brethren wade through their afflictions, in their dangerous circumstances at this time. (Alma 53:13–15)

In this passage, the people of Anti-Nephi-Lehi demonstrate their agency by choosing to fight in the interest of a cause they deem to be just: defending the Nephites.[25] Whereas they viewed their past killing in war as murder since it served an unjust cause, to the extent that they were not even willing to kill in self-defense, they also seem willing to reevaluate and make different choices over time and in different circumstances. While immediately after their conversion the Anti-Nephi-Lehies insisted on burying their swords and refraining from even defensive killing to signify their repentance and ensure their redemption, they now seem to have become sufficiently confident in their redemption from past murders that they are willing to use violence in defense of others. However, the Nephites prevent them from doing so, insisting that they abide by what Helaman₁ interprets to be their past oath and covenant. In other words, despite the Nephites' initial comprehension of the Anti-Nephi-Lehies' moral reasoning as a testament of their repentance of past murders, over the intervening decade, the Nephites have come to ignore the original reasoning of the people of Anti-Nephi-Lehi and impute to them a strict and non-adaptive promissory obligation. As a result, the Nephite leader Helaman₁ denies them the ability to exercise their moral agency, "over-powering" and "compelling" them to stay out of the conflict.

At the same time, although this strict promissory logic leads Helaman₁ to treat the older adult men as objects or at best static subjects without dynamic moral agency, he does permit their sons to take up arms. As they do so, the sons begin to call themselves Nephites and make a covenant to protect the land and defend the liberty of the Nephites and themselves, revealing a more traditional Nephite form of moral reasoning based on promissory obligation and a traditional just war rationale, at least according to Mormon₂'s account (Alma 53:16–18). Helaman₁ also interjects himself in a literally paternalistic role, calling the stripling warriors his sons, with them calling him "Father" (Alma 56:10, 56:46)—notably after having compelled their fathers not to fight, denying their agency and erasing them from the narrative.[26] This moment is thus to some degree a moment of assimilation, further signified by the fact that Mormon₂'s narrative never again refers to the people of Anti-Nephi-Lehi or even "the people of Ammon."

Cultural Resilience: Anti-Nephi-Lehi's Moral Logic in the Words of Samuel₂ the Lamanite

However, there is also evidence that the assimilation of the young men is not complete. They continue to hold to the teachings of their mothers, who assured them that God would be with them, protecting them, and, implicitly, that they would be justified in fighting such a war because it would be for a worthy cause of defending their Nephite brethren whom they loved (Alma 56:46–48). This again demonstrates the Anti-Nephi-Lehies' distinct ethic of war—that is, that killing in war is murderous and sinful only in certain circumstances, when a war is unjust, and not in others where a war is just. Despite favorably citing the warriors' recitation of their mothers' words, Helaman₁, ironically, had failed to fully understand those women's moral logic as he had prevented their husbands from joining the fight under that same rationale.

Further evidence that the assimilation of the Anti-Nephi-Lehies was not complete comes a generation later, when it becomes clear that the moral reasoning that motivated the people of Anti-Nephi-Lehi has survived beyond the persistence of that distinct group identity and is serving as a foundational belief of the majority of Lamanites, who have converted to a belief in Jesus Christ. Samuel$_2$ the Lamanite, a missionary to the Nephites (whom Mormon$_2$ depicts as the more wicked group at this time), recounts that most of the Lamanites have also buried their weapons of war. He notes that that they too view their past killings in war as *sins* (Helaman 15:9), reiterating the Anti-Nephi-Lehies' original moral reasoning about sin, repentance, and redemption and their revisionist views of killing in war. The words of King Anti-Nephi-Lehi echo across generations in Samuel$_2$'s words, even after the proximate generation had been assimilated by Helaman$_1$ and his Nephite contemporaries, permitting cultural resilience and rebirth.

It is difficult to know the exact mechanisms of this cultural transmission as the Nephite record fails to continue the story of the people of Anti-Nephi-Lehi. However, it is possible that the assimilation of the two thousand sons was not as complete as Helaman$_1$'s rhetoric and Mormon$_2$'s narrative implies and that they eventually returned to their families and continued to preserve their cultural traditions. It may be even more likely that the *daughters* of the people of Anti-Nephi-Lehi—who Mormon$_2$ neglects to mention but who certainly existed—remained unassimilated as they continued living with their parents rather than joining up with Helaman$_1$. These daughters, absent from Mormon$_2$'s account, likely would have been taught the same moral lessons that their mothers taught their brothers. They also would have likely continued to teach their children those lessons. This would have prepared those same children to engage in an act of cultural renewal in the days of Samuel$_2$ the Lamanite, presumably alongside other Lamanites who had never joined the people of Anti-Nephi-Lehi. In this act, these grandchildren of the original generation of Anti-Nephi-Lehi and their Lamanite peers once again enact the ritual of burying their swords, presumably the same swords that their fathers—which likely included the two thousand stripling warriors—had taken up again. Notably, this time they maintain their Lamanite identity rather than adopting the Anti-Nephi-Lehi moniker or another like it. This could suggest that they were disillusioned with the way Nephites had attempted to assimilate the people of Anti-Nephi-Lehi and refused to call them by their chosen name, opting instead for retaining the more persistent Lamanite identity of their forebearers, even while insisting upon its compatibility with Christian belief.

The Book of Mormon's Internal Subversion of Its Use as an Assimilation Tool

Since its publication in the 1830s, the Book of Mormon has often been used as a tool of assimilation and colonization. As Elise Boxer writes:

> The Book of Mormon is not just a reflection of Mormon settler colonialism, but has been used to create a discourse that silences Indigenous voices and perspectives regarding their own history as a people on this continent. . . . The use of the Book of Mormon as a historical and religious text of Lamanite identity and history on this continent erases the way Indigenous Peoples view their own creation as a people, their connection to the land, and their identity as a people. Instead, Indigenous Peoples are made to fit into Mormon creation stories and religious belief system.[27]

The story of the people of Anti-Nephi-Lehi subverts this use of the Book of Mormon as an assimilation tool from within the book itself. It does so by narrating those processes and illustrating how distinctive modes of moral reasoning, even when merged with an ostensibly more universalistic set of beliefs such as a Christian gospel, can create intergenerational cultural resilience despite colonialist, assimilationist, and genocidal efforts. The people of Anti-Nephi-Lehi and the Lamanite inheritors of their beliefs decolonized the teachings of Christ as related by Nephite missionaries, integrating these teachings with their own moral reasoning and creating a new ethic of killing in war as sin. This story illustrates how moral reasoning taught by parent to child—and perhaps especially mother to daughter—can act as a tool of cultural resurrection and resilience in the face of assimilation pressures, persisting or resurfacing in future generations who seek to nurture or reclaim that moral voice. Likewise, Indigenous peoples today are decolonizing Mormonism by adapting, synthesizing, and critiquing Latter-day Saint teachings with their own Indigenous values and belief systems, creating a more just and peaceable form of Mormonism with the power to resonate across generations.

Notes

1. Annual Mormon Studies Conference: Indigenous Perspectives on the Meaning of "Lamanite," April 29, 2023, https://mormonstudies.cgu.edu/annual-mormon-studies-conference-indigenous-perspectives-on-the-meaning-of-lamanite/.

2. Dennis R. Defa, "The Goshute Indians of Utah," in *A History of Utah's American Indians*, ed. Forrest S. Cuch (Salt Lake City: Utah State Division of Indian

Affairs and the Utah State Division of History, University of Utah Press, 2000), https://issuu.com/utah10/docs/history_of_utah_s_american_indians/s/10988.

3. Zak Podmore, "Here's How San Juan County Reached This Historic Moment and Why the Tension in Southeast Utah Won't End Anytime Soon," *Salt Lake Tribune*, July 7, 2019, https://www.sltrib.com/news/2019/07/07/heres-how-san-juan-county; Zak Podmore, "San Juan County Voters Defeat Ballot Measure to Study Change in Government," *Salt Lake Tribune*, November 8, 2019, https://www.sltrib.com/news/2019/11/08/san-juan-county-voters; Zak Podmore, "Navajo Nation Applauds Expected Extension of San Juan Voting Rights Deal," *Salt Lake Tribune*, February 25, 2021, https://www.sltrib.com/news/2021/02/25/navajo-nation-applauds; Native American Rights Fund, "Protecting Bears Ears National Monument," https://narf.org/cases/bears-ears; and B. "Toastie" Oaster, "What Indigenous Leaders Think about Co-Managing Bears Ears with the Feds," *High Country News*, July 22, 2022, https://www.hcn.org/articles/indigenous-affairs-bears-ears-what-indigenous-leaders-think-about-co-managing-bears-ears-with-the-feds.

4. Grant Hardy, *Understanding the Book of Mormon: A Reader's Guide* (New York: Oxford University Press, 2010).

5. Rolf Straubhaar, "Unpacking White-Heritage Mormon Privilege: A Latter-Day Saint Pursuit of Critical Consciousness," in *Decolonizing Mormonism: Approaching a Postcolonial Zion*, ed. Gina Colvin and Joanna Brooks, 103–113 (Salt Lake City: University of Utah Press, 2018).

6. See Elise Boxer, "The Book of Mormon as Mormon Settler Colonialism," in *Essays on American Indian and Mormon History*, ed. P. Jane Hafen and Brenden W. Rensink, 3–22 (Salt Lake City: University of Utah Press, 2019); Elizabeth A. Fenton, "Nephites and Israelites: *The Book of Mormon* and the Hebraic Indian Theory," in *Americanist Approaches to the Book of Mormon*, ed. Elizabeth A. Fenton and Jared Hickman, 277–97 (New York: Oxford University Press, 2019); Thomas W. Murphy, "Lamanite Genesis, Genealogy, and Genetics," in *American Apocrypha: Essays on the Book of Mormon*, ed. Dan Vogel and Brent Lee Metcalfe (Salt Lake City: Signature Books, 2002); Thomas W. Murphy, "Imagining Lamanites: Native Americans and the Book of Mormon," https://search.proquest.com/docview/305307387 (accessed Nov. 10, 2023).

7. See Angelo Baca, "Porter Rockwell and Samuel the Lamanite Fistfight in Heaven: A Mormon Navajo Filmmaker's Perspective," in Colvin and Brooks, *Decolonizing Mormonism,* 67–76; Elise Boxer, "'This Is the Place!': Disrupting Mormon Settler Colonialism," in Colvin and Brooks, *Decolonizing Mormonism*, 77–100; Zachary McLeod Hutchins, "'I Lead the Way, Like Columbus': Joseph Smith, Genocide, and Revelatory Ambiguity," in Fenton and Hickman, *Americanist Approaches to the Book of Mormon*, 391–419; *In Laman's Terms: Looking at Lamanite Identity*, Takin' It Back Productions, University of Washington, 2008; Sarah Newcomb, "Lamanite Truth," *Lamanite Truth*, https://lamanitetruth.com/ (accessed Nov. 10, 2023); S. Ata Siulua, "Withering as a Rose: Tongan Indigeneity, Mormonism and the Curse of the Lamanites," https://mormonstudies

.cgu.edu/annual-mormon-studies-conference-indigenous-perspectives-on-the-meaning-of-lamanite (accessed Nov. 10, 2023).

8. See Moroni Benally, "Decolonizing the Blossoming: Indigenous People's Faith in a Colonizing Church," *Dialogue: A Journal of Mormon Thought* 50, no. 4 (2017): 71–78; Joanna Brooks, "Mormonism as Colonialism, Mormonism as Anti-Colonialism, Mormonism as Minor Transnationalism: Historical and Contemporary Perspectives," in Colvin and Brooks, *Decolonizing Mormonism*, 163–85; Gina Colvin, "A Maori Mormon Testimony," in Colvin and Brooks, *Decolonizing Mormonism*, 27–46; Ignacio Garcia, "Empowering Latino Saints to Transcend Historical Racialism: A Bishop's Tale," in Colvin and Brooks, *Decolonizing Mormonism*, 139–60; Robert Joseph, "Lamanite Identity in a Māori Context," https://mormonstudies.cgu.edu/annual-mormon-studies-conference-indigenous-perspectives-on-the-meaning-of-lamanite (accessed Nov. 10, 2023); Farina Noelani King, "Aloha in Diné Bikéyah: Mormon Hawaiians and Navajos, 1949–1990," in Hafen and Rensink, *Essays on American Indian and Mormon History*, 161–82; Armando Solórzano, "Who Is a Lamanite, Anyway? Latinx Interpretations of the Term, Its Impact, and Reformulation," https://mormonstudies.cgu.edu/annual-mormon-studies-conference-indigenous-perspectives-on-the-meaning-of-lamanite (accessed Nov. 10, 2023); Stanley J. Thayne, "Mormonism and the Catawba Indian Nation," in Hafen and Rensink, *Essays on American Indian and Mormon History*, 113–36; and Thayne, "'We're Going to Take Our Land Back Over': Reading *The Book of Mormon* from an Indigenous Space," in Fenton and Hickman, *Americanist Approaches to the Book of Mormon*, 321–40.

9. See Brooks, "Mormonism as Colonialism"; Colvin, "Maori Mormon Testimony"; P. Jane Hafen, "Afterword," in Colvin and Brooks, *Decolonizing Mormonism*, 263–73; Joseph, "Lamanite Identity in a Māori Context"; Murphy, "Imagining Lamanites."

10. See Murphy, "Lamanite Genesis, Genealogy, and Genetics"; Lori Elaine Taylor, "Joseph Smith in Iroquois Country: A Mormon Creation Story," in Hafen and Rensink, *Essays on American Indian and Mormon History*, 41–60.

11. Thomas W. Murphy, "Decolonization on the Salish Sea: A Tribal Journey Back to Mormon Studies," in Colvin and Brooks, *Decolonizing Mormonism*, 47–66.

12. Hafen, "Afterword"; Murphy, "Decolonization on the Salish Sea."

13. See Kimberly Matheson (Berkey) and Joseph M. Spencer, "'Great Cause to Mourn': The Complexity of *The Book of Mormon*'s Presentation of Gender and Race," in Fenton and Hickman, *Americanist Approaches to the Book of Mormon*, 298–320; Deidre Nicole Green, *Jacob: A Brief Theological Introduction* (Provo, UT: Neal A. Maxwell Institute for Religious Scholarship, BYU, 2020); Joshua Madson, "A Non-Violent Reading of the Book of Mormon," in *War and Peace in Our Time: Mormon Perspectives*, ed. Patrick Q. Mason, J. David Pulsipher, and Richard L. Bushman (Salt Lake City: Greg Kofford Books, 2012), 13–28; Eduardo Obregón Pagán, "A Decolonial Reading of the Book of Mormon: Sociopolitical Under-Currents in the Book of Mormon World," https://mormonstudies

.cgu.edu/annual-mormon-studies-conference-indigenous-perspectives-on-the -meaning-of-lamanite (accessed Nov. 10, 2023); Fatimah Salleh and Margaret Olsen Hemming, *The Book of Mormon for the Least of These*, vol. 1: *1 Nephi-Words of Mormon* (Salt Lake City: Common Consent Press, 2020); Fatimah Salleh and Margaret Olsen Hemming, *The Book of Mormon for the Least of These*, vol. 2: *Mosiah-Alma* (Salt Lake City Common Consent Press, 2022).

14. Taylor, "Joseph Smith in Iroquois Country."

15. Thomas W. Murphy, "Other Scriptures: Restoring Voices of Gantowisas to an Open Canon," in Hafen and Rensink, *Essays on American Indian and Mormon History*, 23–40.

16. See Eugene England, "Why Nephi Killed Laban: Reflections on the Truth of the Book of Mormon," *Dialogue: A Journal of Mormon Thought* 22, no. 3 (1989): 32–51; Joshua Madson, "Non-Violent Reading of the Book of Mormon"; Hugh Nibley, *Since Cumorah: The Book of Mormon in the Modern World*, 2nd ed., ed. John W. Welch (Salt Lake City: Deseret Book, 1988), 295–96.

17. Duane Boyce, *Even unto Bloodshed: An LDS Perspective on War* (Salt Lake City: Greg Kofford Books, 2015).

18. J. David Pulsipher, "The Ammonite Conundrum," in Mason, Pulsipher, and Bushman, *War and Peace in Our Time*, 1–12.

19. Section 98 of The Doctrine and Covenants of The Church of Jesus Christ of Latter-day Saints (Salt Lake City, UT: The Church of Jesus Christ of Latter-day Saints, 2013); Patrick Q. Mason and J. David Pulsipher, *Proclaim Peace: The Restoration's Answer to an Age of Conflict* (Provo, UT: Neal A. Maxwell Institute for Religious Scholarship, BYU, 2021).

20. Baca, "Porter Rockwell and Samuel the Lamanite Fistfight in Heaven," 76.

21. For a discussion of theories for why the people chose this name, see Michael Austin, "What Were the 'Anti-Nephi-Lehies' Against and Why Does It Matter Today? #BOM2016," *By Common Consent*, July 7, 2016, https://bycommon consent.com/2016/07/17/what-were-the-anti-nephi-lehies-against-and-why -does-it-matter-today-bom2016/ (and the comments).

22. Just war theory is generally divided into ideas about *jus ad bellum* and *jus in bello*—that is, what is a just cause for fighting a war and what is just conduct within war. The primary fissure between traditional and revisionist theorists of war ethics—and the one most relevant in the case of the people of Anti-Nephi-Lehi—concerns whether these two sets of ethical considerations can be morally disentangled from each other. Traditional just war theory—as formulated in Michael Walzer's *Just and Unjust Wars*—treats *jus ad bellum* and *jus in bello* as morally independent: One can (and should) behave ethically in war regardless of whether the war is being fought in a just cause. Over the past two decades, scholars who have come to be known as the revisionists of just war theory have critiqued this basic premise and the principles that flow from it, such as the moral equality of combatants and noncombatant immunity. Most notably, Jeff McMahan argues that the moral defensibility of killing in war

cannot be separated from the question of whether the war is just or unjust in the first place. See Michael Walzer, *Just and Unjust Wars: A Moral Argument with Historical Illustrations* (New York: Basic Books, 1977); Jeff McMahan, *Killing in War* (Oxford: Oxford University Press, 2009).

23. At the same time, Mormon$_2$ did include a significant level of detail about the agency exercised by the Lamanites, even if recognizing it requires careful excavation and a degree of skepticism toward the surface narrative or the quoted words of Ammon$_2$. Those details must have been present in the Nephite records that he was abridging, in addition to some primary records of Lamanite/Anti-Nephi-Lehi statements and thoughts. Mormon$_2$ also clearly admired the faith and dedication of the Anti-Nephi-Lehies, albeit often with a paternalistic and pedestalizing lens.

24. This story could even be read as a clever way that the Anti-Nephi-Lehies engineered to gain possession of some Nephite lands without bloodshed, but in light of the heavy casualties they bore during the attacks from their erstwhile fellow Lamanites in Alma 24 and 27, it is unlikely that their commitment to nonviolence toward their Lamanite attackers was a purely strategic means to obtain Nephite lands. Rather, their nonviolent ethic seems genuinely motivated by a repentance, redemption, and testament logic.

25. Mormon$_2$ writes that they desired to take up arms to defend "their country." It is unclear whether they are referring to their own country or that of the Nephites, or if they view those as one and the same, but given the context of the verse, wherein they express compassion for the plight of the Nephites, whom they still view as a distinct social group, and given the lack of a direct threat to Jershon at this time, it is likely that "their country" is referring to the country of the Nephites. This is reinforced in Alma 56:7, where Helaman$_1$ writes to his fellow Nephite General Moroni$_1$ that the fathers had desired to "take up their weapons of war in our defence."

26. In Alma 56, Helaman$_1$ also reveals his biases when he begins his epistle to his fellow Nephite general Moroni$_1$ about these two thousand young men by a gratuitous reference to long-standing Nephite stereotypes about Lamanites: "Now ye have known that these were descendants of Laman, who was the eldest son of our father Lehi; Now I need not rehearse unto you concerning their traditions or their unbelief, for thou knowest concerning all these things" (Alma 56:3–4).

27. Boxer, "'This Is the Place!'" 4.

9

The Perils of Apparel

Clothing and Dress Ethics in the Book of Mormon

ARIEL BYBEE LAUGHTON

In one of the first chapters of the Book of Mormon, the patriarch prophet Lehi₁ recounts to his family an extended vision he received from God in which the cosmic struggle of the righteous to come unto God is presented to him as an extended allegory. Among the vision's many symbols is a building, "great and spacious," that towered over the earth, filled with people who were mocking and jeering at the righteous who were below them. He gives few details about the building or its inhabitants except that the people in the building were "old and young, both male and female; and their manner of dress was exceedingly fine" (1 Nephi 8:26–27). Lehi₁'s son Nephi₁ later explains that the building represented "the pride of the world; and it fell, and the fall thereof was exceedingly great" (1 Nephi 11:36). For Lehi₁ and Nephi₁, clothing in this vision is interpreted as a critical marker of unrighteous pride and concern for the approval of "the world and the wisdom thereof" (1 Nephi 11:35). The extravagant dress of the building's inhabitants symbolizes the worldliness and the excessive self-regard of the unrighteous who persecute the humble followers of God below, and it plays an integral part of a trajectory that leads to the ultimate fall of the great building.

As demonstrated by this vision and its interpretation, clothing is a means of communication within a community.[1] Questions of appropriate or ethical dress pertain to every community that uses clothing as well as to those that choose not to. As with many other physical items, clothing and nakedness are imbued with meanings by the community in which they are produced or performed, and they reflect to some extent the values and ethics of that community.[2] For Lehi₁ and Nephi₁, the clothing of the people in the building has both social and theological implications that communicate what is for them an objectionable ethos. Many other Book of Mormon narrators refer frequently to clothing and in due course develop an ethics of dress rooted in both theological and socioeconomic concerns. For them, clothing has both a physical presence and a range of symbolic meanings. These meanings are most often constructed in the context of concerns about pride, worldliness, wealth, and social division. Together, they reflect an ethics of dress that contrasts sharply to many modern understandings of clothing and dress and encourages reassessment of current modesty ideologies in the Church of Jesus Christ of Latter-day Saints and other religions with programs of proscriptive dress.

This chapter draws attention to the ways Book of Mormon prophets ascribe both social and theological meaning to clothing in order to produce a series of dress ethics rooted in concepts of socioeconomic justice and righteous humility. My assessment first considers the numerous textual proscriptions against fine dress and then reviews injunctions against nakedness, or the state of being completely without clothes, with reference to either oneself or others. Prohibitions against both fine apparel and nakedness reflect the prophets' concerns over increasing socioeconomic division in society as well as the spiritual degeneration of their people as they become oriented toward the acquisition of temporal and worldly things instead of God. In context of these proscriptions against fine clothing and nakedness, I review the few positive references to clothing made in the book and suggest some basic ethical guidelines for dressing oneself and others. Finally, I relate Book of Mormon dress ethics to some teachings about appropriate dress that have been set forth by various leaders and committees of the Church of Jesus Christ of Latter-day Saints, which is currently the largest religious denomination that accepts the Book of Mormon as scripture and an ethical guide.

Proscriptions against Fine Dress

Lehi₁'s vision and Nephi₁'s subsequent interpretation represent only the first of many references to clothing. Throughout the book, numerous prophets develop an ethics of dress that is firmly tied to teachings on wealth, social status, and concern for the poor. These teachings are deeply concerned with the dangers of "fine clothing," or rich and ostentatious dress that reflects social and economic inequities in their societies. For these prophets, such an imbalance reflects the larger decline of religiosity and righteousness among the people, placing society as a whole in danger of God's chastisement.

Similar to the Hebrew Bible's narration of the cyclical faithfulness and unfaithfulness of the Israelite people to God, the Book of Mormon recounts the ebb and flow of the righteousness of the Nephites, a group of people brought out of Israel and to America at the time of the Hebrew prophet Jeremiah (perhaps sixth to seventh century BCE). The Nephite narrative follows a cyclical pattern: The people are righteous, they receive blessings from God because of their righteousness, and then, sooner or later, they decline into sin and unrighteousness and must be called back to God by prophets (in addition to other social, political, or natural phenomena), whereupon they usually repent and return to righteousness.

In this progression of cyclical stories, fancy or ostentatious dress frequently appears as a symbol or marker of spiritual and moral decay. Nephi₁ further develops the connection between clothing as an indicator of unrighteous pride or worldliness as he recounts another vision in which he sees worldly wickedness represented as a different structure: a "great and abominable church," founded by the devil (1 Nephi 13:6). Nephi₁ notes specifically the "gold and silver and the silks and the scarlets and the fine-twined linen, and the precious clothing, and the harlots," which he was told by an angel were "the desires of this great and abominable church" (1 Nephi 13:7–8). He associates fine and expensive clothing with markers of wealth and sex to portray a church whose desires have become disoriented from God and have devolved into a lust for worldly things.[3] Likewise, at a later point, Nephi₁ condemns the corrupt churches that he prophesies will come forth at a future time that "rob the poor because of their fine sanctuaries; they rob the poor because of their fine clothing; and they persecute the meek and the poor in heart, because in their pride they are puffed up" (2 Nephi 28:13). The desire for expensive clothing and opulent places of worship leads churches not only to avarice and lust but also to outright theft and intentional persecution of the poor.

Further developing Nephi₁'s warning against persecution of the poor, the prophet Jacob₂ warns his people that "because some of you have obtained more abundantly than that of your brethren[,] ye are lifted up in the pride of your hearts, and wear stiff necks and high heads because of the costliness of your apparel, and persecute your brethren because ye suppose that ye are better than they" (Jacob 2:13). Jacob₂ is concerned that the economic inequities growing in his society are leading to unholy personal pride and undesirable social stratification. The wearing of expensive clothing is inspiring within the rich a feeling of superiority to the more economically disadvantaged. According to Jacob₂, such perceptions are not only unjustified but lead to God's judgment and condemnation of the individual who holds them (Jacob 2:14). He asserts that these people must instead "think of your brethren like unto yourselves, and be familiar with all and free with your substance, that they may be rich like unto you" (Jacob 2:17).

The well-dressed are to share their wealth in order to elevate those around them to a similar status.

Later Book of Mormon prophets continue to associate fine clothing with unrighteous worldliness, self-aggrandizement, and socioeconomic division. Alma₂ recounts that the heretic preacher Nehor starts to "be lifted up in the pride of his heart, and to wear very costly apparel" as people begin to embrace his religious teachings and give him money for his new church (Alma 1:5). For Alma₂, Nehor's expensive clothes stand as evidence of his personal corruption and indicate the falseness of his message. Subsequently, Alma₂ registers his despair to see faithful members of the Nephite church falling into sin after a time of remarkable material prosperity. Having acquired great riches, luxurious fabrics, many flocks and herds, and much gold and silver, they become "lifted up in the pride of their eyes, for they began to wear very costly apparel" (Alma 4:6). For Alma₂, the fine dress of the Nephite believers is an indication that the people of the church have become corrupted by the development of great personal pride in their wealth. He understands this unrighteous arrogance, manifest in their rich clothing, as an indication that the people have become too worldly and focused on wealth (Alma 4:8). Furthermore, it has led them to persecute unbelievers and to turn "their backs upon the needy and the naked and those who were hungry, and those who were athirst, and those who were sick and afflicted" (Alma 4:8, 4:12). In contrast to those who hoarded their riches and neglected the needy, Alma₂ praises other church members who were "abasing themselves, succoring those who stood in need of their succor, such as imparting their substance to the poor and needy, feeding the hungry, and suffering all manner of afflictions for Christ's sake" (Alma 4:13). These blessed redeemed who have retained the remission of their sins by sharing what they have (Alma 4:14) stand in sharp contrast to the unrighteous wealthy clad in fancy dress. The rich must desist from "the wearing of costly apparel and setting your hearts upon the vain things of the world" (Alma 5:53). For him, dressing in fine clothing is inexorably linked to worldliness and vanity and leads to oppression of the poor.

Similar prohibitions against fine dress appear again as Alma₂ recounts his missionary journey undertaken with the purpose of reconverting the Zoramites, a sect of Nephites who have broken away from the mainstream church and built their own places of worship in a new city. When Alma₂ arrives in their city and attends one of their worship services, he is appalled to see the Zoramites praying to God from a high podium in their synagogues and expressing denial of Christ while asserting their exclusive status as God's people chosen to be saved while "all around us are elected to be cast by thy wrath down to hell" (Alma 31:12–18). Alma₂ expresses his consternation at these teachings and practices in the form of a prayer that condemns the fine clothing and ornamentation of the Zoramites at length:

> Behold, O God, they cry unto thee, and yet their hearts are swallowed up in their pride. Behold, O God, they cry unto thee with their mouths, while they are puffed up, even to greatness, with the vain things of the world. Behold, O my God, their costly apparel, and their ringlets, and their bracelets, and their ornaments of gold, and all their precious things which they are ornamented with; and behold, their hearts are set upon them, and yet they cry unto thee and say—We thank thee, O God, for we are a chosen people unto thee, while others shall perish. (Alma 31:27–28)

While Alma$_2$'s initial account of the Zoramite worship he witnessed had not included any mention of their mode of dress, he now recounts their fine clothing and adornment as evidence of their pride, vanity, and worldliness.[4] He decries the Zoramites as hypocrites who pray to God while their true love is their own material finery. For Alma$_2$, the Zoramites' understanding of their own election led to prideful arrogance, but their ideological conflation of worldly prosperity with religious salvation is even more egregious. Alma$_2$ understands fine clothing and jewelry to function within the Zoramite religious culture as a distinctive marker of election.[5] Because the Zoramites love their fine dress so much, they do not allow that the poor—those who have been "cast out of the synagogues because of the coarseness of their apparel" (Alma 32:2)—to have access to worship and fellowship with the "chosen" people, condemning them to perish because of their lack of material prosperity. For Alma$_2$, this high heresy, the result of intermingling gross materialism with salvation theology and its resulting oppression of the poor, justify his extensive (and mostly unsuccessful) missionary journey to reclaim them.[6]

The Book of Mormon later relates a post-mortal appearance of the resurrected Jesus Christ to the Nephite people. After teaching the people at length, reorganizing their religious worship, and performing numerous miracles (3 Nephi 11–28), Christ departs. Their society, however, is radically altered. According to the narrator-prophet Mormon$_2$, all people in the land (both the Nephites and their hereditary enemies, the Lamanites) were converted to the Lord, there were no longer any disagreements or disputes, everyone kept the laws and treated one another fairly, and all things were held in common among every person, resulting in a society without economic or social divisions (4 Nephi 1:1–3). This utopian state persists for two hundred years and results in great economic prosperity for the people (4 Nephi 1:23). However, Mormon$_2$ recalls, "In this two hundred and first year there began to be among them those who were lifted up in pride, such as the wearing of costly apparel, and all manner of fine pearls, and of the fine things of the world" (4 Nephi 1:24). From this point, the people stop holding everything in common and begin to have private property again, resulting in the division of society into classes and the building up of multiple churches that deny Christ's true church (4 Nephi 1:24–26).

It is notable that Mormon$_2$ separates this ideal society's great economic prosperity from the time when people begin to garb themselves in expensive clothing and ornamentation as a display of their pride and feelings of superiority to others. For him, great wealth seems to naturally result from the unified and egalitarian society that results from the conversion of all to Christ. It is when unrighteous pride begins to inspire some to distinguish themselves from others around them by donning finer clothing and jewels than others that this ideal society fractures and breaks down into economic and class divisions and the church fragments into various competing sects. Wealth alone is not detrimental to society, but the pride it inspires in certain individuals, manifest by their fine dress and ornamentation, is insidious and destructive to the community.

Many years later, the last Nephite prophet, Moroni$_2$, who has lived to see the entire destruction of his people by their enemies because of their wickedness (Moroni 8:6–8), prophesies that the book he is writing will come forth at a future time when people have again become profoundly sinful and churches have become defiled, prideful, and materialistic (Moroni 8:26–33).[7] Looking far into the future, he warns later readers of the Book of Mormon:

> Jesus Christ hath shown you unto me, and I know your doing. And I know that ye do walk in the pride of your hearts; and there are none save a few only who do not lift themselves up in the pride of their hearts, unto the wearing of very fine apparel, unto envying, and strifes, and malice, and persecutions, and all manner of iniquities; and your churches, yea, even every one, have become polluted because of the pride of your hearts. For behold, ye do love money, and your substance, and your fine apparel, and the adorning of your churches, more than ye love the poor and the needy, the sick and the afflicted. (Mormon 8:35–37)

Again, the wearing of fine clothing is understood to be the manifestation of unrighteous pride and the gateway to sin. As with Alma$_2$ and Mormon$_2$, Moroni$_2$ associates expensive dress with pride, contention, greed, envy, hard feelings, social discord, and sin in general. Moroni$_2$ prophesies that the prideful well-dressed will corrupt the churches as their love of material goods, including their nice clothing, supplants caring for the poor and needy.

Most often, Book of Mormon narrators interpret clothing in light of both theological and socioeconomic concerns. The prophets understand fine clothing to be a symbol of society's degeneration into unrighteous pride and link its wearing to the rise of undesirable social divisions in society. For writers like Alma₂ and Mormon₂, these social divisions result from the failure of the finely dressed to adequately care for the poor and the needy. Fine clothing serves as a symbol of turning one's focus away from the things of God and toward the things of the world.

Proscriptions against Nakedness

While presenting a strong socio-theological invective against fine clothing, the Book of Mormon demonstrates almost equal consternation over nakedness. Because nakedness is an integral part of any clothing system and, like clothing, conveys meaning and performs various social and theological functions in a community, it is profitable to consider the symbolic nature of nakedness as part of the ethics of dress more broadly developed in the Book of Mormon.[8] Considering how nakedness is understood sheds further light on why the Nephite prophets employed clothing as a key theme in their expression of the decadence and degradation of their society. Both forced nakedness and self-imposed nakedness have consistently negative connotations and become an implicit point of reference for prophetic admonitions concerning the poor.

Nakedness receives its earliest chronological treatment in the Book of Mormon when Jacob invokes the term in context of describing the state of the wicked after the resurrection. After humans are raised from the grave as immortal and incorruptible souls, Jacob asserts, they (presumably, the wicked) will have "a perfect knowledge" of all their guilt, uncleanliness, and nakedness, while the righteous will be fully aware of their own purity and be clothed in a "robe of righteousness" (2 Nephi 9:14). This new complete knowledge of one's "nakedness" that accompanies the resurrection echoes Adam's and Eve's sudden realization of their own nakedness after eating the forbidden fruit (Genesis 3.6–11) and may account for Jacob's association of nakedness with sin and guilt in this passage.[9] The guilty will stand ashamed in the nakedness of their sin, while the righteous feel joy in finding themselves clothed in purity. While Jacob does not connect this teaching to ethical issues at this point, this naked/clothed dichotomy lays a foundation for his own further reflection on wealth and poverty in Jacob 2:17–19 as well as in the writings of several other Book of Mormon authors.

For example, narrators such as Alma$_2$ and Moroni$_2$ invoke imagery of the "naked" poor to serve as a foil for the finely dressed unrighteous. As mentioned earlier, Alma$_2$ contrasts those who, because of their prosperity, become proud, worldly, and wear "very costly apparel" to those needy who are naked and suffering hunger, thirst, and sickness because of the former's neglect (Alma 4:6, 4:11). Likewise, Moroni$_2$ creates a strong juxtaposition between wearing fine clothing and giving proper care to the hungry, needy, and sick. After berating his readers for selling themselves for "that which will canker," he asks, "Why do ye adorn yourselves with that which hath no life, and yet suffer the hungry, and the needy, and the naked, and the sick and the afflicted to pass by you, and notice them not?" (Mormon 8:39). Moroni$_2$ constructs a direct juxtaposition between "dead" material adornment and living human beings, contrasting the "adorned" rich to the naked poor to amplify this disparity. By putting on one's body fine material goods "which hath no life," one becomes blind to the material needs of the sentient (and thus more important) beings around them who stand in need.

As demonstrated by Alma$_2$ and Moroni$_2$, nakedness serves as a point of differentiation between righteousness and unrighteousness in the Book of Mormon. The naked poor are not considered righteous or unrighteous because of their nakedness; rather, their nakedness serves as a symbol of the corruption of those who are finely dressed. Further richness is added to this understanding of nakedness when it is considered in light of two other contexts in which nakedness occurs in the book: nakedness in prison and nakedness among the Lamanites.

First, Mormon$_2$ recounts with distress how Alma$_2$ and his missionary companion Amulek are denied food and water and are also bound and stripped of their clothes when they are imprisoned in Ammonihah as punishment for their teaching (Alma 14:22). Their forced nakedness is one of the multiple abuses they suffer while imprisoned, including being forced to witness the murder of women and children, being mocked and ridiculed, and being physically beaten. By taking their clothes, the Ammonihahites remove their social status and assert their own power over Alma$_2$'s and Amulek's authority in the community. This forced nakedness is intended to degrade, dishearten, and humiliate the prisoners.[10] In a similar narrative, the missionary prophet and Nephite prince Ammon$_2$ is dismayed to arrive in the Lamanite city of Middoni and find his brother Aaron$_2$—also a son of the Nephite king—and their friends not only in prison but also naked and with their skin "worn exceedingly" because of their shackles (Alma 20:29). The stripping of this Nephite prince of his clothing—and thus of his dignity, significant social status, and authority—by his Lamanite captors associates the forced nakedness with an especially profound level of shame, humiliation, and punishment.

While the Book of Mormon portrays forced nakedness as a humiliation and a social crime, self-chosen nakedness has different (yet still strictly negative) connotations. The Lamanites, the hereditary enemy of the Nephites, are often described as being "naked," presumably at their own instigation. The prophet Enos describes the Lamanites as "wild, and ferocious, and a blood-thirsty people, full of idolatry and filthiness; feeding upon beasts of prey; dwelling in tents, and wandering about in the wilderness with a short skin girdle about their loins and their heads shaven" (Enos 1:20). When they come up to battle against the Nephites at various junctures, they are described as being naked in similar terms, their heads shaved and wearing a leather covering over their genitals (Mosiah 10:8; cf. Alma 3:5, Alma 43:20).

These authors also report that the Lamanites arrive with various weapons and apparel on their bodies. While asserting that the Lamanites were "naked" except for their loincloths, Mormon$_2$ notes also "their armor, which was girded about them, and their bows, and their arrows, and their stones, and their slings, and so forth" (Alma 3:5; cf. Mosiah 10:8). As with the poor of Antionum, it is not clear that the Lamanites were "naked" in that they were entirely without apparel.[11] Rather, Book of Mormon narrators refer to Lamanite "nakedness" as a means of expressing what they understand to be increasing Lamanite savageness. While the Lamanites claim a common ancestor with the Nephites in the prophet Lehi$_1$, the two peoples quarrel and diverge and the Lamanites are cursed by God and become idle, "full of mischief and subtlety, and did seek in the wilderness for beasts of prey" (2 Nephi 5:24). Ensuing allegations of Lamanite nakedness, accompanied by reports of their laziness, shaved heads, and minimal coverings, are intended to communicate the Lamanites' continued degeneration into abject ferity as well as their lack of cunning in battle. Lamanite "nakedness" is starkly contrasted to the "thick clothing" of the Nephites, who had been prepared with abundant dress as well as a diverse range of weapons, breastplates, and head and arm shields (Alma 43:18–19).[12] Nakedness not only suggests Lamanite social degeneration but also a lack of foresight and preparation that leaves them vulnerable to the attacks of their enemies and "exceedingly afraid" when they see the Nephites (Alma 43:21). On the other hand, ample thick clothing serves as a symbol not only of Nephite civility but also of their wise preparation and superior battle acumen.[13] For Mormon$_2$, victory in battle is obtained long before the first engagement as it is greatly determined by the level of preparation manifest in an army's state of dress and preparation. Being adequately, even abundantly, and appropriately clothed is safe, smart, and shows preparation, while nakedness shows lack of foresight and vulnerability.

In short, the Book of Mormon associates nakedness not only with poverty and the wickedness of the rich but also with shame, humiliation, degradation, loss of social status, power and authority, punishment, idolatry, filthiness, civil decline, nomadism, ferity, vulnerability, a lack of preparation, and even intellectual inferiority. These cultural associations with nakedness suggest something more of why the nakedness of the poor is of deep concern to the prophets. The link between nakedness and poverty, prison, and the degraded state of one's enemies reflects a community where the nakedness of the needy might be understood not only as a pressing moral issue but as a widespread ethical catastrophe. The economic and social conditions of an unjust society stripped the poor from their clothing as well as food, shelter, and other basic necessities and drove them into the shame, suffering, and loss of social status similar to how prisoners stripped of their clothing and subject to other punishments suffered. Through association with the Lamanites, poverty's nakedness reflected the forced denigration of the poor into a state of fierce savagery and moral destitution. The poor who were not sufficiently dressed were in a state of vulnerability and unpreparedness for whatever lay ahead, just as were the Lamanites who came up to battle insufficiently dressed.

In context of these understandings of nakedness, it is clear why Alma$_2$'s preaching companion Amulek insists that faith in Christ's atonement and continual prayer are not enough to secure personal salvation: "For after ye have done all these things, if ye turn away the needy, and the naked, and visit not the sick and afflicted, and impart of your substance, if ye have, to those who stand in need . . . your prayer is vain, and availeth you nothing, and ye are as hypocrites who do deny the faith" (Alma 34:28). The state of being poor was not only pitiable but a grievous sin on the heads of society's more well-heeled that was so egregious that it had the power to negate any other good deed done in the hope of salvation. Furthermore, Mormon$_2$ attributes the Nephites' lack of military success to "their oppression to the poor, withholding their food from the hungry, withholding their clothing from the naked," and myriad other sins (Helaman 4:12). All members of the church are to impart what they had to "every needy, naked soul" (Mosiah 18:28).

For these prophets, nakedness is the manifestation of both moral bankruptcy and social degeneration, leading to God's withholding of post-mortal blessings as well as those being immediately sought in the interest of preserving society from destruction in battle. The prophets frame care of the poor, including clothing the naked, not as an act of benevolent charity but rather as a mandatory act of restoring justice in society and returning both the self and society to a correct relationship with God. They do not speak to the poor and encourage them to find means to clothe themselves.[14] Instead, nakedness is understood to be a condition inflicted on the poor and perpetuated by those who neglect their obligations to God as well as to society.

Ethical Dress of the Self

While most teachings about clothing in the Book of Mormon consist of warnings and prohibitions against fine clothing and nakedness, some guidance as to the ethical use of dress is provided. For example, Zeniff, the leader of a small Nephite city, warmly recalls a time of peaceful prosperity for his people when the men of the community tilled the ground and raised crops, and the women were tasked to "spin, and toil, and work, and work all manner of fine linen, yea, and cloth of every kind, that we might clothe our nakedness" (Mosiah 10:5). Strikingly similar variations of this verse occur in Helaman 6:13 ("their women did toil and spin, and did make all manner of cloth, of fine-twined linen and cloth of every kind, to clothe their nakedness") and again in Ether 10:24 ("they did have silks, and fine-twined linen; and they did work all manner of cloth, that they might clothe themselves from their nakedness").[15] Each of these passages is situated within descriptions of peaceful and prosperous times resulting from great industry and innovation. Mormon$_2$ describes the women spinning cloth during a time of peace and free trade between the Nephites and Lamanites, when both peoples become exceedingly rich due to mining of gold and an abundant success with crops and flocks (Helaman 6:7–12). Moroni$_2$ recounts the industry of the Jaredites who are trading broadly, mining precious metals, successfully farming, and inventing new tools (Ether 10:22–28). In these contexts, the people's ability to weave cloth and to cover up the undesirable nakedness of their bodies signifies their civilization's prosperity and abundance.[16]

In addition, all three passages mention the excellent quality of the cloth that is made. Mosiah 10:5 and Helaman 6:3 both mention the production of fine linen, and Ether 10:24 specifically mentions the Jaredites' production of silks in addition to fine linen and other clothing. As mentioned earlier, the prophets elsewhere decry the wearing and possession of such fine fabrics. Nephi$_1$ associates silks, fine-twined linen, and other precious cloth with the "great and abominable" church (1 Nephi 13:7–8). Alma$_2$ attributes the growth of pride among the people to several factors, including their riches and wearing of silks and fine-twined linen (Alma 4:6). In these three passages, however, the wearing of these fine fabrics is seen in a positive light as a mark of the community's success and prosperity. There are at least three caveats that allow for positive endorsement of fine clothing that also provide more general ethical principles for the wearing of clothing in a moral and socially responsible manner.

First, the production and wearing of good-quality clothing may be praiseworthy as it becomes an endeavor of the *community* on behalf of the *community*. The women (or people) toil and spin so that clothing might be provided to all. The importance of the distribution of the clothing throughout the community is further attested in Alma 1. Mormon₂ recounts that the righteous Nephites had an abundance of silk, fine-twined linen, and good-quality cloth (Alma 1:29) but also states that these people did not wear "costly apparel" (Alma 1:27). He considers these Nephites to be righteous because "in their prosperous circumstances, they did not send away any who were naked, or that were hungry, or that were athirst, or that were sick . . . and they did not set their hearts upon riches; therefore they were liberal to all . . . having no respect to persons as to those who stood in need" (Alma 1:30). Having accumulated great wealth, the people presumably use their silk and linen to ensure that there is no naked individual in the community.[17] While they most likely wore and used the fine materials they produced and accumulated, they nevertheless are not considered to be clad in "costly" apparel because they liberally shared their material possessions, and the poor in their community were sufficiently provided for.[18]

Second, while emphasizing the moral imperative of providing for the naked and needy, the Book of Mormon prophets consistently value the hard labor required to meet the needs of oneself, one's family, and one's community (e.g., Mosiah 27:4). Thus, Mormon₂ and Moroni₂ cast in a positive light the physical "toil and spin" of the women (people) to produce the fine clothing in the aforementioned verses. Elsewhere, the Nephite king Benjamin reminds his people that he has toiled with his own hands in service to his people to prevent the levying of heavy taxes to support the monarchy (Mosiah 2:14).[19] Similarly, ordained Nephite priests are required to labor in order to support themselves despite the demands of their offices (Mosiah 18:24, 27:5; Alma 1:6). The physical labor of each individual in the community ensured the equality of all members (Alma 1:26). The work performed while toiling and spinning infuses the fine clothing that is produced with virtue and righteousness as it signals not only care for all in the community but also reflects the shared value of hard work that ensures equality between all members in the community.[20]

Third, the prophets often prioritize the importance of attitudes about clothing over the quality or abundance of clothing itself. Thus the Book of Mormon presents varying estimations of fine clothing's moral value through the lens of the perceived intent of the wearer and also the work the clothing is seen to perform in the community where it is worn.[21] Fine clothing donned by individuals for the intent of expressing personal economic or social superiority to other members of the community expresses an incorrect orientation toward worldly possessions, overdeveloped care for temporal concerns, and leads to social stratification, economic disparity, and unjust treatment of the poor and needy. By contrast, the stated goal of the fine cloth produced in Mosiah 10:5 and elsewhere is to allow the people "to clothe [their] nakedness." While this phrase gives the impression that the clothing itself was simple and utilitarian even though made out of good-quality materials, perhaps it indicates less about the appearance of the clothes and more about what Mormon$_2$ perceived to be a proper attitude about clothing. As mentioned earlier, Mormon$_2$ considered the prosperous of Alma 1 to not be wearing "costly apparel" despite their accumulation of a good deal of fine silks and linens because they were sufficiently giving of what they had and caring for the poor in the community. Their focus was oriented away from personal social aggrandizement and toward ensuring that the whole community was clothed, cared for, and prosperous.

Toward the end of the Book of Mormon, this ethos is further developed as Jesus visits the Nephites and reiterates for their religious leaders some teachings similar to those of Matthew 6:28–33, encouraging the people to "consider the lilies of the field" (3 Nephi 13:28):

> Wherefore, if God so clothe the grass of the field . . . even so will he clothe you, if ye are not of little faith. Therefore take no thought, saying, What shall we eat? or, What shall we drink? or Wherewithal shall we be clothed? For your heavenly Father knoweth that ye have need of all these things. But seek ye first the kingdom of God and his righteousness, and all these things shall be added unto you. (3 Nephi 13:30–33)

Jesus teaches that correct attitudes about clothing, at least for some designated disciples, include eschewing any care for appearance or clothing. No thought at all was to be given to any bodily covering or other physical necessity, but all focus was to be on spiritual matters with trust that once one's priorities were correctly focused on the kingdom of God rather than the physical world, God would provide what was necessary for maintenance and clothing of the body.[22] To be clothed by God was a manifestation of one's correct orientation toward him and would allow God's righteousness to be manifest in his disciples.[23]

Ethical Dress: Others

Jesus promises that God will dress his disciples as magnificently as he does the lilies of the field. Likewise, the Book of Mormon places no limitations on richly dressing and adorning others out of one's own abundance. Providing clothes to others is considered an expression of correct orientation toward God rather than worldly things and a commitment to unity and equality in the community. Book of Mormon narrators also interpreted the clothing of others to be a manifestation of personal righteousness. Personal endeavors to clothe the naked kept the giver in a state of personal holiness. Benjamin teaches that "for the sake of retaining a remission of your sins from day to day . . . I would that ye should impart of your substance to the poor, every man according to that which he hath, such as feeding the hungry, clothing the naked, visiting the sick and administering to their relief, both spiritually and temporally, according to their wants" (Mosiah 4:26). Clothing and otherwise caring for the poor is understood to be a powerful prophylactic against personal sin. While counseling moderation in some respects, Benjamin also asserts that a beggar was never to be denied his request unless the giver was in a state of poverty so dire that he had nothing to give (Mosiah 4:25, 4:27). "For behold, are we not all beggars?" he reasons. "Do we not all depend upon the same Being, even God, for all the substance which we have, for both food and raiment, and for gold, and for silver, and for all the riches which we have of every kind?" (Mosiah 4:19). For Benjamin, humanity's abject poverty before God and dependency on his mercy for all demands that if even the poorest members of a community have a shirt to give, it must be given when asked for by another in need.

With similar concern for the poor and needy of his community, Jacob$_2$ asserts not the common impoverished state of all before God but rather the potential of the entire community to become "rich" through sharing. He decries the pride of his people manifest in their wealth and wearing of expensive clothing as it is leading to social divisions in the community (Jacob 2:13). But rather than condemning material prosperity, he interprets riches in a positive light: "Think of your brethren like unto yourselves, and be familiar with all and free with your substance, that they may be rich like unto you" (Jacob 2:17). For Jacob, the ethical objective of a righteous society is to make all equally "rich" through the prosperous sharing their material means with the less prosperous. After one has sought the kingdom of God and "obtained a hope in Christ," riches might be righteously sought out and obtained if done so with the intent to "clothe the naked, and to feed the hungry, and to liberate the captive, and administer relief to the sick and the afflicted" (Jacob 2:19). Jacob$_2$ imagines a society where the personal accumulation of wealth is a context for altruism through its distribution within the community and the elevation of every member to prosperity. All will be cared for and richly clothed if everyone will share what they have. But Jacob$_2$ also promises material prosperity to those who seek the kingdom of God first, entwining his teachings of charitable giving with a gospel of prosperity. Riches will be given to the righteous whose priorities are in correct order and whom God knows will clothe the naked with them.[24]

In general, the Book of Mormon prophets encourage the generous disbursement of one's material goods to others. The only situation in which clothing another person is completely condemned is when the receiver is deemed a false prophet. The prophet Samuel$_2$ condemns the Nephite people for giving money, "costly apparel," and support to false prophets who teach things that are pleasing to hear rather than things that are true (Helaman 13:27–28).[25] For Alma$_2$, Nehor's wearing of fine clothing is an integral part of what proves he is a false prophet. Nehor teaches that the priests and teachers of the church should not be laboring manually but should be supported by their congregations, and many people give him support and money, leading him to be prideful and wear "very costly apparel" (Alma 1:6).[26]

Conclusion: Book of Mormon Dress Ethics versus Modesty

The Book of Mormon demonstrates an ethics of clothing based on its dual concern for social justice and religious rectitude. While its prophets connect the wearing of fine dress and ornamentation to worldliness, unholy pride, the nakedness of the poor, and corrosive social division, it is clear that their common pejoratives, such as "very fine apparel," refer to more than the simple material realities of the clothing. They seem untroubled by the fineness or costliness of dress if such clothing is provided to all members of the community, if all labor and toil together for its production and procurement, and if it is worn while maintaining a correct orientation toward God, with an attitude of humility and well-prioritized social aspirations to help the poor. These guiding principles yield a series of ethical guidelines for the wearing of clothing that account for both divine mandates against pride and materialism as well as the socioeconomic work that the production and wearing of clothes performs within the community.

With respect to contemporary dress ethics, it is useful to consider these Book of Mormon principles in relation to the teachings of the Church of Jesus Christ of Latter-day Saints. While the book does not (and need not) serve exhaustively as a theological and ethical measure for the doctrines and practices of the church, Latter-day Saints represent the largest denomination of those who read the Book of Mormon as sacred scripture and engage with it frequently as a source of spiritual guidance in their everyday lives. With respect to dress, modern church teachings diverge significantly from the attitudes and concerns of Book of Mormon authors.

Latter-day Saint leaders have long established various policies and guidelines of appropriate dress for its membership, but the most widespread and best known of these dress ethics has been articulated in terms of "modesty" and has been directed almost exclusively at women and women's dress. In his 1951 address to students at Brigham Young University, church leader Spencer W. Kimball decried increasing sexual immorality in the world and cited "the immodest dresses that are worn by our women, and their mothers" as a significant cause of the problem. For Kimball, women's immodest clothing—including strapped and strapless evening gowns, low-neck dresses, tight sweaters, backless attire, and shorts—was leading to sexual sin and a deterioration of society in general.[27] Kimball's connection of female dress to sexual sin gained a good deal of traction in the church in the 1960s, largely in reaction to the contemporary sexual revolution, and in the decades that followed, church leaders with growing frequency attributed what they perceived to be the declining sexual morality of the world to the immodest clothing of women in particular. Inappropriately clad women were increasingly blamed for the unchaste thoughts and actions of men.[28] Women were encouraged to eschew unisex clothing in favor of more feminine styles that seemed to church leaders to promote traditional gender roles and chastity among its members.[29]

From the 1960s to the present, the Church of Jesus Christ has published various manuals, newspaper editorials, and pamphlets outlining appropriate standards of dress for its members. The most prominent of these, *For the Strength of Youth*, directed toward the church's teenage members, was first published in 1965 and is still in print (and in digital formats) today. While the pamphlet has undergone many revisions, until its most recent revision in 2022 it continuously provided instruction focused on women's modesty, with prohibitions of short shorts, short skirts, midriff-revealing shirts, sleeveless, and low-cut clothing, directed specifically at young women (while young men were vaguely told to "maintain modesty").[30] The Gospel Topics essay "Modesty," currently on the church's website, continues to stress a connection between modest dress and sexual chastity, warning that women's suggestive clothing can stimulate inappropriate desires and lead to sexual sin.[31]

In general, Latter-day Saint leaders have promoted a dress ethos of modesty that is deeply gendered and focused on the female body as the site where the sexual morality of society is created, with women bearing responsibility for its maintenance. These principles are deeply at odds with the ethics of dress encountered in the Book of Mormon. Based on the conjuncture of socioeconomic concerns and theology, Book of Mormon prophets understood the moral value of dress to be determined by its spiritual impact on the individual and socioeconomic impact on the community. With the single exception of the toiling and spinning women (Helaman 6.13; Mosiah 10.5), discussions of clothing are never gendered. Clothing is never linked to manifestations of proper or improper sexual behaviors or gender roles. On the other hand, the Latter-day Saint ethics of modesty originate from concerns for gender and sexuality in conjunction with Latter-day Saint doctrines about the sacredness of the body and procreation. Rather than communicating unrighteous pride and a lack of care for the poor that puts the community at risk, "immodest" clothing is understood to communicate *women's* openness to sexual sin and *women's* transgression of gender roles that threaten the well-being of society.

In 2022, Latter-day Saint Church leaders revised the *For the Strength of Youth* pamphlet and excluded all references to the term "modesty." Young members are now encouraged to formulate a personal standard of dress based on personal inspiration from God and their understandings of the body's sacred nature.[32] The new pamphlet asserts that styles for both women and men should emphasize the divine nature and destiny of the wearer and not seek to draw inappropriate attention to the physical body. All are encouraged to let "moral cleanliness" guide choices about clothing.[33]

This disavowal of "modesty" indicates a remarkable sea change in Latter-day Saint clothing rhetoric, particularly with the removal of gendered teachings about dress directed to women and concerning women's bodies. Yet emphasis remains on making clothing choices based on the maintenance of bodily holiness and "moral cleanliness," or sexual morality. Dress continues to be understood to be an indicator of the sexual, and righteousness hinges on correct sexual behaviors. In contrast, the Book of Mormon presents a different standard for ethical dress, with clothing understood to indicate pride or humility, and morality hinging on the social and economic equality in a community. What would a reconciliation of the ethics of these two distinctive systems yield? The question of what revisions must be made to modern Latter-day Saint dress ethics in light of its defining and authoritative scripture, the Book of Mormon, awaits further consideration.

Notes

1. This is a foundational principle of clothing studies established by scholars such as Malcolm Barnard in his *Fashion as Communication* (London: Routledge, 2002).

2. This idea has developed from Anna-Katharina Höpflinger's assertion that clothing communicates sociocultural categories as well as religious worldviews. See Höpflinger, "Between Regulation, Identification, and Representation: Clothing and Nudity from the Perspective of the Study of Religion," in *Clothing and Nudity in the Hebrew Bible*, ed. Christoph Berner, Manuel Schäfer, et al. (London: T & T Clark, 2019), 5–10.

3. Nephi$_1$ also attributes the disoriented desires for worldly praise to this church's taking captive and destroying "the saints of God" (1 Nephi 13:9). While the reference is unclear, a few Latter-day Saint leaders—most notably, Bruce R. McConkie (who served as an LDS apostle from 1972 to 1985)—have interpreted the "great and abominable church" as a reference to the Catholic Church. See Bruce R. McConkie, *Mormon Doctrine*, 1st ed. (Salt Lake City: Bookcraft, 1958).

4. Alma$_2$'s condemnatory listing of the "costly" apparel of the Zoramites is somewhat reminiscent of the condemnation of the daughters of Israel in Isaiah 3:16–26, a passage transcribed in its entirety and without direct commentary earlier in the Book of Mormon (2 Nephi 13:16–26).

5. Parrish Brady and Shon Hopkin argue that Mormon$_2$ uses the clothing of the rich and poor Zoramites metaphorically to illustrate the digression/progression of the wicked and righteous in Alma 31–44. See Brady and Hopkin, "The Zoramites and Costly Apparel: Symbolism and Irony," *Journal of Book of Mormon Studies* 22, no. 1 (2013): 40–53.

6. After thoroughly condemning the practices and doctrines of the Zoramites, Alma$_2$ ends his prayer by pleading: "O Lord, wilt thou grant unto us that we may have success in bringing them again unto thee in Christ. Behold, O Lord, their souls are precious, and many of them are our brethren; therefore, give unto us, O Lord, power and wisdom that we may bring these, our brethren, again unto thee" (Alma 31:34–35). The charity and universality of this all-encompassing plea stands in stark contrast to the divisive prayer of the Zoramites as recounted by Alma$_2$ in Alma 31:15–18.

7. While Moroni$_2$ does not specify the time he sees in his vision or give any defining details, LDS readers commonly understand that his prophecies refer broadly to the centuries since the Book of Mormon was discovered and translated. See Ezra Taft Benson, "A New Witness for Christ," *Ensign* (Nov. 1984): 6; L. Tom Perry, "Blessings Resulting from Reading the Book of Mormon," *Ensign* (Nov. 2005): 6–8. Moroni$_2$'s father, Mormon$_2$, who was the editor and commentator of most of the book, attributed the destruction of Nephite civilization to both the wickedness of the people generally (Moroni 6:16–22) and to the lasting negative influence of one Gadianton, who formed a covert crime ring that perished and then resurged multiple times in Nephite society for hundreds of years (Helaman 2:13).

8. See Höpflinger, "Between Regulation," 5, 9–10.

9. The Genesis narrative recording the fall of Adam and Eve from Eden was known to Book of Mormon prophets by means of the "brass plates" taken from Jerusalem (see 1 Nephi 4:4–29) that contained, among other things, the five books of Moses (1 Nephi 5:11). Lehi, Jacob's father, teaches about Adam and Eve's spiritual and physical fall and descent from Eden in 2 Nephi 2:14–20.

10. Eric Silverman asserts that in most cases, disrobing intends to strip away "a person's identity and status while affirming the authority of the superior." See Silverman, *A Cultural History of Jewish Dress* (London: Bloomsbury, 2013), 9. As with the poor in the land of Antionum, Alma₂ and Amulek may not have been totally naked in prison, or at least not for the entire duration. After they miraculously break their bonds and cause the prison walls to fall down, they "straightaway came forth into the city" instead of seeking food and clothing (Alma 14:28).

11. While Book of Mormon prophets frequently decry the nakedness of the poor, it is not clear that they were referring to the poor being completely without clothes. As previously mentioned, the poorest class of people in Antionum were considered by the higher classes of their society to be "dross" and "filth[y]" and were excluded from communal religious worship because of the "coarseness of their clothing" rather than their lack of clothing altogether (Alma 32:2–3). It is not clear whether these poor were simply more fortunate than other "poor" who were totally naked or whether the prophets would have also considered the poor of Antionum to be among the "naked" because they needed the administration of food and clothing when they left their land to join with the Nephites (Alma 35:9). For a similar consideration of how naked the "naked" of the Hebrew Bible were, see Rainer Kessler, "'When You See the Naked, Cover Them!' (Isa. 58:7): The Clothing of the Poor as an Act of Righteousness," in Berner and Manuel Schäfer, *Clothing and Nudity in the Hebrew Bible*, 334–35.

12. Cf. the contrasting description of the Lamanites in Mosiah 10:8 to the hardworking and fully clothed Nephites in Mosiah 10:4–5.

13. Even when the Lamanites return to fight garbed in thick skins, the Nephites still win by out-preparing them. See Alma 49:6–9. For Mormon₂ (who narrates this story), the victory seems less about the quality of fighting and more dependent on an army's adequate preparation with clothing and weapons.

14. In fact, the prophet-king Benjamin finds it morally reprehensible that someone would withhold help from a beggar who they judged to be unworthy and deserving of his lowly situation: "Whosoever doeth this the same hath great cause to repent; and except he repenteth of that which he hath done he perisheth forever, and hath no interest in the kingdom of God" (Mosiah 4:16–18).

15. It is notable that the references in two of these passages to *women* toiling and spinning (Mosiah 10:5; Helaman 6:13) are the only occasions in the Book of Mormon in which clothing and dress are tied to a specific gender. The authors imply that women are the correct producers of clothing for the community, in contrast to a nongendered "they" who toil and spin in Ether 10:24.

16. See also Ether 9:16–20. Because the Book of Mormon situates itself in the tradition of the Hebrew Bible and speaks frequently of Adam in context of the

creation and fall narratives (e.g., 1 Nephi 5:11; 2 Nephi 2:22, 2:25; Alma 22:13, 42:5; Mormon 9:12), it is reasonable to argue that this repeated valuation of toiling and spinning and of covering one's nakedness may stem from the primordial garden narrative where Adam and Eve discovered their nakedness and by their own industry sewed together fig leaves to cover it (Genesis 3:7).

17. Cf. 2 Nephi 26:30–31: "Wherefore, if they should have charity they would not suffer the laborer in Zion to perish. But the laborer in Zion shall labor for Zion; for if they labor for money they shall perish." Charity is to be extended to those who labor, and they must labor also for the good of the community rather than to get ahead in it.

18. On the other hand, Mormon₂ states that the unbelievers of the community who don't achieve the same material prosperity as the righteous are guilty of wearing costly apparel as well as laziness, idolatry, theft, whoredoms, murder, and unrighteous pride (Alma 1:31–32).

19. Cf. Noah₃, a despotic Nephite king condemned for levying heavy taxes upon his people to support his laziness, idolatry, and sexual perversions (Mosiah 11:3–4, 11:6).

20. It must be acknowledged that Mormon₂'s statement that Nephite women in particular were specifically tasked with the labor of making cloth in Helaman 6:13 suggests a society with deeply divided gender roles and displays something of the limitations of Nephite egalitarianism at this period.

21. Daniel Becerra has noted how wealth "affects and reflects personal and communal morality" in the Book of Mormon. Economic and moral discourse converges and discussions of wealth are theological and tied to the people's relationship to God. See Daniel Becerra, "Samuel the Lamanite and the Ethics of Wealth in the Book of Mormon," in *Samuel the Lamanite: That Ye Might Believe*, ed. Charles Swift (Provo, UT: Religious Studies Center, BYU, 2021), 109–110.

22. Similarly, Nephi₁ and Jacob₂ both refer to a "robe of righteousness" or divine protection within which God may choose to enfold the worthy (2 Nephi 4:33, 9:14; cf. Isa. 61:10).

23. While the "take no thought" notion of Jesus's teaching inspired generations of Christians toward ascetic practices of the body, the Book of Mormon lacks any reference to extreme forms of dress beyond nakedness and advocates moderation in appearance. Eschewing costly apparel in favor of giving to the poor, Mormon₂ reassures readers that the righteous Nephites nevertheless still appeared "neat and comely" (Alma 1:27). In doing so, he excludes any notions that nakedness or bodily neglect might be coded as positive in the Nephite religious context. On the other hand, the Book of Mormon allows that divesting oneself of clothes through the rending of garments in righteous indignation or in making a covenant before God is honorable and praiseworthy, such as are performed publicly by Captain Moroni₁ and the Nephites who join his cause of liberty (Alma 46:11–12, 46:19–24). Notably, their ensuing state of undress is never referred to as "nakedness."

24. Susan Easton Black discusses the promises of temporal wealth for the righteous that are found throughout the Book of Mormon in her "Lest Ye Become

as the Nephites of Old," in *The Book of Mormon: The Keystone Scripture*, ed. Paul R. Cheesman, 256–68 (Provo, UT: Religious Studies Center, BYU, 1988).

25. While less explicitly stated, a similar modification of priestly teachings in exchange for material goods may have been taking place among the people of King Noah$_3$ in Mosiah 11:3–11.

26. Perhaps it is because of Nehor that Alma$_2$ seems especially sensitive when a later theological challenger, Korihor, brings similar accusations against him. Korihor accuses Alma and other priests of taking financial advantage of their congregations (Alma 30:27) and Alma$_2$ heatedly responds at length (Alma 30:32–35).

27. Spencer W. Kimball, *A Style of Our Own: Modesty in Dress and Its Relationship to the Church*, An Apostle Speaks to Youth, No. 4 (Provo, UT: Brigham Young University, 1951), not paginated.

28. See Katie Clark Blakesley, "'A Style of Our Own': Modesty and Mormon Women, 1951–2008," *Dialogue* 42, no. 2 (2009): 22–26. Notable among these leaders was Elder Mark E. Petersen, who taught at the general conference of the church's general women's organization, the Relief Society, in 1962: "What tempts the boys to molest the girls today more than any one thing . . . is the mode of dress of our girls," claiming that when "such sights are placed before their eyes, almost like an invitation, can you blame them any more than the girls who tempt them, if they take advantage of those girls?" (quoted in Blakesley, 25).

29. Blakesley, "Style of Our Own," 26–28.

30. *For the Strength of Youth* (Salt Lake City: Church of Jesus Christ of Latter-day Saints, 2011), 7.

31. "Modesty," Church of Jesus Christ of Latter-day Saints (accessed February 24, 2023), https://www.churchofjesuschrist.org/study/manual/gospel-topics/modesty?lang=eng.

32. "For the Strength of Youth," Church of Jesus Christ of Latter-day Saints (accessed February 24, 2023, https://www.churchofjesuschrist.org/study/manual/for-the-strength-of-youth/06-body?lang=eng&id=11#p11.

33. "For the Strength of Youth," 5.

10

An Ethics of Authority and the Authority of Ethics

The Book of Mormon Talks Back

MICHAEL D. K. ING

God,
grant me the courage to question my leaders;
the humility to accept their answers;
and the prudence to know when courage becomes arrogance
and humility becomes complicity.

Several years ago, there was a discussion on one of the Mormon blogs named after the longest-running LDS Church periodical, *Millennial Star*. The topic was the attempted sacrifice of Isaac, the son of Abraham, in the Bible. In critically reading the story, one participant asked whether anyone would seriously consider taking the life of their children if the president of the church had asked them to do so. One of the hosts of the blog said, "With the testimony I have of the living prophets, if President [Thomas S.] Monson were to call upon me to sacrifice one of my children, I would do so."[1] The host did go on to explain how he believed the prophet would never ask such a thing; nonetheless, I think his general sentiment about the moral authority of LDS Church leaders is shared and, furthermore, the church has actually fostered this kind of moral reasoning.

This chapter looks to the Book of Mormon in addressing the relationship between moral authority and ecclesiastical authority. More specifically, it draws from the text (primarily 3 Nephi 6) to reveal the trouble of conflating these authorities. Theoretically, this chapter explores the question of what happens when the Book of Mormon becomes critical of the authorities who claim authority to interpret it. This chapter is a kind of taking back (and talking back to) authority. My aim is to open up more space for extra-ecclesiastical moral authority within Latter-day Saint Church culture. This includes space for legitimately disagreeing with the church as a matter of conscience, space for church leaders to admit wrongdoing, and the need for the church to develop a more robust mode of ethical reflection that goes beyond the language of loyalty.

This chapter is organized into three sections. The first describes the current state of Latter-day Saint culture, where moral authority is coupled with ecclesiastical authority. The second shows how portions of the Book of Mormon reveal an uncomfortable truth—namely, that ecclesiastical authority is not above corruption and can sometimes present itself in ways that suggest those with such authority aim to take the place of God. The third section provides preliminary ideas to limit ecclesiastical authority in ways that create space for other forms of moral reasoning. My hope is that this chapter continues a conversation that builds to articulating more robust forms of moral reflection within Latter-day Saint culture.

Faith Obedience: The Might of the Priesthood Makes Right

"No true Latter-day Saint will ever take a stand that is in opposition to what the Lord has revealed to those who direct the affairs of his earthly kingdom."[2]

Latter-day Saints have been troubled by September 11 long before 2001. On September 11, 1857, a Latter-day Saint militia executed 120 men, women, and children passing through Utah on their way to California. The event became known as the Mountain Meadows Massacre.[3] How otherwise good people could perpetrate such horrendous acts is a perplexing moral issue.

Approximately 150 years later, in the wake of September 11, 2001, another Latter-day Saint, Assistant Attorney General Jay S. Bybee, provided legal advice to the president of the United States on captured Taliban and other suspected terrorist operatives. The memo, in part, endorsed enhanced interrogation techniques, which included waterboarding, extreme sleep and food deprivation, enclosures in coffin-like spaces, and intimidating prisoners who had been forced to strip naked. These techniques were developed by another Latter-day Saint, John Bruce Jessen, and his business partner, James Elmer Mitchell—psychologists who ran a consulting company called Mitchell Jessen and Associates. The United States government paid Mitchell Jessen over $80 million partly to help develop this program.[4]

In September 2003, Alyssa Peterson, a Latter-day Saint and soldier in the 311th Military Intelligence Battalion of the 101st Airborne Division, was sent to Iraq to do interrogations. Peterson had recently completed an undergraduate degree in psychology and had studied Arabic at the Defense Language Institute. After only two days of working in what they called "the cage," Peterson refused to be involved. It is unclear exactly what she was asked to do, but other colleagues described the use of enhanced interrogation techniques. Peterson was reassigned but also reprimanded for showing too much "empathy" for the prisoners. On September 15, 2003, she took her own life with her military-issued firearm. She left behind a notebook that tied her death to her participation in the interrogation tactics of the cage.[5]

This is a deeply tragic story, made all the more ironic by the fact that Bybee, Jessen, and Peterson are all members of the church. To state this more baldly, one of the members of the LDS Church designed a program to intentionally harm, humiliate, and systematically abuse potential terrorists; another member gave official endorsement to implement it; and another Latter-day Saint was then tasked to carry it out. After two days of practicing it, this final Latter-day Saint took her own life. Perhaps the deepest point of irony in this story is that, ostensibly speaking, the only one of the three who did something "wrong" was Peterson in dying by suicide. Bybee went on to become a circuit judge in the court of appeals for the Ninth Circuit. Jessen was actually called as a church bishop in 2012, only to step down a week later, not because of an institutional reprimand but because, in his own words, "I just felt it would be unfair for me to bring that controversy to a lot of other people."[6] And although the church has recently softened its rhetoric on suicide, it is still unequivocal that suicide is "not right."[7]

While these situations are more complicated than I have portrayed, it is fair to at least say that Latter-day Saints lack a robust tradition of moral deliberation. I will go even further to say that in place of a deliberative ethics, an ethics of authority has taken up shop. In other words, the idea that the *might* of priesthood authority *makes right* is a well-documented tradition within LDS culture. The problem, to put it in theoretical terms, is that ecclesiastical authority has become synonymous with moral authority, and the church's language of morality is the language of loyalty (usually framed as "obedience") to the church and its leaders.

This is best captured by the term "faith obedience," which comes from the title of Elder R. Conrad Schultz's talk in the April 2002 LDS General Conference. He stated:

> One of the sneaky ploys of the adversary [i.e., the devil] is to have us believe that unquestioning obedience to the principles and commandments of God is blind obedience. His goal is to have us believe that we should be following our own worldly ways and selfish ambitions. This he

does by persuading us that "blindly" following the prophets and obeying the commandments is not thinking for ourselves. He teaches that it is not intelligent to do something just because we are told to do so by a living prophet or by prophets who speak to us from the scriptures. Our unquestioning obedience to the Lord's commandments is not blind obedience. . . . We might call this "faith obedience."[8]

Faith obedience, while not blind, is unquestioning. We ought to do things when told to do so by prophets. Their word is necessary and sufficient. Other authorities in the church before and after Schultz have expressed this idea of faith obedience. Perhaps the best example is attributed to Heber J. Grant (1856–1945), seventh president of the church, who is purported to have said, "Always keep your eye on the President of the Church and if he ever tells you to do anything, and it is wrong, and you do it, the Lord will bless you for it." The provenance of this quote is unclear, but the life it takes on is worth noting. Elder Marion G. Romney (a member of the Quorum of the Twelve Apostles) quotes this in General Conference in 1960 and repeats it in 1972; President Ezra Taft Benson quotes it at Brigham Young University in 1980; and the Relief Society and Priesthood Manual for the church repeats it in 2014.[9]

This quote is interesting for several reasons. Most relevant, it highlights a long-standing tension recognized by philosophers between what is right and what is good. In this case, the good of faith obedience wins out over what is right. This view is perhaps best explained as a kind of benevolent paternalism. In other words, we live in a world where what is right is not always clear, but if anyone knows what is right, it will be the prophets of the LDS Church. We cannot trust in ourselves in the same way we can trust in them. Their position puts them in closer proximity to the right, so we ought to rely on them, even if they end up being wrong. Said differently, we ought to take their view as right because we lack the authority to see as they do. Even if they end up being wrong, their authority ensures that they will be wrong far less often than we will.

This benevolent paternalism is frequently reinforced by assurances that God will not allow the prophet to lead the church astray. The penultimate chapter of the LDS scriptural canon concludes with these words of President Wilford Woodruff (1807–1898): "The Lord will never permit me or any other man who stands as President of this Church to lead you astray. It is not in the programme. It is not in the mind of God. If I were to attempt that, the Lord would remove me out of my place."[10] The idea is that prophets are *capable* of choosing poorly; however, God will not permit the leader of his church to do so (at least in any major way). Prophets are fallible, but they will not stray.[11] As expressed in an LDS children's hymn: "Follow the prophet . . . don't go astray; follow the prophet . . . he knows the way."[12]

Because of prophetic authority, and because of prophetic assurances of their own "instrayability," members of the church are not in a position to correct ecclesiastical authority. As President Henry B. Eyring explained in the April 2019 General Conference, where he quoted President George Q. Cannon (1827–1901): "God has chosen His servants. He claims it as His prerogative to condemn them, if they need condemnation. He has not given it to us individually to censure and condemn them."[13] Ahmad S. Corbitt, first counselor in the Young Men General Presidency, builds on these words in a 2022 address to LDS chaplains titled "Activism vs. Discipleship."[14] After quoting Eyring, Corbitt explains, "All needed and appropriate changes in the Kingdom of God are God's work to bring to pass." Regular members of the church advocating for change, according to Corbitt, represent a "modern-day verbal stoning [of the prophets]." This kind of advocacy is "one of the most masterful deceptions of our time astutely spun by the 'liar from the beginning' who 'deceiveth the whole world' [i.e., the devil]."

President Dallin H. Oaks, currently next in line to lead the LDS Church, has taken a similar position, explaining that it does not matter if the criticism one offers is correct. In 1985, Oaks said the following to all Church Educational System teachers:

> Criticism is particularly objectionable when it is directed toward Church authorities, general or local. Jude condemns those who "speak evil of dignities." (Jude 1:8.) Evil speaking of the Lord's anointed is in a class by itself. It is one thing to depreciate a person who exercises corporate power or even government power. It is quite another thing to criticize or depreciate a person for the performance of an office to which he or she has been called of God. It does not matter that the criticism is true. As Elder George F. Richards, President of the Council of the Twelve, said in a conference address in April 1947, "When we say anything bad about the leaders of the Church, whether true or false, we tend to impair their influence and their usefulness and are thus working against the Lord and his cause."[15]

Oaks repeats parts of this in 1987, 1991, and 2007.[16] In the 1987 retelling, which was published in the church publication *Ensign*, he added: "The counsel against speaking evil of Church leaders is not so much for the benefit of the leaders as it is for the spiritual well-being of members who are prone to murmur and find fault. The Church leaders I know are durable people. They made their way successfully in a world of unrestrained criticism before they received their current callings. They have no personal need for protection."

Oaks's warning about criticism coincides with the benevolent paternalism mentioned previously. Members should not criticize leaders of the church, not because the criticisms are inaccurate or because the leaders cannot handle it but because it will encourage other members to distrust the leadership. Members are prone to fall away, while prophets are in a league of their own. Faith obedience requires recognizing your inadequacy when compared with church leaders. The might of their priesthood authority makes them right.

Less Than the Dust of the Earth: Moral Vulnerability in the Book of Mormon

The idea that a group of people can be above criticism and the idea that ecclesiastical authority dictates moral authority are both challenged in the Book of Mormon, particularly in the last third of the text. The twelfth chapter of Helaman largely consists of the reflections of the main editor, Mormon$_2$, after recounting several tumultuous years between competing groups of Nephites as well as Lamanites, all taking place shortly before the birth of Jesus. Mormon$_2$ laments:

> O how foolish, and how vain, and how evil, and devilish, and how quick to do iniquity, and how slow to do good, are the children of men; yea, how quick to hearken unto the words of the evil one, and to set their hearts upon the vain things of the world!
>
> Yea, how quick to be lifted up in pride; yea, how quick to boast, and do all manner of that which is iniquity; and how slow are they to remember the Lord their God, and to give ear unto his counsels, yea, how slow to walk in wisdom's paths!
>
> Behold, they do not desire that the Lord their God, who hath created them, should rule and reign over them; notwithstanding his great goodness and his mercy towards them, they do set at naught his counsels, and they will not that he should be their guide.
>
> O how great is the nothingness of the children of men; yea, even they are less than the dust of the earth. (Helaman 12:4–7)

This is not a pretty picture of humanity. We are foolish, vain, and evil; slow to follow the counsels of God; quick to boast of our own power. We do not want God ruling over us; preferring, perhaps, to instead exalt one of our own. Indeed, what a splendidly savage rejoinder: how great is our nothingness. Mormon$_2$ argues that we are deeply vulnerable creatures when it comes to being good.

This expression of human vulnerability is reminiscent of Elder Dieter F. Uchtdorf's reading of Matthew 26 in the Bible, which relates that at the Last Supper, Jesus tells his twelve apostles that one of them will betray him.[17] Verse 22 reads, "They were exceeding sorrowful, and began every one of them to say unto him, Lord, is it I?" Uchtdorf picks this up in General Conference in 2014, and although he does not use the term that I will use to describe the situation, he essentially highlights the problem of self-deception wherein we come to believe that there is no way the "it" could be "I." As Uchtdorf states, "I'm not sure why we are able to diagnose and recommend remedies for other people's ills so well, while we often have difficulty seeing our own." In contrast to this, the scene at the Last Supper is one of vulnerability—each member of Jesus's inner circle is open to the possibility that *they* might betray Jesus. Devout readers might initially believe they themselves would never do such a deed, but the text seems to speak to this impulse: If one of the apostles was capable, why not I? The lesson seems to be that our fortitude for the moral is never beyond reproach, including times when we have been chosen by God himself. When it comes to moral frailty, there is no difference between the twelve apostles and the rest of humanity. Furthermore, we all can easily deceive ourselves into thinking that we are morally invulnerable.

A few chapters, and about thirty years later, following his lamentation on vulnerability, we again find Mormon$_2$ describing a tumultuous scene, in what the book designates as the twenty-sixth year since the sign of Jesus's birth. A reprieve in the fighting that occupied the previous years has occurred and the people get a chance of sorts to start over. This time is described in 3 Nephi 6:4 as a time of "great order in the land." The twenty-eighth year is marked by peace and prosperity, but in the twenty-ninth year, people begin to be "distinguished by ranks" of rich and poor as well as educated and uneducated. This fuels animosity, building to verse 14: "And thus there became a great inequality in all the land, insomuch that the church began to be broken up; yea, insomuch that in the thirtieth year the church was broken up in all the land save it were among a few of the Lamanites who were converted unto the true faith." The situation seems akin to other Latter-day Saint narratives of spiritual decline and apostasy.[18] People fall away from the authoritative church until only a small group belongs to the true faith. In this instance, the Lamanites preserve this true faith. The story continues by explaining the source of the falling away: "Now the cause of this iniquity of the people was this—Satan had great power, unto the stirring up of the people to do all manner of iniquity, and to the puffing them up with pride, tempting them to seek for power, and authority, and riches, and the vain things of the world" (3 Nephi 6:15). Readers learn in verse 17 that this search for power, authority, and riches leads these people into "a state of awful wickedness." Things take a turn, however, in verse 20: "And there began to be men inspired from heaven and sent forth, standing among the people in all the land, preaching and testifying boldly of the sins and iniquities of the people." Readers are not told much about these inspired men. Since the text has just mentioned that the true faith was preserved by only a small group of Lamanites, followed by the report of these inspired men sent by inspiration from heaven, the remaining church does not appear to be the source for these men (the text would probably identify them as Lamanites if that were the case). Indeed, they do not appear to be called by church leaders, nor do they seem concerned with ensuring that their agitation for change is sanctioned by ecclesiastical authority.

There is precedent for aspects of this in the Book of Mormon. Earlier in the text, Lehi₁ and Abinadi appear to gain their authority for activism directly from God, as does the later prophet Samuel₂ the Lamanite. More broadly speaking, this is something of an Old Testament trope where prophets appear at dark moments with a voice of warning. Notably, the Old Testament prophets are not necessarily connected with priesthood authority. Jeremiah, for instance, who supposedly lived at the same time as Lehi, received his charge as direct communication from God:

> Thus says the Lord: Stand in the court of the Lord's house, and speak to all the cities of Judah that come to worship in the house of the Lord; speak to them all the words that I command you; do not hold back a word. It may be that they will listen, all of them, and will turn from their evil way, that I may change my mind about the disaster that I intend to bring on them because of their evil doings. (Jeremiah 26:2–3)[19]

Jeremiah delivers his message in the temple courtyard, where readers discover that the people choose not to turn from their evil ways: "And when Jeremiah had finished speaking all that the Lord had commanded him to speak to all the people, then the priests and the prophets and all the people laid hold of him, saying, 'You shall die!'" (Jeremiah 26:8). Interestingly, the priests and prophets are implicated in the act of seeking to kill Jeremiah for speaking the words God had given him.

There are two points worth noting about these passages. First, the moral authority of those inspired from heaven does not come from being sanctioned by the institutionalized authority of the priesthood. Second, even those involved in running the religious institution of the time were capable of not only being deeply wrong on moral issues but even seeking to kill God's appointed messenger.

The vignette from the book of Jeremiah is furthermore central to the narrative of the Book of Mormon itself, where the rejection of Jeremiah's (and Lehi₁'s) message provides the reason for Lehi₁'s family to flee Jerusalem before it was destroyed as promised by Jeremiah. Thus, the entire Book of Mormon is a text born from men called by God who were not only unsanctioned by ecclesiastical structures of the time but also targets of violence by those structures.

Returning to 3 Nephi 6, readers find a similar reaction to the men inspired from heaven: "Now there were many of the people who were exceedingly angry because of those who testified of these things; and those who were angry were chiefly the chief judges, and they who had been high priests and lawyers" (3 Nephi 6:21). The chapter goes on to explain that the judges began sentencing these "prophets of the Lord" to death, usurping the authority of the governor who otherwise held sole authority to execute these kinds of sentences. Eventually, word of this reaches the governor, who has the judges arrested and tried in court. The chapter concludes with a narrative of moral corruption:

> Now it came to pass that those judges had many friends and kindreds; and the remainder, yea, even almost all the lawyers and the high priests, did gather themselves together, and unite with the kindreds of those judges who were to be tried according to the law. And they did enter into a covenant one with another, yea, even into that covenant which was given by them of old, which covenant was given and administered by the devil, to combine against all righteousness. Therefore they did combine against the people of the Lord, and enter into a covenant to destroy them, and to deliver those who were guilty of murder from the grasp of justice, which was about to be administered according to the law. And they did set at defiance the law and the rights of their country; and they did covenant one with another to destroy the governor, and to establish a king over the land, that the land should no more be at liberty but should be subject unto kings. (3 Nephi 6:27–30)

Two issues are raised here that merit further discussion—the composition of the group that conspired against the prophets sent from heaven and the nature of their covenant. These verses explain that judges, lawyers, and high priests, as well as their friends and families, opposed the group of inspired men. Judges and lawyers are roles within the governing structure of the time. They do not necessarily overlap with the organization of the church at this point in the Book of Mormon. The category of high priest, however, is almost uniformly associated with the church.

The term "high priest" appears twenty-eight times in the Book of Mormon; in all but one usage (besides 3 Nephi 6) it is clearly an ecclesiastical term (and in the one outlying usage, the ecclesiastical reading is not ruled out). In many usages it refers to a single individual—*the* high priest—who was the leader of the church, as in the following passage: "Alma was their high priest, he being the founder of their church" (Mosiah 23:16). The term can also refer to a group of church leaders: "Helaman and the high priests did also maintain order in the church; yea, even for the space of four years did they have much peace and rejoicing in the church" (Alma 46:38). Importantly, the term appears with frequency in Alma 13, where high priests are the select group called after the holy order of God:

> Now they were ordained after this manner—being called with a holy calling, and ordained with a holy ordinance, and taking upon them the high priesthood of the holy order, which calling, and ordinance, and high priesthood, is without beginning or end—
>
> Thus they become high priests forever, after the order of the Son, the Only Begotten of the Father, who is without beginning of days or end of years, who is full of grace, equity, and truth. And thus it is. Amen. (Alma 13:8–9)

High priests, therefore, are men called with a "holy calling" and ordained into the priesthood with a "holy ordinance." They are men who commit to the "order of the Son"; they are leaders of the church. As such, it seems reasonable to think that the high priests mentioned in 3 Nephi 6 are those who had held ecclesiastical authority within the church of the time. Interestingly, the footnote in the current edition of the Book of Mormon on the term "had been high priests" (in 3 Nephi 6:21) refers readers to a study guide entry for "Apostasy of Individuals." Thus, even the authors of the footnotes understand the high priests who seek to destroy the prophets of the Lord as people affiliated with the church. It is worth stressing that the inspired men of 3 Nephi 6 are not the leaders of the church. Instead, the leaders are as vulnerable as anyone else.

In addition, 3 Nephi 6 explains that "all the lawyers and the high priests" entered into a covenant, depicted here and elsewhere in the Book of Mormon as an agreement coming straight from the devil. In 3 Nephi 6 this covenant requires destroying believers in the renewed church, getting the judges who had killed the men inspired from heaven off the hook, and "establishing a king over the land."

The trouble of kingship is a constant refrain throughout the Book of Mormon. The books of Nephi, Mosiah, Alma, and Ether warn about the dangers of having a king as ruler. These books echo texts in the Bible where the criticism of kings is not only about better and worse forms of government for the welfare of the people but also about the ways kings come to take the place of God—they rule over and come to control people, and they become beyond reproach. In the book of Judges, after Gideon's victory over the Midianites, the children of Israel petition him to become their king. He retorts, "I will not rule over you, neither shall my son rule over you: the Lord shall rule over you" (Judges 8:23). In the Book of Mormon, the brother of Jared warns his people who are demanding a king, "Surely this thing leadeth into captivity" (Ether 6:23). The trouble, in short, is that kings take the place of God—they demand worship, they demand fealty, and they will extract it if necessary.

In 2014, the same year that Heber J. Grant's quote about following the prophet even if wrong appeared in the Relief Society and Priesthood Manual, and the same year Dieter F. Uchtdorf delivered his "Lord, is it I?" address, Elder Lynn Robbins gave a talk at General Conference titled "Which Way Do You Face?" The talk begins:

> "Which way do you face?" President Boyd K. Packer surprised me with this puzzling question while we were traveling together on my very first assignment as a new Seventy. Without an explanation to put the question in context, I was baffled. "A Seventy," he continued, "does not represent the people to the prophet but the prophet to the people. Never forget which way you face!"[20]

This quote is interesting for several reasons. First, it is delivered to the general membership of the church to signal where Robbins's loyalty lies—he takes direction from the prophet, not "the people." While the primary audience is the general membership, there is also a way in which his audience is the prophet or church authorities themselves: Lesser authorities perform their obedience to higher authorities by quoting them or pledging their loyalty to them in front of the general membership. This demonstrates their commitment to ecclesiastical authority. Second, this quote is interesting for what it lacks: Robbins does not face God in the story; rather, he faces the prophet. The prophet stands in for God. While the idea of the prophet representing God is widely taught in the LDS Church, the framing of the idea in this manner, in combination with many other similar expressions, serves to erode the gap between God and the prophet such that the prophet becomes God-like.

Some years before Robbins's talk, Elder Kevin R. Duncan delivered a talk at April 2010's General Conference titled "Our Very Survival."[21] As the title suggests, the primary point of his talk is to show how we are saved (in the multifaceted sense of the term). It turns out that our salvation depends on our devotion to the prophet. Duncan explains: "Surely one of the crowning blessings of membership in this Church is the blessing of being led by living prophets of God. Trusting in and following the prophets is more than a blessing and a privilege. President Ezra Taft Benson declared that 'our [very] salvation hangs on' following the prophet." In short, we can only be saved by being obedient to the prophet. The royal imagery is also interesting, as if we are "crowned" into a royal family under the direction of a king.

Duncan goes on to quote the address mentioned above that Ezra Taft Benson delivered in 1980 at Brigham Young University titled "Fourteen Fundamentals in Following the Prophet."[22] Benson's address lays out key characteristics of the prophet, including the following: "The prophet is not required to have any particular earthly training or credentials to speak on any subject or act on any matter at any time" and "The prophet is not limited by men's reasoning." His fourteenth fundamental point is an encouragement and warning: "[Follow] . . . the living prophet and the First Presidency . . . and be blessed; reject them and suffer." In explaining these points, Benson relates the experience of an LDS Church leader who encountered a member who disagreed with the prophet on a civic matter. This leader remarked, "Now I tell you that a man in his position is on the way to apostasy. He is forfeiting his chances for eternal life. So is everyone who cannot follow the living prophet of God."[23]

In theory, there is a gap between God and the prophet, but in practice the president of the LDS Church, his counselors, and members of the Quorum of the Twelve Apostles have become kings in the Kingdom of God. Indeed, we stand when they walk into a room, remain seated until they stand at the end of a meeting, and watch them enter and exit in order of seniority. The adage "obedience is the first law of heaven" is repeated frequently in the church. The General Authorities have become the sources of law, and their authority has become more than a preeminent value; it has become untouchable and the basis for determining what is ultimately right and good. Authority has become the law itself and those with authority have become the sacred.

The Book of Mormon teaches by contrast that moral authority need not stem from ecclesiastical authority. It actually warns readers that those in ecclesiastical authority can usurp moral authority, attempting to establish themselves as kings beyond reproach. In the concluding section, I build on this warning to suggest limits on ecclesiastical authority that allow for the flourishing of moral deliberation.

The Limits of Authority

Ecclesiastical authority has become a sacred cow (or perhaps a golden calf) in the LDS Church. It must be domesticated if the religious tradition is to remain an integral part of more members' lives. A problem that ecclesiastical authority presents is that it crowds out room for careful thinking, which is the very room necessary for members of the church to choose to trust in the revelations of those in authority. It is worth noting that I am not advocating that LDS Church leaders should not make moral claims, nor that they should not make those claims on the basis of revelation, which by definition is not open to the same kind of examination that moral deliberation is otherwise open to. Rather, I am advocating that we ought to be more reflective about the ways in which claims to authority can obscure what is right and even become abusive.

We must strike a balance such that within the church we leave enough room for leaders to effectively say, "Trust me on this one," while also having sufficient room to permit thinking critically about claims, policies, and doctrines they make or state. In 1945 a church magazine printed the infamous statement "When our leaders speak, the thinking has been done."[24] It has been nearly eighty years since that time, and church leaders have worked to distance themselves from this quote; however, we have yet to adequately explore this room for thought. With that in mind, I propose the following limitations to ecclesiastical authority:

1. Authority cannot call for actions that are otherwise unethical while precluding an arena for questioning the call to action.
2. Authority cannot trump what is right solely for the sake of maintaining authority.
3. When those in authority provide reasons for policy, they cannot revert to justifying the policy on the basis of authority when the reasons are questioned.[25]
4. When those in authority entirely control the parameters of scrutinizing authority, authority has gone too far.
5. When those in authority do not take responsibility for the unintentional harms caused by exercising authority, authority has gone too far.
6. Respect for authority can come in many forms. Questioning how decisions were reached is not inherently disrespectful, even if that questioning entails strong disagreement.

The material discussed throughout this chapter demonstrates the need for most, if not all, of these limitations. They are rooted in the basic idea expressed in the Book of Mormon that moral vulnerability is inherent to being human and that the church, as a human-run institution, is similarly vulnerable. More particularly, the Book of Mormon shows that those in authority can gloss over their vulnerability and project invulnerability as a way to usurp the position of God. These limitations help to foreground a shared vulnerability as we strive to build Zion.

The 121st section of the Doctrine and Covenants limits ecclesiastical authority on similar grounds and highlights the virtues by which ecclesiastical authority is properly exerted. In part, it reads:

> We have learned by sad experience that it is the nature and disposition of almost all men, as soon as they get a little authority, as they suppose, they will immediately begin to exercise unrighteous dominion. . . .
>
> No power or influence can or ought to be maintained by virtue of the priesthood, only by persuasion, by long-suffering, by gentleness and meekness, and by love unfeigned;
>
> By kindness, and pure knowledge, which shall greatly enlarge the soul without hypocrisy, and without guile—
>
> Reproving betimes with sharpness, when moved upon by the Holy Ghost; and then showing forth afterwards an increase of love toward him whom thou hast reproved, lest he esteem thee to be his enemy. (Doctrine and Covenants 121:39, 41–43)

Here, the *might* of priesthood authority does not *make right*. Rather, the authority of the priesthood is limited by what is moral and does not define what counts as moral. LDS scholar Roger Terry makes an interesting point regarding these passages: "If we truncate verse 41 before it runs off into the list of qualities a leader should employ in exercising priesthood authority, a very important lesson comes suddenly into focus: 'No power or influence can or ought to be maintained by virtue of the priesthood'—period. A man cannot maintain power or influence over somebody simply by virtue of the fact that he holds the priesthood or occupies a priesthood office; nor should he try because if he does, he loses the *power* of the priesthood."[26] This is not the standard reading of the text, but it does highlight how ecclesiastical authority is dependent on moral authority in ways that moral authority is not dependent on ecclesiastical authority. Moral authority stems from what we might call Christ-like virtues; it does not stem from ecclesiastical authority. People with these virtues are those we want influencing our lives. These passages also offer a caution about leadership: "Almost all" people are prone to rely on their authority to exert influence. This is unrighteous dominion, not because they are asserting their authority in domains where others have authority but because they are asserting their authority at all. Authority is never a sufficient reason to exert power over someone.

This creates some complications with regard to revelation, as leaders in the church are put in positions of receiving revelation that has bearing on others. Resolving these complications, however, comes down to trust. Believing that someone has received revelation is to trust them, and trust takes time and effort to cultivate. Trust is easier lost than won and trust is not something that can be asked of others with too much frequency. The reasons we trust are not because someone is in a position of authority over us; rather, we trust because people have demonstrated that they are competent in their roles and that they have our best interests at heart. In other words, we trust leaders when they demonstrate they are trustworthy people with Christ-like virtues. Furthermore, their demonstration of virtue is not predicated on those immediately below them in the hierarchy insisting they are virtuous; rather, their virtue is conveyed throughout the community in a multitude of meaningful ways, and their competency in their roles is never beyond critique.

It is also worth noting that we are not alone in dealing with these issues. Other religious communities navigate similar tensions and they may provide useful resources in addressing them. One way this issue has played out in Catholicism, for instance, is represented in a 1969 comment made by future head of the Catholic church, Joseph Ratzinger:

> Over the pope as the expression of the binding claim of ecclesiastical authority there still stands one's own conscience, which must be obeyed before all else; if necessary even against the requirement of ecclesiastical authority. This emphasis on the individual, whose conscience confronts him with a supreme and ultimate tribunal, as one which in the last resort is beyond the claim of external social groups, even of the official Church, also establishes a principle in opposition to increasing totalitarianism.[27]

These kinds of claims stand in contrast to statements made by President Oaks regarding a loyal opposition within the LDS Church: "There is no warrant for this concept in the government of God's kingdom."[28] Perhaps Ratzinger's point about the expression of conscience as opposition to increasing totalitarianism can be taken to heart.

I opened this article with a serenity prayer. I would like to close with it as I believe it strikes a healthy balance between the role of the LDS Church and the role of a member of the church when determining what is right:

> God,
> grant me the courage to question my leaders;
> the humility to accept their answers;
> and the prudence to know when courage becomes arrogance
> and humility becomes complicity.

Notes

1. rameumptom, April 22, 2014, 6:12 p.m., "comment on," Bruce Nielson, "'Liberal' and 'Orthodox' Views on the Faith of Abraham," *Millennial Star* (blog), April 21, 2014, http://www.millennialstar.org/liberals-and-orthodox-on-the-faith-of-abraham/comment-page-1/#comment-120828.

2. Bruce R. McConkie, "The Caravan Moves On," General Conference, October 1984, https://www.churchofjesuschrist.org/study/general-conference/1984/10/the-caravan-moves-on?lang=eng.

3. For more on the Mountain Meadows Massacre, see Ronald W. Walker, Richard E. Turley, and Glen M. Leonard, *Massacre at Mountain Meadows: An American Tragedy* (Oxford: Oxford University Press, 2008).

4. Zach Hagadone, "The Silent Partner: How an Eastern Idaho Farm Boy Became a Contract Torturer," *Salt Lake City Weekly*, June 17, 2015, https://www.cityweekly.net/utah/the-silent-partner/Content?oid=2860760.

5. Greg Mitchell, "The U.S. Soldier Who Killed Herself after Refusing to Take Part in Torture," *Huffington Post*, Oct. 12, 2014, https://www.huffingtonpost.com/greg-mitchell/the-us-soldier-who-killed_b_5972886.html.

6. "Psychologist Who Helped Devise CIA Interrogation Program Lost Mormon Role," Reuters, Dec. 11, 2014, https://www.reuters.com/article/us-usa-cia-torture-psychologists/psychologist-who-helped-devise-cia-interrogation-program-lost-mormon-role-idUSKBN0JQ00H20141212.

7. The Church of Jesus Christ of Latter-day Saints, *General Handbook*, 38.6.20, "Suicide," https://www.churchofjesuschrist.org/study/manual/general-handbook/38-church-policies-and-guidelines?lang=eng#title_number115.

8. R. Conrad Schultz, "Faith Obedience," General Conference, April 2002, https://www.churchofjesuschrist.org/study/general-conference/2002/04/faith-obedience?lang=eng.

9. *Conference Report of The Church of Jesus Christ of Latter-day Saints* (Salt Lake City: Church of Jesus Christ of Latter-day Saints, 1960), 78; Marion G. Romney, "The Covenant of the Priesthood," General Conference, April 1972, https://www.churchofjesuschrist.org/study/general-conference/1972/04/the-covenant-of-the-priesthood?lang=eng; Ezra Taft Benson, "Fourteen Fundamentals in Following the Prophet," Brigham Young University devotional, February 26, 1980, https://speeches.byu.edu/talks/ezra-taft-benson/fourteen-fundamentals-following-prophet/; *Teachings of the Presidents of the Church: Ezra Taft Benson* (Salt Lake City: Church of Jesus Christ of Latter-day Saints, 2014), 153.

10. Doctrine and Covenants, "Official Declaration 1, Excerpts from Three Addresses by President Wilford Woodruff Regarding the Manifesto."

11. On the notion of "instrayability," see Holly Welker, "The Mormon Version of Infallibility," *Religion Dispatches*, March 24, 2014, http://religiondispatches.org/the-mormon-version-of-infallibility/.

12. Duane E. Hiatt, "Follow the Prophet," *Children's Songbook*, https://www.churchofjesuschrist.org/music/library/childrens-songbook/follow-the-prophet?lang=eng.

13. Henry B. Erying, "The Power of Sustaining Faith," General Conference, April 2019, https://www.churchofjesuschrist.org/study/general-conference/2019/04/34eyring?lang=eng.

14. Ahmad S. Corbitt, "Activism vs. Discipleship: A Message for Chaplains of the Church of Jesus Christ of Latter-day Saints," October 4, 2022, https://cdn.vox-cdn.com/uploads/chorus_asset/file/24159863/Brother_Corbitt_Chaplain_seminar.pdf.

15. Dallin H. Oaks, "Reading Church History," address to Church Educational System teachers, August 16, 1985, https://archive.org/details/reading_church_history_1985_oaks.

16. Dallin H. Oaks, "Criticism," *Ensign* (Feb. 1987), https://www.churchofjesuschrist.org/study/ensign/1987/02/criticism?lang=eng; Dallin H. Oaks, *The Lord's Way* (Salt Lake City: Deseret Book, 1991), 346–47; "Elder Oaks Interview Transcript from PBS Documentary," Church of Jesus Christ of Latter-day Saints' Newsroom, July 20, 2007, https://newsroom.churchofjesuschrist.org/article/elder-oaks-interview-transcript-from-pbs-documentary.

17. Dieter F. Uchtdorf, "Lord, Is it I?" General Conference, October 2014, https://www.churchofjesuschrist.org/study/general-conference/2014/10/lord-is-it-i?lang=eng.

18. Most relevant is Taylor Petrey, "The Greater Apostasy? Responsibility and Falling Away in LDS Narratives," *Peculiar People* (blog), July 15, 2013, https://www.patheos.com/blogs/peculiarpeople/2013/07/the-greater-apostasy-responsibility-and-falling-away-in-lds-narratives/; see also Miranda Wilcox and John D. Young, eds., *Standing Apart: Mormon Historical Consciousness and the Concept of Apostasy* (New York: Oxford University Press, 2014).

19. Citations follow the King James version, which is used widely in the LDS Church.

20. Lynn G. Robbins, "Which Way Do You Face?" General Conference, October 2014, https://www.churchofjesuschrist.org/study/general-conference/2014/10/which-way-do-you-face?lang=eng.

21. Kevin R. Duncan, "Our Very Survival," General Conference, October 2010, https://www.churchofjesuschrist.org/study/general-conference/2010/10/our-very-survival?lang=eng.

22. Benson, "Fourteen Fundamentals in Following the Prophet." A good portion of Duncan's talk quotes Benson's; it is worth noting that Duncan's talk was not the only one to draw liberally from Benson's address at the April 2010 conference.

23. For a more recent example of this kind of rhetoric see Elder Kevin S. Hamilton's January 24, 2023, BYU devotional: "As I visit with members across the Church, I sometimes hear things like 'I don't support the Church's policy on (you fill in the blank).' Or 'I don't agree with the way the Church does (this or that).' Could I suggest an alternative approach? Substitute the word *Savior* or *Lord* or *Jesus Christ* in place of 'the Church'—as in 'I don't support the Savior's policy on (again, you fill in the blank)' or 'I don't agree with the way Jesus Christ does (this or that).'" "Why a Church?" https://speeches.byu.edu/talks/kevin-s-hamilton/why-a-church/.

24. "Sustaining the General Authorities of the Church," *The Improvement Era* 48, no. 6 (June 1945): 354, https://bhroberts.org/records/4J8pVf-09zPB9/improvement_era_publishes_an_article_teaching_that_when_the_leaders_of_the_church_have_spoken_the_thinking_has_been_done.

25. An example of this is the 2015 policy banning the children of same-sex couples from being baptized, which was subsequently repealed in 2019. At first, church leaders offered several reasons for the policy (see Sarah Jane Weaver, "Elder Christofferson Provides Context on Handbook Changes Affecting Same-Sex Marriages," LDS Church News, Nov. 12, 2015, https://www.thechurchnews.com/2015/11/12/23213606/elder-christofferson-provides-context-on-handbook-changes-affecting-same-sex-marriages). After pushback, President Russell M. Nelson described it as "the mind and will of the Lord" that was his "privilege . . . to sustain." Russell M. Nelson, "Becoming True Millennials," Worldwide Devotional for Young Adults, BYU-Hawaii (Jan. 10, 2016), https://www.lds.org/broadcasts/article/worldwide-devotionals/2016/01/becoming-true-millennials?lang=eng.

26. Roger Terry, "Authority and Priesthood in the LDS Church, Part I: Definitions and Development," *Dialogue: A Journal of Mormon Thought* 51, no. 1 (2018): 12.

27. Joseph Ratzinger, "Gaudium et Spes," n. 16, in *Commentary on the Documents of Vatican II*, vol. 5, ed. Herbert Vorgrimler (New York: Herder and Herder, 1969), 134.

28. Dallin H. Oaks, "Opposition in All Things," General Conference, April 2016, https://www.churchofjesuschrist.org/study/general-conference/2016/04/opposition-in-all-things?lang=eng.

11

The Ethics of Memory in the Book of Mormon

COURTNEY S. CAMPBELL

Remember. Few imperatives are reiterated more frequently in the Book of Mormon than the responsibility to remember and its corollary of refraining from forgetfulness. The content of the responsibility to remember contains both religious and moral dimensions. Persons and communities are admonished to remember the merciful nature of God's interactions with his children and the foundation of faith in Christ. Communities are repeatedly called to remember the legacy of the foundational narratives and experiences from which the community originated. The recollection of a history of captivity and oppression of predecessor communities provides a moral vision for the challenges faced by a contemporary community. Conversely, communities that have lost their religious and moral direction are critiqued for having forgotten their origins and legacy, an intimation that at the root of such waywardness is a prideful communal self-sufficiency. The appeal to remember can thus have a twofold function of an invitation to covenantal relationships and a calling to accountability.[1] The call to remembrance may be applied to personal responsibilities or, more broadly, invoke a responsibility of communal and collective memory. Furthermore, the reader of the text is not exempted from the responsibility of remembrance. Readers are invited in various ways to remember the narratives and teachings so they can "learn to be more wise" (Mormon 9:31) than the communities whose destruction is narrated and to acquire a witness of the truth.

The insistent imperative of remembrance situates the Book of Mormon within philosophical and literary discourse about the ethics of memory. The ethics of memory fuses together responsibilities of remembrance of preceding generations and commitments of care to future generations. In this chapter, I explore this embedded ethics of memory through three organizing themes: the moral voice of prophetic criticism, the moral logic of covenantal relationship, and the commitments of a moral witness. My approach relies on methods of moral analysis to provide an interpretation of selected narratives in the text that manifest generalizable moral wisdom.

The prophetic critiques of communities in the text and of anticipated future communities who will read the text situates the prophetic figure or witness in the role of an embodied moral memory. Moreover, as observed by religious social ethicist Richard B. Miller, "religions with prophetic traditions" are resources of principles, narratives, and exemplars that cultivate commitments of empathy, solidarity, and responsibility in broader civic life.[2] The prophetic narratives of the Book of Mormon are thereby illustrative of how a moral voice can extend beyond the generative religious community and be resonant or meaningful for ethical issues in society.

The moral logic of a covenantal ethic presumes recollection of a relationship-creating gift of love or act of deliverance; the Israelites whose Exodus narrative is formative of the identity of the communities of the Book of Mormon are reminded of their divine deliverance from slavery in Egypt prior to the articulation of the covenant responsibilities (Exodus 20:1). This pattern of deliverance→ memory→ covenant informs the formation of four principal covenant communities in the text: the people of King Benjamin, the refugee community of Alma$_1$, the Anti-Nephi-Lehies, and the peaceable community created through the ministry of the resurrected Christ.

I construct the concept of moral witness by integrating one of the foundational covenant responsibilities, that persons should "stand as witnesses" of God (Mosiah 18:8), with the characteristics of a moral witness portrayed by philosopher Avishai Margalit. The moral witness serves as a memory for future generations, narrating a human tragedy, its lessons, and its meanings, for the benefit of persons and communities distanced in time and space. As Margalit expresses the point, "The hope with which I credit moral witnesses is a rather sober hope; that in another place or another time, there exists, or will exist, a moral community that will listen to their testimony."[3] The prophetic moral voices of the Book of Mormon are not only moral witnesses, but the overarching commitment of the text as a whole to preserving a legacy for future moral communities also marks the Book of Mormon itself as a moral witness.

The Moral Voice of Prophecy

My exposition of the moral voice of prophetic criticism in the Book of Mormon initially draws on the account of social criticism developed by social philosopher Michael Walzer. Social criticism consists of protest directed against the "institutions and activities of everyday life," a practice that Walzer argues originates historically and morally in the biblical prophetic tradition. What makes the Hebrew prophets "inventors of the practice of social criticism" is their distinctive reliance on "a moral frame" to validate their condemnation of corruption in the kingdoms of Israel and Judah. The prophetic critique of covenantal infidelity, political self-interest, economic injustice, social marginalization, and religious exclusion manifests a structure of moral argumentation comprised of four primary features: an indignant indictment of hypocrisy, criticism of behaviors and institutional arrangements that advantage privileged elites, the search for core community values, and a demand that everyday life accord with these core values. The moral argument of the Hebraic prophet seeks to be a catalyst for remembrance, indignation, and repentance within a community, especially among the religious and political elites who influence the communal ethos. Remarkably, the biblical prophets find an audience for their moral criticism, and Walzer seeks to understand the social puzzle of "why people . . . not only listen, but copy down, preserve, and repeat the prophetic message."[4]

Walzer's claim that prophecy is a moral voice of criticism of ruling elites, communities, and societies offers an interpretive lens for the prophetic voice that emerges in the Book of Mormon. This voice is exemplified in the call to accountability of the early Nephite community by Jacob$_2$, the criticism of Abinadi against King Noah$_3$ and his priests, the witness of Alma$_2$ and Amulek to the legal elites and rulers in the city of Ammonihah and to the economically privileged Zoramites, the call to repentance of Zarahemla and the entire Nephite nation by Samuel$_2$ the Lamanite, and the biting indictments Moroni$_2$ expresses against the contemporary society that would bear the promise and the burden of receiving the sacred text. The narrative trajectory of the moral voice of prophecy moves from communal to social to universal.[5] The prophetic critique is invariably directed at the self-serving economic motivations and exclusionary hypocrisy of the ruling political, economic, and religious elites of a community that perpetuates persistent violations of a common morality of minimal decency.[6] Communities characterized by a moral epistemology of "knowing evil" (Mosiah 16:3) and perpetual practices of "iniquity" and "abominations" in the face of a prophetic witness to remember and reform jeopardize the capacity for moral agency, embody moral callousness, and place themselves in peril of dissolution. My exposition of the moral voice of prophecy will focus on the Abinadi narrative, as supplemented by converging features in the prophetic critiques of Jacob$_2$, Alma$_2$, Samuel$_2$, and Moroni$_2$.

Abinadi is the first martyr explicitly mentioned in the Book of Mormon; his narrative is filtered through the memories of Limhi and Alma$_1$, who each formed covenant communities in response to Abinadi's witness. The context for Abinadi's prophetic criticism is the prospective demise of a community that had departed from the main body of Nephites and whose leadership had passed from its initial leader, Zeniff, to his son Noah$_3$ (Mosiah 11–12). Noah$_3$ and his self-appointed priests, the ruling and religious elites of the community, are portrayed as materialistic hedonists: They seek riches for their own pleasure and engage in "riotous living" exemplified in concubinage and "wine-bibbing," or drunkenness (Mosiah 11:14–15). The elites further violate the common morality by a practice of lying and flattery of the people and yet have persuaded themselves that their actions are justifiable and blameless—that is, they exemplify moral self-deception.

The elitist ethos of hedonism does not leave the community unscathed: Noah$_3$ imposes severe tax burdens on the people that support an extensive building project as well as idleness, idolatry, and the concubinage lifestyle of the ruling elites. The onerous taxes create a circumstance of moral complicity as they cause the "people to labor exceedingly to support iniquity" (Mosiah 11:6). Noah$_3$'s people are not without blame, however, as they perpetrate "all manner of wickedness" (Mosiah 11:2), language signifying moral corruption. The people emulate the idolatry and the infidelities of their ruling elites; a battle with the Lamanites incites the people to "delight in blood, and the shedding of the blood of their brethren" (Mosiah 11:19). Responsibility for this communal moral corruption and the bloody hands of the armies is nonetheless laid at Noah$_3$'s feet: The narrative prefaces its account of community wickedness with the observation that "he did cause his people to commit sin" and concludes by commenting that the people's blood lust occurs "because of the wickedness of their king and priests" (Mosiah 11:2, 11:19). The authority of the elites seems to compromise the agency of the people, and their immoral rule places the community so proximate to the cusp of dissolution that a prophetic call to accountability is necessary.

Abinadi's witness to and against the ruling and religious elites and the community as a whole exemplifies the moral voice of prophetic criticism. The moral meaning of prophecy can be constructed through an argumentative structure comprised of seven core features: communal positionality, calls to accountability, a recollecting of moral memory, exposure of moral hypocrisy, narrative re-storying, neglecting the vulnerable, and moral hope.

Positionality: A Connected Critic

The communal positionality of a prophet is important to their credibility.[7] Abinadi is a *part* of Noah$_3$'s community, described initially as "a man among them [the people]" (Mosiah 11:20), and his prophetic voice is brought to bear against his community and their rulers. Yet, he is also *apart* from the community, having eventually to use a disguise to fulfill his divine mandate (Mosiah 12:2). What Abinadi is *not* is an outsider, speaking to a community whose history, teachings, and practices he is uninformed about. He is a "connected critic" who is knowledgeable about the formative narratives, beliefs, and values that comprise the religio-moral culture of his community.[8]

Moreover, Abinadi and other prophetic witnesses not only speak against evil but also have themselves suffered from its infliction: They are humiliated, scorned, beaten, persecuted, maliciously targeted, deprived of food and clothing, incarcerated, exiled, and compelled to witness atrocities, all of which may be a prelude to martyrdom. They are not insulated from the wrongs inflicted by the communities they critique and call to repentance. The bearer of prophetic moral criticism is not a detached onlooker or social observer of community moral decline but bears with others the burdens attendant to moral corruption. This personalized experience of evil and suffering generates an integrity and authenticity to the moral voice of prophecy that is integral to the authority and credibility of a moral witness.[9] A prophet's experience of the suffering inflicted upon the Messianic "suffering servant" can cultivate a Christ-like empathy and solidarity, virtues required to bear witness on behalf of persons oppressed by the powerful social elites.

Calls to Accountability

Prophetic criticism is a calling to *accountability* directed to an entire community, but particularly those ruling elites who are responsible not simply for governance but for shaping the communal ethos and way of life. A moral voice that critiques the powerful from within the community witnesses to the fragility and tenuousness of power grounded in unjust and exploitative relationships; it represents, in Walzer's memorable phrasing, "the subversiveness of immanence."[10] This subversive character means the prophetic call to accountability and its implicit indictment initially issues in a challenge by Noah$_3$ to Abinadi's authority and credibility: "Who is Abinadi, that I and my people should be judged of him?" (Mosiah 11:27).[11] Abinadi informs Noah$_3$ and the community that their evil and wrongdoing are known to God and that in the absence of repentance, they will experience famine, pestilence, loss of liberty, and death. The moral argument of a prophet is not a pleasant picture, and the people, conditioned by the communal ethos of the rulers to self-deception and callousness, seek to evade accountability by indicting Abinadi for his evil speaking of the king who has "not sinned" and of his "guiltless" people (Mosiah 12:14).

A prophetic call to accountability honors the essential parameters of moral experience: It presumes the rulers and the people have knowledge of faith-filled beliefs and right morality and have exercised their moral agency to choose or "know evil," even to the point of constructing a prevailing cultural narrative that reframes evil as good. The community's rejection of accountability means that it is on the cusp of compromising the minimal moral conditions to preserve personal agency and communal sustainability. The wisdom of the moral voice of prophecy is that rulers and their people are not judged by a person they treat as alien to the community and lacking credibility as a communal critic, but rather the source and authority for judgment is the community's own narratives, norms, and laws that constitute a minimal morality. The community is accountable at the very least for neglecting a responsibility of remembrance.

Moral Memory

Given the protestations of innocence and evasions of accountability, a moral voice of prophecy appeals to a common historical narrative, the communal tradition, and an inherited moral legacy to remind the community of its social and moral identity and to elicit the gratitude, self-reflection, and humility necessary for the needed reforms and repentance. Walzer contends that "the prophetic message depends upon previous messages" and is "parasitic upon a previously accepted and commonly understood morality."[12] A prophetic voice, then, is an embodied *moral memory* of the community engaged in a project of moral excavation: The ethics of prophetic memory calls a community to accountability through remembrance and recovery of its formative narratives, norms, and identity.[13]

Abinadi initiates his exposition of communal moral memory by recollecting for Noah$_3$ and his priests that the community's founding narrative and identity from the biblical Exodus are comprised of *deliverance from* "the house of bondage," a voice of moral irony as the community's rebellion has placed it on the cusp of being *delivered into* captivity. The formative narrative of deliverance conveys moral norms and identity: Abinadi reiterates the Mosaic covenant and requirements of the Decalogue for rulers and priests who failed to internalize, teach, and live by the foundational moral law (Mosiah 12–13:26). The moral voice of prophetic criticism presumes a responsibility of remembrance and critiques the community for its forgetfulness of its formative narratives, its ingratitude toward the moral legacy of the past, and its moral amnesia.[14] The prophetic appeal to moral memory refutes the community's claims to innocence and repudiation of accountability.

Forgetting foundational narratives and norms, moreover, can jeopardize the identity and sustainability of a community. Notably, a perennial pattern in the six prophetic calls to accountability is that the Nephite communities (or their latter-day counterparts) forget the origins of their economic prosperity in divine blessings; this moral amnesia invariably creates class divisions that erode the community's cohesion, unity, and justice.[15] When a framework of common rules and practices is systemically neglected, supplanted by a narrative reframing of good and evil, and accountability evaded, the conditions for moral agency and for minimalistic social cohesion are eroded. The moral voice of prophecy exposes the community as lacking a story, a moral memory, and therefore a moral identity. It is a morally lost community.

Moral Hypocrisy

The prophetic moral critique reveals an emerging chasm between the forgotten responsibilities and virtues of communal morality and the current practices of the rulers and the community by which they assert their innocence and immunity from accountability. It exposes the pervasive tendency of humans to "draw near [God] with their lips, but their hearts are far from [God]"[16]—that is, to religious and moral hypocrisy. In Abinadi's witness, the ruling elites of Noah$_3$ are morally hypocritical on three grounds: (1) The hypocrisy of the *heart*: Noah$_3$'s priests have "not applied [their] hearts to understanding" the Mosaic moral law. The responsibilities of the foundational communal covenant are "not written in [their] hearts," which instead have been given over to the "study of iniquity" (Mosiah 12:27, 13:11). This obliviousness to the law reiterates the moral amnesia of the rulers and their neglect of the community-preserving responsibility of remembrance. If the inner self or "heart" lacks integrity, hypocrisy in various forms is almost certain to follow. (2) The hypocrisy of *hedonism*: The materialistic hedonism of the ruling elites, manifested in the self-serving pursuit of riches and in infidelity, violates the common morality of prohibited actions. It represents a double standard of morality, an ethic of indulgence for the rulers and an ethic of burdens for everyone else in the community. This moral duplicity provokes Abinadi's caustic indictment "If ye teach the law of Moses, why do you not keep it?" (Mosiah 12:29). (3) The pretense to *teaching*: While Noah$_3$'s priests affirm that they "teach the law of Moses," Abinadi observes that they "pretend to teach" (Mosiah 12:25): Their corrupt, self-serving intentions vitiate their community instruction and instead become an occasion for the people to sin. The religious elites are accountable not only for having failed to *observe* the precepts of the communal morality but also for failing to *understand* what they are to teach and for failing to *teach* their people the right ways of worship and morals. The protestations of innocence mask an underlying moral corruption of power, pride, and pretense that the moral voice of prophecy "pulls down" and exposes (Alma 4:19, 60:36).

Abinadi's indictment of these three realms of moral hypocrisy is echoed in the criticism of the Lamanite prophet Samuel₂ to the Nephite community of Zarahemla. Samuel₂ attributes the "wickedness and abominations" of the people to a moral corruption of the heart or inner self that is manifested in a quest for "treasures" and "riches." That is, the Zarahemla community has engaged in a form of idolatry in which material wealth supplants God. This materialistic idolatry displays a hypocritical failure of religious imagination and moral memory: The people "always remember" their riches but "do not remember" the divine hand in their prosperity or to extend expressions of gratitude. The morally corrupt heart and self-absorbed materialistic preoc-cupations issue in violations of communal morality, including "great pride, . . . envyings, strifes, malice, persecutions, and murders, and all manner of iniquities" (Helaman 13:17–23). The community's moral hypocrisy is further expressed through practices of devoting its material excess—gold, silver, and costly apparel—to payment of "foolish and blind guides" who speak flattering words that "there is no iniquity" (and so no accountability). The community esteems such persons as "prophets" even while true proph-ets who call the people to accountability for their wrongs are slandered as "false prophets" and evicted from the community (Helaman 13:24–30). The incorrigibility of moral self-deception and hypocrisy is almost intractable, and Samuel₂, as with Abinadi, makes prophetic recourse to a new story, the story of Christ.

Narrative Re-storying

The moral legacy of communal identity is a baseline standard for account-ability, but insofar as this has been forgotten and neglected, the moral voice of prophetic critique commonly situates the received communal morality within a new or different story. That is, the prophetic voice recovers com-munal moral integrity often through a pedagogy of narrative re-storying. Jesus's teaching on the foundational requirements of *Torah*—love of God and love of neighbor—memorably re-stories these responsibilities for an audience of Jewish priestly and legal elites through the Good Samaritan parable.[17] Jesus's parable does not present a new morality but situates the received requirements of love within a different story—a different moral reality—that transforms the moral world of the Jewish community beyond exclusionary boundaries.

Abinadi is similarly confronted with a question of textual interpretation that has perplexed Noah₃'s skeptical priests. Immediately following his indictment of hypocrisy and his remembrance of the Mosaic morality, Abinadi re-stories this morality by framing it as a "type" and "shadow" of the salvation narrative in which God will come to earth, assume human form, and offer himself as a sacrificial atonement that provides the deliverance of resurrection and the grace of redemption. Christ is re-storied by Abinadi from lawgiver and judge to the suffering servant of Isaiah's Messianic prophecy, a narrative that conveys an entirely different and transformational religious and moral reality. The Messianic narrative similarly enables Abinadi to confer on the prophets and communities of believers a re-storied identity as the "seed" of the Messiah (Mosiah 12:20–24, 13:28–35, 14–15, 16:14–15). Persons whose identity had been bound to the house of "Israel" as a "remnant" or "branch" are now invited to assume responsibility through the covenant name of "Christ." The communal morality does not change (yet), but the moral reality is radically re-storied. The prophetic pedagogy of narrative re-storying offers a way to restore the wholeness and moral identity of a community that has lost its story and is on the verge of dissolution. Though Noah₃ and the priests respond to Abinadi's re-storying invitation with an accusation of blasphemy, the story is foundational in every new moral community.

Passing by the Poor

Jesus's parable as well as repeated prophetic and priestly teaching in the Book of Mormon indict a further form of moral hypocrisy among religious leaders and communities highlighted by the metaphor of "passing by" or neglecting the needs of the poor and vulnerable.[18] This form of hypocrisy reflects moral callousness and neglect of the community's memory of when they themselves comprised the poor and the stranger and required deliverance beyond their own means. Moral neglect constitutes a wrong of omission, although it is frequently embedded in wrongs of commission toward the vulnerable of a community. Although this "bypassing" neglect can be inferred in the Abinadi narrative from both the communal context and the consequences of his moral critique, his call for communal accountability does not explicitly incorporate this wrong. However, the Nephite communities historically are continually reminded of a responsibility to "impart of [their] substance" to the vulnerable and are repeatedly summoned to repentance for their moral neglect.[19]

The moral voice of prophetic criticism regarding neglect of the vulnerable is especially prominent in Alma₂'s discourse to the Zoramite community and

Moroni$_2$'s indictment of latter-day religious communities.[20] The narrative of Alma$_2$'s mission among the dissenting Zoramites reveals that Zoramite pretensions to holiness and chosenness mask a materialistic preoccupation: The hearts of the Zoramite elites are "set upon" wealth, "fine goods," and "precious things." The Zoramite religious exclusivity then becomes a pretext for the economically privileged to exclude the poor from their worship and communal life even though the poor have performed the labor to construct community synagogues. Like Noah$_3$'s community, the Zoramite poor are exploited for the benefit of the economic elite (Alma 31:24–30, 32:1–5). Moroni$_2$ similarly critiques the "pollutions" of latter-day religious communities that create a hypocritical moral myopia at the very core of the materialistic conditions of modern life. The language of "pollution" is morally potent as it designates a violation or desecration of that which is sacred and thereby interweaves textual themes of purity and uncleanness.[21] In Moroni$_2$'s prophetic critique, the desecration of the sacred involves in important respects a deeply mistaken materialistic pursuit by societies, especially by religious communities, including a quest for acquisition of wealth, substance, apparel, and adornment of churches. Moroni$_2$'s moral argument with modernity drips with the irony of materialistic and hedonistic hypocrisy and moral myopia as he portrays contemporary communities preoccupied with "that which hath no life" even as living persons are bypassed and neglected: Moderns "suffer the hungry, and the needy, and the naked, and the sick and the afflicted to pass by you, and notice them not" (Mormon 8:35–40).

The prophetic call to accountability and its exposure of moral hypocrisy is almost invariably accompanied by indignation at a community's exploitative treatment of its vulnerable. The moral problem is not that the rich elites live well but that they live well at the expense of the poor. While not explicit in the Abinadi narrative, it is noteworthy that the successor communities that receive a religious and moral legacy from Abinadi each incorporate a responsibility for the vulnerable into their communal practice. Alma$_1$, who recorded and taught the words of Abinadi to a new community of believers, has instructed his followers to "impart of their substance of their own free will and good desires towards God, . . . to every needy, naked soul" (Mosiah 18:27–28). Noah$_3$'s son and successor, Limhi, similarly directs his people that, despite their tributary taxation by the Lamanites, "every man should impart to the support of the widows and their children, that they might not perish with hunger" (Mosiah 21:17). Given these directives to communities that derive their origins from Abinadi's teaching, it seems entirely possible that his prophetic legacy includes a communal responsibility for the poor.

Prophetic Hope

The moral voice of the prophetic seeks to unify past, present, and future communities in a common narrative with moral integrity. The prophetic passion of Abinadi is forged by the confluence of fidelity and gratitude to predecessor generations, indignation at the wrongs of the elites and the community, and hope for recovery and renewal of religious and moral possibilities—if not with Noah$_3$'s people, then through subsequent communities and generations. It is an abiding hope in the possibility of remembrance, recovery, and renewal that leads Abinadi to express in the conclusion of his sermon, "Teach [the people] that redemption cometh through Christ the Lord" (Mosiah 16:15). That benediction would make no sense were the community to die with Abinadi. The moral voice of prophecy thereby anticipates the continuation of teaching, the preservation of the prophetic legacy, among an audience that will outlive the prophet; the call to accountability also calls a community into being from the chaos of the present. It is a profound statement of responsibility toward and hope in future communities. Abinadi's witness leads to his martyrdom, as Noah$_3$ authorizes his death by fire,[22] but death does not get the last word, nor do Abinadi's words die with him; new moral communities are birthed from the martyrdom of Abinadi by the priest Alma$_1$ that enact the morality of covenant.

The Moral Logic of Covenant

Covenant is an organizing theological concept of the text (even those who do evil are portrayed as entering into covenants) and of the contemporary LDS religious community that received and has been formed by the text; however, ecclesiastical teaching has short-shrifted the moral meaning of covenantal responsibility by interpreting it as a form of contractual agreement with specific "terms" and "conditions" delineated by God.[23] The thin notion of covenant as a transactional agreement for specific performance misses the thick moral culture and transformational relationships embedded in covenantal morality.[24] Here I construct a moral logic of covenantal responsibility and relationship that draws on textual narratives of the four *moral* communities that exhibit a covenant morality: the covenant of King Benjamin's people, the covenant of Alma$_1$'s people at baptism and in their subsequent communal practice, the covenant of nonviolence of the people of Anti-Nephi-Lehi, and the covenant of the peaceable community called into being by the ministry of the resurrected Christ. This moral logic of covenant is initiated by an ethics of gift that shapes the moral culture of the community and is memorialized and remembered over time through ethical features of calling, promise, responsibility, public witness, transformation, and narratives and ritual of renewal.

A covenantal relationship and morality are embedded in a distinctive moral reality that contrasts with contractual transactions: A covenant is initiated through the offering of a *gift*. This gift for the four moral communities created through prophetic invitation, as well as in the paradigmatic Exodus narrative incorporated into the communities' religious and moral identity, pertains to deliverance from bondage, oppression, and injustice. The covenant-creating gift can take the form of physical deliverance from enslavement or oppression to other communities or a redemptive deliverance from the bondage of sin. Without the merciful mediation of divine deliverance, the community story would have turned out very differently for persons considered "the most lost of all mankind" (Alma 24:11). The gift creates a state or condition for ongoing life that the recipient could not achieve on their own and so cultivates a moral posture of trustful reliance. The truthfulness of the narrative in which the gift is embedded inhibits self-deception and fosters virtues of humility, gratitude, memory, and solidarity necessary to the formation of a moral community.[25]

While the moral voice of prophetic criticism is focused on a call to accountability, the gift ethic symbolizes a *calling to relationship* of covenant with both God and with other persons in community. A covenant invites a morally distinctive form of relationship that shapes a moral culture and moral responsibilities. Consequently, the initial response to the gift of deliverance is structured by three moral features: communal recognition of the gift (or rebellion against it as a form of manipulation), the exercise of choice in accepting (or refusing) the gift, and responsive expressions of gratitude (or self-sufficient prideful disavowal). This is to say that freedom, liberty, and agency are embedded in the relationship-generating gift, without which the possibility of morality and the capacity for moral choice are empty. Noah$_3$ and his people rejected the proffered relationship and chose the path of rebellion, refusal, and pride in response to Abinadi's prophetic criticism, while the communities of Alma$_1$ and Limhi chose relationship and a covenantal culture. These formative experiences of responsive morality cultivate the virtues of dependency, trust, and solidarity and confer a liberating moral valence on covenantal morality relative to the transactional language of "agreement." A covenant seeks to bring out of the circumstances of oppression and bondage a morality of gift-gratitude rather than of command-obedience or the mutual self-interest that characterizes contractual relationships.

The gifted character of covenantal relationships underlies and reinforces a process of *mutual promise* that solidifies and enacts the relationship. God is represented in the Book of Mormon as a being who makes and fulfills "all his promises" to persons and to communities (Alma 37:17–18). The practices of promise making and promise keeping are narratively memorialized in the divine gift of deliverance of the Israelite, Jaredite, and Lehite communities from conditions of oppression and chaos to a land of "promise." The responsive promises of moral agents and communities bind themselves to a covenantal relationship with God and a moral covenant of presence and unity with members of the community that should shape future actions. The content of the paradigmatic responsive promise is expressed by Alma₁ to his community of exiles: (a) a calling into relationship so that the community desires to be known as "the children of God"; (b) the creation of a covenantal culture in which community members display presence through lightening the burdens and providing comfort for others; and (c) the bearing of "witness" to and before God (Mosiah 18:8–11). A covenantal relationship thereby reflects what theologian Joseph Allen refers to as "entrustment"— that is, "to place ourselves or something we value in the other's hands."[26] The concept of entrustment is displayed prominently in the covenant of the Anti-Nephi-Lehies to refrain from violence and place their lives (and eternal life) in the hands of God and their adversaries (Alma 24:20–21).

A moral community that is responsive to the gift-based promises of protection, posterity, and prosperity willingly *assumes responsibilities* that define and shape their relationship with the divine and for their common life; the gift of deliverance offers the grace and freedom to create and to serve in relationships mediated by care, succor, solidarity, and service rather than power and exploitation (Mosiah 2:17–21). It is therefore important to recognize how the gift-based relationship precedes the issuing of commandments. The commandments express a moral infrastructure of gift, calling, freedom, relationship, promise, and trust; the morality of commands will be empty and even incoherent in the absence of the morality and culture of covenant. The moral logic of covenant provides a distinctive and new moral motivation of grace and gratitude that shifts focus from specified actions or prohibitions to the relationships the actions cultivate.

The formation of a covenantal relationship includes a *public witness* or ritual that embodies the promissory commitment. This public witness reflects an inner change of disposition and identity centered (as with the call to accountability) on the "heart" and memorializes the gift, call, and relationship in and through embodied actions. The people of King Benjamin who experienced a mighty change of heart that issued in a disposition to do good continually have their names recorded; the followers of Alma₁ witness to the desire of their hearts to enter a covenantal relation with God and members of their community through the ritual of baptism; the Anti-Nephi-Lehies attest to the forgiveness of their sins by a merciful God through a collective action of burying their swords in the earth; the community formed by the ministry of the resurrected Christ manifests the sacrifice of a broken heart through participating in the sacrament ritual.[27] The public witness of covenantal morality expresses an aspiration for moral integrity, a consistency between the inner self and external action, in contrast to the hypocrisy that invites the moral voice of prophetic criticism. The public nature of this witness generates a common purpose and a shared accountability; "publicness" is a standard for assessing an authentic covenant in marked contrast to morally corrupt covenants based in power and greed that issue in the conspiracies of "secret" combinations.

While a minimalist morality of prohibitions construes human relationships as transactional interactions that leave the parties unchanged once the interaction ends, a covenantal morality is, by contrast, laden with *transformative* potential in identity and relationships that is open-ended in time. The covenantal transformation is symbolized in the experience common to each of the covenant communities of having a new name or identity conferred upon them, such as the "children of Christ," the "children of God," or the "people of God." The metaphor of "children" itself bears the transformationalist possibilities: In his discourse, King Benjamin invites his people to abandon their natural selves, draw on the salvific gift of Christ's atonement, and "become as a child." The call to covenantal relationship thereby involves a transformative process and the conferral of a new identity so profound it is analogous to a new birth: It cultivates virtues pertaining to the inner life, including humility, submissiveness, meekness, and patience as well as the coordinating covenantal virtues of faith, hope, and love (Mosiah 3:18–19; cf. Alma 7:23, 13:28). Of course, the names that are symbolic of transformed identities must be lived into over time; a community created by a gift must now undertake the responsibility of becoming a moral community.

The moral logic of covenantal relationships persists and endures over time and is bequeathed as a moral legacy for future generations through inscribing memory *in narratives and rituals of renewal*. The core content of the enduring responsibility of remembrance consists of the narratives and gift of deliverance from which the call to covenantal relationship was generated. As theological ethicist William F. May contends, "A covenant . . . ratifies and extends into the future an alteration of identity towards which the original exchange of gifts moves."[28] A covenantal memory encompasses remembrance of the merciful nature of God, the deliverance from the "captivity of our fathers," and the salvific sacrifice of Christ remembered in the sacramental ritual.[29] The practice of covenantal remembrance conveyed through narrative, symbolism, and ritualized renewal marks off a moral community from communities that are so imperiled by their spiritual and moral amnesia that a prophetic call to accountability is necessary as their moral memory.

The morality and relationship of covenant thus originates in an ethics of gift and is sustained through time by an ethics of memory and a communal responsibility of remembrance. Past is made present to give moral shape to the future. The concern for shaping a future moral culture, a commitment of moral legacy to lineage, posterity, and future generations so that such communities can learn wisdom that escaped predecessor generations, is a distinguishing feature of the moral witness.

The Book of Mormon as Moral Witness

Philosophical reflection on the moral responsibilities of communities in relation to the Holocaust and other twentieth-century atrocities has led to the emergence of an ethics of memory.[30] This moral conception and its underlying cultural context seem particularly relevant to an exposition of the moral legacy of the Book of Mormon given that the Nephite and Jaredite prophets are witness to two genocides. My interpretation relies primarily on the intrinsic features of an ethics of memory that philosopher Avishai Margalit contends comprise a moral witness.

Margalit understands a moral witness to be a "special agent of collective memory"—that is, the moral witness is not engaged in personal memoir but is the voice and memory of a community. This agentic voice of responsibility confers a "special moral authority" on the moral witness.[31] Margalit proposes several defining characteristics or "marks" of a moral witness: The identity of the moral witness is comprised of an experiential encounter with evil and suffering, a willingness to assume personal risk, a commitment of service with a moral purpose, and a hope in the persistence of moral community. My contention is that these characteristics are embedded in the narratives of both prophetic calls to accountability and prophetic calls to covenantal relationship delineated in the preceding sections. In short, the prophetic voices *in* the text and the prophetic voice *of* the text are moral witnesses. I will argue for this claim by focusing on textual illustration of the marks of moral purpose, experienced evil, and hope.

Margalit recognizes there can be different purposes for narrating a story or critique of a moral and existential atrocity like the Holocaust, including historical documentation, investigative chronicling, and advancing political objectives. While these are valid purposes, the moral witness is engaged in a distinctive practice of creating meaning to the events by serving others with a moral purpose: They relate a painful and tragic narrative to benefit the welfare of communities both present and envisioned. A moral purpose is exemplified in the moral voice of prophecy in the Book of Mormon by Mormon₂'s refusal to lead his armies and instead to "stand as an idle witness" by relating both the destruction of his people and the prophetic legacy for future generations (Mormon 3:16). A moral purpose is likewise disclosed in a concluding admonition of Moroni₂ concerning one rationale for preserving the Nephite record of rebellion, moral atrocity, and genocide: "I know that ye shall have my words, . . . that ye may learn to be more wise than we have been" (Mormon 9:30–31).

The moral purpose is especially pertinent in prophetic calls to account-ability or relationship given an underlying experience of prophetic anguish and encounter with evil.[32] Prophetic anguish reflects a confluence of per-sonal indignation, shared grief with suffering persons, and divine pres-ence and vulnerability. The moral voice that calls to accountability is often accompanied by a sense of powerlessness in relying on the agency of ruling elites or a community to reverse the communal religio-moral trajectory. This moral sensibility of anguish and moral distress is prophetically personified in Alma₂'s experience of "being weighed down with sorrow, wading through much tribulation and anguish of soul" following the initial rejection of his message by the people of Ammonihah. Subsequently joined by Amulek, a converted citizen of Ammonihah, in the ministry and following a second rejection, Alma₂ and Amulek are bound and compelled by their captors to witness a horrific martyrdom of women and children who experience the same torturous death by fire as Abinadi. Amulek's anguish (or "pain") evokes his exclamation "How can we witness this awful scene?" and his experienced powerlessness leads him to propose calling on divine interven-tion to prevent the evil. Alma₂ informs Amulek that he is constrained from such a divine recourse and observes that God allows the atrocity in part so that "the blood of the innocent shall stand as a witness against them [the people of the city]" (Alma 14:8–11). The discourse of "witness," a central component of covenantal responsibility, applies both to prophetic anguish over helplessness to prevent a massacre of martyrs and to the moral voice of the victims themselves.

The indignation at moral corruption and the anguish of futility of the call to communal accountability experienced by Abinadi, Alma₂ and Amulek, Samuel₂, and other prophetic voices is given its most poignant expression by Mormon₂, who acknowledges that his ministry to his people was "without faith" and "without hope" since "the day of grace was passed with them" (Mormon 2:15, 3:12, 5:2). Moreover, his inner pain over the destruction of his people is revealed in a wrenching lamentation: "My soul was rent with anguish, . . . O ye fair ones" (Mormon 6:16–20). The prophetic experience of powerlessness in an existential encounter with evil manifests the characteristics of a moral witness. A prophetic moral witness becomes a voice for the voiceless, enacts the covenantal commitment to share the burdens and mourning of the vulnerable, and embodies the Messianic narrative of the suffering servant.

Prophetic anguish regarding the futility of accomplishing the moral purpose contextualizes what Margalit designates as "the heroic" if "sober hope" of a moral witness: "In another place or in another time, there exists, or will exist, a moral community that will listen to their testimony."[33] The narrative of the moral witness then addresses multiple audiences of moral accountability, extended in space and envisioned in time, and in the face of all evil evidence to the contrary, affirms hope in the sustainability and recovery of a moral community. A present generation may reject the moral voice of prophecy and kill the messenger and the martyrs for the message; it may reject a call to accountability or the gift and call to relationship, but the wrenching anguish of moral distress is balanced by hope that future generations will embrace the promise of communal peace, unity, and justice cultivated by covenantal relationships.

The hope Margalit attributes to a moral witness is pervasive in the prophetic narratives in the Book of Mormon and may be said to confer to the entire text the character of a moral witness. Virtually every primary author manifests hope for and confidence in the openness of a future moral community to their narrative record. I provide just a few illustrations here. The metaphor shared by Lehi$_1$, Nephi$_1$, and Moroni$_2$ that their writings and "the words of the righteous . . . will cry from the dust" to future generations manifests the core hope of a moral witness.[34] The petitionary prayer of Enos that God would "preserve a record of my people, the Nephites; even if it so be by the power of his holy arm, that it might be brought forth at some future day unto the Lamanites, that, perhaps, they might be brought unto salvation," similarly expresses vindication through a future community (Enos 1:13, 18). Alma$_2$ situates this moral hope within the covenantal morality of promise: "For he [God] promised unto them [our fathers] that he would preserve these things for a wise purpose in him, that he might show forth his power unto future generations" (Alma 37:18).

It is morally meaningful that Mormon$_2$ prefaces his anthologizing by voicing the hope that the record "perhaps some day . . . may profit them" (Words of Mormon 2). His most compelling expression of moral hope occurs, however, when he temporarily assumes the posture of an "idle witness," given the futility of moral purposiveness for his own people. His moral identity changed, Mormon₂ immediately addresses numerous future communities and generations, including the twelve tribes and the house of Israel, the "remnant" of Lehi's posterity (Lamanites), non-Israelites (the Gentiles), and ultimately the "world" and "all the ends of the earth" with an epistolary ethic of universal accountability: "Every soul who belongs to the whole human family of Adam; . . . must stand to be judged of your works, whether they be good or evil" (Mormon 3:20). He interweaves the hope of a moral witness for future communities into his narrative of the destruction of his people twice more, informing future communities of the purpose of his words and the preserved record as a whole, that Jesus Christ is the Son of God, and God will both remember and fulfill his covenants.[35] He is a moral witness even in the midst of a communal apocalypse.

When Moroni₂ assumes responsibility for preserving the narrative, there is no longer a moral community or a community. He is the sole and lonely survivor of the Nephite nation, so his words, marked by the observation that "the whole face of this land is one continual round of murder and bloodshed," are necessarily those expressing the hope of a moral witness, directed to "whoso receiveth this record" (Mormon 8:1–8, 8:12). Moroni₂ acknowledges the prayers of prophetic predecessors on behalf of the preservation of the record, which "shall come even as if one should speak from the dead," and then indicates he has been given prescient revelatory insight into the moral nature of the future world that will receive the record: "I speak unto you as if ye were present. . . . Jesus Christ has shown you unto me, and I know your doing." This "doing" is not, however, the "doing good" of covenantal morality but rather exposes a world of religious "pollution," moral corruption, and hypocrisy attributable to the same materialistic preoccupations and the vices of pride, envy, and malice that contributed to the destruction of his people. As with other moral voices of prophetic criticism, Moroni₂ bitingly indicts—three times in four verses— this envisioned society of the future, and notably its religious underpinnings, for its moral callousness and indifference regarding the socially vulnerable (Mormon 8:8–16, 8:26, 8:35–40, 9:30–31). Delivered with indignation, Moroni₂'s prophetic indictment leaves a question about whether there is moral hope for latter-day communities. The hope of the moral witness ultimately resides in the witness of the sacred record.

The ethics of memory in which the hope of a moral witness is embedded couples the responsibility of remembrance of the covenantal ethic with a responsibility to posterity and to future generations. These dual responsibilities extend the moral community and the moral legacy of covenant in space and time.[36] This consistent aspect of prophetic calls to accountability and to relationship entails that the record itself, the text we know as the Book of Mormon, represented as preserved for the benefit of moral communities in another place or another time, bears the identity of a moral witness.

Conclusion

I have used the emphatic imperative to "remember" in the Book of Mormon to explore and interpret a constructive ethics of memory. This ethics of memory has been framed through the moral voice of prophetic criticism, an exposition of the moral logical of covenantal morality and relationships, and the concept of moral witness that narrates a history to shape the moral culture of future communities.

The expansive moral reality of the Book of Mormon has meaning and revelatory value beyond the religious tradition formed by the book. Its emphasis on the radical dependency of persons on divine gifts and on community presence and solidarity reveals the moral myopia and hypocrisy at the core of cultures of materialism. Its focus on the common life of covenantal communities presents a compelling moral critique of a self-absorbed individualism. The moral voice of prophecy and of covenantal morality resists the reduction of relationships to impersonal, transactional interactions (an inevitable feature of a materialistic ethos) and fosters personal and communal transformation through an ethic of gift, calling, promise, and embodied practices that sustain covenantal relationships. The moral centrality of relationship and the responsibility of remembrance illuminate the moral amnesia that befalls communities in the absence of a shared story or narrative.

The Book of Mormon is more than a moral critic for contemporary society, however, for its moral visions offer constructive alternatives for creating moral communities out of strangers. Notably, May contends that American political identity is best framed in covenantal rather than contractualist understandings: "A covenantal sense of the human condition helps supply the cultural soil out of which the national identity emerges and from which it irregularly draws its life."[37] The covenantal morality embedded in the sacred text aligns with and preserves the moral memory of this covenantal sensibility as the contemporary political community founders on the shoals of polarizing self-interest. Furthermore, as displayed in the textual narratives of the Nephites donating their land and protection to the Anti-Nephi-Lehi refugees and that community subsequently providing sanctuary to the excluded Zoramite refugees, the defining characteristic of a morally capacious covenantal ethic resides in the normative responsibility assumed by the community to care for and provide material substance to assist the burdens borne by the vulnerable. The contemporary parallel for enacting the covenantal responsibility to the vulnerable concerns the regional, national, and global refugee crisis, a question for which the twenty-first-century LDS Church has drawn on both scriptural resources and its own moral memory and narrative identity as a religion of persecuted exiles to offer safety, security, shelter, and skills to involuntarily displaced peoples and political and religious refugees.[38] Those moral resources do not resolve or translate into a political resolution, but they do re-story and frame a moral vision about the stranger and the refugee.[39]

The narrative prophetic and moral voice of the text thereby offers resources of moral memory and moral witness for civic responsibility and matters of social justice. The prophetic calls to accountability and relationship in the text make compelling recourse not only to narrative but also to analogy, parable, metaphor, symbol, and memory. The moral voice is manifestly humanized and humanizing, perfused with lamentation, grief, and indignation, and occasional glimpses into the ineffable. The moral voice is prophetic in nature, engaging in criticism that attests to the vital role of moral agency and accountability. In the hopeful aspiration of its writers and the text as a whole to bequeath a moral legacy for future communities, the Book of Mormon is not only a religious witness but also a moral witness that invites readers to gift relationships that exemplify the highest of human possibilities.

Notes

1. The text invokes the language of "remember" (or variations) 221 times and uses the language of "forget" (or variations) 26 times. (See https://gospelcougar .blogspot.com/2007/12.) For illustrative examples, see 1 Nephi 7:12–14; Mosiah 1:3–17, 4:11, 6:3; Alma 5:6, 9:8–13, 29:10–12, 36:2, 36:29; Helaman 5:6–12, 13:22; Moroni 10:3, 10:18–19.

2. Richard B. Miller, *Friends and Other Strangers: Studies in Religion, Ethics, and Culture* (New York: Columbia University Press, 2016), 147, 205. See also Alexis de Tocqueville, *Democracy in America*, ed. J. P. Mayer (New York: Doubleday, 1969); and Stephen L. Carter, *The Culture of Disbelief: How American Law and Politics Trivialize Religious Devotion* (New York: Basic Books, 1993).

3. Avishai Margalit, *The Ethics of Memory* (Cambridge: Harvard University Press, 2002).

4. Michael Walzer, *Interpretation and Social Criticism* (Cambridge: Harvard University Press, 1987), 58–74. See also Walter Brueggemann, *The Prophetic Imagination* (Minneapolis: Fortress Press, 2018).

5. These six illustrative narratives are found in Jacob 2–4; Mosiah 11–18; Alma 8–14 and 31–34; Helaman 13–16; and Mormon 8–9.

6. See chapter 3 of this volume for an exposition of the morality of minimal decency.

7. See the related observation of Jesus: "A prophet is not without honor, but in his own country, and among his own kin, and in his own house" (Mark 6:4).

8. Walzer uses this phrase to distinguish the Hebraic prophets. Walzer, *Interpretation and Social Criticism* 33, 57. There is a diverse dynamic of communal positionality in other illustrations of prophetic criticism in the Book of Mormon but community connection is vital. Alma$_2$ is initially treated as an outsider with no standing among the people of Ammonihah but subsequently teaches with Amulek, a member of the community. Samuel$_2$ is clearly an outsider to the people of Zarahemla, but his prophetic witness is paired with the ministry of Nephi$_3$. Moroni$_2$ is distanced in time and space from modern society, but the religious and moral conditions of modern life have been revealed to him such that he can attest, "I know your doing" (Mormon 8:35).

9. Margalit, *Ethics of Memory*, 170–71. Miller develops a compelling account of the authority-conferring virtues of moral and social critics that are centered on integrity. See Miller, *Friends and Other Strangers*, 91–95.

10. Michael Walzer, *Thick and Thin: Moral Argument at Home and Abroad* (Notre Dame, IN: University of Notre Dame Press, 1994), 47.

11. See the following for similar challenges to prophetic voices: Alma 9:2, 9:6, 10:2–4, 10:12; Helaman 16:1; Mormon 8:35.

12. Walzer, *Interpretation and Social Criticism*, 59, 63.

13. My language of moral memory adapts the assertion of Alma$_2$ that the sacred records "enlarge the memory of this people" (Alma 37:8).

14. The ethics of memory in prophetic critiques is further illustrated in Jacob$_2$'s argument of communal accountability for its concubinage practice—"Ye know that these commandments were given unto our father, Lehi; wherefore you have known them before" (Jacob 2:34)—and in Alma$_2$'s initial indictment of the people of Ammonihah: "Ye have forgotten the tradition of your fathers" (Alma 9:8–10).

15. Daniel Becerra has observed that in the Book of Mormon generally, there is a "correlation" between prosperity and moral discourse. See Daniel Becerra, "Samuel the Lamanite and the Ethics of Wealth in the Book of Mormon," in *Samuel the Lamanite: That Ye Might Believe*, ed. Charles Swift, 107–125 (Provo, UT: BYU Religious Studies Center, 2021).

16. See Isaiah 29:13; Matthew 15:7–9; 2 Nephi 27:25, Church of Jesus Christ of Latter-day Saints, *The Pearl of Great Price: Joseph Smith—History*, 2024, 19.

17. Luke 10:25–37. I develop this argument more fully in Courtney S. Campbell, *Bearing Witness: Religious Meanings in Bioethics* (Eugene, OR: Cascade Press, 2019), 98–124.

18. The language of the powerful "passing by" the poor is used in both the Good Samaritan parable (Luke 10:25–37) and in Moroni$_2$'s critique of latter-day communities (Mormon 8:35–39).

19. 2 Nephi 28:13; Jacob 2:17–19; Mosiah 4:26, 18:27–28; Alma 1:27, 4:12, 5:53–55, 34:27–28; Helaman 4:12; Mormon 8:35–40. Although I have

categorized neglect of the vulnerable as a wrong of omission, some passages clearly imply it comprises a wrong of commission, as when Nephi₁ claims that the materialistic quest for "fine" clothing and sanctuaries constitutes "robbery of the poor" (2 Nephi 28:13).

20. Daniel Becerra argues that this wrong is embedded in Samuel₂'s prophetic critique. See Becerra, "Samuel the Lamanite," 115–20.

21. The basic claim is that a person who is "unclean" cannot enter the presence of God. For illustrations, see 1 Nephi 10:21, 15:34; 2 Nephi 9:14–16; Jacob 1:19; Mosiah 2:28; Alma 7:21, 11:37, 40:26; Mormon 9:14. For a relevant discussion of biblical codes of moral purity, see L. William Countryman, *Dirt, Greed, and Sex: Sexual Ethics in the New Testament and Their Implications for Today* (Philadelphia: Fortress Press, 1990).

22. Abinadi's death is a reminder of the etymological and conceptual connection between "witness" and "martyr," a connection reinforced in the new community of Alma₁ by a covenant that requires participants to be "witnesses of God . . . even until death" (Mosiah 18:10).

23. Wouter Van Beek, "Covenants," *Encyclopedia of Mormonism*, 1992, https://eom.byu.edu/index.php/Covenants; Church of Jesus Christ of Latter-day Saints, "Gospel Topics and Questions: Covenant," https://site.churchofjesuschrist.org/study/manual/gospel-topics/covenant?lang=eng; Church of Jesus Christ of Latter-day Saints, "Bible Dictionary: Covenant," https://site.churchofjesuschrist.org/study/scriptures/bd/covenant?lang=eng.

24. My interpretation is indebted to the concept of covenantal ethics developed by William F. May, *The Physician's Covenant: Images of the Healer in Medical Ethics*, 2nd ed. (Louisville, KY: Westminster John Knox Press, 2001); and Joseph L. Allen, *Love and Conflict: A Covenantal Model of Christian Ethics* (Lanham, MD: University Press of America, 1995).

25. Campbell, *Bearing Witness*, 159–62.

26. Allen, *Love and Conflict*, 32.

27. These illustrations are drawn from Mosiah 5:2, 18:7–11; Alma 24:7–18; 3 Nephi 18:1–12.

28. William F. May, *Testing the National Covenant: Fears and Appetites in American Politics* (Washington, DC: Georgetown University Press, 2011), 93.

29. See Mosiah 1:3–6, 4:11, 28:16; Alma 5:6, 9:8–13, 29:10–12, 36:2, 36:28–29, 60:20; Helaman 5:5–12; 3 Nephi 18:1–12; Moroni 10:3, 10:18–19.

30. Some influential examples include Jeffrey Blustein, *The Moral Demands of Memory* (Cambridge: Cambridge University Press, 2008); W. James Booth, *Communities of Memory: On Witness, Identity, and Justice* (Ithaca, NY: Cornell University Press, 2006); and Margalit, *Ethics of Memory*.

31. Margalit, *Ethics of Memory*, 17.

32. Prophets are a type of Christ in experiencing sorrow, pain, and anguish regarding communities exhibiting the characteristics of rebellion. See 2 Nephi 26:7; Alma 3:7, 8:14, 13:27, 31:31–33; Helaman 7:6; 3 Nephi 7:15; Mormon 2:19, 2:27.

33. Margalit, *Ethics of Memory*, 155, 167.

34. See 2 Nephi 3:19–20, 25:3, 25:8, 25:21–22, 26:15–16, 27:13, 29:2, 33:13; Jacob 4:3; Mormon 8:23, 9:30; Ether 12:22; Moroni 10:27. For discussion of the "sepulchral voice" of the dead to the living, see Jillian Sayre, "Books Buried in the Earth: *The Book of Mormon*, Revelation, and the Humic Foundations of the Nation," in *Americanist Approaches to the Book of Mormon*, ed. Elizabeth Fenton and Jared Hickman, 21–44 (New York: Oxford University Press, 2019).

35. Mormon 3:16–22, 5:9–21, 7. Mormon$_2$'s purposes are incorporated into the title page of the Book of Mormon. See Daniel H. Ludlow, "The Title Page," in *The Book of Mormon: First Nephi, the Doctrinal Foundation*, ed. Monte S. Nyman and Charles D. Tate Jr., 19–34 (Provo, UT: Religious Studies Center, BYU, 1988).

36. See Kimberly Matheson's chapter, "Epic History, Ethical Pedagogy: The Book of Mormon's Scene of Instruction," in this volume for discussion of multiple audiences of reception.

37. May, *Testing the National Covenant*, 93.

38. See Patrick Kearon, "Refuge from the Storm," April 2016 General Conference, https://www.churchofjesuschrist.org/study/general-conference/2016/04/refuge-from-the-storm?lang=eng; and Linda K. Burton, "I Was a Stranger," April 2016 General Conference, https://www.churchofjesuschrist.org/study/general-conference/2016/04/i-was-a-stranger?lang=eng

39. See May, Testing the National Covenant, 119–25.

12

Further Visions

Practical Ethics and the Book of Mormon

KELLY SORENSEN

In the garden of practical and applied ethics topics that Book of Mormon speakers address, directly and indirectly, there are many seedlings and flowers—many more than this volume could accommodate. In this closing chapter I note some of them. Even here I cannot be comprehensive, and I certainly cannot note all of the relevant scholarship. My aim is simply to invite further work on these and other topics.

For simplicity, I will use the terms "ethics/ethical" and "morals/moral" synonymously below. And I will generally use terms like "obligation," "moral permission," and "moral requirement." Some may regard these terms as a foreign or modern imposition on the text, since the Book of Mormon does not itself use these exact terms. But it does use related words like "duty" and "obliged," and words like "ought" and "should" are especially common in the text.[1]

The sections below work progressively through different levels of expanding communities. Beginning from the self, I turn to the family, then to communal interactions, to economic obligations to the poor and to refugees, to the state and its disruption by war, to Indigenous people, to past and future generations, and finally to the earth and nature. At the end of this chapter, I provide suggestions for further reading illustrative of emerging scholarly discussions on practical ethics that incorporate Book of Mormon teachings or narratives.

Are There Moral Obligations Concerning Oneself?

The Book of Mormon suggests an ethic of personal moral transformation. Jesus Christ tells audiences in both the New Testament and the Book of

Mormon to become perfect (Matthew 5:48; 3 Nephi 12:48). This imperative to develop oneself morally includes both making and keeping promises and covenants, on the one hand, and the cultivation of virtuous character attributes, on the other. The process of moral development also seems to have both individual and communal aspects; an individual's moral development often seems tied to the community's moral development. Obligations to self are inextricable in important respects from obligations to community.

Writers of devotional literature for popular audiences on the Book of Mormon frequent the theme of personal moral transformation. This popular discourse emphasizes, as do Book of Mormon teachings, that a transformed moral identity is enabled only through the atonement and redeeming grace of Christ. That is, personal moral transformation is not a matter of "works-righteousness" but grace liberating and enabling moral agency. As illustrated by Daniel Becerra's chapter in this volume, "Moral Psychology and the Book of Mormon," personal moral transformation can occur across many vectors of the self, including heart, mind, soul, spirit, and body.

What Responsibilities Do Parents Have to Children and Vice Versa?

The very first line of the Book of Mormon, "I, Nephi, having been born of goodly parents," situates the family as a school for moral character, with apparent reference to both mother and father. Family relationships are the primary context for moral formation and the transmission of legacy through multigenerational lineage and identity, especially once the narrative begins to follow the vicissitudes of one family (that of Alma₁) quite closely across more than a century of history. Nephite prophets are portrayed as devoted and sometimes anguished fathers bestowing blessings and counsel to their posterity. Amy Easton-Flake has pointed out that the principal moral role granted to fathers, rather than to mothers, among the Book of Mormon's Nephites suggests that it was intended to be received in the nineteenth-century American context as against the social grain.[2] Strikingly, the valiant faith displayed by the sons of the Anti-Nephi-Lehies—Lamanites by ethnicity or culture—is instead attributed to the teachings of their mothers (Alma 56:47–48). The volume thus arguably portrays variation among cultures as to how moral formation within the family unfolds. The moral context of family is also emphasized through the frequent identity of persons becoming "children" of God or of Christ.

Despite all this, the narratives of family in the Book of Mormon are notably complex. The dramatic opening chapters about the family of Lehi₁ and Sarah portray intra-familial group loyalty, contention, and violence, as well as tensions about ownership of family heritage items. The generational legacy of this beginning family is two nations in almost perennial conflict with each other. The Nephite prophet Jacob$_2$ compares the family life and marital fidelity of the Lamanites favorably relative to those of his Nephite community. Mormon$_2$ subsequently narrates a patrilineal multigenerational family story full of conflict, rebellion, and moral transformation that spans much of the remaining history, ultimately concluding with the conveying of responsibility for the records to his son Moroni$_2$ as their society is annihilated. Family is thus as often the site of sorrow and disaster as it is of happiness and hope.

Given the extended focus on family interactions, the Book of Mormon invites more attention regarding what family members morally owe to each other and whether these relational responsibilities have priority over responsibilities to non-family members. In an illustratively complex story, for instance, the high priest Alma$_1$ rejoices at his wayward and antagonistic son's being struck down for several days, taking advantage of the opportunity to draw the community of faith to witness divine intervention on behalf of the church. At the same time, it is also true that Alma$_1$ asks the gathered community in this story to pray for his son, and the community's prayers seem to play a role in his redemption and healing (Mosiah 27). The relative strength of familial moral obligations among other obligations is also worth exploring.

Questions about the scope of what counts as family need attention, along with questions about the ethics of familial adoption (in individual cases like Laban's servant Zoram, adopted in some sense into Lehi$_1$'s family; and political cases like the national adoption of the Anti-Nephi-Lehies). Also of importance are questions about the statuses of occasionally mentioned plural wives and concubines, prostitutes, household servants or slaves, and others that contribute to, are situated at the periphery of, or disrupt familial life.

How Should I Converse and Interact with Others?

Book of Mormon figures frequently express concern about "contentions." Sometimes the words "contentions" and "wars" are proximate in the text; sometimes, instead, the words "contentions" and "disputations" are proximate. Occasionally (most overtly in father–son conversation about moral issues), the text dwells on how to speak boldly but not overbearingly (see Alma 38). And there are rich narratives about how both strangers and non-strangers speak to and relate to each other.

The book invites attention to the ethics of civility. It is of particular interest that the narratives in the First Book of Nephi dwell often on how religious language might be received as "hard" speech, perhaps playing a role in setting up the division between the Nephites and the Lamanites. The text thereby can offer further visions about moral obligations with respect to the words and speech one offers to others. Ideals relating to unity are similarly prescribed in various ways as is the expectation that individuals can enact responsibilities to seek the welfare of others by conferring esteem to others similar to regard for oneself.

How Should I Act When I Have Wronged Someone, and How Should I Act When Dealt with Unjustly?

Along with first-order questions about moral rightness and wrongness, there are second-order questions about what one should do in response to a case of moral wrongness. Repentance, a frequent topic in the Book of Mormon, usually focuses on what one should do in response to one's own moral wrongdoing. And certain Book of Mormon voices—most notably king Benjamin—dwell on how many ways one might offend in social relationships and the processes of forgiveness. More broadly, perhaps there is a sense in which communities and other groups can repent for their collective wrongdoings, too—the narrative of the Anti-Nephi-Lehies invites this kind of question.

The category of "moral repair" includes these questions, but it is still broader since one can also ask what response morality requires of someone who is not directly responsible for a harm or wrong—a bystander or third party. (A particularly interesting story to investigate here might be that of Ammon's intervention in a dispute between Lamoni and his father in Alma 20.) Determinations of who in a conflict has been the initiator of harm or offense and who the recipient is can be complex, suggesting a context for cultivating the capacity for righteous judgment emphasized in a sermon of Mormon$_2$. Indirect responsibility and responsibility associated with long chains of causality also raise questions about obligations of moral repair. It is potentially of interest that some prophetic voices in the book, the early figure of Jacob$_2$ as well as king Benjamin, express concern over being responsible for sins committed by those they did not preach to sufficiently to rid themselves of the guilt of their would-be hearers.

Should I Seek Out Economic Prosperity?
What Are the Moral Obligations of Persons Who Experience Prosperous Conditions?

Directly after the climactic appearance of Jesus Christ in the Book of Mormon, a peaceable community is established that lives in a state of economic equality for approximately two hundred years, distinguished by having "all things in common among them" and the absence of "rich and poor." The Book of Mormon is intriguingly silent about how this radical economic egalitarianism was achieved. What is clear from the narrative is that the economic commons ended as some sought out "fine things of the world" and organized churches "unto themselves to get gain" (4 Nephi 1:26).

The formative Book of Mormon communities receive a covenantal promise of "prosperity"—sometimes framed in economic terms—conditioned on their righteousness. The moral basis for prosperity may underwrite a distinction that emerges in several places in the text between "obtaining riches" and "getting gain," the latter a condition of self-serving avarice that issues in economic stratification. The prophet Jacob$_2$, in the first explicit moral sermon, while acknowledging the validity of the Nephite quest for "seeking riches," admonishes the community for attributing their wealth to their own actions rather than to divine providence and stipulates a provision that riches are to be used to advance the welfare of the poor and the needy in the community (Jacob 2). Several narratives of communal history, and the text as a whole, manifest a perpetual concern with the distribution of material wealth and prosperity. The question of communal responsibility for the poor is reiterated in the narrative of Nephite king Benjamin and that of the covenanted community of Alma$_1$; the neglect of this responsibility informs Moroni$_2$'s biting critique of latter-day religions near the end of the Book of Mormon (Mosiah 4, 18; Mormon 8). The collective witness of these narratives is that economic inequality is profoundly morally undesirable; educational and economic class distinctions are the cause of much community disorder and disintegration.

Questions remain about the source and scope of moral obligations to address economic equality—obligations by the state, by the religious community, by the family, and by individuals. For instance, how important to the Book of Mormon's message is the apparent distinction drawn by king Benjamin between a Christian's appropriate response to the beggar, which is immediate and unquestioning, and a Christian's appropriate response to the poor, which is wise and focused on the long term? Questions also remain about the relative strength of these obligations and about the morally permissible or required means of bringing about greater economic equality. Especially important to such questions may be the fact that the volume eventually distinguishes between the responsibilities of the church to the poor and the responsibilities of the state to the poor.

What Should One Do about Refugees and Stateless Persons?

A recurring narrative in the Book of Mormon is the ordeal of several diverse communities of religious persecution and political oppression and their subsequent deliverance. The text begins with the departure of Lehi₁'s family from Jerusalem into a wilderness journey of eight years because of threats against Lehi₁'s life, and Nephi₁ subsequently leads his own followers away from the earliest Lehite community. Two communities, one founded by the prophet Alma₁ and the other by Limhi, are delivered from political, religious, and economic oppression of the priests of Noah (Mosiah 22–24). The Anti-Nephi-Lehies, a community of converted Lamanites, are provided a sanctuary from threats against the community by the Nephites, and the Anti-Nephi-Lehies in turn provide a refuge from persecution and oppression for a community of believers ostracized by the Zoramites (Alma 27, 35).

Although the Book of Mormon does not use the term "refugee" in these contexts, it does provide morally meaningful narratives regarding the responsibilities of oppressed communities to seek deliverance and the responsibilities of prospective host communities to offer sanctuary and refuge from persecution. This narrative framing corresponds with the duties assumed by the historical community of Israel to love the stranger—for the people of Israel had once been strangers in the land of Egypt—as well as the parabolic command of Jesus to the early Christians: "I was a stranger, and ye took me in" (Matthew 25:35).

These narratives have been drawn upon in the past decade by LDS ecclesiastical leadership in the context of refugee crises in the Middle East and North Africa and in sub-Saharan Africa. New initiatives have emerged regarding humanitarian responsibilities for refugees and for refugee resettlement. The Book of Mormon narratives of flight, deliverance, and sanctuary can provide an important lens for discerning ethical responsibilities of communal care for those who have sought to escape political and religious persecution.

What Obligations Does One Have to People in Terms of Gender, Race, Indigeneity, and Temporal Generation?

There are few women, named or unnamed, in the Book of Mormon. So it may seem to have little to say about women and gender more generally. But perhaps these issues are still underexplored. Daniel Peterson suggests that Nephi₁'s vision includes a reference to Heavenly Mother.[3] And there remains more to be said about women like Abish, Sariah, and the unnamed Lamanite queen (Alma 19). Strikingly, a meta-interpretation through a close reading of Sariah's words and other texts early in the book by Kimberly Matheson and Joseph Spencer suggests that the Book of Mormon offers a signal to readers that Lehi$_1$'s family carries a costly undervaluing of women into the rest of the book's thousand-year narrative. Other readings, like Carol Lynn Pearson's, offer something of an ethics of gender through attending to the book's absences on this issue.[4]

On race and ethnicity, two main views have become prevalent in the last decades. The topic is clearly important in the Book of Mormon: Tensions and violence are often associated with perceived differences in appearances and purported skin color. One view treats passages ostensibly about skin color attributions as metaphorical. Another view treats these passages as literal, along with a meta-interpretation that a key point of the book is to exhibit the horrific costs of racial and ethnic violence.

On indigeneity, the book invites consideration about obligations to the Indigenous peoples of the Americas ravaged by European colonization. On the one hand, Nephi$_1$ writes favorably about a presumably European explorer who travels to the Americas (1 Nephi 13). But on the other hand, the title page of the Book of Mormon (traditionally taken to be written by Moroni$_2$) addresses the Indigenous people of the Americas as its first and crucial audience and concern. The survival and future well-being of these Indigenous Americans is secured early in the book by their morally exemplary behavior (Jacob 3:6).

Connections among temporal generations suffuse the Book of Mormon. The book's dominant figures, Nephi$_1$, Mormon$_2$, and Moroni$_2$, address themselves in various ways to future readers. Their modes of address suggest moral obligations incurred by those future readers: obligations to hear, remember, and act on the warnings represented narratively through the experiences of two self-destructing civilizations and by Moroni$_2$'s direct and dire warnings in particular.

The ethics of gender, race, indigeneity, and temporal generation—all of these issues call for more interpretive work.

What Is the Ethical Significance of Religious Liberty?

The Book of Mormon makes strikingly modern claims about the importance of religious freedom and the need for separating religious beliefs and discipline from civic laws. The high priest Alma$_1$, in confronting dissenters from the church of God, initially requests that the Nephite king Mosiah$_2$ render judgment on the dissenters, but Mosiah$_2$ refuses and defers to Alma$_1$'s authority over the church (Mosiah 26). Subsequently, the narrative discloses that a primary moral and legal reason for a political transition from monarchy to a system of judges among the Nephites was to ensure that each person was answerable and accountable for their sins. While the communities are organized around basic laws necessary for a cohesive community, such as prohibitions against murder, robbery, theft, and lying, applicable to everyone, laws did not restrict freedom of belief or prescribe particular forms of religious preaching or worship: "the law could have no power on any man for his belief" (Alma 1:16–18).

The issues of religious liberty continue to resonate for members of the LDS Church because of the legacy of nineteenth-century persecution from both state coercion and anti-Mormon sentiment among the general populace in frontier communities. A principle of religious freedom and equality is inscribed into the Eleventh Article of Faith authored by Joseph Smith. The LDS Church has been particularly prominent in advocating for religious liberty protections even while seeking to ensure protections from discrimination in civic law for members of the LGBTQ+ communities.

What Kind of Political Order/State Deserves My Allegiance?

Order matters everywhere in the Book of Mormon in a way that seems to undergird specific types of organization: religious, communal, political, and familial, with overlaps among these types. That order should exist, and order and organization of certain sorts, is a stance that arises throughout the book in what seems to be an ethical/moral tone: Readers sense that people *morally should* form and maintain certain kinds of communities that enable personal moral transformation and help realize the common good. Sometimes God initiates the founding of these types of order; sometimes human beings do, with God participating in the development of order with intriguingly varying degrees of engagement.

Religious order and authority are often in the book's foreground. The introduction into a religious community through a baptism ritual is connected with ethical duties and covenantal responsibilities to "mourn with those that mourn" and "comfort those that stand in need of comfort," as well as to "stand as witnesses of God at all times and in all things" (Mosiah 18:9). The community described, albeit only briefly, in the fourth book of Nephi perhaps serves as a model for the ideal society in the Book of Mormon.

Absent from many contemporary lists of applied ethics topics is what one might call community ethics, of which religious community and order is one subset. Some communities in the Book of Mormon may, on close reading, operate outside both political and religious frameworks, as least as contemporarily understood.

Various frameworks of political order and authority figure importantly in the book, from monarchy to a distributed-power system of judges. Diverse narratives highlight efforts of some political dissenters, particularly those who wish to establish rule by kingship, to subvert political order and to use violence to suppress sedition and reinstate the rule of judges (Alma 59–62). These narratives provide moral visions of questions of political legitimacy, formation, and structure.

Is Violence Ever Permissible?

The Book of Mormon narratives have proven to be fertile ground for different interpretations of the ethics of war and violence among LDS scholars. The text includes narratives of interpersonal violence by prominent characters such as Nephi$_1$ and Ammon$_2$, a narrative of a community of converted Lamanites—the Anti-Nephi-Lehies—who make a covenant to renounce violence but whose sons subsequently become valiant warriors, and several narratives in which Nephite leaders such as Moroni$_1$ and Helaman$_1$ lead their nations in defensive wars to protect their freedom, property, and religion. Ultimately, the communal histories of two prominent nations—the Jaredites and the Nephites—are brought to an end by interminable warfare.

These narratives raise questions about the compatibility of a social practice of war with the gospel of peace proclaimed by Jesus Christ. They invite discussion as to whether narrative descriptions of action from historical communities carry normative force for contemporary communities. They require reflection about the moral differences, if any, between interpersonal violence and intra- and inter-communal war. LDS scholars have made use of various ethical categories and concepts—including self-defense, pacifism, nonviolence, and just war—to illuminate the moral meaning of the Book of Mormon on issues of violence and warfare, although without any interpretive or substantive agreement.

How Should I Regard the Earth and Nature?

The Book of Mormon discloses a pronounced narrative of "the land" as a promised destination for families and communities under divine direction; the Lehi$_1$ and Sarah family, and many other groups in the book, urgently seek out what is commonly referred to as "a land of promise" or a "choice land" and, subsequently, as "the land of our fathers." The "land" becomes a refuge from evil, an opportunity for community formation, and a place of intergenerational memory. The narrative language suggests that much more is at stake in land possession than mere property ownership.

Nature can not only elicit an aesthetic of beauty but also provide an ethic of place and identity, as displayed in the observation of Mormon₂ that "the waters of Mormon, the forest of Mormon, how beautiful are they to the eyes of them who there came to the knowledge of their Redeemer" (Mosiah 18:30). Nature is commonly invoked as a symbol for religious commitment and insights; symbols like valleys, mountains, rivers, wilderness, trees, and fruit can also be a catalyst for humility and repentance, as when the Nephite king Benjamin reminds his people, in language that echoes the Genesis creative narrative, that they are "less than the dust of the earth" (Mosiah 2:25; cf. Helaman 12:7–8). In these respects, "the earth and all things that are upon the face of it" point beyond nature and humanity to a witness of God and Christ (Alma 30:44).

That said, it is not clear that there is a conception in the Book of Mormon of the land, animals, or species being conferred with a moral status of intrinsic value independent of their purposes for human welfare. The text clearly offers exemplary sacred spaces, but the Book of Mormon is mostly unexplored relative to its implications for environmental ethics or what the LDS tradition has frequently framed as an ethic of stewardship.

A Human Life That Goes Well

Some account of well-being—an account of what makes a human life go well—informs and stands behind many of the practical ethics matters above. More work needs to be done on the view of well-being held by various Book of Mormon authors. Benjamin refers to "the blessed and happy state of those that keep the commandments of God (Mosiah 2:41), and Jesus describes the requisite characteristics for blessedness as well (3 Nephi 12). Asked in terms of contemporary philosophical theories of well-being, we might wonder whether being in this state of blessedness is to have a set of objectively intrinsically valuable things in one's life, like happiness, knowledge, relationships with God and family and others, and moral goodness, or whether this state reduces to a single objective intrinsic good like happiness. Benjamin seems to have believed the latter. But other texts suggest a broader list of intrinsically good elements that jointly constitute human well-being.

Human well-being, however conceived, is only one candidate type of intrinsic value. There are other candidate intrinsic values. Equality, desert, beauty, and nonhuman living things may also be intrinsically valuable— intrinsically valuable along with human lives that go well. Perhaps the Book of Mormon can be mined here for insights, or at least for further questions.[5]

Further Reading

Becerra, Daniel. "Ethical Approaches to the Book of Mormon," *Journal of Book of Mormon Studies* 32 (2023): 97–115.

Becerra, Daniel. "Samuel the Lamanite and the Ethics of Wealth in the Book of Mormon," in *Samuel the Lamanite: That Ye Might Believe*, ed. Charles Swift, 107–125 (Provo, UT: Religious Studies Center, BYU, 2021).

Boyce, Duane. *Even unto Bloodshed: An LDS Perspective on War* (Salt Lake City: Greg Kofford Books, 2015).

Bushman, Richard. "The Book of Mormon and the American Revolution," *BYU Studies Quarterly* 17, no. 1 (1976): 1–17.

Colvin, Gina, and Joanna Brooks, eds., *Decolonizing Mormonism: Approaching a Postcolonial Zion* (Salt Lake City: University of Utah Press, 2018).

Couch, Robert. "Desiring Riches: A Radical-Practical Critique of Modern Business," in *Reapproaching Zion*, ed. Samuel D. Brunson and Nathan B. Oman, 35–60 (Salt Lake City: Common Consent Press, 2020).

Davis, Richard. *The Liberal Soul: Applying the Gospel of Jesus Christ in Politics* (Draper, UT: Greg Kofford Books, 2014).

Easton-Flake, Amy. "'Arise from the Dust, My Sons, and Be Men': Masculinity in the *Book of Mormon*," in *Americanist Approaches to the Book of Mormon*, ed. Elizabeth Fenton and Jared Hickman, 362–90 (New York: Oxford University Press, 2019).

Givens, Terryl L. *Wrestling the Angel: The Foundations of Mormon Thought: Cosmos, God, Humanity* (New York: Oxford University Press, 2015).

Green, Deidre Nicole. *Jacob: A Brief Theological Introduction* (Provo, UT: Neal A. Maxwell Institute, 2020).

Halverson, Jared M. "'Because of Faith and Great Anxiety': Jacob and the Challenges of Mental Health, in *Jacob: Faith and Great Anxiety*, ed. Avram R. Shannon and George A. Pierce, 273–308 (Provo, UT: Religious Studies Center, BYU, 2024).

Hardy, Grant. *Understanding the Book of Mormon: A Reader's Guide*. (New York: Oxford University Press, 2010).

Handley, George B., Terry B. Ball, Steven L. Peck, eds., *Stewardship and the Creation: LDS Perspectives on the Environment* (Provo, UT: Religious Studies Center, BYU, 2006).

Handley, George B. *The Hope of Nature: Our Care for God's Creation* (Provo, UT: Maxwell Institute, BYU, 2020).

Harris, Sharon J. *Enos, Jarom, Omni: A Brief Theological Introduction* (Provo, UT: Neal A. Maxwell Institute, 2020).

Harris, Sharon J. "Saving the House of Israel: Collective Atonement in the Book of Mormon," in *Latter-day Saint Perspectives on Atonement*, ed. Deidre Nicole Green and Eric D. Huntsman, 115–30 (Chicago: University of Illinois Press, 2024).

Hickman, Jared. "The *Book of Mormon* as an Amerindian Apocalypse." *American Literature* 86, no. 3 (2014): 429–61.

Holland, Jeffrey R. "The Mormon Refugee Experience," https://newsroom. churchofjesuschrist.org/article/elder-holland-transcript-mormon-refugee -experience.

Mason, Patrick Q., and J. David Pulsipher, *Proclaim Peace: The Restoration's Answer to an Age of Conflict* (Provo, UT: BYU/Maxwell Institute/Deseret Book, 2021).

Mason, Patrick Q., J. David Pulsipher, and Richard L. Bushman, eds., *War and Peace in Our Time: Mormon Perspectives* (Salt Lake City: Greg Kofford Books, 2012).

Matheson, Kimberly, and Joseph M. Spencer, "'Great Cause to Mourn': The Complexity of *The Book of Mormon*'s Presentation of Gender and Race," in *Americanist Approaches to the Book of Mormon*, ed. Elizabeth Fenton and Jared Hickman, 298–320 (New York: Oxford University Press, 2019).

Oaks, Dallin H. "Going Forward with Religious Freedom and Nondiscrimina-tion," *BYU Studies Quarterly* 61, no. 1 (2022): 117–28.

Pearson, Carol Lynn. "Could Feminism Have Saved the Nephites?" *Sunstone* (March 1996): 32–40.

Peterson, Daniel C. "Nephi and His Asherah," *Journal of Book of Mormon Studies* 9, no. 2 (2000): 16–25.

Pulsipher, J. David. "Defend Your Families and Love Your Enemies: A New Look at the Book of Mormon's Patterns of Protection," *BYU Studies Quarterly* 60, no. 2 (2021): 163–83.

Quick, Devon. "The Promise of Prosperity: Its Meaning and Relevance," *Religious Educator* 24 (2023): 45–63.

Salleh, Fatimah, and Margaret Olsen Hemming. *The Book of Mormon for the Least of These*, Vols. 1–3 (Salt Lake City: BCC Press, 2020, 2022, 2023).

Spencer, Joseph M. Spencer. "The Presentation of Gender in the Book of Mormon: A Review of Literature," *Journal of Book of Mormon Studies* 29 (2020): 231–63.

Thomas, John C., and Robert T. Smith, eds. *Religious Liberty and Latter-Day Saints: Historical and Global Perspectives* (Provo, UT: Religious Studies Center, BYU, 2023).

van Uitert, Rebecca. "Undocumented Immigrants in the United States: A Discus-sion of Catholic Social Thought and Mormon 'Social Thought' Principles," *Journal of Catholic Legal Studies* 46, no. 2, (2007): 277–314.

Vail, Coby. "Refugee Resettlement in Utah: Lessons on Community and Reli-gious Engagement," https://berkleycenter.georgetown.edu/responses/refugee-resettlement-in-utah-lessons-on-community-and-religious-engagement.

Welch, Rosalynde Frandsen. "Theology of the Family," in *The Routledge Handbook of Mormonism and Gender*, ed. Amy Hoyt and Taylor G. Petrey, 495–508 (New York: Routledge, 2020).

Welch, Rosalynde Frandsen, and Diana Brown, eds. *Are We Not All Beggars: Reading Mosiah 4* (Proceedings of the Latter-day Saint Theology Seminar Book, 2023).

Wright, Walker A., "Ye Are No More Strangers and Foreigners," *BYU Studies Quarterly* 57, no. 1 (2018): 65–103.

Notes

1. Some might argue that a virtue-based understanding of ethics is a better conceptual fit for the premodern setting of the Book of Mormon and that the book's most fundamental evaluative focal point is properly the human agent's moral character and dispositions, with terms like "duty" and "obligation" reducible to fundamental virtue and character. Becerra's chapter in this volume opens the door to additional work in this direction. Whether virtue and character are the book's most philosophical fundamental moral evaluative focal points or not, Becerra's inventory shows that people in the book often think about morality in terms of moral psychological terms like "heart," "mind," "spirit," and "body/flesh." But different groundings are conceivable. Perhaps the book's terms of "duty" and "ought" float on top of a philosophical ethics of virtue and character, where duties and obligations are explained in terms of what people of virtue and character tend to do. But perhaps instead duty and obligations are fundamental, with virtue language floating on top of some other, deeper metaethical foundation—a Kantian moral respect owed to beings with certain rational and agential capacities, a consequentialist state of affairs, divine commands, or something else. Figures in the Book of Mormon do not seem to be interested in metaethics, but thinking about metaethics may help us see things in the text we would otherwise miss—or perhaps the text can help us see things in practical ethics, ethical theory, and metaethics that we would otherwise miss. This is another direction for "further visions" about ethics and the Book of Mormon.

2. Amy Easton-Flake, "'Arise from the Dust, My Sons, and Be Men': Masculinity in the *Book of Mormon*," in *Americanist Approaches to the Book of Mormon*, ed. Elizabeth Fenton and Jared Hickman (New York: Oxford University Press, 2019), 362–90.

3. Daniel C. Peterson, "Nephi and His Asherah," *Journal of Book of Mormon Studies* 9, no. 2 (2000): 16–25.

4. Carol Lynn Pearson, "Could Feminism Have Saved the Nephites?" *Sunstone* (March 1996): 32–40.

5. I thank the other authors of this volume for generous contributions to this chapter.

Contributors

DANIEL BECERRA is assistant professor of ancient scripture at Brigham Young University. His primary research interests concern moral formation in late antiquity (ca. second–seventh centuries CE), particularly within Christian ascetic contexts. He also researches topics relating to theology and ethics in the Book of Mormon.

COURTNEY S. CAMPBELL is the Hundere Professor in Religion and Culture and director of the Medical Humanities Program at Oregon State University. His research interests focus on applied ethics in biomedicine, death and dying, nonviolence and war, and religious communities. He is the author of *Bearing Witness: Religious Meanings in Bioethics* (Cascade Books, 2019) and *Mormonism, Medicine, and Bioethics* (Oxford University Press, 2021) and is a fellow of the Hastings Center.

RYAN W. DAVIS is associate professor of political science at Brigham Young University. He writes about the value of autonomy in ethics, political philosophy, and philosophy of religion. He has published scholarly articles in leading journals such as the *Journal of Political Philosophy*, the *American Journal of Political Science*, the *Journal of Politics*, and the *Journal of the American Philosophical Association*.

MICHAEL D. K. ING is professor of religious studies at Indiana University, Bloomington. He is the author of *The Dysfunction of Ritual and Early Confucianism* (2012) and *The Vulnerability of Integrity in Early Confucian Thought* (2017), both with Oxford University Press.

ARIEL BYBEE LAUGHTON is an independent scholar of the history of early Christianity. Her primary field of research includes the writings of the Latin Church Fathers from the third to sixth centuries, especially those concerning women, gender, and sexuality. She has also published on Latter-day Saint historical perspectives of post–New Testament Christianity and LDS engagement with early Christian atonement theologies.

KIMBERLY MATHESON is the Laura F. Willes Research Fellow at the Neal A. Maxwell Institute for Religious Scholarship. Her research centers on the Book of Mormon, Christian contemplative practice, and the continental philosophy of religion. She has published several articles in the *Journal of Book of Mormon Studies* as well as various philosophy and religion journals and is the author of *Helaman: A Brief Theological Introduction* (Brigham Young University, 2020).

RACHEL ESPLIN ODELL is an international relations expert and an advocate for ethical government. She holds a PhD in political science from MIT, where she wrote her dissertation on the politics of the international law of the sea. She is a foreign affairs analyst at the US Department of State, but the views in her chapter (ch. 8) are her own and not necessarily those of the US government. She previously worked as a research fellow and analyst at the Quincy Institute for Responsible Statecraft and the Carnegie Endowment for International Peace. Esplin Odell also served on the board of directors of Mormon Women for Ethical Government (MWEG) from 2019 to 2023 and helped develop MWEG's foundational Principles of Ethical Government.

KELLY SORENSEN is associate dean of academic affairs and professor of philosophy and religious studies at Ursinus College. He teaches and writes about ethical theory, biomedical ethics, environmental ethics, and metaethics. He is the coeditor of *Kant and the Faculty of Feeling* (2018) with Cambridge University Press.

JOSEPH M. SPENCER is associate professor of ancient scripture at Brigham Young University. His work focuses on philosophy, theology, and scripture. Professor Spencer has served as the editor of the *Journal of Book of Mormon Studies*, as the associate director of the Latter-day Saint Theology Seminar, as president of the Book of Mormon Studies Association, and as the coeditor of the Introductions to Mormon Thought series (published by the University of Illinois Press). He is the author of seven books, including *A Word in Season: Isaiah's Reception in the Book of Mormon* (University of Illinois Press, 2023) and, with several colleagues, *Book of Mormon Studies: An Introduction and Guide* (Brigham Young University Religious Studies Center, 2022).

Index

motivation, 105, 136–38. *See also* moral psychology

murder. *See* violence

nakedness, 174–77, 180–88, 196
narrative ethics, 41–42, 95–123, 152–73, 220–21, 229–32
natural man, 19–22, 33
nature, 24–28, 62–64, 70–71, 125–26
Nephi₁, xi–xii, 2–3, 50, 53, 84–85, 132–33
Nephites, 2–7, 84–85, 107–9, 127–28, 132, 150, 175–76
nonviolence, 128–33, 150–53. *See also* violence; war

obedience, 23, 196–200, 205–6
obligation, 88, 146, 162–64, 236, 248n1
oppression, 127–28, 177–78, 183, 218, 222–24, 241

paternalism, 135, 147, 152–55, 158, 164–67, 198–200, 222–24
peace 29–33, 65, 244
permissibility, 125, 129, 132, 136–39
persecution, 46, 176, 179, 241–43
persuasion, 95–123
politics. *See* governance
prayer, 23, 41, 65, 195, 209–10
pride, 27, 46, 51, 174–80, 184–90
Priesthood, 196–98, 200–4, 208
promises and oaths, 138, 146, 153, 162–67, 225. *See also* covenants
prophet/prophetic, 2–5, 52, 84, 118, 198–99, 205–6, 220
prophetic ethics, xiii, 51–52, 84–85, 97, 154, 175, 183–84, 190, 214–23, 227–32
prosperity, 177–81, 184–88, 239–40, 245

racism, 3, 6, 58, 136, 242
rationality, 62–64, 71, 76n61, 96
redemption, 78, 155–68
refugees, 129–32, 232, 241

religion and morality, 14, 39–43, 54, 75n58
religious liberty, 242–43
reparation, 147–49, 165, 239
repentance, 8, 43, 162, 166–68, 239
resilience, 145–46, 154–55
righteousness: and clothing, 175–76, 180–81, 185–87, 190; and happiness, 20–21, 27, 30–31

saint, x, 20–22, 32–33
salvation, 8, 78, 87–92, 178
Samuel₂ (the Lamanite), 5, 149, 151, 154–55, 167–68, 188, 220
scene of instruction, xii, 95–123
Scheffler, Samuel, xi, 77–85, 88–92
self-defense, 128–33, 152, 164–66, 244
sexual immorality, 53, 189–90
sin, 20, 30–32, 161–68, 174–81, 183, 187, 189–90
Smith, Joseph, 1, 139, 147–50
Spirit (Light) of Christ, xi, 44, 53, 60, 68–71, 75n51
supererogation, 138
syncretism, 149, 152–55, 159

truth, 1, 8, 29, 63–73, 133–36

values/valuing, 77–82, 88–92, 96, 245
violence, 3, 31, 50, 58, 128–33, 137, 145–46, 150–69, 244. *See also* nonviolence; war
virtue/virtues, 13, 22, 27–29, 47–48, 125, 136–40, 208–9, 236–37, 248n1; and vices, 27–28, 46, 230
vulnerability, 200–201, 207–8

Walzer, Michael, 172n22, 214, 218
war, 7, 128–33, 137, 145–53, 162–69, 172–73n22, 244. See also nonviolence; violence
wealth, 9, 47, 51, 175–80, 185–88, 222, 240
well-being, 245
wickedness, 27, 30–33, 46, 183
women, 58, 184–85, 189–90, 241–42

The University of Illinois Press
is a founding member of the
Association of University Presses.

Composed in 11.5/13 Adobe Garamond Pro
with Gotham display
by Lisa Connery
at the University of Illinois Press

University of Illinois Press
1325 South Oak Street
Champaign, IL 61820-6903
www.press.uillinois.edu